# Beyond Belief:
# Agnostic Musings for
# 12 Step Life

# Beyond Belief: Agnostic Musings for 12 Step Life

## Finally, daily reflections for nonbelievers, freethinkers, and everyone

Joe C.

Rebellion Dogs Publishing
23 Cannon Road, Unit # 5
Toronto, ON Canada M8Y 1R8
news@rebelliondogspublishing.com
http://rebelliondogspublishing.com

*Beyond Belief: Agnostic Musings for 12 Step Life*
By Joe C.
Foreword: Ernest Kurtz, PhD
Editors: Amelia Chester, Joan Eyolfson Cadham
Cover Design: Sarah Beaudin

Library and Archives Canada Cataloguing in Publication

C., Joe, 1960-
        Beyond belief : agnostic musings for 12 step life / Joe C ; editors, Amelia Chester and Joan Eyolfson Cadham.

Includes index.
Issued also in electronic format.
ISBN 978-0-9881157-0-5

        1. Substance abuse--Popular works. 2. Twelve-step programs.
I. Chester, Amelia II. Eyolfson Cadham, Joan, 1940- III. Title.

HV4998.C45 2013          616.86'03          C2012-905255-8

The brief excerpts from *Pass it On, Twelve Steps and Twelve Traditions, Living Sober, Alcoholics Anonymous Comes of Age, The Big Book* and "Box 4-5-9" are reprinted with permission from Alcoholics Anonymous World Services, Inc. ("AAWS") Permission to reprint these excerpts does not mean that AAWS has reviewed or approved the contents of this publication, or that AAWS necessarily agrees with the views expressed herein. A.A. is a program of recovery from alcoholism only—use of these excerpts in connection with programs and activities which are patterned after A.A., but which address other problems, or in any other non-A.A. context, does not imply otherwise. Additionally, while A.A. is a spiritual program, A.A. is not a religious program. Thus, A.A. is not affiliated or allied with any sect, denomination, or specific religious belief.

*Rebellion Dogs Publishing—a voice of reason in the recovery community. Visit our website for community, merchandise and the latest in blogs and resources— now with more bite and less dogma.*

# FOREWORD

## by Ernest Kurtz, PhD
*(author of The Spirituality of Imperfection and Not-God: A History of Alcoholics Anonymous)*

ONE MEANING OF REFLECTION, according to the *Oxford English Dictionary*, is "the action of turning (back) or fixing the thoughts on some subject; meditation, deep or serious consideration." This treasure of a book offers spurs to reflection and more. Drawing on a rich variety of often surprising sources, each day's reading provides not a mere bite but a full meal of thoughts for the coming or just-past day. Since my mornings tend to be rushed, *Beyond Belief* soon moved itself into my mid-afternoon "break" period, where it could shed more leisurely light both backwards and forwards.

*Beyond Belief* terms its offerings *musings* rather than "meditations." The O.E.D. gives the first meaning of the verb muse as "to be absorbed in thought; to meditate continuously in silence; to ponder." *Absorbed* . . . *ponder*: this book is not light reading. I have not so far wanted to fight with it, but I do find *Beyond Belief* often challenging, sometimes provocative, unfailingly stimulating.

The book is aimed at a general 12-Step readership, but it is mindful that there heretofore exist no such aids for unbelievers, freethinkers, and the unconventionally spiritual. Given that the latest Pew survey found that twenty percent of the American people list their religious affiliation as "None," it is certainly time that the Recovery world took into consideration this population's needs. *Beyond Belief* addresses that need in a confident, non-aggressive way. I doubt that any believer will find anything objectionable in its pages. This believer, for one, finds much that is spiritually helpful.

If I have one criticism of this book it is that its musings are too rich. On quite a few pages I wished to pause and think after virtually every sentence. For many, reading *Beyond Belief* will require a pen or pencil in hand and perhaps a notebook on the side.

This is the first daily reflection book of which I know that offers a lengthy "Notes" section as well as a full Bibliography. The Notes are far more than mere citations, often presenting brief additional discussion and even new material that more frequently than not is as rich as the text itself.

In addition to the Notes and Bibliography, the end-matter of *Beyond Belief* contains a full Index that allows searching out individual musings on just about any topic. Having problems with "ego"? Check out May 29, August 8, September 24 or seven other dates. Polishing your gratitude? Flip to March 2, June 16, November 12 or eleven other dates.

*Beyond Belief* will enrich anyone interested in living a 12 -Step life.

# PREFACE

A FUNNY THING HAPPENED to me on my way to the new millennium. I realized that I had been a closet agnostic for a lot of my recovery. I had stayed clean and sober without the white light experience of an intervening God who grants sobriety, serenity or anything Bill W.-ish. We hear "fake it until you make it" in the rooms, and that's what I did. Decades into my faking it, I hadn't made it, in as far as feeling the presence of God. I felt like an imposter in Twelve & Twelve meetings.

Then came the Internet. I found a community of nonbelievers in recovery. Although a minority in Twelve Step culture, we are not freaks of nature. Some of my new nonbeliever friends had their own agnostic groups and some just fit their way into the mainstream fellowship, either apologetically or obnoxiously. I am now, truly, no longer alone. I don't have to feign belief in order to feel like I belong.

There is no shortage of daily meditation books for addicts who are predisposed to a worldview that includes a deity. But when I went looking for a daily reflection book not based on a monotheistic worldview, I couldn't find one, so I wrote one. It took four years. Art, philosophy, religion, comedy, science and the folk-wisdom of Twelve & Twelve rooms are all drawn upon within these pages.

This book speaks in an agnostic voice. Nonbelievers have something to add to the recovery conversation. There is no bias against faith in God or other deities. *Some of my best friends believe in God.* I don't consider them absurd and they don't see me as inferior. Non-theists are not intellectual holdouts. Non-theists are not more evolved. Beliefs are like favorite colors. If I like green and you like yellow that shouldn't interfere with our discussion of addiction and recovery.

The Big Book's chapter "We Agnostics" draws a line in the sand: "God either is or He isn't. What was our choice to be?" (*Alcoholics*

*Anonymous*, 53) Nature abhors a vacuum and a state of nothing can't exist in either the material or spiritual world. This kind of binary thinking made sense in the autocratic world of 1939. But in a democratic, pluralist society, all-or-nothing thinking is a cognitive distortion—a philosophical assumption that everything is right or wrong, good or evil, superior or inferior. In this millennium, people can hold opposing views and be equals in the same community. Our Traditions, lovingly and tolerantly, make room for more than one truth. That's a good thing, because the only problem with the truth is that there are so many versions of it.

If you believe in God and I do not, we both *let go…* then, I don't know. Maybe God scoops up our will, puts His hand on our shoulders and guides us in the right direction. I don't think so but maybe you're right. The *action* in the Step that we both take is *letting go.* The theology of what happens next is an interesting discussion but irrelevant to getting sober and living well, *à la* Twelve Steps. Unity is not about uniformity of beliefs; it's about a common purpose. Firm on principles, our methods stay flexible.

In the mid-1970s, when I got clean and sober, an Alcoholics Anonymous advertisement regularly ran in my local newspaper. It read, "If you want to drink and can, that's your business. If you want to quit and can't, that's our business. Call AA…" The ad included the local Intergroup phone number. What it conveyed to me was that if I wanted to drink, AA had nothing for me except warm regards. If I had no problem quitting by myself, AA would mind its own business. But if I wanted to quit and could not stay stopped, AA was one way that worked.

Our creed includes some common beliefs:
(1) Addiction is an incurable, progressive illness.
(2) One day at a time, we can stay sober.
(3) Self-reliance was insufficient for us to get and/or stay sober.
(4) Honesty, open-mindedness, self-evaluation and a willingness to make amends and help others are tools to get and stay clean and sober (recovery).

Some of us consider these tenets facts. Some of us concede that these tenets don't hold up as facts when subjected to scientific scrutiny. Nonetheless, as facts or ideas, they are our creed. These ideas are true for us and we feel it in our guts.

Alcoholics Anonymous started as a conversation between two amateurs who couldn't make it on their own. Others joined the conversation. They weren't experts, either. Since 1935, there hasn't been a generally recognized expert on addiction, prevention or recovery inside AA. As far as I know, none of the other 500 organizations that have taken the Twelve Step tenets and run with them have produced an expert either.[1] I have friends in AA, NA, SLAA, OA, FA, CA, Al-Anon, GA, ACA and other Twelve & Twelve fellowships. I call myself a qualified member in some of these meetings. In other cases, I have gone to meetings to support a friend or to satisfy my own curiosity. I have read and learned new things from each group's literature.

When referring to the Steps and Traditions, this book uses an addiction-generic, faith-neutral translation of the Steps adopted by some Twelve & Twelve agnostic groups. The Steps aren't considered sacred by every member, certainly not every nonbeliever. Many members with a variety of worldviews interpret, omit or replace Steps in a way that works effectively for them. The agnostic interpretation of the Twelve Steps used in this book isn't poetry and these Steps aren't universally embraced, not even by every agnostic or atheist Twelve Step member. I find in these agnostic Steps the essence of what the original Twelve Steps ask of us. They reflect the thought and action required to combat the destructive control of addiction and the artful balancing act of living clean and sober. Every member decides to work or dismiss each Step and how to interpret them. The variation used in this book is designed to not leave anyone out of the conversation.

The notion of taking artistic liberty with the program offends those in the Twelve Step orthodoxy. Bill Wilson was quite clear about the inherent liberty that groups and their members enjoy. Buddhists replaced the word "God" with "good" so that the practice of the Steps could be compatible with their non-theistic belief. Bill wrote, "To some of us, the idea of substituting 'good' for 'God' in the Twelve Steps will seem like a watering down of A.A.'s message. But here we must remember that A.A.'s Steps are suggestions only. A belief in them as they stand is not at all a requirement for membership among us. This liberty has made A.A. available to thousands who never would have tried at all had we insisted on the Twelve Steps just as written."[2]

Much of the language for the new millennium hasn't been crafted yet. The words "atheist" and "nonbeliever" describe someone by what they are not. "Freethinker" as a description of non-theists might seem to suggest that all religious people have rigid viewpoints, which isn't fair or true. Language lags behind culture. For example, all of us believe women and men have an equal right to vote. We no longer use the word "suffragist" to describe ourselves. One day, none of us will have to describe ourselves by what we do not believe.

Look at how far we've come from when the Twelve Step phenomena started. Society is more culturally diverse and more globally connected. Our understanding of addiction and recovery has expanded with our growing experience. Naturally, language evolves, too. Terms like "John Barleycorn" or patriarchal phrases like "This is the Step [Six] that separates the men from the boys" sound goofy to today's reader.[3] In time, the language in this book will sound just as dated.

Some of the newest fellowships are devoted to Century Twenty-one problems. Who, in the mid-1980s, could have conceived of addiction to online gaming? OLGA is a new millennium fellowship that presents the age-old Steps using a new-age language. Each new fellowship speaks the language of the day. For the most part, the newer the fellowship, the less emphasis is placed on God and the less the addict is referred to using a masculine pronoun.

Twenty-first century stewardship of Twelve & Twelve fellowships is in transition. Around the year 2005, the first of Generation X celebrated their 40th birthdays. In North America alone, children born between 1965 and 1980 number 51 million. Some have been sobering up, getting active and preparing to captain Team-Recovery. No second generation runs the family business just like Mom and Dad did. Gen X alcoholics and addicts are by no means Baby Boomer clones. Demographers describe this version of Homo sapiens as educated, individualistic and flaunting an unabashed disdain for structure and authority. Gen X faces our age-old addiction problem with an enigmatic attitude.

Right behind Gen X we see 75 million North American Millennials (Generation Y or Gen Next, born from 1981 to 2000). These youth were wired to the net before they got wired from addiction. Before the end of this century, the new bleeding deacon will be the multi-tasking, gadget-dependent, silver-haired web-surfer.

Hey, change is not inevitable—there is always extinction. When *hardening of the attitudes* is allowed, organizations will reify. Members tend to vote to keep things the same, more than to embrace change. In my own recovery, I experienced population growth in Alcoholics Anonymous from less than one million in the mid-1970s to a doubling twenty years later. For the generation of AA members that came before me, perpetual growth was all they knew. Early in the 1990s, AA population stalled at two million members and it remained +/- 10% of that high water mark for two decades.[4] Smaller, newer fellowships are growing. Technically, AA population is an outside issue to other fellowships. Yet as the granddaddy of *Twelve Steppery*, AA is something we all have some connection to. Is AA more likely to sustain the same numbers indefinitely? Will it increases or decrease in population?

Survival of the Twelve Step movement depends on the delicate balancing act of sticking to our principles while adapting to our environment. We could grow; alternately, we could stall and shrink. Imagine if we celebrated the 100th anniversary of the Twelve Steps, with the few thousand faithful members huddled around the carefully preserved 164 pages of the Big Book. Like other change-resistant cultures such as the Amish or Mennonites, the world would view us as charming, harmless and irrelevant.

Bill Wilson wrote, "A.A. will always have its traditionalists, its fundamentalists and its relativists."[5] Each camp looks at stewardship differently. For example, anonymity means something different to most members with twenty-first century dry dates than it does to baby-boomer old-timers. Spiritual lingo, rituals and what defines "outside issues" are all subject to review by Generation-Next.

Nonbelievers as a demographic are something that this millennium is getting used to. A survey conducted by *Pew Forum on Religion & Public Life* (2012) reveals that the " 'Nones' are on the rise." People who identify themselves as being unaffiliated with a religion rose from 15% to 20% between 2007 and 2012. While 13 million American adults identify as atheists/agnostics, another 33 million have no particular theistic view.[6] This news falls on the heels of a 2011 Survey in the UK that shows that 29% of British and Welsh respondents and only 35% of Scottish respondents claim to be religious. In Canada the 2008 Harris-Decima poll reported that 72% of Canadians believe in a god, 23% do not believe and 6% offered no opinion (rounded numbers).[7]

The daily musings in this book are written in the customary *we* voice. I know—only obnoxious people talk this way in meetings. However, this is the customary style used in self-help writing. There are imperfections with the English language and they become even more pronounced using this *we* voice. Technically, "God of our understanding" should be "Gods of our understanding." If two people believe in God, the God of one's understanding is a different one than the other's—hence, *Gods*. "Clearing away the wreckage on our side of the street" would be more grammatically correct as "our sides of the street" but nobody talks that way. "Our drug of choice" should be "our drugs of choice" and "our inner-child" should be "our inner children" to be consistent with the plural "our." As an editorial turning point there was no way to be grammatically correct and not come across as awkward. Most daily reflection books are penned in a *we* voice so *we do too*, despite the ambiguity.

As it turns out, each of the 365 pages is a continuation of an ongoing discussion in the rooms. I dare not take ownership of any of these ideas or interpretations. I have been in Twelve Step meetings, pondering the questions of the universe, for so long that I dare not draw the line between original thought and ideas crafted from the wisdom of meetings and coffee shops. I have been studying Twelve Step books and attending meetings, conferences, Step studies, service meetings and retreats for over 13,000 twenty-four hour periods. It's safe to say that this book captures neither originality nor expertise. The days reflect lessons learned in and out of the rooms and questions that continue to amuse or perplex me.

I don't hope or expect to find bobble-headed agreement with every thesis on every day. Agree or disagree, be inspired or be skeptical. Please treat these pages as part of a never-ending dialogue. I didn't start this conversation. Let's keep it going. We're all in this together.

# January 1

*"The Tao is a world unfolding according to its own laws.*
*Nothing is done or forced; everything just comes about.*
*To live in accord with the Tao is to understand non-doing*
*and non-striving. Your life is already doing itself.*

*Jon Kabat-Zinn, PhD (born 1944)*

---

Have we become human *doings* who have forgotten how to *be*? Does a day of not doing and not striving sound un-recovery? In western culture, we are encouraged to make New Year's resolutions, ostensibly to correct our flawed lives. Taoism suggests that we are worthy just the way we are. So is the world around us. How would our days, years or lives look if we felt 100% worthy already? Forget the resolution! Non-doing and non-striving sound like practices that should come naturally; "Don't worry, be happy." So, how have we become habitually self-critical? Some Twelve & Twelve members may always be striving to get good enough, yet never be satisfied.

Each day this year, we will look to wisdom, humor and contradiction to propel the Good Ship Recovery. We don't strive to create the energy in our world; we work with it. This year, we examine and reexamine what we think we know. We start by questioning whether or not we are flawed, and if flawed, whether or not we need to be fixed. Are we navigating through life consciously, sailing along on the energy that presents itself, or are we struggling against the elements?

We don't need to conform to embrace the fellowship's Tradition of unity. Each of us is as unique as our own thumbprint. Non-doing and non-striving are symbiotic with a program of action. Being still allows for a wider vantage point than the tunnel vision of full-speed-ahead.

Non-doing and non-striving are not exactly Twelve Step, Twelve Tradition clichés. Am I set in my ways or open to new ways of seeing?

# January 2

*"Every form of addiction is bad, no matter whether the narcotic be alcohol, morphine or idealism."*

Carl Jung (1875–1961)

---

Why is everything we love so damned addictive? Food, work, spending, sex, and even being right—all of these things are the rewards of good living. A sense of mastery at work or play adds to a sense of well-being unless we take ourselves too seriously. Intimacy fulfills us when we aren't plagued by codependency. Solitude is rewarding when we aren't isolating. Healthy recovery involves maintaining what is good in life without going overboard.

"More is better" is the addict's refrain. As kids, did we balk at the steady-as-she-goes tortoise winning the race with the rabbit? We emulated the rabbit, not the tortoise, and our lives were an attempt to re-write the ending. Jung's "narcotic" is not to blame for our plight. Addiction is our responsibility. Some of us stop one dependency only to discover a new addiction that will fill the emotional void. Maybe a gambler manages boredom with drink, or an alcoholic becomes a workaholic or exercises beyond what is healthy or recreational. Many addictions began as innocent distractions.

Consider this addicts' metaphor about managing multiple compulsions: We have four cans of stinky garbage and only three lids. No matter how quickly we cover the exposed can, another lid has to be borrowed to cover the freshly exposed stink. Keeping a lid on addiction by *putting a lid on it* seems futile. Awareness is no cure for the smell. At some point we have to dispose of the garbage.

Jung also said, "Who looks outside, dreams; who looks inside, awakes." Addiction came from indulgence, from taking in what we found *out there*. There was not enough *out there* to fill the void *in here*. If our solution is something new, found *out there*, it won't fill the void either—it's just a better dream. The solution, when found inside, when we internalize our recovery, can finally fill the void. We awaken to clean living and we make it our own.

Am I predisposed to addiction? Can I distinguish between my habits/indulgences and deadly obsessions? Is my recovery a dream or am I awake?

# January 3

*"All change is not growth; as all movement is not forward."*

*Ellen Glasgow (1873–1945)*

---

In what author James Howard Kunstler calls "symptoms of impaired consensus," something for nothing delusions and faith that wishing upon a star can make it so lead to what Kunstler calls "toxic psychology." He argues, "It was exactly this magical thinking that came to infect the realm of capital finance and has so far come close to destroying it... After a while I began to understand what lay behind the plea for 'solutions.' They were clamoring desperately for rescue remedies that would allow them to continue living exactly the way they were used to living, with all the accustomed comforts." Kunstler uses the example of the Aspen Environment Forum, where great thinkers bandied about ideas such as alternative fuels for cars that could postpone the inevitable demise of the current system.[8] No one brought up the idea of ending our dependence on automobile transportation. No one talked about more mass transit, more efficient communities where people could walk to what they needed. Forum chatter stalled at bandage remedies (small change) and fell short of the innovation and sacrifice needed to make real progress.

Rocking chairs create motion—but where do they get us? How often have we heard (if not said ourselves), "I need a new sponsor, job or daily reflection book," with the idea that change is growth. Action, such as reading or going to meetings, isn't necessarily progress. We may learn something new and maybe even develop a new vocabulary. Is this growth? Only if we apply the new information and commit it to better living will change morph into growth.

Do I know in my heart and my head that I need determination and a change in behavior in order to convert temporary enthusiasm into real growth?

# January 4

*"You will never wake up sober and wish you'd had
a drink last night."*

*Heard around the rooms*

---

This might be heard in a Step One meeting in AA but it could be applied to acting out in any process or substance addiction or codependent relationship. When we are new or struggling, craving preoccupies us like hunger would the starving. An early AA slogan, "Think, think, think", is brain medicine. Let's face it—what kind of addicts would we be if our minds weren't Petri dishes for impulsive thoughts? Thinking these thoughts through to their most likely outcomes can go a long way toward disarming opportunistic impulses. Craving? Keep thinking. Another fond saying around the rooms is, "My brain would kill me if it didn't need the transportation." Who can relate?

Automatic thinking can highjack our conscious mind with a rash idea. Maybe it's a good idea. Even if it is, we are not committed to it. Being mindful instead of compulsive, we don't stop looking for ideas just because we found one. After all, if we just came across one good idea, maybe we have stumbled upon a goldmine of good ideas, so why wouldn't we keep digging? An idea is only a bad idea when it's our only idea.

How protected am I today from craving or other cunning, impulsive thoughts? Can "Think, think, think" remind me not to get married to my first idea even if it's a good one? When I have "What's the use?" thoughts, can "Think, think, think" save me from impulsivity? Has impulsivity recently led to regret?

# January 5

*"It is impossible for a man to learn what he thinks
he already knows."*

Epictetus (AD 55–AD 135)

---

"Keep an open mind" is easier to say while pointing an index finger at another. It's quite a different matter when we consider the three fingers pointed back at us. Epictetus spoke the truth nearly two thousand years ago and it's true today. To give what we know perspective, let us consider four quadrants of knowledge:

| Box I:<br>*What we know we know* | Box II: *What we know<br>we do not know* |
|---|---|
| Box III: *What we do not<br>know we do not know* | Box IV: *What we do not<br>know we know* |

Box I gives us a sense of mastery: "I know my shit." Box II keeps us humble: "I need to learn that." Box III, as this quote suggests, addresses our blind spots: "What could possibly go wrong?" Box IV is our unconscious wisdom, sometimes revealing itself to us at the most opportune times: "I didn't know I had it in me."

Research suggests that an addict's mind produces compromised neurotransmissions that further frustrate our cognitive capacities. What we call a *wet* brain or *fried* brain is a brain that has been damaged. We are aware of some of this damage, and some evades us. Meditating and applying "Think, think, think" before we jump to conclusions or open our mouths are tools that assist us in recovery. Counting to ten before saying or doing something impulsive can help mitigate the damage caused by being a few cards shy of a full deck. Asking ourselves, "What else could this mean?" can help highlight the difference between being certain and being right.

How can I change my thinking and vocabulary to be less handicapped by my own ignorance, blind spots or overconfidence?

# January 6

*"Experiencing the pain of my life gave me back my vitality; first pain, then vitality. The price of repressing feelings is depression. I also had to resist the usual way of learning. If you are forced to do something, you cannot have fun. But for me, having fun is the first condition for creativity."*

*Alice Miller (1923–2010)*

---

What a concept: recover from addiction and have fun, not apart from, but as part of the process—not an arduous process but the creative process. The Twelve Steps can seem so solemn at times but recovery is an adventure. Alice Miller is sharing from one of her thirteen books, *The Drama of the Gifted Child*, about dealing with her own unmet childhood needs.[9]

If we were our own coaches preparing ourselves for the Olympics we would encourage and celebrate progress. We would think up stimulating, entertaining activities to keep us sharp and motivated. Being able to prevent drudgery from seeping in over the long haul would be a competitive advantage. For Olympic success we also have to be brutally realistic. We don't deny the new pain that life brings, nor do we leave old pain buried. In recovery we face unresolved life dramas like an athlete reviews the flaws and kinks of their performance. We all have imperfections. Masking defects or denying them do not, an Olympic performance, make.

Vitality flows to the surface after experiencing and purging the pain. Like stretching and strengthening our muscles, discomfort is never indefinite suffering; it waxes and it wanes. Unused muscles hurt more than those in use all the time. Repressed pain hurts more than feelings we deal with as they come up. Our confronted hurt no longer haunts us; our psychic circulation flows and vitality is restored. Recovery, like exercise, need not be dull or repetitive. Just as rest is part of a training regimen, there is time for fun and laughter in our recovery routines. Fun helps us strengthen and heal.

What can I do today to make my recovery fun and creative?

# January 7

*"Myths can sometimes express philosophical ideas that more exact language can never get across. Mythological language is infinitely suggestive."*

*Alan Watts (1915–1973)*

---

Poets, songwriters, filmmakers, painters and popstars use mythological archetypes like good (God) vs. evil (Devil). Egyptian, Greek, Norse, Eastern and Aboriginal parables are full of great stories. Artistic interpretations of these stories neither mock nor advocate religion. Mythology, religion and cultural customs anecdotally tell and preserve our narratives.

Those of us with theistic or religious convictions are well served by keeping Twelve Step discussion about higher powers at an anecdotal level. Atheists can stand up for what they believe in without being evangelical, too. Differing experiences need not be barrier-building. Who can take issue with us if we maintain humble ambivalence toward our dearest beliefs? If we want our communication to be inoffensive, we avoid absolute or rigid language. An atheist that zealously reacts to a religious parable by offering "proof" of the non-existence of an omnipotent being misses the life lesson of the story. Conversely, the religious zealot who discounts the spiritual contribution of the nonbeliever is suffering the same *hardening of the attitudes* that builds unnecessary barriers. There is a time for intellectual stubbornness and a time to rise above it. Do we look for fault like there's a reward for it? Who made us the truth police?

Art can answer questions that academia cannot and vice versa. We can be grounded in reality *and* have active imaginations; one isn't superior to the other. Contempt makes our world smaller. Tolerance is a good start, but we strive for appreciation of others. A childlike curiosity about art, philosophy, religion or history opens our minds. I don't need to believe in Cain and Abel or Dr. Jekyll and Mr. Hyde to let their stories tell me more about myself and my world.

Can I find value in science, faith and mythology as guideposts to a rich and full life?

# January 8

*"Moral cowardice that keeps us from speaking our minds is as dangerous to this country as irresponsible talk. The right way is not always the popular and easy way. Standing for right when it is unpopular is a true test of moral character."*

Margaret Chase Smith (1897–1995)

---

What this Joseph McCarthy-era senator had to say about moral dangers to the USA could be applied to our fellowship as well. Speaking without thinking is detrimental; so is staying silent out of cowardice when an unpopular opinion may need our support. Bill Wilson's *Concept V* crafted the traditional "Right of Appeal" for just this reason. Wilson writes, "The well-heard minority, therefore, is our chief protection against an uninformed, misinformed, hasty or angry majority."[10] A minority opinion can be right. We can't stay silent when witnessing discrimination or harassment. Minority rights are inherent—they don't need to be granted by the majority; they must be respected.

Senator Smith made it clear that a fair and democratic society required pluralism and not binary thinking. In her democracy, everyone had rights: the right to criticize, the right to hold unpopular beliefs, the right to protest and the right to independent thought. Margaret Smith spoke up against McCarthy, a member of her own political party. McCarthy's position was that the democratic world could not make peace with communism, and that the eradication of communism was necessary for a free and democratic world. Communist thought or skepticism of the American establishment was intolerable and un-American in McCarthy's view. Smith's leadership would lead to the censure of Joseph McCarthy, whose career would fold before his alcoholism unraveled, eventually ending his life in 1957.

When others anger and say, "special interest groups can't highjack the agenda," will I speak up and say, "While that is true, even the most unpopular position deserves our thoughtful consideration"?

*"Sometimes we find ourselves becoming involved in the lives of others as a way of avoiding fulfilling our own potential and vision. This saps us of the energy that we need to be 'spending' on our dream—and then we wonder why we feel aimless and annoyed."*

*Visions, Debtors Anonymous*

Here are some great balancing acts: a life of service to others that includes personal commitments, connecting with community without losing our personal identities, finding partnership without codependency, *mothering* without *smothering* our children. Demonstrating gratitude to be in the service of others is good. Martyrdom is either overextending ourselves or narcissistic.

How do we keep balance in our relationships? First we remember the motto, "progress, rather than perfection." A Step Ten exercise involving checking in with ourselves or others can help keep us on target like a sailor who constantly adjusts sails and measures his or her heading. Feelings are like a barometer to help us gauge how we're doing in service or in managing confrontations. How did we feel about it afterward? The "aimless and annoyed" feeling mentioned above can be our compass. If we feel good, we're on track. If we are frustrated, let's take inventory.

Transactional Analysis uses a *Dramatic Triangle* comprised of three roles: Perpetrator, Victim and Rescuer.[11] The Rescuer secretly wants recognition for heroism or encourages constant dependency from the Victims he or she helps. There is no true satisfaction in living a role or label; it's inauthentic. Uncomfortable feelings signal that our motivations are off-base. The idea that we cripple our children by making life easy for them reminds us that, in service, we do not do for others what they can clearly do themselves. To paraphrase a parable: we teach others to fish; we don't catch and cook every fish they will ever need.

I realize I don't do relationships perfectly. Today, how are my boundaries with others?

## January 10

*"The inherent instability of the human organism makes it imperative that man himself provide a stable environment for his conduct. Man himself must specialize and direct his drives. These biological facts serve as a necessary presupposition for the production of social order."*

The Social Construction of Reality
*by Peter Berger & Thomas Luckmann*

---

"Our common welfare should come first. Personal recovery depends upon A.A. unity."[12] Rules that unify a society are fabricated—not natural law. Adherence to agreed upon rules legitimizes a society's subjective reality. Our Traditions are not rules per se; they are our manifesto. The interdependence of unity and recovery is not a scientific fact; it is our creed. The principle of unity is the premise of our Traditions. Maybe we could walk away from the fellowship and never fall prey to addiction again. But wouldn't we want to know the meetings were here if we needed them or someone else did?

Unity is not uniformity. Some members go to a lot of meetings; one a day might not be enough at times. For others, attending two meetings per week shows a lack of imagination. We each find our rhythm by trial and error. We don't have to like or be like everyone else to respect our common welfare. We get our say in meetings, but we don't always get our way. Our fellowship doesn't police or expel members for noncompliance. With no rules to enforce, we may appear to be a society of anarchists. Bill Wilson took some heat from friends in medicine and academia for encouraging a lawless society. It was seen as irresponsible. Left to our own devices isn't man selfish? "Homo-empathicus," a Jeremy Rifkin term coined in his contrarian book, *The Empathic Civilization,* suggests that we are naturally empathetic and social.[13] Tradition One suggests that we are all in this together—all for one and one for all.

Do I speak of unity, and then get impatient when others criticize or express their opinions? Unity makes room for even the most unpopular opinions. Do I balance the needs of the many along with my needs?

# January 11

*"This is how change happens, though. It is a relay race, and we're very conscious of that, that our job really is to do our part of the race, and then we pass it on, and then someone picks it up, and it keeps going. And that is how it is. And we can do this, as a planet, with the consciousness that we may not get it, you know, today, but there's always a tomorrow."*

*Alice Walker (born 1944)*

---

Alcoholics Anonymous was borne of many ideas and experiences already in play. Seeing addiction as a medical condition and not moral depravity was a huge step forward. Prior to that, we addicts could be despised or pitied and society could be quite detached from our eventual demise. Once labeled a medical condition, people thought twice about writing us off. Alcoholics and addicts had a self-image adjustment to make too, accepting that they were morally no worse than any medical patient. Addiction and treatment are a continuum and one day we may forgo the medical diagnosis of addiction for some greater understanding. Many would resist embracing such a revolutionary idea. Let's neither rashly adopt any new promise of a solution to an age-old problem, nor be dogmatically resistant to change for the better. Remember that it was once commonly accepted that addiction was the Devil's work.

All progress is a team effort, whether it involves treating addiction, global consciousness or maintaining a cleaner planet. In all noble objectives, whether a grassroots movement or a United Nations debate, the baton is handed from member to member around the table to help a movement to initiate and continue positive change. In Twelve & Twelve fellowships, service commitments celebrate the spirit of rotation. The cause, the goal and the end are celebrated, although the champions of positive change are often anonymous. Our program, like a living organism, is inter-dependent and constantly changing. We each have a temporary but impactful role to play.

In and out of the fellowship, am I mindful that my service is temporary but can still be impactful? Do I have a tendency to see my role as either grandiose or insignificant?

*"Many of us still do not want to use the word "insanity" to describe our own behavior and thinking. Denial and delusion come from addictive and co-dependent impaired thinking. Considering that insanity involves distortion of reality, addicts and co-addicts need to regain perspective on what is real and what is not. Spirituality will elude us if we cling to delusion."*

The Gentle Path Through the Twelve Steps *by Patrick Carnes*

---

Addicts suck at assessing risk. We take risks others wouldn't. It's not brave; it's insane. We deny our addiction with three reality blocks that Dr. Carnes identifies as (i) ignoring, (ii) distorting and (iii) lacking reality.[14] Medical consensus now suggests that we addicts have identifiable brain chemistry irregularities that prevent outside stimuli or internal safety mechanisms from alerting us to danger. Have our selective memories and blind spots distorted our reality? Wow—that's crazy!

Old-timers have come to terms with this. We hear them joke, "Half of what I remember never happened." Memory loss, blackouts or psychic distortion may be symptoms of trauma. For some, Step work reveals psychological problems that are beyond the scope of peer-to-peer help. Some memories may take years to come back; some blank spots never come back. Have we been gambling without a full deck?

Addiction begets isolation. Isolation makes us more self-absorbed. Compulsion to control and overcompensation for real or perceived inadequacies put us further and further away from reality—more evidence that people like us really shouldn't be running with scissors.

Do I take issue with the word "insane" when I consider Step Two or any of the other Steps that reference my behavior? How do I describe my addictive thinking and behavior? How much of that *old* thinking and faulty brain chemistry is still with me today?

# January 13

*"Where does one go from a world of insanity?*
*Somewhere on the other side of despair."*

T.S. Eliot (1888–1965)

---

Step Two says, "We came to believe ..." Belief isn't a choice; it's a compulsion. Altered beliefs require evidence, arguments and trust. Hope can be felt but it's hard to articulate. Despair, on the other hand, we know and can articulate clearly. We only know that "somewhere on the other side of despair" is something that is not despair. In game show terms we choose Door # 2, sight unseen, for a life that is not what this is, not where addiction has brought us. Without the intellectual comfort of proof, gut instinct guides us to believe (or hope) that Door # 2 is a better choice. We make a sane choice from an insane place. We know not the way but we feel like we are given a second chance. We have a moment of clarity and/or faith. We choose an unknown in choosing the promise of life over wasting away.

We hear this *power* defined by people as a "spiritual awakening," "collective unconsciousness," "god-consciousness" or "our higher selves." Various mental constructs or symbols give definition to our Step Two experiences. Words don't have to be readily available at decision time—hindsight will help us narrate how Step Two worked for us. We reach out for help from power(s) beyond our own resources, for guidance and strength in our resolve for continued abstinence and self-improvement.

Recovery is rarely a straight line; we are more likely to go back and forth than to commit with finality. We are comfortable in meetings one day and resistant the next day. That's OK; those who put up a fight over the program do better when the shit hits the fan later in life. One day we will have a narrative to articulate the other side of addictive despair. Making a decision, without knowing the outcome, requires faith. Choosing "that, not this" is a good enough start as we come to— and then come to believe.

How important is the language I use to explain what I think and feel about Step Two today?

# January 14

*"It is generally inadvisable to eject directly over the area you just bombed."*

U.S. Air Force Manual

---

Who says military intelligence is an oxymoron? This looks like pretty good advice. To many, this is a familiar scenario. The practical lesson, even for pacifists, is that the safe confines of our metaphorical cockpits may have to be abandoned due to the unexpected. Do we have a safe place to land if we need to eject? Like the metaphor that warns of burning our bridges behind us, we should think through our exit strategies, in case things don't go our way. Our households, the boss's office, our home groups or our social networks might not be sanctuaries if we unloaded a shit-storm the last time we were there.

We take responsibility for our actions in recovery and we become mindful and more considerate of how our actions impact on others. Less "bombing" will lead to less hiding, less apologizing and less chaos—and we will endure less retaliation, too.

We all need a safe place to vent and the right time to do it. Sometimes we have wrath that we feel compelled to unleash. Restraint is a sign of maturity. Some letters, emails and speeches are best when they aren't delivered. It can be healthy just to get our feelings out on paper. How much more do we get from hitting the send button and dropping the bomb—and at what cost?

Life is unpredictable. Like our pilot who has to eject from his war plane, we never know from whom we might need help or mercy tomorrow. We stand up for what we believe. We are also cautious about imposing our will on others. War is the utter failure of diplomacy.

How good am I at diplomacy? Can I express my needs and wants without being threatening or passive-aggressive?

# January 15

*"Being unwanted, unloved, uncared for, forgotten by everybody,*
*I think that is a much greater hunger, a much greater poverty*
*than the person who has nothing to eat."*

### Mother Teresa (1910–1997)

---

Mother Teresa devoted her life to relieving suffering in developing nations. Most of us don't live either her life or the lives of those whom she touched. The dilemmas of people living in extreme poverty fall into a different category, in the Maslow Hierarchy of Needs, than those faced by someone stressed out about overtime and mortgage payments.[15] Some of us have travelled and seen real suffering for ourselves. Few of us stayed to help and fewer still traded in our creature comforts for lives of Mother Teresa-like servitude.

So when we consider how this quote applies to each of our lives, it is not without gratitude and a pause for thought that addiction and the emotional hardships of recovery, at their worst, are privileged problems. Yes, we can die from emotional bankruptcy forty floors up, looking down on Las Vegas (our problems are very real) but our upside is more than most earthlings can dare contemplate.

Human suffering has some constants that transcend environment. We look back at our early days and see how our bitching about money troubles and other shortfalls were surface wounds. Below the surface of our chaotic lives was greater fear—the fear of being unwanted, unloved and forgotten. We lived with walls to keep people out; we also feared that we didn't matter to the same people we were trying to keep out. In our self-pity we felt entitled and manipulated others. We drove people even further away. Regardless of our neighborhoods, we created our own ghettos of despair. We could easily have died there—many do. Whether we are living the good life now or barely see the possibility through the fog, we have opportunities for better lives. Yes, we have problems, but we have choices that many people dare not dream of.

What is important to me today? What do I have to be grateful for today?

# January 16

*"We may be self-employed and have the idea that we cannot charge much because we love what we do or that we are justified only by suffering. But buyers don't care about our struggle; they only want to know if a product fits their needs. In fact, if a book or film is produced in joy, that feeling shines through and attracts buyers."*

*"Turning Work into Play,"* Workaholics Anonymous

---

Work takes up a large percentage of the best years of our lives. What purpose do we see in our labor? Work is a good reflection of the state of our recovery. No one in the office cares what Step we are on, just that we do what is asked of us. Some of us find a higher purpose in our work while others find ourselves out of sorts vocationally. Work recognition might be a source of a daily buzz. Do we look to wealth or prestige to give our lives meaning? If work is a means to an end, that's not selling out. But if we are courting it to feed psychic needs we might feel used and abused at the end of the work relationship. Motives and intentions are keys to creating a healthy working environment. *Games People Play* by Eric Berne offers many good ways to identify and inventory our behavior and to recognize when we are being drawn into the games other people play. Not every conflict is our fault or responsibility to solve.

Work can also be a way to get right with the world, to be what we could not be in addiction. We can make amends for the selfish rut that obsessive-compulsiveness reduced us to. Like today's quote says, attitude counts for a lot. People won't remember what we did or said so much as the attitude we projected. Dignity doesn't come from a title; we bring dignity to the workplace and as our integrity grows, so will our job satisfaction.

Just for today, can I reflect on what I have to contribute instead of what I need and want? Life is like a mirror. When I smile at the mirror of life, life smiles back at me. If I wait for the mirror to smile first... that's a long wait. I spend a lot of my life at work. What am I going to do with that time?

*"Now we were truly feeling some sense of deep release from the past! We were free of much guilt for our misdeeds, from the shame of having fallen short of our inner values. In many instances, the values we had thought were ours had turned out to be someone else's."*

*Sex and Love Addicts Anonymous, "The Promises"*

---

How do we achieve authenticity? Have we adopted popular beliefs and rituals to win approval or get along? Do we claim to be individuals while extolling values that are either inherited from our parents or in direct defiance of them? Defiance isn't a value; it's a reaction. What is it that we stand for? It takes time to find our true voices and personal convictions.

So much of Twelve Step recovery requires tearing down façades, leaving us feeling vulnerable and ashamed. Understanding shame helps us understand the cycle of faking our way through life. The truth can set us free. It is never too late to build a foundation for our lives on legitimate values. If we fed insatiable needs with sex, drugs and consumer goods, knowing our values won't suddenly make us boring. However, we grow more confident and calm. Our values can't be bought or stolen and we know it. We may be popular or we may be ridiculed. The approval of others is no longer the measure by which we find our self-worth. We still like things and people but we aren't slaves to our needs anymore.

Early in the recovery process we may mimic others we admire. It's like trying on clothes in a store—each of us looking around for what is *really me*. Our authentic voices will change from time to time—we are dynamic, not stagnant. If we are open, perceptions and priorities may change. Writing, thinking, meditating and talking it out can help us find inner truth. Resisting the urge to fall back on our old coping techniques makes us feel strong.

The promises follow Step Nine which, for me, is about taking responsibility and having dignity. Can I feel the difference between my own integrity and winning the approval of others?

# January 18

*"Insanity in individuals is something rare but in groups, parties, nations and epochs, it is the rule."*

Friedrich Nietzsche (1844–1900)

---

Nietzsche was a follower of Arthur Schopenhauer, a German philosopher/writer who also influenced Einstein, Jung and Freud. Schopenhauer looked at truth as an embryonic force that must overcome two difficult hurdles—ridicule and violent opposition—before reaching universal acceptance. *Group conscience* demands more love and insight than popular opinion. It asks what is right, rather than what we want.

Picture two wolves and one sheep voting on what's for dinner. Is that democracy? Organizations can look democratic while keeping up appearances. Forward thinking that doesn't account for the very human tendency to resist change and sabotage progress is *coo-coo*. Many crazy people sound lucid until you check the facts. So we don't take everyone at face value. It pays to apply the same discretion and discernment to countries, companies, societies and our home groups, too.

Tell AA how its message would resonate with more people if the literature had a gender-neutral facelift. Most concede that changing "To Wives" to "To Loved Ones" and "God as we understand Him" to "God of our understanding" would convey the same message without the patriarchy. The language would be more inclusive, making AA more effective at its primary purpose—bringing hope to the *still suffering*. If our primary purpose is to keep the regulars comfortable, then who needs change? As a group we need to deeply explore our intent.

Remember how devoid of reality our arguments were when we were new? Rigorous honesty—is that for crisis management or is it our way of life? Progress rather than perfection is still the mantra when looking at both personal and group welfare. Dogma and fear of change will always cripple us humans but our crazy group and our crazy fellowship needs us and we need them. Rule # 62 reminds us to not take ourselves too seriously.[16]

Can I reach my potential with a flawed but workable program? Am I an example of willingness to adapt? How well do I take to other people's ideas about change?

# January 19

*"You will not be punished for your anger;
you will be punished by your anger."*

*Buddha (563BC-483 BC)*

---

Anger is the most misunderstood of feelings. Being angry is natural; it is spontaneous, honest and legitimate. Our difficulty with expressing feelings is a great catalyst for our addictions. There are no "bad" feelings; there are, however, "bad" ways to process or react to our feelings.

Resentment is repressed anger. Repression is what punishes us. Dr. Gabor Maté argues that small "d" depression (feeling blue) isn't a feeling, but a coping mechanism. The premise is that we are overwhelmed by feelings and avoid our anger (or grief, or shame), leading to numbness and then depression. Depression (or anxiety) is the result of constipated feelings. Melodramatic expressions of anger, on the other hand, may be a smokescreen for repressed sadness.[17] How do we take stock of feelings if we don't know if our feelings are genuine or camouflage?

Misguided help on the topic of anger abounds. As kids, we are taught that expressing anger is over-reactive, selfish or forbidden and that ignoring anger will make it go away. As adults, heart patients are told, "Don't get angry." We owe it to ourselves and to our loved ones to learn how to express anger in safe, effective and healthy ways. Step Four encourages us to inventory our hurt. Learning to label feelings is a good start for those of us who identify as emotionally handicapped; investigation leads to understanding. Today's author, Buddha, also said, "To understand everything is to forgive everything."

Understanding comes more from experiencing the Steps than from reading about and listening to them. Writing, talking, doing the exercises—these are parts of the process. Have we been assertive in expressing our feelings or do we side-step into aggressive or passive-aggressive reactions? All this takes time and the progress is slow. We focus on being better with time—not being perfect.

Do I feel better or worse after I express anger? If I feel better when I *let it all out*—great. What if I feel worse afterward? What angers me now and do I need practice and training to express myself?

# January 20

*"Deceit: Only fools hope to live forever by escaping enemies.*
*Age promises no peace though the spear spares them."*

Havamal: The Sayings of the Vikings

---

*Havamal* is a guide for living—heathen wisdom of Scandinavian forefathers—and has endured by being passed from Viking to Viking for 1,000 years. These principles helped them survive Christian crusades and various invaders while other civilizations were completely assimilated. The stewards of these noble truths gained no obvious reward. It's a little like the Twelve Steps—we pass on the way from one addict to another with no obvious payoff. All the original one hundred members are gone but here we are, carrying their message, some of us citing chapter and verse and some of us describing our transformations in our own words.

Addicts know a thing or two about avoidance. Procrastination pains us more than simply confronting our problems or foes. The goal in avoidance is to dodge pain, but the sense of impending doom is often harsher than any hostility or humiliation that we face by taking our lumps. It's not that we literally face being gored like our Norse brethren, but don't tell our active imaginations that we have it so much easier. Those of us who long for control and approval don't expect satisfaction from the angry customer we need to call back, the ex we need to deal with or the amends we need to make. We even put good things off. A member was asked, "Did you call them? You had this great job prospect!" "No," replies the addict, "If I call and they say 'no,' I won't have a great job prospect anymore."

When we feel overwhelmed by too many calls, years of taxes or hours of cleaning, we can reduce the task to the ridiculous—we do our work for ten minutes. It's not enough to solve the problem, but it gets us started. If we stop, we find it wasn't so bad and we aren't anxious about putting another ten minutes in again sometime soon. If we keep going, great; doing it is always easier than thinking about it.

What do I want or need to at least get started on today?

# January 21

*"If you ask people about these problems, you will most likely find they have faith that somebody intelligent is looking at these things for us. That isn't a justified faith. We have to do our thinking for ourselves. We can't let other people do our thinking for us. Because a lot of people have ulterior motives and they will try to steer us in the wrong direction. A lot of them don't know what's going on even though they are in positions of power."*

*Albert Bartlett, PhD (born 1923)*

---

Our author isn't anti-serenity, but today's challenge is to know when it's time to be assertive. There is a serene spiritualist and a cantankerous malcontent in each of us. If these two personalities of ours are integrated we can be happy and useful. Government, employers and most of those around us would love to see us positive and grateful, mindful of the small things and not too critical. Subversive rattling of the cages challenges the status quo and isn't the best way to win friends or gain approval.

Every addict has cognitive dissonance. We were sure that everything would be OK when we were out there, blind to how we were affecting ourselves and others. After finding recovery and a noteworthy increase in manageability in our lives, we generally want to hold on to that warm feeling. Isn't someone else looking after the big issues? Bartlett challenges us to think sanely and soberly about the well-being of the world around us. Why shouldn't it start with us? In recovery we have unique skills that we have learned from the Steps and the Traditions, which we can share with the outside world. World leaders are seeking out life on other planets—we don't even know how to sustain life here. Isn't that a little crazy? When our heads clear from addiction we will see that not all the crazies are inside these rooms. Our time will come to make a stand.

Even within my program, my family and my home group, disturbing the apple cart can be better than killing people with kindness. Am I sometimes lazy with unjustified faith that everything will be OK? Serenity, courage and wisdom are enigmas more than absolutes. Do I see chaos in the world and turn my head away, leaving it for someone else to solve?

# January 22

*"A horse is dangerous at both ends and uncomfortable in the middle."*

### Ian Fleming (1908–1964)

---

Hmmm, a conundrum... Does Ian Fleming mean, "Forget the horse, take the Aston Martin; it's faster and more comfortable?" Or is the horse a metaphor for life? Are addicts often James Bond-esque, boredom-averse escape artists? The uncomfortable middle is a balanced life focused on here and now. Compare that to a life of extremes at "both ends." Binging and purging, recklessness and rigidity—these are not uncomfortable; they are dangerous. Addicts relate to escalating extremes leading to riskier behavior. The abnormal becomes acceptable because normal has gotten boring. Happiness and productivity are possible when we finally learn to feel at home with the calm and routine of our lives. We still have freedoms, risks and extravagances, but within limits.

Psychologists who study Subjective Well-Being (SWB) find that the things that make us happiest or most fulfilled are things we do only 5% of the time. For example, people tend to report higher SWB at meal times.[18] Even those who are stressed out in the morning, afternoon and night find that breaking bread, often with friends or family, is a pleasant part of the day. Eating all the time or being obsessed with eating is no joy. Wagering on a horse can make a day at the track exhilarating, but to be addicted to gambling means more and more extravagant stimulation is needed to find the same satisfaction. We often hear the term "progressive disease," and many of us can see how our extreme behavior got worse. Thoughts of suicide were seriously entertained as either the only escape or our just rewards. We don't have to ride the garbage truck all the way to the dump but lots of us did—losing almost everything.

The key to progress is improvement, not perfection. Fun and rewards are parts of a balanced recovery. So is boredom. An inability to find pleasure in regular things is normal in early recovery; the medical term for this is "anhedionia." It passes as our intensity-addicted brains *rewire* themselves into clean and sober living.

Have I learned to thrive in the middle of life or make peace with mild discomfort? Am I still triggered? Am I an intensity junky? Do I fidget or want things "shaken, not stirred" when all is quiet?

# January 23

*"To decide is to walk facing forward with nary a crick
in your neck from looking back at the crossroads."*

*Betsy Cañas Garmon (born 1985)*

---

So many addicts and codependents on a train to ruin, so few recovered or recovering. What separates one group from the other? We all reach a crossroads. Some of us concede defeat to addiction and others come to another decision. There is no such thing as "no decision." We learn this in time. "Maybe I will quit tomorrow" isn't a non-decision. It's a choice for today; we know tomorrow never comes. Some addicts/codependents never get a second chance. Addiction takes hold and we think time is on our side. Russian roulette doesn't go as many rounds as we had hoped. Some people get snuffed out quickly, while some of us have cat-of-nine-lives chances.

Non-addicts face crossroads in their lives, too. But our brain chemistry is disturbed. Years of intoxication have damaged survival skills that help to evaluate risk and foresee consequences. Each of us has been at that crossroads. We chose recovery. Most members who have persisted through the Steps don't look back with longing. Our daily reprieve may never be 100% free of all compulsions. Some of these will be nuisances and some could be more serious, forcing us to start over with a new bottom line. Will we get new kinks in our necks at new crossroads of smoking, gambling, shopping, internet or any other new addiction standing between us and a manageable life of freedom?

Stats on who recovers and who dies of addiction are hard to collect. Addicts are notorious liars and we don't always show up for focus groups. No one knows with certainty what becomes of those who go back out. We don't even know for certain what the future holds for us.

All I know for sure is that I made a decision. Do I recommit every day or forget about it and get on with life? Do I look back? If so, does it bring longing and fear or gratitude and commitment?

## January 24

*"A.A. was not invented! Its basics were brought to us through the experience and wisdom of many great friends. We simply borrowed and adapted their ideas."*

Bill W., letter, 1966[19]

---

Hero-worshipers infer that the hand of God rested on Bill Wilson's shoulder as he wrote the Big Book. Bill didn't think so. The man had a message, the message started a movement, and the members reified the message into a monument. The next M-stop on the alliteration train will be a mausoleum, on which may be inscribed, "AA was great and then members grew afraid of change, so it stayed the same and withered away." Are we afraid to keep borrowing and adapting new ideas, as our founders did? Bill W. did not believe in change for change's sake, but he anticipated the need for adaptation.

AA founders learned from R. Peabody's book, *The Common Sense of Drinking*, from The Oxford Group, Dr. Silkworth, Dr. Jung, William James and many other sources. Did founders ask to be canonized and to have their words enshrined as the alpha and omega of recovery talk, or did they want us to pay it forward, preparing the program for tomorrow's newcomer?

Even if the granddaddy of Twelve Steppery is bogged down in a reifying quagmire, over 500 new fellowships have been inspired by or in retaliation to AA. That's good. Every new fellowship has an easier time adjusting to the language of the day, unfettered, or at least less fettered, by dogma or bleeding deacon finger-waving.

Here is a partial list from Wikipedia of Twelve Step anonymous programs that have adapted the wisdom and experience of AA or reacted to it: Adult Children of Alcoholics, Al-Anon, Alateen, All-Addicts, Gam-A-Teen, Life Ring, Moderation Management, Nar-Anon, Rational Recovery, SMART Recovery, S.O.S. and Survivors of Incest Anonymous. Other programs offer support for people who struggle with clutter, codependency, debt, and addictions to cocaine, crystal meth, food, gambling, marijuana, narcotics, online gaming, pills, smoking, heroin, sex and love, and work.

Do I balance an appreciation for the past with the courage to change when it comes to Twelve & Twelve legacy?

# January 25

*"Like it or not, you'd better accept reality the way it occurs; as highly imperfect and filled with most fallible human beings. Your alternative? Continual anxiety and desperate disappointment."*

A New Guide to Rational Living *by Albert Ellis and Robert Harper*

---

Page 63 of *Alcoholics Anonymous*, says of Step Three, "The wording was, of course, quite optional so long as we expressed the idea, voicing it without reservation." More modern fellowships use the term "higher power" instead of the original "God as we understood Him." Secular interpretations of Step Three include "Made a decision to turn our will and our lives over to the program, the fellowship or the collective wisdom of those who have come before us." Today's authors offer a materialist variation of Step Three: accept life on life's terms. This Step is about a decision, not about a definition. We don't require answers to the great questions of the universe. A decision starts our Step Three process. "I let go and I don't know" is a good start. Understanding comes later.

From a Cognitive Behavioral Therapy perspective the Steps are a mental reframing of the way we see and react to the world. *Self-will* is not useless. It needs reining in. Our *self-will* has become reactive, defiant and ultimately self-destructive. Like a computer infected by viruses, willpower isn't garbage, but our brains need scanning, and reformatting, to eliminate and contain damage. All of us resist abdicating our power but how do we get a new result without doing something new?

The third Step is not about having to accept anyone else's beliefs or having to deny our own. If we want recovery then we are going to have to try a few things outside our comfort zone. "Faith without works is dead." Whether we believe in a deity or not, the Step is the same—we resign ourselves to the limits of addiction. Now what? We can explore some or all of the nine Steps that follow. The choice is ours—that's the empowering payoff of Step Three.

How would I word Step Three? Is it a daily event or a one-time thing? How open-minded am I?

# January 26

*"Most of us play the game of Hypocritical Procrastination quite unconsciously, and we have endless variations. One group of people, whom I call the Travelers, react to a task by remembering they have some very important chores to do elsewhere. Or they travel elsewhere hoping to find some very important chores to do. An uncontrollable urge moves them away from the work to be done."*

The Procrastinator's Handbook
*by Rita Emmitt*

---

Other games are described in the handbook. In one game we play the *Perfect Preparer*, who always reads one more book on Step Four instead of doing an imperfect but perfectly adequate inventory now. The *Socializer* goes to a meeting to see friends or talk program, relieving the tension without solving the problem. The *Straighteners* can't work on the next Step in a cluttered environment so they do laundry, dishes or participate in whatever distraction can be called "getting organized." The *Happy Helper* is the procrastinator who comes to the aid of another before continuing with personal work—regardless of the "help" being asked for or needed.

As busy fellowship members we look devout, but are we avoiding important tasks that scare us? When we are busy-busy, we ask ourselves if we are making life better and acting responsibly, or mistaking tension-relieving activity for actual problem solving. When we find ourselves avoiding, we need not scold ourselves; we examine our cold feet with child-like curiosity. Why are we afraid and/or what are we avoiding? If what we "need" to do is for our benefit, what is behind the avoidance? Is it simply a fear of change? Is it laziness or is it something else? We reflect on the possibilities (without using rumination as another form of procrastination).

Can I be mindful of my procrastination games today? What is my modus operandi for avoidance?

# January 27

*"Truth is a pathless land. We cannot come to it through any organization, through any creed, through any dogma, priest or ritual, nor through any philosophical knowledge or psychological technique. We must find it through the mirror of relationship, through the understanding of the contents of our own mind, through observation, and not through intellectual analysis or introspective dissection. We have built in our images a sense of security—religious, political, personal. These manifest as symbols, ideas, beliefs. The burden of these dominates thinking, relationships and daily life.*
*"These are the causes of our problems for they divide us from each other in every relationship."*

*Jiddu Krishnamurti (1895–1986)*

---

This truth that will set us free is not one truth arrived at by following the one true path. Employing binary thinking, we see a right path and a wrong path. We open our eyes. Between all the zeros and ones we see infinite possibilities. Truth isn't awaiting us at any destination. Life is *here*, not *there*. *There* is the carrot in front of the donkey. Having the carrot is an illusion, a tomorrow that never comes. We are the ass pursuing the carrot. *Now* is where we find truth, "through the mirror of relationship, through the understanding of the contents of our own mind, through observation." These instructions are in the present tense. Our time on earth is finite but the depth of our experience is infinite—insofar as we are present in our unfolding lives. Symbols, ideas and beliefs give a comforting narrative to yesterday and tomorrow. They tell *a* story but they aren't *the* story. With our newfound liberty comes responsibility, or at least the choice to take responsibility.

With so much commercially packaged truth, morality and comfort pitched at me daily, am I on a path of my own choosing? Do I stop seeking and simply observe, sometimes? There's a lot of truth right here, right now. Do I still catch myself peddling my own brand of truth as good medicine for everyone?

# January 28

*"Eternity isn't some later time; it has nothing to do with time. Eternity is that dimension of here and now which thinking and time cuts out. If you don't get it here you won't get it anywhere. The experience of eternity here and now is the experience of life.*

*Joseph Campbell (1904–1987)*

---

Google "Joseph Campbell" and see how he brings mythology to life. Avoiding literal interpretations of religions, his faith was in the meaning—the universal truth of the parable. We hear in the rooms, "Religion is for people who are trying to avoid hell; spirituality is for people who have been through it." Horror and despair are sometimes precursors to wonder. At three days of sobriety it seems unimaginable to ever be free from craving. At three decades of recovery we juggle doubt and clarity, nirvana and agony, longing and loathing, being peaceful and being possessed. We keep smiling while playing the game of life because no one gets out alive yet eternity is present in every moment lived. Eternity is here; eternity is now.

Addicts tend to squirm out of quiet, mindful moments. "I would rather stick needles in my eyes than meditate" is a reactive refrain for many. Mr. Campbell's words remind us that eternity is lost when we spend this moment regretting yesterday and getting anxious about tomorrow. Reflecting on the past and preparing for the future aren't misguided activities. The trick is to do these things without getting lost in them. Waiting and regretting steal away more bountiful options for life's experience right now. Eternity is now or never. If we don't get it here, we won't get it anywhere.

What a moment I am having, and another, and another. What am I waiting for? Can I enjoy the awe of this moment? Will I? When?

# January 29

*"You know quite well, deep within you, that there is only a single magic, a single power, a single salvation ... and that is called loving. Well, then, love your suffering.
Do not resist it, do not flee from it.
It is your aversion that hurts—nothing else."*

*Hermann Hesse (1877–1962)*

---

Picture people at meetings saying, "I am grateful to be an addict." There is a post-traumatic *gain* from addiction. That gain is our new attitude in recovery. Love and acceptance bring a more positive or objective perspective to suffering. Capitulation about our addiction allows us to progress away from wishing things had turned out differently.

Pain aversion is part of the survival instinct. We have to be practical and mindful about our reactions. It's not an on/off switch that allows us to say, "I love suffering now." Pain avoidance is an automatic defense we develop in childhood. We first debunk the idea that welcoming pain is masochistic or self-indulgent. Hesse suggests that avoidance or repression is responsible for our suffering. Popular psychology suggests that depression and anxiety are not so much feelings themselves as coping mechanisms that numb out, disguise or repress anger, shame, grief, fear or any unbearable suffering.

In the same way our shadows cast larger-than-life images from the late-day sun, our feelings appear bigger than us. If we move away from the shadow, it grows, reinforcing our impulse to keep our distance. However, if we move toward it, the shadow shrinks to its right size. Expressing and/or experiencing suffering is the only way emotions can run their course and free us. The notion of each of us being our own loving parent incorporates protecting and preparing our inner child. Good parenting teaches respect for feelings, not fear. Loving our suffering is like loving a bratty kid. A child has an inherent right to love and compassion; they don't need to earn it.

When I face the truth of my life and stop trying to evade reality, don't I generally find myself saying, "What was the big deal?"

*"The beginning of self-knowledge: recognizing that
your motives are the same as other people's."*

*Mason Cooley (1927–2002)*

---

Step Five is a leap of faith—sharing secrets at the risk of being judged and rejected. We recognize that our "motives are the same as other people's." Like others, we seek approval, want to control and resist being controlled. We long for "this" and we loathe "that."

This is one advantage of sharing Step Five with another Twelve Step member: as a layperson, the member hears us and may identify with our experience and/or feelings. Members may share their own secrets—something that a professional or religious leader would be reticent to do. Some of us finally feel like authentic members of the fellowship after opening up. We stop acting. We let someone know who we really are. Many of us are solitary or guarded people. We once thought that we did not want to join a fellowship; we could do it on our own. When we admit to ourselves and another human being the exact nature of our wrongs, we value having fellowship. We admit our own need for intimacy and community.

We share dark secrets. But what is the "exact nature of our wrongs," referred to in Step Five? We seek perspective on our triggers—we want to know why we hold back or lash out. This "exact nature" may make sense over time, if not in a flash. More than *confessing*, we are *relating* to another about who we are and why we do what we do. Being accepted makes us feel part of the human race, no better and no worse. Some of us see this step as our first true act of intimacy.

Keeping secrets, while sometimes necessary, keeps me from crossing an important threshold in this program of trust. Do I share the darkest of my secrets? In so doing, can I see how I am no lesser or greater than others?

# January 31

*"There is a crack in everything. That's how the light gets in."*

*Leonard Cohen (born 1934)*

---

Brains judge stuff. Sometimes our brains get it right, sometimes they don't. Some things are better understood when observed instead of judged. Judgment causes narrow focus—helpful sometimes, but not always. Our damage—our cracks—are characteristics that maybe we judge too soon to appreciate fully. When we judge our own damage as an aberration we isolate, overcompensate or blame someone else for our imperfection. Some of us went to therapy or Adult Children of Alcoholics and only got part way through the process. We delegated blame to our parents, employers or lovers and that made us victims. The reward for proving someone else is to blame is not very fulfilling.

What if we could stop criticizing ourselves and/or blaming others? Could we see everyone's unique damage as the "cracks" that let the light in? "The light," or enlightenment, comes from suffering—the damage (cracks). We all have unique pain and we can all gain a unique insight from it. We can appreciate the beauty of this in us and in others. There is no more need to judge ourselves or others. We can still practice discernment but we don't hold others in contempt. If we see the unique insight that each damaged person gains from their personal damage and the subsequent knowledge they have to share with the world, won't we find them less irritating? Those who aren't learning from others may be trapped in the judging game—always comparing and qualifying others, never being authentic for fear of having the tables turned and being persecuted by others.

Can I catch myself when I am quick to judge and smile at the beauty of the cracks in the world? Humility helps me remember that I only catch a little of what's going on with me and in the world I live in. Today, what if I try to observe more and judge less?

# February 1

*"The real miracle of individuation and reclamation of the Wild Woman is that we all begin the process before we are ready, before we are strong enough, before we know enough; we begin a dialogue with thoughts and feelings that both tickle and thunder within us. We respond before we know how to speak the language, before we know all the answers, and before we know exactly to whom we are speaking."*

*Clarissa Pinkola Estés (born 1945)*

In Jungian psychology, integration and unification of the self come through the resolution of successive layers of psychological conflict such as egomania and inferiority complexes. Compulsions like binging and purging become exacerbated in addiction and polarize rather than unify our personality traits. Overindulgences lead to self-loathing and swearing off. We demonize these base instincts and think of being freed forever from these *shortcomings* once we have identified them and turned them over. "Not so fast," says Dr. Jung. Integrating these extremes into a well-functioning whole is what he calls "individuation." There is no victory of good over bad, but rather an integration of yin and yang. We don't choose Dr. Jekyll over Mr. Hyde; they shake hands and we learn to manage better with all of who we are.

The Steps are a process of reprogramming—with time and help, we find new coping strategies, honestly appraising ourselves and resisting overcompensation or feeling ashamed and secretive about ourselves. From disillusionment to enlightenment, we draw our extremes to the middle, humbly doing the best we can with our imperfection, in an imperfect world. We have faith at times and we are fearful at times as we trudge along and adapt. Fear and fantasy are always part of us but this individuation is a changing of the guard. We are still affected by, but not enslaved by, our all-or-nothing extremes.

Do I see that turning over or eliminating "character defects," as the original literature phrased it, is just one way to articulate the reclaiming or recreating of my life and the world I live in?

# February 2

*"Zen is not some kind of excitement, but
concentration on your usual everyday routine."*

*Shunryu Suzuki (1904–1971)*

---

In our first months many of us feel as though recovery is like a walk on thin ice. We want recovery but we aren't convinced that our addictive predispositions won't shatter the thin layer that holds us and swallow us into the frigid water below. When our circumstances graduate from being completely unworkable to being merely uncomfortable, urgency diminishes. We can live with uncomfortable—why keep struggling with all this rigorous and absolute business? Save it for crisis management. We can all point to examples of people who have been settling for *good enough* for years. Recovery gives us choice and dignity. If we feel good enough, and coasting is our Shangri-La, we aren't wrong to move on to other things. We don't have to defend our recovery to anyone.

Some of us have been on the run for so long that avoidance became a habit. If we focus on what is before us and the thoughts, feelings and sensations that come our way, we will get to know ourselves better. We might like who we are. We might not choose escapism over reality. Our loved ones and surroundings are a different experience when we live in real time. If we dream and dread, reminisce and regret the whole day away, we lose what matters most, our "usual everyday routine."

As I read now, breathing in the words and ideas, do I imagine how Zen-like I am right now, or how I will be soon? It sounds good but am I cut out for living in the moment? Being more present is an exercise that takes practice and gentle encouragement—not scolding myself. I can get just a little better each day.

# February 3

*"No human being could possibly maintain the extremely high standards we often demand; we find ourselves falling short, as all people must whose aims are unrealistic. And discouragement and depression set in. We angrily punish ourselves for being less than super-perfect."*

Living Sober, 41

---

Being kind and fair to ourselves is learned. "Being Good to Yourself," Chapter 16 of *Living Sober*, discusses the importance of tender loving care (TLC) in our recovery. Some of us will diligently work through Twelve Step workbooks and when asked to write down our symptoms we will fill every line and then start writing in the margins. Or maybe there is no time for writing because we have two more books to read on self-analysis. We try to leave no stone unturned. Then, when the book directs us to take some leisure time or treat ourselves, we roll our eyes and say "Yeah, right!" We push through because we have a belly full of hurt and no time for this all-in-good-time B.S. In fact, we are making up for lost time. With luck, at this point we check in with a running mate or sponsor. At some point when we are either laughing at or defending our behavior, she or he might say that we are missing the point of the process. Each Step, first taken in our conscious minds, has to be absorbed to take hold.

Absorption happens during rest and play. Some describe being kind to ourselves in thoughts and actions as reprogramming our subconscious minds. If we want the benefits of the work to last, we have to concede that (a) we can't get it all done in one sitting, (b) we will never get it 100% right all of the time and (c) being gentle with ourselves is part of healing. Sponsors tell us to go meditate on this fact because, after all, meditation comes so easily to restless addicts. Sponsors are such comedians.

Step work takes diligence, not deprivation? Maybe the "Easy does it" bumper sticker should be scraped off the bumper and put on the dashboard where I can see it. Do I see *living sober* as trying to transcend the human experience or embrace it? What TLC do I have planned for myself today?

# February 4

*"It would be impossible to precisely describe addiction in a way that is agreeable to everyone. However, the disease seems to affect us in the following general ways. Mentally, we become obsessed with thoughts of using. Physically, we develop a compulsion to continue using, regardless of the consequences. Spiritually, we become totally self-centered in the course of our addiction. Looking at addiction as a disease makes a lot of sense to a lot of addicts because, in our experience, addiction is progressive, incurable, and can be fatal unless arrested."*

N.A.—It Works How and Why

---

If playing the semantics game is delaying our progress, let's consider how progress can be made without holding out for exact, scientific definitions. If our brains are stalled, we can follow gut instincts. We look for how we identify with others. We hear that obsessive-compulsive disorders can affect us to the core. Addiction took hold out of an insatiable need to self-medicate to keep us from deep-down hurt. Our drug of choice kept getting one more chance, all the while plotting our demise. Detoxification left us bare and vulnerable to anxiety, remorse, boredom, doubt and self-loathing. These ideas don't have to be scientifically proven if we identify with them. The point is that we are talking a common language, one addict to another.

We have real consequences from our misdeeds. We often feel a sense of impending doom. We are lonely and yet we isolate from others. We get some comfort from meetings but stay behind a wall that says, "I am different; I am not like everyone else." News Flash: everyone is different. We can belong without being assimilated. Early days of newfound freedom may or may not come with a pink cloud. If they do, we remember that what goes up must come down.

Temptation is everywhere in the early days. We preempt what tempts—we improve the odds by altering our environment. The experience of many suggests that the best chance at recovery involves incorporating a three-fold recovery plan—physical, mental and spiritual. We find exercises to re-teach ourselves, first to cope but ultimately to thrive.

Do I resist the idea of a three-fold disease? Am I always open to new ways of seeing? Am I stalled by semantics and definitions?

## February 5

*"When it comes to getting things done, we need fewer architects and more bricklayers."*

Colleen C. Barrett (born 1944)

---

A story is shared around the rooms about the search for a higher power. A hiker falls over a cliff and clings to a thin root that won't hold him for long. He cries out, "God, if you are there, show yourself and I will believe." A voice responds, "I am here. Let go absolutely." The hiker looks down below to 200 feet of certain death and asks, "Who else is up there? I want to talk to someone else."

We can imagine that the hiker is the bricklayer, looking to the architect for direction in a moment of crisis. But in questioning the direction given from the *architect of the universe*, the hiker is calling upon this greater power to render services, not to give direction.

We are both the architects and the bricklayers in life and every day calls for both skill sets. Most days require more bricklaying and less big picture detailing. In recovery we learn that there is only so much value in evaluating how to proceed in the Steps. The value comes from the work—pushing our boundaries and doing it—more than from drafting a course of action. The maxim, "no task too big or too small" is a recovery mantra. Living life as it comes breathes life into serenity, courage and wisdom. We don't learn it from a book—it's on the job training, one brick at a time.

Playing architect all the time is a subtle form of avoidance. "Clearing away the wreckage of the past," this is work for our architect—the thinking, analyzing, problem-solving self. No matter how good our minds are, they're unskilled at doing our hearts' work. To heal, repressed feelings have to be experienced—not just examined and compartmentalized. Our bricklayer does the heavy lifting, which is experiencing and expressing our feelings. We may even employ another architect—a therapist or sponsor. They don't do the work; they help direct us. The house isn't repaired without the bricklaying no matter how savvy the architect or architects.

In this metaphor, more bricklaying is needed in recovery and life. Do I kid myself when I try to *think* my way out of *feeling* by planning when it's time to work? Can a compass and protractor do the job when a wheelbarrow is needed? If I am avoiding, what am I avoiding?

## February 6

*"They may forget what you said, but they will
never forget how you made them feel."*

*Carl W. Buechner (born 1926)*

---

We have all recommended a speaker, a musical act or a guilty pleasure that has affected us. When asked, "Why? What's so special about this person/place/thing?" we can't find the words to express what we got out of it, or put another way, what it got out of us. We can't articulate the experiences intellectually—we feel them. Maybe this sense goes back to when we were babies and we had to navigate the world without having the advantage of language—we responded to our own and to others' feelings. We knew when we felt safe, stimulated, scared, tired or hungry.

So regardless of whether or not we consider ourselves wordsmiths or tongue-tied, we leave impressions on people—feelings that last. So what got us sober? Was it the words that were said at a meeting that persuaded us to keep coming back or was it how the meeting (the members at the meeting) made us feel? When we meet newcomers for the first time, we sometimes panic in our attempts to find the right words to say, when, as it turns out, words are secondary. The same is true at home and work. People respond to how we make them feel. Communication is said to be 7% about words; the rest is tone and body language. That's why a smile is understood around a world divided by almost 7000 languages. So how do we get better at exuding good feelings? Mindfulness training is one way. This includes compassion-meditations, directed at self-compassion and wishing others well. This helps prepare us for interacting with pure intent. Our intentions speak louder than our words.

How do I feel about the others in my world, today? Do I wish them well? If my intention is sincere, the words I communicate with will be good enough.

# February 7

*"The dogmas of the quiet past are inadequate to the stormy present. The occasion is piled high with difficulty, and we must rise with the occasion. As our case is new, so we must think anew and act anew."*

*Abraham Lincoln (1809–1865)*

---

Abe had a way of shaking the foundation. He may have been killed by dogmatic conservatives with the goal of preserving the existing order. Every society has examples of violent opposition to progressive revolution. Breaking away from *what is and what should always be* can have harsh consequences. A 2010 Pew Research Center survey showed that in some Muslim countries, over half the population supports execution as a fair punishment for leaving the faith.[20] Artists or politicians with freethinking idealism may die for what they believe in if they advance an idea that departs from the status quo. Being an apostate or heretic can rattle the cages of the faithful among us. This can unfold in the form of deadly violence or more subtle forms of harassment or discrimination.

The inability or unwillingness to adapt is fatal. We all resist change. Lincoln warns us of our own tendencies toward rigidity. Intolerance and dogmatic reflex are generally borne of fear. If someone proposes change to our comfortable routines, what do we do? We may reactively dismiss the new idea. The Big Book says, "At some of these we balked. We thought we could find an easier, softer way. But we could not. With all the earnestness at our command, we beg of you to be fearless and thorough from the very start. Remember that we deal with alcohol—cunning, baffling, powerful!"[21] Is alcohol so much more powerful than ritualistic routines that we cling to for comfort? Fearlessness is needed to defend against complacency—not just for Step One, but for our whole lives.

Every member, group and fellowship is well-advised to evaluate rituals and literature. How do they measure up to present and future needs? How do our groups look and feel to the newcomer? In many ways, the newcomer is more objective about us than we are. A newcomer can help us stay firm in principle and flexible in method and language.

What do I say or do out of habit? Do I talk in clichés? What changes would I like to make? Am I adaptive and open to change? Do I welcome change in my life or resist all the way?

# February 8

*"If we focus only on our eating behavior—which is merely a symptom of the problem—to the exclusion of the rest of the program, we are using OA only as a diet program and eventually will go back into our disease. To sustain our plan of eating for any length of time, we must embrace the whole program."*

"The Tools of Recovery," Overeaters Anonymous

---

Food didn't cause eating disorders. Alcohol didn't create a single alcoholic nor did betting make the gambler. Love doesn't make us codependent and orgasm doesn't cause sex addiction. Many drugs and activities trigger dopamine and create a chemical reaction that leads to addiction in some people.[22] In many cases, emotional problems predisposed us to seek relief. Seeking led to dependency, which led to addiction and a downward spiral.

Only the first Step of any Twelve Step program refers to activity or substance as being to blame for our dysfunctions. This doesn't minimize the clear and present danger that addictive behavior poses, or the urgency to admit our powerlessness. The point is that the Steps are solution-focused, not problem-focused. Once we have accepted addiction in our lives, we make an important break from isolation and self-sufficiency. Our minds and imaginations are opened to a wealth of experience and strength that we find in others. We look back at life through personal inventory to identify patterns, triggers and ways our self-will shortchanged us and those we love. So it goes, through the Twelve Steps—it isn't about resisting temptation; it's about healing.

*Stockholm Syndrome* sometimes affects the hostages of addiction.[23] We grew attached to our abuser/drug of choice. Freedom from bondage came with a strange suffering; we lost a bad habit but an old friend, too. Some will demonize addiction and others will mourn the loss. A more balanced approach is to admit to addiction, take responsibility and ask for help when needed.

Have I said my good-byes to addiction and moved on? Is my program about stopping or living? It's not like I will be bored or alone after Step One. I will have freedom and I will have choice. Is the program a problem solver that I apply and move on from, or a way of living for me?

# February 9

*"If you trust, you will share, if you share you will express
your feelings, if you express your feelings you will
discover yourself, if you discover yourself you will heal."*

*Adult Children of Addicts*

---

Everyone speaks at a meeting, not so much for others but for selfish benefit. Secondary or tertiary benefit is almost accidental. When we express ourselves we are having out-loud conversations with ourselves. If we are authentic, new realizations flow in real time. From these realizations, growth and healing can follow. The value of what we take from others is in identifying with the personal processes of others which touch us in some way. Sometimes it is easier to see our patterns and schemas in the foibles of others than to see through our own self-deception.

If we hear ourselves say, "I didn't hear what I needed at the meeting," perhaps our expectations were askew. We heard what others needed to say. Was there anything in their experience that we could identify with or gain from? If so, great; if not, maybe that means "not yet."

We need never feel offended, persecuted or contradicted at meetings. Even if someone's finger and gaze is directed right at us, we know they are expressing what they need to hear/say and this is true for them in this moment. We need never take comments personally. People are talking "to" the group, not "as" the group. We all express ourselves from our own unique perspectives and from this moment in time, regardless of how we say it—I, you or we. This is a selfish program. Meetings, like sponsors, are guides. If we are only at meetings for fellowship, others are our leaning posts.

Today's quote contains wisdom that may be lost if we rush. Reflection isn't a game show. We don't slap our hands on the buzzer as fast as we can and guess the meaning. We are reflective instead of reactive because this is not a competition.

Am I in tune with the nuances of what a selfish program means? Do I take responsibility in my program? Do I see meetings as a place for self-discovery?

## February 10

*"There is somebody who knows better than anybody,
and that is everybody."*

*French aphorism*

---

Gaining a consensus or gauging popular opinion isn't the same as an informed group conscience. The most democratic aspect of Twelve & Twelve life is that if we are here today, we are tied for first place in influence; we are each entitled to one vote, just like everyone else. Tenure and martyrdom don't earn a second vote no matter what. If we value our fellowship, and want it to be here for the next generation, we need to be aware of the issues and contribute to the conversation as responsible members.

Criticizing our fellowship or group isn't disloyal. Literalists and radicals both love the fellowship. The minority view deserves a second chance. Opinion is sentiment and although it may be popular, we must weigh it against what is true and just. If we are resisting an idea, have we just dug our heels in? Respecting Traditions doesn't mean resisting change. Oh, we don't have to change—there is always extinction.

Tradition Two gives each group considerable power over its affairs.[24] We have servants, but no leaders. General Service and Intergroup act as service bodies. They don't govern the groups; the only rules groups and individuals have are the rules they choose for themselves. Individuals don't have to adhere; they can join or start another group. Group reps in each fellowship work on behalf of the group conscience. They bring the issues to the table and carry the group conscience up (or down or across) the ranks. Business meetings are where sobriety is put to the test; both principles and personalities are in play. Around the rooms we hear, "AA is about what you could expect from a fellowship run by drunks." Replace the first and last words of that sentence with any other fellowship and it still makes sense. We are tested when asked to support a group conscience that we don't agree with. Do we all do our share of the work? Are any jobs in the fellowship too big or too small for us?

Do I spend time reading or learning about service work? If I am a member of more than one fellowship, do I balance service fairly between them? What does "We all get our say, but that doesn't mean we can all have our way," mean to me?

# February 11

*"A typical day in the life of a heavy metal musician*
*consists of a round of golf and an AA meeting."*

Billy Joel (born 1949)

---

We can't speak to this musician's golf game but statistically speaking, the metal-head in each of us likely displayed addictive tendencies before the age of twenty-five, maybe as teenagers. What makes chemical dependency a youth problem is that 95% of drug and alcohol addicts started using before the age of twenty-five. Treatment professionals in the USA report that less than one in ten youth that fit addiction criteria find their way to treatment.[25]

Do enabling parents talk themselves into believing their kids will grow out of it? Is our social infrastructure unable to deal with the fact that our children are drinking? And what might the statistics be for youth addicted to food, porn and gambling? All of these are easily available to the average teenager. Studies show that reduction in the size of the brain region known as the *hippocampus* has been found to be common in adolescents being treated for alcohol dependence. This renders reasoning and other brain functioning more vulnerable to intoxication at younger ages. Morbidity and mortality related to booze is highest in twelve to seventeen-year-olds. The National Institute of Alcohol Abuse and Alcoholism studied youth alcohol abuse from 1991 to 2002 and found that the younger we started drinking, the more likely we were to abuse alcohol. Depending on parental factors, the under-sixteen-year-old drinker's risk of alcoholism is 20%, at the low end, rising to close to a 60% chance of addiction where there is family addiction history. Starting at sixteen, the risk is still high, reducing at age twenty-one to the 10% range—the normal risk for any drinker.[26]

For those of us who are teenage addicts, for those of us who saw signs we ignored back then, and for those of us with kids at risk, the age at which we or they start is an important factor. What none of this explains, and what maybe Billy Joel can elaborate on, is—what causes rock stars to go golfing each day?

At what age did I start demonstrating addictive tendencies? Statistics and facts keep changing in addiction and recovery. Do I spend the right amount of time keeping up to date?

# February 12

*"After listing his complaints, Bill asked (some thirty years before the Rolling Stones) whether he was ever to get any satisfaction, and Father Dowling answered, 'No, never!' In the shape he was in, Bill found the priest's certainty astounding, but Dowling was merely elucidating a central tenet of Christianity (or any moral system) that extols selflessness: virtue must be its own reward; we cannot expect any satisfaction for doing what we know we must."*

Bill W.: A Biography of Alcoholics Anonymous
Cofounder Bill Wilson
*by Francis Hartigan*

---

Bill Wilson may not have lived the life of the promises described in the Big Book. He suffered from depression and financial woes, wrestled with his own infidelity, failed at quitting smoking and died of emphysema. Wilson's reward for creating AA was harsh criticism for his stewardship. Brokering a consensus on the Twelve Steps between the atheist-sympathisers and the predominantly Christian members was an act of diplomacy. He met every personal criticism with a turned cheek. Bill was quick to say that many had risen to greater spiritual heights than he had. In fact, he thought of himself is a flawed individual and considered, in his later writing, a lifetime of constant struggle with his own character defects.

Many considered him a lousy sponsor, maybe because he never said "no" and he spread himself too thin. Dowling saw Bill as saintly. Bill saw the priest as someone he could talk frankly to, and feel heard and understood by. We are all reminded that a spiritual journey will surely bring meaning to life, but it won't likely look like what we imagined success to be. *Trudging* the road of happy destiny foreshadows a future of forward movement that is both satisfying and tough going.

Am I up for doing the next right thing, willing to follow my values without being tied to outcomes or reciprocity?

*"Step Ten: I will continue to evaluate my own actions and admit to myself what choices were wrong."*
*TeenAddictionAnonymous.com*

---

An airplane leaves from the departure city en route for its destination thousands of miles away. Sixty minutes after departure the plane finds itself slightly off course. What does the pilot do? Seeing he/she is going the wrong way, will she or he fly back to the departure city and try again, or does the pilot make a slight in-air adjustment to put the plane back on course? We see the irrationality of starting all over again when a slight adjustment will do. If recovery is our airplane, values are our bearings; any time we are off course, we can turn back in the heading of living within our values. We accept that we will get blown off course from time to time. We don't start all over, we simply alter our course. Step Ten is the compass or barometer to show us when we are off course in life.

If the pilot sees an engine is on fire, it would be foolish for her or him to push on just because it's never been a problem before. Sometimes our *recovery plane* has to be landed at the nearest, safest airport for a rigorous inventory of the working parts. Unexpected turbulence or sheer flying hours can reveal wear or damage that need attention. A regular Step Ten can sometimes reveal a recurring theme, highlighting a need for more intense inventory. For some of us this means outside help in the form of counseling, therapy and/or another Twelve Step program. Just like the pilot flying the plane, we affect other people's welfare by the choices we make.

Is a rational pilot flying my *recovery plane*? Am I living consciously or on auto-pilot? Do I respond attentively, calmly and open-mindedly to the messages my control panel gives me?

# February 14

*"Sometimes he caught himself listening to the sound of his own voice. He thought that in her eyes he would ascent to an angelical stature; and, as he attached the fervent nature of his companion more and more closely to him, he heard the strange impersonal voice which he recognized as his own, insisting on the soul's incurable loneliness.*
*We cannot give ourselves, it said: we are our own."*

*James Joyce (1882–1941)*

---

We come into this world alone and we leave alone. Author Joyce asks of the time in between, "What gives our lives value?" We may walk a mile in another's shoes to gain both empathy and perspective but life is still a solitary experience. Even if we are in a great relationship, we are not one person with the other. Finding peace when we are alone, without succumbing to isolation, is a learned quality for most. Addicts often still have to learn about true communion with one or many without the reactive withdrawal or the need to manipulate and direct the other(s).

We lack perspective if we see ourselves as the central characters in our own dramas—the hub of the universe. Isolation can take place either by avoiding others or while hiding in plain view of everyone, behind masks. Working the Steps is an exercise that fosters balance and inter-dependency. When working on some Steps, we humbly accept the aid of others, and some are worked in isolation, encouraging meditation and list-making. Steps Ten through Twelve are guides to help us to be good family members, work associates or community members. Being good isn't about being perfect, but it involves making adjustments.

What are my tendencies around solitude—do I avoid it or overindulge? Am I healthy about my alone time? Have I grown more comfortable in my own skin in recovery? Do I find a balance between reliance and personal responsibility?

# February 15

*"I don't think you can become an outstanding runner unless you get a certain amount of enjoyment out of the suffering. You have to enjoy absorbing it, controlling it and—ultimately—overcoming it."*

Derek Clayton (born 1942)

---

In his book *The Masters of the Marathon*, Clayton connects the dots from suffering to growth and ultimately to achievement. Recovery is like a marathon: the achievement is enormous but the route requires one step or breath at a time. No one runs the race for us but there are many running shoulder-to-shoulder with us. Success is personal, based on our individual goals, not the group's goals. We don't know if we can do it at first but we are open, willing and determined. Our outcomes are not certain. Do we enjoy our suffering as the author suggests? Is that sick or what?

Suffering is part of life but it need not define or limit our lives. Running from suffering to a drug of choice or codependency made an adversary out of suffering—something to be avoided. Some of us practice mindfulness and bring out the welcome mat to greet pain and suffering along with any other thoughts, sensations or feelings. We neither seek nor avoid pain. We don't get overwhelmed by the sensations or feelings, nor do we revel in playing the victim. Experience shows that no hardship is insurmountable. If we treat life like a game or puzzle to be solved, we look for options and solutions, thoughtfully and patiently. We navigate around the challenges: (i) caving in to catastrophic thinking, (ii) jumping to conclusions, (iii) overcompensating or (iv) denying our struggles. Suffering, like running, doesn't have to be an all-day affair. It's part of life, not life itself. It is part of the human experience to make mistakes and improve as we go.

Can I take pride in my ability to face life fearlessly and unconditionally, rolling with the punches? Stability comes from facing pain and that, in turn, makes me a good example to others.

# February 16

*"Is this surrender or a ceasefire?"*

*Heard around the rooms*

---

Recovery involves resignation. Around the rooms we are also reminded that the surrender to recovery isn't giving in; rather it is letting in—letting the Steps and fellowship help us. Steps Two and Three mean for many that we are not going it alone, on our own wits. We start letting people in, becoming more vulnerable and authentic in the process. We feel and believe that we are not alone.

But this laconic quote asks a bold question: are we giving up or are we taking a breather? How often have we said to ourselves or others, "This time it will be different. You can depend on me. I am going to stop and I am going to change"? Chronic slippers look beaten and they sound full of conviction after every setback. But are they done, once and for all? Addicts and alcoholics will take meetings into detox and treatment centers, engaging with the most desperate of addicts. They may have been clean and sober once. Maybe they thought they had the world by the tail. But low bottom addicts are not shocked to find they have fallen so far. These are the addicts who have fallen from grace before.

Detox patients confide that they don't honestly know if they will stay clean, sober and true when that locked door opens and the big cruel world pulls them back. This is desperation. Why do good people not make it? Maybe they don't understand powerlessness. An unauthentic ¾ effort at recovery just isn't a guarantee of recovery or even ¾ of the benefit. Therapist and author M. Scott Peck said that if stopping doesn't feel strange we don't understand the depth of the pain involved: "In its major forms, giving up is the most painful of human experiences."[27]

Step work reveals a series of barriers and new challenges that test us. Will they be dealt with? We can always procrastinate. Some of us get lulled into new outlets that trigger our obsessive-compulsive dispositions. Secondary addictions are no surprise to many of us in the fellowship.

Am I entirely ready? Can I admit a need for help? Is there at least one other member with whom I am vulnerable—someone to whom I surrender and let go with, absolutely? In Step One I resign myself to the fact that there is no cure for addiction. Surrender is never conditional. Have I surrendered or simply declared a ceasefire?

# February 17

*"There's no life without humour. It can make the
wonderful moments of life truly glorious,
and it can make tragic moments bearable."*

*Rufus Wainwright (born 1973)*

---

"A funny thing happened to me on the way to a meeting…" Healthy members and groups make room for humor; it has a healing quality. True, there is much about the tragedy of addiction that is no laughing matter. Many of us hide our insecurities by playing the clown—also true. Although we need never take our addictions lightly, Rule # 62 reminds us never to take ourselves too seriously.

Sometimes the best thing a well-meaning member can do is honor our pain and show empathy. Conversely, laughing in our faces may loosen a bundle of worry that is trapped in our imagination. Some of us have a knack for turning a phrase or finding the light-sided irony in any situation. Some of us just don't know how to tell a joke. Inevitably, boundary issues need to be taken seriously when we are joking around.

There are many ways we can lighten tension without a punch line. Steering someone's preoccupation to a lighter topic we know they care deeply about can help soften moods. Going to some sketch comedy, a funny movie or sitting at home playing music can have the same healing effect as hearing the right thing at the right time.

Some of us remember humor in the meetings as a turning point. We were new, perplexed and didn't know what to make of this Twelve Step program. But we recall people laughing hysterically at unimaginable horror shows. We thought, "You people are sick—you're my people!"

Why so serious? Is there something I really need to lighten up about?

## February 18

*"Without a knowledge of mythology much of the*
*elegant literature of our own language cannot*
*be understood and appreciated."*

*Thomas Bulfinch (1796–1867)*

---

Like literature, psychology draws upon archetypes. Carl Jung refers to an archetype as a pattern in our present life relived or derived from our past, as in "She always falls for that 'type'," which could mean just like her dad, the emotionally unavailable type or some pattern cued from her subconscious. If we are weary from psychotherapeutic navel gazing, Twelve Step work, or the latest *How to be a Better You* bestseller, we can try reading a fable or going to a movie to learn about the human experience in a more entertaining way. We are taught and entertained by archetypes in Egyptian, Norse, Greek, Celtic, Eastern, Biblical and Aboriginal mythology. Metaphorical stories illustrate the gods' roles in the natural world and how they touch human life.

The Bible indulges in stories of flooding, parting the sea, resurrection and eternity. Stories only dumb us down if we take them literally and don't dig for the meaning. "Archetype" is a Greek word. Over the next few days we'll look at a few key mythological characters in Greek history and see how they play out in addiction and recovery. We may not know them by name, but we've played these characters or battled these foes in real life.

Mythology was created, in part, to help us understand our world. Do I have superheroes or dramatic characters I identify with? What is it about them or their dilemmas I identify with? Do I see how art and folklore metaphorically reveal truth about my life and world?

# February 19

*"No one is useless in the world who lightens
the burden of it for anyone else."*

*Charles Dickens (1812–1870)*

---

The classic character who carried the weight of the world on his shoulders was Atlas, burdened by the spite of Zeus, punished for insubordination. Atlas was the strong silent type, enduring his burden without complaint. We may have played this character at some point in our lives. Alternately, influential Atlas-like characters may have left an impression on us that forged our beliefs or values.

If we have this *Atlas complex*, we are carrying assumptions that are not right-sized. Some of us are a wee bit codependent. If we carry the burden of the world on our shoulders, we are taking on more than our own lot in life. Codependency has been defined as inverted narcissism or co-narcissism. So instead of being preoccupied with self, self is lost and our worth is tied to how another is perceived or how they perceive us. Symptoms include issues with sex, trust, boundaries, repression, obsessive-compulsive disorders, passiveness, caretaking, controlling behavior and low self-worth.

If we don't suffer this martyrdom, but grew up with someone who did, what were the messages they gave us about life and the world we live in? Have those messages created any false premises that we are still living by? Writing, talking or therapy can help us identify the guilt and/or persecution complexes that we are consciously or unconsciously balancing and then focus our energy on letting them go.

What does carrying the weight of the world on my shoulders tell me about myself and those around me who indulge in this role? Do I ever say or think, "So-and-so needs me and they would be lost without me" or "It is my role to keep it all together. Whatever price I pay, I will never be free of my situation"? How about, "Don't worry about me—I can handle it"? Can I help to lessen the burden of others, without spiraling into an *Atlas complex*?

## February 20

*"Suffering produces endurance and endurance produces character and character produces hope."*

The Bible, English Standard Version (Romans 5:3-4)

---

A brother of the Greek Titan Atlas, Prometheus was punished by Zeus for showing compassion to humans by offering them fire, which is often a metaphor for knowledge. As punishment, Prometheus was tied to a rock before his liver was eaten out of his torso by a raven. This suffering would be unrelenting and faced every day, until Prometheus apologized. Prometheus, the rebel, never gave in, never sold out and suffered the same anguish daily until thirteen generations later, when he was rescued by Hercules.

Ambiguous grief is an infliction upon life experience that has no healing or resolution such as a missing loved one who is never found, or being diagnosed with HIV, MS or another chronic, degenerative condition. These are examples of plights for which time offers no cure; the song remains the same tomorrow. Be it a consequence of our addictions or a seeming slap in our sober face, any of us may face a Promethean lot in life.

Without glorifying suffering, the quote above reminds us that, one day at a time, we can endure the unthinkable. Troubles faced can build character. There is always hope—hope that tomorrow could be different and hope that no matter how far down the scale we go, we will see how our experiences can benefit others. The great challenge for us is to face life-altering realities without falling prey to escapism, delusion or victimhood. Our plights need not define us. They can just be facts of life.

Many burdens have more choices and possibilities than I can see. No matter what I face, can I be strong and clear-minded? Imagination is a crucial tool in managing life's plights.

# February 21

*"The most important kind of freedom is to be what you really are. You trade in your reality for a role. You give up your ability to feel, and in exchange, put on a mask."*

Jim Morrison (1943–1971)

---

As we finish up for now with Greek mythological roles, let's look at a few other roles we have played or roles that have been inflicted on us by others. As Zeus, we are controlling, dominating and persecuting. Echo is the nymph without her own voice or an original thought, doomed to a copy-cat existence. Narcissus is the self-absorbed god who sees the world through his eyes only, devoid of empathy. Hera, the ultimate codependent, jealous wife of Zeus, is always playing detective and is preoccupied with what others are doing. Remember Icarus? He was given an escape from Crete by way of wings made by his dad from wax and feathers. The one rule that the father Daedalus imposed was to not fly too close to the sun. Icarus couldn't resist the intoxication of flight, and as he kept going higher, the heat of the sun melted the wax. Icarus crashed into the sea and drowned. Sound like anyone we know? How would we like to be Daedalus, who tried to warn him?

These are just a few classic traps that rob us of autonomy. As we perform these roles, our real lives are passing us by and we mimic feelings and reactions, true to these characters, instead of struggling with our authenticity. These roles (masks) and parables are alive and well in psychology, Hollywood, religion and a Twelve Step, Twelve Tradition meeting "coming soon to a room near you."

If I need to work on finding my authenticity, what steps do I need to take to peel away the masks? If I know who I really am, when I am tempted to hide do I see how being authentic, faults and all, is a positive example to others? The courage to be real, and true to myself, is a prerequisite for freedom.

# February 22

*"My sponsor says that in order to stay sober we need to have a spiritual thirst. I don't run across a lot of people, even in recovery, who share the same kind of thirst that I have. It's relentless, inextinguishable. I know that it's because I'm sicker than most that, I'm more desperate for spiritual answers than many others. I'm lucky because I have to practice."*

The 12-Step Buddhist *by Darren Littlejohn*

---

*The 12-Step Buddhist* is a candid portrayal of one member's dance with recovery. We follow Littlejohn through the Twelve Steps only, therapy only, Buddhism only, and combinations thereof. From medication to meditation, describing what it was like and what it's like now without pretense or apology, he gives a lively take on AA and NA dogma, how to spot a Buddhist Guru fraud in the western world and why Lamas just don't get addiction or addicts.

This quote speaks volumes about the constant, determined search that is required to find our own personal answers, recovery, potential and peace. You can tell how tall a building is going to be by the size of the hole in the ground. Is our enlightenment dependent on how desperate we are, or how bad our circumstances are? Some of us have surface problems and a part-time approach to recovery is going to yield good enough results to return to righteous living. Some of us come to sobriety broken, yes, but the worst personal anguish of life may be saved for after we are sober. We feel sorrow with greater intensity now that we are stone-cold-sober than we did while living out our addictions.

Is suffering a punishment for not *thoroughly following the path*? Am I lazy? Will I only do as much soul-searching as is needed to get the heat off? Do I call increased good fortune a *good* thing in sobriety and the school of hard knocks a *bad* thing? Do I still hold on to conditions for my surrender or do I accept what life hands me?

# February 23

*"The role of a writer is not to say what we all can say, but what we are unable to say."*

Anaïs Nin (1903–1977)

---

When we are sharing our stories or relating to others in recovery we share the language of the heart. We try to be as candid as possible and speak our own unique truths. Clichés are a quick way to express something we all relate to. Clichés have merit in that they allow us to say so much with few words. But overused, clichés cause others to tune out. When we truly speak from the heart, we don't need catchy phrases. Who knows what it will be about our story that will resonate with another? Not only does our candor tell our version of the truth, but sometimes another will identify with us and find hope.

We hear "I finally found where I belonged" when people talk about coming to meetings. We have all heard something in the company of addicts that transformed our hopelessness into positive expectations. More often, uncovering the truth is a process rather than a revelation. It isn't reading, writing or listening alone. There is a process that leads to transforming us from being overwhelmed to being empowered. Like a chemical reaction, words and witness can sometimes change the teller and listener.

The real meaning of *selfish program* is that we often say what we need to hear—we are the architects of our own recovery. Our own words can sometimes be like postcards from our psyches. Have we ever heard ourselves say, "I don't know where that came from"?

Do I speak from the heart? Do I sometimes talk because my own voice relieves my anxiety? If I listen instead, maybe someone else will say what I am unable to say but need to hear.

# February 24

*"Every second that you experience suffering for others, you collect merit as vast as the sky, and purify eons of negative karma. Each time, you become closer to enlightenment and closer to enlightening other sentient beings."*

*Lama Zopa Rinpoche (born 1946)*

---

Bodhicitta is a Buddhist practice—wishing to bring happiness and relieve the suffering of others as much as possible. No matter what level of nirvana or enlightenment you have achieved, you just ain't top-dog, Buddhist guru material until you reach the state of the altruistic principle of Bodhicitta.

No matter how wounded we are when we come into the program, the Steps and fellowship transform us into people that help others out of reflex. We can't tap people on the head and make them recovered. We cannot take their pain away. But we know with certainty that freedom is possible because, for us, despair was transformed into a glimmer of hope, and then we found recovery. We have stories to tell and we have time to listen. Addiction is such a dark place because it is such a self-absorbed state: our needs are endless and we feel alone. Weeks and months in, we can still be self-absorbed while the enormity of the Steps is still in front of us. Just being at a meeting is being an example to others. Showing levity about our own shortcomings can make others smile. Making peace with our flawed incompleteness can be a symbol of hope for those still undecided about our program. In taking on another suffering member's concerns and helping them find their own brand of salvation we are inadvertently freed from the bondage of our own preoccupations.

Six ideals of Buddhist living are patience, morality, generosity, enthusiasm, concentration and wisdom. We don't learn it then do it—we do it then share what we have learned. These ways of treating ourselves are prerequisites to the path of enlightenment in Buddhism. As Dr. "Dharma" Bob and "Bodhicitta" Bill W. would have put it, "having had a spiritual awakening ... we tried to carry this message ... and to practice these principles in all our affairs."

Am I happy today? Does the happiness I feel come from the things and places I expected it would or am I surprised about what makes me happy today?

*"Empty your mind; be formless, shapeless—like water.*
*Now you put water into a cup, it becomes the cup, you*
*put water into a bottle, it becomes the bottle,*
*you put it in a teapot, it becomes the teapot.*
*Now water can flow or it can crash.*
*Be water, my friend."*

*Bruce Lee (1940–1973)*

---

Bruce Lee, a master of the martial arts, understood that two of the keys to meditation and deeper awareness are relaxation and fluidity. Stress, or more accurately, *distress*, seems normal to the addictive mind. Serenity isn't granted; it is practiced. It comes from within and is a byproduct of meditation, opening the door to strength and greater understanding.

Water is fluid and docile, but don't mess with it—water has power that can overwhelm human strength. Before dismissing meditation as something that will make us dull or wimpy, we are encouraged to try it first. Bruce Lee wasn't reputed to be a wimp. Like many things in life, anxiety and impulsivity can be fully refunded if we don't like what our balanced, meditative self looks like in the mirror. Reacting to chaos is easy, not heroic. Living peacefully is the challenge.

Do I see how meditation makes me more adaptable to my environment, able to fit in and can complement my surroundings? As the water analogy suggests, do I also see the power and force that come from conscious meditation?

# February 26

*"Attraction is beyond our will or ideas sometimes."*

*Juliette Binoche (born 1964)*

---

"Our public relations policy should be guided by the principle of attraction rather than promotion."[28] Our example to newcomers is important. It's not saying the right thing that attracts people to us; they come back if they feel like they were heard. Ultimately, a newcomer's fate has more to do with what he or she does and says than with what we say or do. Our enthusiasm for the newcomer to "come to believe" should be muted. It's their choice to stay or to go. We are not cheering for our fellowships as if they were our favorite sports teams. We're not the "best" and we're not competing with any other system for overcoming addiction or codependency. Absolute statements make us and our fellowships appear cult-like. Statements like "See it our way or help yourself to jail, death or the loony bin" may be sincerely felt but are hardly scientifically irrefutable. Unsubstantiated claims are neither credible nor attractive.

What statistics do we have about people who leave Twelve & Twelve fellowships? We don't do exit surveys or follow-up studies. All we offer that carries weight is our experience. Opinions are like ... well, we all know what they are like, and the smell that comes with the territory.

Ads can let people know that a fellowship is here to help. One such AA ad reads as follows: "If you want to drink and can—that's your business. If you want to stop and can't—that's our business: Call Alcoholics Anonymous [phone number]."

What shall I do when I catch myself being evangelical about recovery, my fellowship, my group or my own point of view? A statement like, "This I believe ..." is sharing. "This is how it is" has crossed the line to *drunk-on-dogma* preaching; I see what is true for me as being universally true. How many personal beliefs or personal experiences do I spout off as though they're universal truths?

# February 27

*"Avoid authorities who offer a universal blueprint for salvation
or a map of your spiritual pilgrimage. Be suspicious of anyone
who claims to have esoteric knowledge of the hidden truth,
God's will, the outcome of history or why we should
bomb Iraq back into the Stone Age.
The great spiritual secrets...are hidden in plain sight."*

*Sam Keen*

---

The small print in Sam Keen's *Hymns to an Unknown God* is that to see these secrets hidden in plain view, we might have to turn ourselves inside-out first. This is true in Step One—once clean and sober the problem (addiction) and the solution (recovery) are crystal clear. However, before we turned ourselves inside-out, the abstinence plan and the suggestion that our favorite process or substance was responsible for an allegedly "unmanageable life" sounded too melodramatic for our reasoning minds.

Once we want to stop, we have to stay stopped. Where do we turn? Well, what's in plain view? There's the Twelve Steps. Why don't we try to just read the black—ignoring the urge to seek out cryptic messages hidden in the white part of the pages? After the Steps, then we have some choices to make. We might want to get on with our lives. There is a myth that all who stray from meetings eventually die in addiction. Sure, some relapses start with skipping meetings but leaving the fold springboards some of us into worthy callings and purposeful lives. Not many of us will face this *all or nothing* ultimatum, but if the time comes, let's not say "no" to life and become so dependent on meetings, in constant fear that the big bad wolf of addiction is around the corner, waiting to pounce.

Let's say, on the other hand, we want to stay—good then; meetings can add value to a rich, full life. Our program can be a lifestyle instead of a single purpose solution. If we do hang around we avoid becoming zealots. It's easy to tell if we fall prey to *bleeding deaconism*. Zealots talk in absolutes and they just aren't funny. People or organizations that can't tolerate a lampooning fear that laughter will crack their clay feet.[29]

I am looking for answers, today—what do I see right in front of me? Am I in recovery because it's what I want, or am I doing it because I am afraid?

# February 28

*"You can't have everything. Where would you put it?"*

Steven Wright (born 1955)

---

Come to think of it—having our dreams come true would result in a serious storage problem. Still, we find ourselves wanting more wealth, more love, more fulfillment and more meaning from our recovery. In the course of healthy, everyday life sometimes we will feel malcontented. The material world, with its commercial trappings, preys on insecurity, selling illusions about products that can satisfy the inadequacy it implants in us. The more we expose ourselves to media, the more likely we will engage in copious consumption and feel less contentment. Western world contentment has been on the decline since the late 1950s. What has been increasing is our exposure to advertising. Google "the story of stuff" for an enlightening connection between consumption, ecology and human well-being.[30]

Those of us from the *Dysfunction-R-Us* club have some core beliefs that may contribute to unrealistic behavior. We may believe that there will never be enough—not enough time, money or love—at least, not for us. We may think we are unworthy: "If people get to know me, they will reject me." Any of these core beliefs can lead to insatiable needs we try to compensate for.

Left unchecked, here are three maladaptive patterns that we may fall prey to: (i) Hyper-consumption: for most of us this includes, but isn't limited to, addiction; (ii) Resignation: accepting as facts beliefs like, "I am undeserving" or "life is futile"; and (iii) Overcompensation: masking our pain in false bravado and insisting that we don't need anything or anybody. These patterns lead to lives of isolation, possibly compounding the cycle of impulsive binging and purging.

Do I have ambition or resentment that comes from a core belief that there isn't enough to go around and/or that my needs just can't be satisfied? Today, can I remind myself that I am fine just the way I am and that I have so much to be grateful for? Is it better to want what I to have than have what I want? Can I be at peace with not having everything I want?

# February 29

*Happy Leap Year! Create-your-own page!*

---

"I had years of therapy to recover from this. A lot of it had to do with being a people-pleaser, being the ultimate good girl. I wanted everyone to like me. I didn't really have a voice. I was afraid of growing up."
Tracey Gold (born 1969)

"Keep me safe in the company of those who seek truth and safe from the company of those who claim to have found it."
Unknown

"Self-pity is easily the most destructive of the non-pharmaceutical narcotics; it is addictive, gives momentary pleasure and separates the victim from reality."
John W. Gardner (1912–2002)

"In a consumer society there are inevitably two kinds of slaves: the prisoners of addiction and the prisoners of envy."
Ivan Illich (1926–2002)

"To dream of the person we would like to be is a waste of the person we are."
Heard around the rooms

"Glory is fleeting, but obscurity is forever."
Napoleon Bonaparte (1769–1821)

"As far as possible, without surrender, be on good terms with all persons. Speak your truth quietly and clearly; and listen to others, even to the dull and the ignorant; they too have their story. Avoid loud and aggressive persons; they are vexations to the spirit."
From "Desiderata" by Max Ehrmann

"Our program makes sobriety a happy existence by helping us to understand ourselves better. Our sobriety is more than simply a period of time in which we are not drinking; it becomes a happy learning experience. Learn to know yourself and your illness. This is how we overcome."
Jean Kirkpatrick, PhD

# March 1

*"This is a basic personality characteristic of creative people...*
*the attitude of naiveté, of acceptance and*
*curiosity about the odd and strange ... the ability to notice and*
*to remark differences in detail."*

*Jane Piirto, PhD*

---

In Western culture, naiveté and wisdom are widely treated as opposites. In Eastern traditional philosophy and religion, the two are symbiotic. The gentle quality of naiveté is a state of openness, a right-minded, limitless way of seeing. A *beginner's mind* may seem counterintuitive to addicts. We often come from impulsive places where we cope by saving time and jumping to conclusions.

Many an addict's life is lived with a think-fast, act-fast, live-by-instinct mentality. Twelve Step founders touted humility as a cornerstone of change. In being humble, in knowing we know only a little, we are open to seeing more than we have seen before. In the practice of mindfulness, a *beginner's mind* observes things that an efficient and goal-oriented, conscious, logical mind doesn't. As we practice a new way of seeing, let's not get hard on our assumptions; they are just trying to help. But new ways of seeing come, ironically, from regressing or revisiting our childlike awe, from a time when we experienced life without applying labels, quantifying or anticipating.

In our Twelve & Twelve business meetings everyone gets just one vote. Thirty years doesn't glean thirty votes. Three months in, a member is entitled to contribute. We don't take the "If we want your opinion, we'll give it to you" approach. The newcomer perspective is a cleaner, less biased look at how we come across, which is just as valuable as long-timer experience. Again, naiveté has merit.

Is doubt a higher state of consciousness than certainty? Is it another arrow in my quiver?

# March 2

*"We do not sing because we are happy,*
*we are happy because we sing."*

*William James (1842–1910)*

---

James lived around some very colorful people. His siblings Henry and Alice were authors, as was his Godfather, Ralph Waldo Emerson. These influences inspired this original thinker in the disciplines of physiology, psychology and philosophy. He left his mark on Bill Wilson and our entire culture.

There is a relationship between our feelings and behavior. In a healthy, balanced state, our feelings influence our actions, but our actions can also impact our sense of well-being. We can counter restlessness by going to a meeting. We can forget ourselves by reaching out to others. When we are in the throes of obsessive-compulsiveness, we don't seem to read and respond to feelings with the same connectedness. When we are experiencing the extremes of feeling either unworthy or entitled, everything is chaotic and our feelings are exaggerated and unmanageable. What to do? Well, we know what seemed to work back in the day. We would check out into oblivion as a way to navigate the rocky road of life.

As we work the Twelve Steps, we become more integrated and connected to our environment and our feelings. Awe and wonderment will be experiences as will grief and fear. In recovery we find that there are times to resign ourselves to sadness or grief—it won't kill us. But we don't wallow. When the time is right we can think of today's quote. The Steps teach us that we can sing regardless of the weather. Singing can ease our suffering and/or demonstrate our gratitude. It is a sober self-medication.

What will I "sing" about today? Do I have theme songs for when I want to express happiness? How about to comfort me or draw out feelings when I am blue? Right thinking can come from right "doing" as we learn over and over again in the Steps. How can I steer my thinking by doing something positive?

# March 3

*"Be not ashamed of mistakes and thus make them crimes."*

*Confucius (551 BC–479 BC)*

---

Cognitive-behavioral therapy (CBT) helps modify behavior by identifying our triggers and reprogramming problematic assumptions (automatic thoughts). Understanding our patterns and cycles gives us a leg up at modeling healthy new behavior, learning social skills and living more consciously. The addiction cycle is circular. When we act out we feel guilt (shame). We relieve the shame by purging, often promising that we will quit. For predictable results, repeat cycle, increasing the dose as required.

The Twelve Steps break this cycle and pave the way for new patterns—a recovery cycle. "Easy does it" is a mantra that helps still our panic when we feel triggered. Reaching out for help, taking inventory, being mindful and changing our habits are all part of transformation. Recovering members who have had experience with formal CBT under professional care tend to catch on quickly, because they have exposed themselves to methods that complement our peer-to-peer fellowship. CBT patients seek alternative interpretations to experiences that used to trigger feelings of worthlessness, resulting from mistakes made in the past. Shame escalates addiction, which has become both a cure and a self-punishment and has started showing diminishing returns. We can curb the self-abuse that results from the idea, "My mistakes are proof of my unworthiness." The new attitude may look like this: "I do what I think is best. I will make mistakes along the way. Who doesn't? To err is human." OMG—Confucius was a cognitive-behavioral therapist!

Just for today I will try rejoicing in my foibles. Can I try not taking my imperfection so seriously? Can I be empathetic to others' shortcomings, seeing as we are all just doing our best?

## March 4

*"I will listen to everything that is said so I will have some
constructive ideas to take home with me and use.
I will not yield to my compulsion to go on talking
after I have made my point—and what I say will
have a direct relevance to the subject of the meeting."*

One Day at a Time in Al-Anon

When we are new to the program, just getting to meetings makes sense. We go with the flow. Some members say the program is learned not by osmosis but by "ass-mosis." Just get our asses into chairs, listen and learn. But when we have been around for a while and have worked the Steps, getting to every meeting isn't a matter of life or death. Do we get lazy about meetings and their purpose?

We owe it to ourselves to get the most out of life—in and out of the program. When we do go to meetings we can think ahead, priming ourselves for being open and present, checking our egos and considering what we might be able to add. It's worth reviewing why we are going to the meeting. Does someone depend on us? Do we have a problem we seek perspective on? Or are we showing a lack of imagination or avoiding another responsibility? Sometimes we go to meetings out of habit and some other activity may be more appropriate.

Hearing ourselves talk can be intoxicating. Once we needed the approval of others and we were willing to do anything to get it. We still enjoy approval but we don't seek it at all cost. Some of us remind ourselves before the meeting that we are here to be genuine, not impressive. If we talk a lot, we can remember that passing is sharing—sharing the time.

Am I planning to attend a meeting today or in the next couple of days? What's my purpose? Will I get there early (if that's important to me) and be ready to get and give what I can?

# March 5

*"I'm not upset that you lied to me, I'm upset
that from now on I can't believe you."*

*Friedrich Nietzsche (1844-1900)*

---

Oh how we want to put our faith in something out there—a lover who stays infatuated, a friend who will always listen, a bank account that never says "funds not available" and a program that shows us the light and the way. We want *it* so badly that we put people on pedestals, we kneel at the altar of false gods and we set our course for the future as the time and the place where we will be worry-free and wanting for nothing. Putting something, someone or some place on a pedestal invites wishful thinking and it allows us to delegate blame. What would one call today's expectations? We call them premeditated resentments or disappointments; but don't worry, it won't be our fault.

With maturity we look inward for solutions from our voice of reason. Most addiction is borne of something that we think is lacking inside of us. We searched and searched for the right *something* to fill the hole. It was never enough, but we somehow believed that everything would be OK. Our escape from reality would protect us and the harmful consequences would never be faced. But if our addiction didn't fill the hole, how would cutting off the supply fill the void? Many of us tried the program and fellowship, putting the Twelve & Twelve bus to happy destiny on probation. Becoming dependent on fellowship is less harmful than process or substance abuse, but are we setting ourselves up to say to the fellowship, upon our first setback, "You lied to me. How can I ever trust you again?"

We can't cure addiction with a better artificial outside agent. The answers we seek come from within. The great thing about fellowships and programs is that they provide the experience, kinship and change of scenery that we need while we get our shit together. But they aren't the answer. The experience of others will help us find our own answers and chart our own course in recovery.

Am I acquainted, or reacquainted, with a voice inside that I can trust? It shouldn't be new to me. In my addiction, didn't I always have a voice inside that asked me, "Who do you think you're kidding?"

# March 6

*"To be willing to work for humility as something to be desired for itself, takes most of us a long, long time. A whole life-time geared to self-centeredness cannot be set in reverse all at once. Rebellion dogs our every step."*

Twelve Steps and Twelve Traditions, 73

---

We are *rebellion dawgs*—sounds like a band! We don't conform or listen to reason. Did our rebellious nature condemn us to addiction or did addiction warp our brains to the point of antisocial selfishness and poor decision-making?

What AA could identify in the middle of the last century, science can explain this century. Addiction cuts down our neurotransmitters' functionality. Dopamine, GABA and glutamate work harmoniously in normal brains but not in the brain of a *rebellion dawg*. Addiction and maybe other obsessive-compulsive disorders create an imbalance of natural chemicals, influencing behavior, mood and decision-making. In a normal brain the consequences of harmful actions are weighed against rewards. When we mess with our brain chemistry our prefrontal cortex cannot effectively warn us of the dangers of bad habits and rash decisions. Our brains are dysfunctional.[31] That's right, *dawg*—our rebellious nature may not be our nature at all. The question of which came first— chemical imbalance or addiction—is up for debate. Relapse, destructive relationships, narcissism, rash decisions about career, recovery or even what downhill ski trail we choose might not be due to the fact that we are born to be wild; our brain chemistry might be short-circuited.

Synaptic plasticity in some addicts, some of the time, restores brain functioning, keeping us apprised of right/wrong and risk/reward considerations. To re-train our thinking from grandiose to humble, from reckless to mindful, will take time and practice. Let's not be hard on ourselves if we suffer setbacks in our sober, sensible, serene living.

Steps Four through Seven are exercises in reflection, understanding and improving my cooperative, proactive and compassionate ways, where only rebellion ruled me before. Do I remember progress, not perfection, in my recovery? Teaching rebellion dogs new tricks takes time and repetition. Good doggy!

# March 7

*"Emotions like sadness, fear, anxiety, or boredom produce 'psychic entropy' in the mind; that is, a state in which we cannot use attention effectively to deal with external tasks because we need it to restore an inner subjective order. Positive emotions like happiness, strength or alertness are states of 'psychic negentropy' because we don't need attention to ruminate and feel sorry for ourselves, and psychic energy can flow freely into whatever thoughts or task we choose to invest in."*

*Mihaly Csikszentmihalyi (born 1934)*

---

Csikszentmihalyi suggests that different types of energy make us feel psychologically drained or invigorated. We know the difference between being in a good mood compared to a bad mood and we have all experienced changes in mood. Our psyches, like the world around us, are inherently active.

Laws of thermodynamics govern energy. Energy can neither be created nor destroyed, but it can be converted. Carbohydrates are potential food energy that converts to kinetic energy in humans. Psychic examples of energy conversion are anger becoming strength or empathy triggering crying. Like a coffee going cold, our energy can wane; this is called entropy. Negentropy is the "flow" in Csikszentmihalyi's book, *Finding Flow*. Athletes or musicians call this being "in the zone." In this state one can seemingly do no wrong—they have mastery, calm and effortless reflexes.

Flow occurs when we feel both skilled and challenged. Flow's opposite is apathy, a risky state for addicts wherein we might not care if we live or die. We indulged to escape the blues and surge back to our *happy place*. Early in recovery it is normal to experience cravings when we feel down. Coping with boredom in recovery is difficult because we have always medicated away our apathy. We cannot always muster the positive feelings we want instantly. An important step toward mastery over our feelings is to be able to identify our sensations and feelings— good and bad. We can recognize that transitioning feelings from good to bad helps prevent us from being overwhelmed or reactive.

Do I know that how I feel is not who I am? What are my reflex reactions to feeling good or bad? Can I be more mindful of how I am feeling and less reactive?

# March 8

*"The more you lose yourself in something bigger than yourself,*
*the more energy you will have."*

*Norman Vincent Peale (1898–1993)*

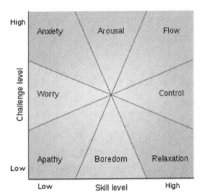

Sometimes just knowing we are worried, anxious or bored can help us separate who we are from what we are feeling. The chart here is from Csikszentmihalyi's book, *Finding Flow*, referred to yesterday.[32] Flow, the opposite of apathy, comes with maximum skill (X axis) and challenge (Y axis). When we add challenge to apathy without skill, this makes us feel anxious. Being more skilled will relax us but only increased challenge raises productivity, which helps us feel good about ourselves. This plays out in a Twelve & Twelve fellowship. If we have become skilled in our own recovery we can still be bored. By challenging ourselves with service work, working with newer members or practicing these principles in new areas of our lives, we elevate our feelings into the top right quadrant of this chart where life is at its best (in the flow).

In today's quote we see that a higher purpose, as much as any higher power, can keep us from spiraling into boredom, worry or other negative emotions. When we are in the flow we may feel spiritual or feel the presence of spiritual forces but rarely can this happen without a purpose greater than self-satisfaction. When we are new, the simple hope of living sober can spur such a pink cloud state. When sobriety is our new normal, waking up with a purpose can guide our energy positively.

As artificial highs intrigue me less, does purposefulness give me the buzz of good, clean living? When do I feel flow?

# March 9

*"One of the most paradoxical aspects of our recovery is that by thinking of ourselves less, we learn to love ourselves more. We may not have expected our spiritual journey to lead to a fresh appreciation of ourselves but it does. Because of the love we extend to others, we realize our own value."*

NA It Works, How and Why

---

What stands between addicts and the happiness that comes from having flow in their lives? A poor self-image has a nagging habit of sabotaging achievement. If we don't feel we deserve it, we tend to police ourselves consciously or subconsciously. It is easy to see that happiness in life is nearly impossible if we are not right with the world and, more specifically, the people in our world. In Step Nine we make restitution for harm done and we feel better about ourselves, increasing our sense of worth. We try harder and achieve more. Others respond better to us, taking cues from our self-image, and flow becomes easier. We don't put up barriers and others are our advocates—cheering us on.

Step Nine is about cleaning up our side of the street so we can look people in the eye, but let's not ignore what caused us to be either emotionally needy or aloof with others. Attachment theory provides a framework for understanding how early relational experiences influence developmental pathways and adult functioning.[33] Abandonment, neglect and/or abuse in our youth can stunt development—cognitively, emotionally and socially. These handicaps lead to escapism, addiction and escalating risky and anti-social behaviors. Attachment disorder can cause codependence (hyperactive attachment) or intimacy avoidance (attachment deactivation) and some of us flip-flop between hot and cold throughout relationships, resulting in the mixed messages, emotional manipulation and hurt feelings that make up our amends list. Ego-maniacs with inferiority complexes are not going to treat others as well as we hope to.

There is a place for cleaning up my side of the street. But do I know the cause of my bad behavior?

# March 10

*"Our membership ought to include all who suffer from alcoholism. Hence we may refuse none who wish to recover. Nor ought A.A. membership ever depend upon money or conformity. Any two or three alcoholics gathered together for sobriety may call themselves an A.A. group, provided that, as a group, they have no other affiliation."*

*Tradition Three*[34]

---

The *Twelve & Twelve* illustrates tolerance of nonconformity by telling the story of Ed the atheist. Ed had to go, according to some of the *faithful* members, because Ed was insisting at meetings that "we are better without this God nonsense." The believers discussed kicking him out, but how? The story takes some artistic liberty and suggests that Ed got drunk, found God and fell in line. "A Vicious Cycle" is the story in this atheist's own words, found in Editions II to IV of the Big Book. Jim B., the member the Ed story was fashioned after, says "the only Higher Power I could concede was the power of the group." Jim was responsible for the addition of the phrase "as we understood Him" to the word "God" in the Twelve Steps of AA. What if "Ed" had been kicked out?

Once Tradition Three came to be, no one could say who was or was not an alcoholic or an AA member. Each group is a group if the members say so. Membership, diagnosis and labels are all self-determined. If we had rules instead of Traditions, we would need enforcement and bureaucracy. Fellowships of all kinds get along without such things; the only requirement for membership is a desire to stop the self-destructive behavior.

Am I ever tempted to judge another member's legitimacy? Do I treat everyone fairly, regardless of background or personality? Do I remember the importance of new members and try to talk to them as equals? Do I ever over-sell the fellowship or rush newcomers? Do I include newcomers the same way I do my friends in the meeting? Do I respect their views?

# March 11

*"Solutions are difficult to come by rationally. The reasoning
mind is like a rudderless ship: It describes interesting patterns
on the water, but it lacks a sure sense of direction.
The rudder of inner guidance comes from
super-conscious levels of awareness."*

J. Donald Walters (born 1926)

---

"Super-conscious"—that's a leap for the restless addict whose mind
strays in the first thirty seconds of meditating. The author of today's
quote, best known in the Kriya Yoga community as Swami Kriyananda,
could be judged by a recovering addict as one who lives an extreme life
of deprivation. We have lived at the other extreme. We see his way of life
as impossibly disciplined and calm while our own lives might include
more melodrama than yoga. We compartmentalize, practice denial and
bow at the altar of avoidance. Right-living is not a place we get to; it
is a direction we are moving in. Maybe we have more work to do than
the next yoga student, and maybe we don't. If the type of meditation
that delivers this super-consciousness sounds like a place we want to be
taken to, let's do our best to think of it as a direction we are headed in—
progress rather than perfection. If we feel like we are worlds away from
a connection with this inner voice, we aren't disqualified. Au contraire,
we have the most to gain.

Let's try periodic meditation for short bursts—maybe two minutes at
a time to start. Let's settle for super-conscious *lite* for a while. Sometimes
we will be swept backward or to one side. So what? We get grounded
again, take a breath and avoid *thinking* about the obstacles; we just point
ourselves in the right direction again. We don't go from unconscious to
super-conscious in one cross-legged session. We practice, one day at a
time.

If I outrun every opportunity for intimacy, if I constantly keep the
crowd amused to temper my loneliness, if I caffeinate my nervous system
with a pot of coffee a day, or figuratively with stimulation-overload, if I
am always a year's wages in debt and ten minutes late, just how exactly
do I meditate my way into the light, let alone into super-consciousness?
Can I be happy with my progress?

## March 12

*"Life is full of misery, loneliness and*
*suffering—and it's all over much too soon."*

*Woody Allen (born 1935)*

---

Pain has been called the touchstone of all spiritual growth. Regardless of what we think about spiritual awakening, we all know rude awakenings. Growing and learning often come the hard way. There may be some question as to the origins of what is thought to be a Chinese proverb (curse): "May you live in interesting times." No one has authenticated the origin of this, but Woody Allen could be the inspiration for the modern cliché, "Life sucks and then you die." He invites us to ponder our tendencies to worry our lives away.

Life is short. In recovery, we get a second chance at a life that was on a trajectory to end tragically. At some point, recovery includes setbacks such as health problems and other misfortunes. The poster child for recovery isn't always the one who has turned it around from rags to riches. Maybe the poster child is one among us who remains stoic in the face of adversity. A second chance isn't a guarantee of a front row seat or a place in the sun. It's just a second chance.

Can I take my recovery one day at time, regardless of what life has in store for me? After all, life doesn't last forever. What am I waiting for?

# March 13

*"Once we adopt a positive mind, positive things will always happen. This belief, like all the other illusions peddled in this culture, encourages people to flee from reality when reality is frightening or depressing ... . The gimmick of visualizing what we want and believing we can achieve it is no different from praying to a god or Jesus who we are told wants to make us wealthy and successful."*

Empire of Illusion, 119, Chris Hedges (born 1956)

---

Many relate to arriving at our first meetings emotionally bankrupt. We come to grips with our *insanity* and move away from absolute despair by changing our lives through the Twelve Steps or other recovery regimens. So what is the other side of the coin of despair? Is it the new us—glossy-eyed, giddy and buzzed on positive expectation? We think not. Dreaming about winning the lottery or yearning for all our troubles to be gone makes us easy prey for gimmicks. *You-Can-Change-Your-Life* books and seminars feed on the gullible—"a fool and their money are soon parted." Subterfuge takes small truths full of integrity and extrapolates them into a seductive language that is vaguely familiar. Then a franchise is made out of our own wishful thinking, preying on our naiveté. The small print says that if we don't get the wealth or relationships we are visualizing, it's our fault. Any request for evidence is treated as subversion and met with clichéd ridicule. Thoughtful intercourse is suspect. Mindless group-speak is "safe." Now that's getting with the program, but the program turns out to be a scam.

Addicts are susceptible to magical thinking and the promise of utopia. Being positive is a good idea but not at the expense of the rich life that mindful inquiry and being at peace with reality will afford. The crazier our world gets the more "Law of Attraction" snake oil will be peddled as a cure for what ails us. Being motivated by positive psychology to take us to "the next level" is one thing; flight from reality to stave off despair is quite another matter.

How do I defend myself today from the allure of quick fixes or the easier softer way?

# March 14

*"How poor are they that have not patience!*
*What wound did ever heal but by degrees?"*

William Shakespeare (1564–1616)

---

Patience is wisdom. Meditation cultivates patience. For those who subscribe to the metaphor of the *addict's mind*, this is not as simple as it sounds. Meditation takes practice. Meditation is a discipline of both learning and unlearning. We who have obsessive tendencies fill quiet moments with rumination or activity, believing that these moments will be made richer by our busy minds. What we fill the quietness with is often clutter. Compare that with quieting our minds and objectively observing our thoughts and feelings right now. Regret and dread distract us from the present moment. Addicts new to meditation will experience boredom, frustration and/or anxiety as they struggle with mindful meditation. A class, a book and/or a mentor may be needed to help train us away from old habits including judgment, obsession and avoidance. Like a runner preparing for his first marathon, we devote our energy and motivation to finding time, keeping our promises and progressing, as Shakespeare says, "by degrees."

Do I know that, to be truly free, I have to cultivate the wisdom to treat recovery as a process, not an event? I already have some discipline—I show up on time for events and appointments that are important to me. How can I apply whatever discipline I do have to practicing meditation so I can gain patience, wisdom and a clear head (by degrees)?

## March 15

*"I suspect the secret of personal attraction is locked up
in our unique imperfections, flaws and frailties."*

*Hugh Mackay (1640–1692)*

---

Is it flattering to be asked to be a sponsor? Often the qualities that attract another member to us are our blatant shortcomings rather than our genius or our acumen in wholesome living. Being asked to sponsor someone is no insult to our recovery, either. Someone struggling with anxiety may be more drawn to someone who has borne the indignities of this calamity more than to someone who knows only peace and prosperity.

"Why me?" is a good question to ask at the start of this new relationship. It serves both parties well to establish what the sponsee's goals are. The needs of the newer member should drive the relationship. The best results come when newer members take responsibility for their own recovery. That way, both members are less likely to fall into old, unhealthy roles such as those of the *Persecutor*, *Victim* and *Rescuer*. (See endnote 11 for further information about transactional analysis and the drama triangle.)

Many sponsorship relationships are temporary and it helps to have that understanding right from the get-go. No two people grow at exactly the same pace and changing circumstances may bring the relationship to a natural conclusion. Hard feelings need not ensue. The end does not mean either member failed to live up to their part of the bargain. Seasons change, needs change and perspectives change. Some sponsor/sponsee relationships last a long time and others don't. Some are informal and never clearly stated. It's nothing personal. It's all a part of the ebb and flow of a peer-to-peer fellowship.

Do I keep my ego in check when I am called upon to help in the program?

# March 16

*"Religion is essentially the art and the theory of the remaking of man. Man is not a finished creation."*

*Edmund Burke (1729–1797)*

---

Twelve & Twelve critics love to point to meetings where, "We are spiritual, not religious," is said just before reciting the Lord's Prayer. They call us "a religion in denial." That's not true, yet we see where they may find compelling arguments.

We can be members without worshiping anything, or practicing or observing sacred rituals. Members who treat literature or meeting rituals as sacred have put human-crafted *stuff* on a pedestal. We should not put people on pedestals; the same is true for anything they write or do. We have what might be called a creed. We share tenets—beliefs that aren't scientifically irrefutable.

We believe addiction is a disease and is incurable. "A pickle will never become a cucumber again" is a popular adage. These are not scientifically agreed upon facts; rather, they are dearly held beliefs. They are our truths, gleaned from the experiences of millions, but from a strictly scientific point of view, they are anecdotal, and to tout them as fact would be quackery. How many of us know why we are addicts? Who could say with certainty what exactly has kept us clean and/or sober? We each have a narrative of what it was like, what happened and what it is like now. We hit bottom and thought we were finished. Recovery was "the art and the theory of the remaking of man." Our journey as addicts and fellowships is "not a finished creation." "More will be revealed" was what our founders told us.

If I make things sacred, do I choke the truth out of them? To date, there is no cure for me, scientific or spiritual. Do I believe I have a reprieve, not a cure? Am I rigid or do I believe in healthy debate?

# March 17

*"Peace has to be created, in order to be maintained.
It is the product of Faith, Strength, Energy, Will, Sympathy,
Justice, Imagination, and the triumph of principle.
It will never be achieved by passivity and quietism."*

Dorothy Thompson (1893–1961)

---

Recovery has to be created in order to be maintained. Many of us don't have sanity to be returned to (Step Two); we have to create it. And the Twelve Steps are not a passive process. Will is not our enemy; it was part of the problem and it will be part of the solution too. Faith, justice, sympathy, imagination—are these not an apt description of the Steps that create peace in each of us? When a snake sheds its skin it lets go of the dead, dysfunctional layer. The new and wholesome skin, the new self, is already inside. It is just a matter of writhing, massaging or employing other kinds of work and energy to get the old skin off. Being likened to a slithering reptile may give us the creeps, but let's take what we can from this metaphor. It doesn't matter if our guidance comes from a higher power or an inner voice—the snake's shedding of its skin is a useful likeness to the process. Our better self, higher self or our Good Orderly Direction is already inside us. It's just a matter of tearing down these walls, this old skin that we have built up for protection over the years. "What an order," indeed. But if we are willing—willing to work up a sweat—the transformation can begin.

Dorothy Thompson is not talking about our personal recovery; she is talking about what it takes to right the wrongs in the world. The great thing about our second chance at life is that we don't have to sit on our hands in white-knuckle sobriety for the rest our lives. We can apply what worked for us in overcoming denial, self-destruction and seeming hopelessness, to the world around us. We can make a difference. We intuitively know how to handle situations that used to baffle us, just as *Alcoholics Anonymous* promised.

What am I doing with my second chance? Am I focused on more, more, more for me? Do I look for ways to apply the power of recovery to the world around me?

# March 18

*"In AA I have learned to take responsibility for my own doings. In ACA, I learned to stop taking responsibility for other people's doings."*

*Heard around the rooms*

"Family" can be a very triggering word. Just say it out loud and get a load of the sensations, emotions and thoughts that follow. Large numbers of AA and Al-Anon members who also identified as Adult Children of Alcoholics (ACAs or ACOAs) experienced a myriad of reactions to the insight that their woes weren't entirely cured by acceptance or by sweeping up their side of the street. Steps Four and Eight chronicle dramas wherein we enacted the role of perpetrator. ACA invites us to examine our life-dramas as the victim, enabler and rescuer, too. Many of our families included victims of victims of victims. Some felt relief from the quote above, while some felt betrayed by their original fellowship for "setting them up" for taking on 100% of the shame and blame. Of course, nobody sets us up for anything; we are peer-to-peer fellowships, each finding our own way, together.

In *Family Interaction: A Multigenerational Developmental Perspective*, authors Anderson & Sabatelli describe families using two dimensions: structures and tasks. Traditional structure (heterosexual couples with natural born children) isn't the only way we define family now but tasks still largely define what a family is and how it functions. Tasks are the business and responsibilities inside the family, and in a dysfunctional home they can be distorted and volatile. An orderly and predictable environment is not provided for children. *Family Interaction* describes rules in a home, as well as *metarules*—the rules about the rules. These rules and *metarules* help to define the structures and tasks. In an alcoholic home the rule might be that we never talk about alcoholism. The *metarule* controls when the rules can be broken. For example, if the rule is to never complain about Dad, an exception may be made when Mom is talking to Aunt Shirley. Rules and *metarules* for breaking the rules—it's hard for kids to get it right.

What was expected and forbidden in my home? What rules had exceptions in my home? Who was allowed to break them and when?

## March 19

*"I'm not afraid of storms, for I'm learning to sail my ship."*
*Louisa May Alcott (1832–1888)*

---

Recovery arms us with the tools to adapt and improvise along the way. We gain hope and expect that we can figure out the new and more complex hardships and troubles that are bound to be part of our lives.

Recovery isn't a better life; it's a better way to deal with life. We once avoided and denied. We emotionally fled or we overcompensated. In recovery we cultivate serenity, courage and wisdom in facing each day. We do the best we can, no matter what the weather.

Storms in life—if we're fortunate to live long enough—are likely to get more threatening but we won't go through them alone if we don't want to. Nor will we go through storms ill-equipped. Still, if we are afraid, that's only natural. With open minds and open hearts it is likely we will get through each storm and grow new coping muscles in doing so.

A storm is brewing. Will I be ready? Will I know where to go for help when I need it? Isn't it true that the greatest struggles in life sometimes become my defining moments?

# March 20

*"Ever notice that anyone going slower than you is an
idiot, but anyone going faster is a maniac?"*

George Carlin (1937–2008)

---

Why can't everyone just save time and see it our way? Carlin plays off of our center-of-the-universe syndrome. We are the focal point. Those in front and behind are extras who scroll up late in the credits of the movies of our lives. Judging others' shortcomings, compared to our qualities, is egotistical. Judging ourselves negatively compared to others' qualities is also egotistical. It still puts us in the middle of the equation. Anaïs Nin (French-Cuban author, 1903–1977) may have beaten Carlin to the punch in her less funny, more existential explanation: "We don't see things as they are; we see them as we are."

Why do we wag judging fingers at others? If we are preoccupied with the wrongs of the world, is there something behind this smokescreen of criticism? Our psychoanalyst will weigh in on this. Sometimes, we are camouflaging pain, fear or self-loathing. Criticism, like procrastination, worry or regret, is a coping technique. When we are right with the world, others do not incite our judgment and rarely do we encourage their hostility. This isn't to say that we will be conflict-free when living rightly, but we will pick our battles instead of exuding antagonism. Perspective matures. Like everyone else, we are trying to move forward in life, doing the best we can. When we are right-minded we see that others have needs and foibles just like we do. We get better at accepting ourselves and others as they are.

Do I look for fault in others like there is a reward for it? If I am critical now, isn't this an automatic thought? If it's automatic, what's behind it? When I catch myself being critical of how everyone else is "driving" along the highway of life, am I putting them down to make myself feel better? Would I feel even better if I was compassionate instead?

# March 21

*"It takes a lot of courage to release the familiar and seemingly secure, to embrace the new. But there is no real security in what is no longer meaningful. There is more security in the adventurous and exciting, for in movement there is life, and in change there is power."*

*Alan Cohen (born 1954)*

---

It takes courage for us as newcomers to part with the familiarity and security of our old way of life. In time, we see how we would have been doomed if we had maintained the trajectory of our old addictive ways. But we do recover and stay clean and sober. The once awkward and absurd Twelve Step program becomes matter-of-fact.

Let's fast forward five or twenty years: consider the apostate. In Twelve & Twelve terms, this could be someone who came to believe in the rooms, began praying to God and got good results. Life improved. They shared their experience, describing how they were lost before finding their way. Years later, this same member wonders if what they believe is real or imaginary. The same turning point could be true of a staunch atheist whose search takes her or him in the opposite direction. Each of us should be able to say, "I felt so sure but now I doubt so much." Being searching and fearless doesn't have to end after a year of recovery. A spiritual journey is a continuum. The same could be said for one who once went to many meetings a week and now finds that their calling is pulling them in another direction. Change is always risky but the alternative is to lose our vitality. We have mythology about those who stray from the pack. Certainly, many relapses occurred after we became complacent about attending meetings. Caution is called for but it is hardly scientific to suggest that all who leave will relapse. Once, Europeans thought that all who sailed west would fall off the end of the flat earth. That widely held belief lacked a few facts, too.

Rashness is foolish but so is rigidity. Is fear a servant that alerts me to danger, or a master that enslaves me in stagnation? Am I as open to change as I was when I was new to the fellowship?

# March 22

*"You may be suffering from an illness which only a spiritual experience will conquer. To one who feels he is an atheist or agnostic such an experience seems impossible, but to continue as he is means disaster, especially if he is an alcoholic of the hopeless variety. To be doomed to an alcoholic death or to live on a spiritual basis are not always easy alternatives to face."*

Alcoholics Anonymous, 44

---

"We Agnostics" was not written by agnostics. It was a grave warning to agnostics: stick to your guns and face certain peril. But the book later concedes, "We know but a little" and "more will be revealed." Many members of Twelve Step fellowships now recover without God, Allah, Hindu's *fave* polytheistic trilogy of Brahma, Vishnu and Shiva, or any other deity. Many doubters have translated the Steps into a secular language that more clearly reflects their beliefs. Atheism is on the rise in America and more so around the world.[35] A spiritual journey is a personal journey and not a universal formula—more so now than when this 1939 passage was written.

For skeptics, this Big Book passage illustrates the line in the sand. It infers that doubters are holding out, not willing to let the "miracle" of sobriety happen. Consider that for the 1930s, in Judeo-Christian America, AA was cutting edge. Today, atheists and theists share their stories with each other and neither need argue how one worldview is more enlightened than another. Neither would refuse help to the other. Sure, some will proselytize and some will roll their eyes, but don't think that in the first days of Twelve Step recovery there was one harmonious, unified group. "Take what you like and leave the rest" has been around from the start. Being beyond belief involves seeing past the narcissism of small differences. None of us have gotten it perfect, no two members are identical and there is no addict whom we would refuse to help find their own salvation.

Do I compare, judge and fault-find or am I beyond belief?

# March 23

---

Today's author knew a thing or two about getting things done. He was a writer, lyricist, politician, botanist, artist, scientist, military man and lawyer. He is credited as having influenced writers Hesse, Emerson and Mann, philosophers Nietzsche and Schopenhauer and composers Beethoven, Brahms and Schubert. This would be but a short list of the people this German skeptic touched and the accomplishments he is known for. Sometimes when we feel like heroes for having suffered through addiction we might want to measure our accomplishments against others.

Before we can try to outpace this overachiever we have to get and stay sober. For members who relapse or bide their time on the sidelines, some of Goethe's words could be a game changer. Momentum, according to Goethe, favors those who have committed themselves to action. We don't stand before the fire pit of life and say, "Pit, give me heat and then I will put some wood on you." We commit to a course of action and "all manner of unforeseen incidents and meetings and material assistance, which no [one] could have dreamed would have come [our] way" occur as a result of this decision.

Many of us say, years later, that "if I had made a list of what I wanted from recovery, I would have sold myself short." Our lives often come to be so much more than we expected. We thought that recovery would be a punishment for owning up to addiction and a whole world opened up to us instead. How much does commitment have to do with success in life? We look to powers of example for clues.

Am I adrift and waiting for something to happen or am I committed to a course of action?

## March 24

*"Shoes block pain, not impact! Pain teaches us to run comfortably! From the moment you start going barefoot, you will change the way you run."*

Born to Run *by Christopher McDougall (born 1962)*

---

*Born to Run* is the story of an aging, battered athlete who refuses surgery, pharmacology, corrective orthotics and surrender to a reality that he is broken. But our athlete can't be fixed and must eventually concede to a diagnosis of chronic degeneration, abandoning the hope of a life that would include carefree running. The author heads off in search of the Tarahumara—an ancient, forgotten tribe of Mexico who hunt by running down a deer until it collapses in exhaustion, without the aid of a single high-tech shoe or electrolyte drink.

Readers follow a growing pack of seekers and runners who uncover troubling facts about how sports injuries have increased with every new breakthrough in running shoe technology. Manufactured comfort makes us soft—we break down more. Our ultra-marathon heroes reconnect with age-old truths, part with learned dependency on the commercial world and save their souls by sunrise. How is this a metaphor for people in recovery?

We wanted to win while avoiding the pain. Every new shelter from pain became a prison from which we sought a new escape. We kept piling on treatments to problems that had been solutions at one time. We fell to record lows and required better coping techniques—quickly! As the above quote suggests, the pain that we were avoiding could have taught us how to live. Imagine that.

What am I running to? What am I running from? When was the last time I ran just for fun?

# March 25

*"You can't think and hit the ball at the same time."*

*Yogi Berra (born 1925)*

---

No one's knack for the obvious is more infamous than Hall of Fame New York Yankee Yogi Berra's. This same truth applies to golf, tennis, skiing and maybe to living life to the fullest. When we're in a game-situation, we can't expect peak performance while analyzing our mechanics. We can practice dance moves in a class but when the music starts for real, we can't dance fluidly and think about dance, too.

Taking time to meditate, visualize or prepare for the day and then taking stock in the evening is how we get better at living up to our potential. In baseball terms, daily inventory is like reviewing the game stats, seeing what's working and what needs improvement. But at game-time (at work, home and play) we trust our instincts. Time won't allow for second-guessing and proper execution. We won't always get it right but how else will we learn other than by swinging and missing?

Because we can't do two things at the same time, if we are being bogged down with self-absorbed angst, a sure cure is to care for someone else. The Dalai Lama said, "If you want others to be happy, practice compassion; if you want to be happy, practice compassion." A key word here is "practice." We are reversing the addictive, narcissistic, hardwired survival mode that found us thinking only about our own personal stats. Compassion is about oneness, not one-upmanship. We don't serve others because we are better than them. We aren't looking for rewards or recognition. Everyone has shyness and fear when it comes to working with others. For some of us, time will reveal that we aren't gifted one-on-one workers. Working on committees or setting up meetings can offer the same escape from the bondage of self.

I have a choice of two gurus today. Do I see that both baseball and Buddhism remind me of the same thing—that not doing and not striving (for selfish things) can bear greater fruit than focusing my attention on myself?

# March 26

*"A life without adventure is likely to be unsatisfactory but a life in which adventure is allowed to take whatever form it will, is sure to be short."*

*Bertrand Russell (1872–1970)*

---

Gawd, Bernie, do you have to be such a killjoy? Whatever happened to live large, die young and leave a good-looking corpse? Now, that's some of that good old thinking that got us here in the first place.

In admitting that we were powerless and that our lives had become unmanageable, several personal beliefs had to be dispelled. We may have felt entitled to our comforts. We may have rationalized that it wasn't so bad, that we had it all under control or that it wasn't our fault—we were the victims of bad breaks and serious misunderstandings. We may not have realized that we were playing Russian roulette and that our days were consequently numbered. In many cases we were blind to the truly self-destructive and counterproductive impact of addiction.

Long after we accept the concepts of powerlessness and unmanageability, many of us will have to stay continually vigilant when indulging in life's pleasures so that they don't blindside our sobriety and we don't get sucked into some new excess. With practice, we naturally recoil from old vices, with little more thought than we put toward breathing or blinking. We won't feel deprived or incomplete anymore. We will be free.

Today, am I living a satisfying life or do I live a life of quiet desperation, sulking about being an addict and feeling hard done by?

# March 27

*"I also saw that I had been self-righteous and smug, thinking*
*I was doing for Bill all that any wife could do. I have come to*
*believe that self-righteousness is one of the worst sins. It is*
*impregnable. No shaft of light can pierce its armor. It keeps its*
*victims apart and aloof from others."*

Lois Wilson, 'Pass It On': The Story of Bill Wilson and How the
A.A. Message Reached the World, 168

---

Lois W., the original Al-Anon member, shares the classic self-concept of someone whose life is harmed by an addict's behavior. Lois was nurse, breadwinner, and decision-maker for herself and Bill. She felt pretty good about her efforts and results. Being unable to cure Bill of alcoholism was a blow to her ego. As much as she wanted to be gracious, she resented that other drunks could do for Bill what she could not.

*Pass it On* is a fascinating discussion of the embryonic stages of Twelve Step recovery. As we read, we imagine facing those challenges of the day, ourselves. There is nothing old-fashioned about self-righteousness. It is like a mind-altering drug in its own right. When we feel superior, all-knowing or persecuted, or as though we're on a crusade, we isolate ourselves with a barrier of uniqueness. Our true motives might fly below our own radar. DENIAL as an acronym has been bandied around the rooms as meaning Didn't Even kNow I wAs Lying. OK, as an acronym it's a stretch—please don't get all self-righteous and miss the point. With walls up and armor on, we lack sensitivity to the nuances of our environments as we cut ourselves off from meaningful stimulation and nurturing. We want approval and control and we are left with nothing but the loneliness of our self-justification.

Am I currently feeling unappreciated or indignant? What's at the root of my discontent?

## March 28

*"Don't ever take a fence down until*
*you know why it was put up."*

Robert Frost (1874–1963)

---

What recovery literature calls "character defects" are like fences. Each one is either keeping fear and danger out or hiding what is going on inside. When we vilify shame, ego, deceit, coercion, seduction, fantasy, resentment, fear or greed, we are susceptible to tearing down those fences without knowing why they were constructed in the first place. We are well-served when we treat Step Four as a fact-finding mission, not a confession of sins. Step Five is a candid discussion from the heart with another erring human who has experienced, firsthand, some of what we are talking about. Step Five is not intended to humiliate us. By writing it down and talking it out, maybe we can understand why these fences were constructed. What were we protecting? What were we keeping out? When was each fence built? Deeper awareness will come in Steps Six and Seven, when we consider life without these crutches and hiding places.

Meditation and mindfulness cultivate intuition and understanding. We relax, breathe and observe our thoughts. Do we think, "Bad thought—go away," or "What is the good thought I must muster to replace the bad thought?" We don't tear down these fences rashly. By treating our feelings, thoughts and sensations as legitimate, we aren't in a rush to burn the house down, along with all the clues. Envy, longing, stress, disappointment and self-condemnation aren't signs of failure. The *judge* inside us is type of fence, too. We note how we feel about these things but we are not quick to draw conclusions.

Some fences (defenses) may still be serving a useful purpose. Can I add a gate so I can come and go until the fence is no longer needed?

# March 29

*"Love comes when manipulation stops; when you think more about the other person than about his or her reactions to you; when you dare to reveal yourself fully, when you dare to be vulnerable."*

Dr. Joyce Brothers (born 1927)

---

Lessons in love originate from the adults of our childhood, movies, radio and first-hand experience. Codependency can be found in many families. And if that's what we lived, is that what we learned? In the early months and years of recovery it's not unusual to walk around with emotional umbilical cords in our hands, looking to plug them in to someone—"I love you so much. Heal me!" We may be more subtle than that but this preconditioning is at the root of the manipulation referred to by today's author. We think we need to control and that we should avoid being controlled, and we also long for approval.

Somewhere along the road we've all heard, "You can't love anyone else until you learn to love yourself." The program teaches us about self-love (or at least helps mitigate self-contempt) as we achieve abstinence, reveal ourselves and try trusting others. Step by step, we learn to love ourselves and our fellows. Love comes as the result of emotional health, and not always as quickly as we'd like. We learn compassion and mend relationships by reversing damage and acting with compassion. We look for ways to love *anonymously*. Who can we do something good for without getting caught? Doing loving things without plotting reciprocity is good daily medicine.

Am I self-reliant in terms of looking after my emotional needs or am I still trying to fill a hole in my heart? Am I ready for love today? The world will never have a shortage of people who are in need of random acts of kindness.

# March 30

*"Were entirely ready to let go of all these defects of character."*

*Step Six, aaagnostics.org*

---

This step was written with some heavy-handed language—words like *entirely ready, all*. Imagine we have cancer and we are asked to become "entirely" ready to have "all" the cancer cells removed from our bodies. How about "entirely" ready to have "all" the plaque removed from our teeth? It's not likely that we would have any resistance to these procedures. So what's our attachment to these defects of character? Are they old friends—partners we have had for as long as we can remember? When everyone seemingly let us down, defects (or defenses) were there for us. If cutting our losses feels like turning our back on an old friend, then how about having a going away party?

Here's an example: let's say that in our inventory we see that in our relationships with others we hid behind masks. Maybe we have a favorite role like *the amiable one* or *the control freak*. We thank those roles for their years of service and protection and tell them that we are now ready to try life on for size without role play. Being ready means trying to live more vulnerably and to resist our fight, freeze and flight reflexes. If we are in therapy we explain this Step. Outside help like psychotherapy can help shed maladaptive behaviors. We uncovered a lot in the inventory Steps and we might think that discovering flaws and owning up to them is a cure. Old habits die hard. Self-knowledge isn't a cure. Knowing we were addicts didn't arrest compulsion—same with simply being able to articulate our flaws in Step Six.

*Entirely* and *all* are evocative words. I am reminded that every member works this Step a different way. There is no rush. Do I accept that I may feel pull-back from characteristics that want to stick around? Do I have the willingness to improve slowly?

# March 31

*"The chief danger in life is that you
may take too many precautions."*

*Alfred Adler (1870–1937)*

---

Some alkies haven't been in a bar since they gave up drinking. They would be offended if offered a de-alcoholized beer. There was a time when some of us put into our bodies any substance that would take us up, down, sideways or backward. But now, in recovery, we are closed-minded to mental health medication because we are suddenly pill-averse. Some of us lived carelessly, and now we overcompensate with our kids, never comfortable with them being out of our sight or playing games that could lead to injury. Pre-recovery was a life of extremes. It's little wonder that in recovery, living life like a loose garment does not come easy. Rigid thinking or *hardening of the attitudes* is a challenge when we really need to find middle-ground.

Recovery gives us choices. Cautious of our decision-making at first, we ask ourselves, "Am I deciding or reacting?" What we want to ask ourselves or discuss with a trusted confidant is whether or not we are considering the pros and cons of each choice. What toothpaste brand to buy may not require a personal inventory but bigger decisions may conjure up our fear. FEAR is an acronym in the rooms: False Evidence Appearing Real. Fear can paralyze us and be a killjoy. Abstinence from the drug of our choice is wise, but do we have to be so absolute in every area of life? Taking chances and getting things wrong is part of the human experience and being more human is the objective of recovery. We made a mess of life. No wonder we can tend to be overly cautious. But it's good to let loose once in a while.

In what areas of my life am I rigid? When am I carefree and flexible? Is freedom of choice part of my natural rhythm or am I driven by risk-aversion or boundless need?

# April 1

*"Don't trust. In alcoholic families, promises are often forgotten, celebrations cancelled and parents' moods unpredictable. As a result, ACoAs learn to not count on others and often have a hard time believing that others can care enough to follow through on their commitments."*

Claudia Black, PhD

---

Dysfunctional homes have common rules and characteristics. "Don't trust" is one of the three rules in maladaptive homes. "Don't feel" and "don't talk" are two more.[36] No parent or caregiver is perfect and these imperfections impact us. To discriminate between imperfection and abusive conduct, we can look at the frequency and severity of the rules and behavior at home. Still, how we were affected is what matters. Can we trust people and do we have healthy boundaries? Adult children of alcoholics report hyper-attachment or intimacy avoidance, numbing out, having a constrained range of feelings and/or minimizing traumatic events.[37]

"Don't feel" conditions us to doubt our instincts and internalize dramatic events. Natural expression is dismissed in many homes with statements like, "That's no way to feel," "Boys don't cry," and "Shouting and screaming is no way for a young lady to behave." Anger is repressed and not expressed. "Don't talk" stifles expression. Secrets sicken the soul, and shyness morphs into either isolation or overcompensation. Denial, fantasy, boundary issues and loneliness become normal.

Recovery households have their own unique mixed messages. These homes feature talk about wellness and gratitude and an expectation to act like everything is fabulous because mom and/or dad are *better*. Basic childhood needs are overlooked with the recovery parent as the centre of the family drama. Damage to kids can go unseen when a dysfunctional parent is still chronically narcissistic. The message to kids is, "Everything is better now—what's the matter with you? Show some gratitude!"

Do I relate to any of these family scripts of "don't trust, feel or talk"? How does that look in my life now?

## April 2

*"Unfortunately, we have come to depend on this quick solution, rather than experiencing and integrating many of life's difficult challenges. As a consequence, we never fully matured. Abstinence is necessary for us, not just because of an allergy to alcohol or sugar, but because only when we begin experiencing life without resorting to quick fixes are we able to grow psychologically and spiritually. This is why coming to terms with my addiction must eventually involve spiritual work, the essence of which is the willingness to face, rather than avoid, pain and suffering."*

A Skeptic's Guide to the 12 Steps *by Phillip Z.*

---

Is growing psychologically and spiritually an addiction cure? Since the 1930s, *problem drinkers* were taught the dangers of inebriation and rationalization. As for the "real" alcoholics of the time, they listened, they agreed, they committed to change, they stopped forever...until shit happened and they fell off the wagon. They didn't have drinking problems, they had living problems.

As this OA Twelve-Stepper articulates in *A Skeptics Guide to the 12 Steps*, if our brain is a deck of cards, we are a few cards short in the reasoning and maturity suits.[38] We don't always maintain promises made to ourselves or loved ones. Our spirits or psyches got distorted. A spiritual cure isn't a magical cure. The quick fix we thought we found in acting out won't be found in recovery. It takes persistence and strength of spirit to walk toward, not run away from, our fears. For some of us this spiritual experience is a mystical one, but for many others it's more practical. Physical abuse, mental deterioration and psychic damage require a holistic approach.

Is recovery a mental, physical and spiritual practice for me? Practically speaking, what does that mean? What does spiritual sickness feel like? What do I do that is spiritually healing?

# April 3

*"Alice came to the fork in the road. 'Which road do I take?' she asked. 'Where do you want to go?' responded the Cheshire cat. 'I don't know,' Alice answered. 'Then,' said the cat, 'it doesn't matter.'"*

Alice in Wonderland *by Lewis Carroll*

---

Conventional wisdom urges us not to be an "Alice." We can't achieve if we don't have a plan and follow it. What does unconventional wisdom tell us? The Cheshire cat doesn't seem concerned about the outcome of Alice's decision. Not every decision is all-or-nothing. When we don't know which way to turn in life, we may be stricken with anxiety: "Do I leave a job or stay, end a relationship or work it out?"

A sage asks the right question. We ask ourselves, as did the cat, "What do we want?" If we have a clear preference then the direction is obvious. Sometimes, like Alice, we don't know what we want. Sometimes the only wrong decision is no decision, because by waiting another day, we are another day older and no closer to clarity. Likely, neither choice will be a path to Easy Street or to irreparable damage. All choices have unexpected consequences. Travelling in either direction will bring unpredictable adversity and/or opportunity. How we deal with the opportunity and adversity is what matters. Rash decisions don't serve us well but many choices will have to be made without all the facts—a best guess will just have to do.

Do I tend to stand by my choices in life or second guess everything I do? Is getting it wrong being wrong, especially when I cannot anticipate the outcome?

# April 4

*"Steps and Traditions represent the approximate truths which we need for our particular purpose. The more we practice them, the more we like them. So there is little doubt that AA principles will continue to be advocated in the form they stand now. If our basics are so firmly fixed as all this, then what is there left to change or to improve? The answer will immediately occur to us. While we need not alter our truths, we can surely improve their application to ourselves, to AA as a whole and to our relation with the world around us."*

*Bill W., A.A. Grapevine, February 1961[39]*

---

Bill Wilson touches on the risk/reward of change. AA's founders left the world resigned to the idea that AA had to adapt to survive. Bill's hope was that the fellowship would have the resolve to make hard decisions without the luxury of certainty, just as he and Dr. Bob had. By the time of this 1961 writing, new anonymous programs were springing up: Al-Anon, Narcotics Anonymous and Gamblers Anonymous. These new fellowships took their opportunities and recognized, "While we need not alter our truths, we can surely improve their application."

Today, there are Twelve & Twelve fellowships for multiple substances and processes. Food, sex, drug, smoking addicts and co-addicts enjoy a multiple-choice of fellowships. This century brought internet-gaming, internet-anon fellowships and teen-based recovery. All of these new groups had a much easier time adapting the language, rituals and literature to present day culture. AA is slow to adapt. Why is that? Fear of change is a greater motivator than desire for change. If change is resisted, membership will erode. If membership ever shrinks to a point that results in the world viewing AA as quaint, harmless and irrelevant, fear of extinction may outgrow fear of change.

Is my role as a steward to reify the message and canonize founders, or to prepare the program for the next generation? In what ways could my fellowship be more inviting to today's newcomer? Can changes be made without forfeiting the integrity and intention of these proven principles? The truth is in the integrity of the principles, not the language they were written in.

# April 5

*"Many of the things I thought I did unselfishly turned out to be pure rationalizations to get my own way about something. This disclosure doubled my urge to live by the Twelve Steps as thoroughly as I could."*

*An Al-Anon founder*

---

So let's get this straight—we can't trust our own thoughts. "My brain would kill me if it didn't need the transportation" is one morbid anecdote heard around the rooms. Another is "How can you tell when a codependent is rationalizing? Their lips are moving." Our brains black out certain truths, rewrite inconvenient personal histories and dress up our motives to adapt to charades of our self-concepts. When we have moments of clarity like the one mentioned above, what to do? Do we cling to illusion or dig deeper for greater clarity? Our self-awareness enhances life for us and the ones we love.

The classic literary conflicts—man vs. himself, man vs. man and man vs. nature—make for a thrilling movie, play or song. It is not so entertaining in real life. For recovering addicts and codependents it's easy to personify our deluded alter egos and blame our *addict minds*. We learn to take ownership of the games our brains play on us. Today, we are stone-cold-sober and we still entertain delusions. Addicts don't have a monopoly on self-deceit. We are like everyone else, just more so. We feel more, think in overdrive and rationalization has its way with our childlike minds.

Both vigilance and self-compassion are keys that unlock our potential. If we can remember that nobody has to be blamed, there's less need to criticize ourselves or others. We can accept our lives, our pasts and others with candor and compassion. The goal is to understand, not to blame.

Do I feel entitled to my point of view? Do I stand by and take responsibility for my attitude and opinions? Do I tend to see my view of things as the ultimate truth?

# April 6

---

Balance, *Part I*: Before recovery we lived lives of extremes—binging and purging, acting out and going on the wagon. Grinning and bearing the gut-wrenching transition on the way up and on the way down—this was par for the course in our lives of chaos. Peace and moderation may make us feel restless or uncomfortable. Duh—recovery is unnatural, at first anyway. Regret or a sense of impending doom can disturb our efforts to stay in the moment. A balanced life may seem lacking, leaving us mourning the intensity of the gambler's life. Many of us admit we don't know what balance looks like or feels like. What limited experiences do we have to draw upon? Balance is unfamiliar to the recovery community. Driving a car on a dark road at night, we see only the little bit of life that appears in our headlights. We can get all the way across the continent without seeing the whole road; a little at a time is good enough.

Today will I "step with care and great tact and remember that Life's a Great Balancing Act"? Is my identity tied to "living on the edge"? Do others see me as a chaotic character or do I give others the impression I am balanced and level-headed? Did I have a "street" persona that I fear will be lost in recovery? Do I feel whole, or like the hole in the donut now that I am in recovery? Tomorrow we reflect more on balance in a mad, mad world.

*"I find it kind of funny. I find it kind of sad. The dreams in which*
*I'm dying are the best I've ever had.*
*I find it hard to tell you 'cause I find it hard to take.*
*When people run in circles it's a very, very mad world."*

"Mad World" by Roland Orzabal

---

Balance, *Part II*: Dreams of death can be about change and transformation. The death card in Tarot is about one thing ending and another beginning. When a snake sheds its old skin it doesn't die; it begins a more vibrant life. How do recovery, balance and enlightenment look in a mad world?

Our world seems to be in perpetual chaos. In a consumer-based world we are pressured to use-and-dispose and then shamed about our treatment of the environment. We are sold the dreams of "have it now and pay later," and then debt brings anxiety and guilt so we buy more to relieve tension. Many of us cycle through excess, compulsion and obsession in step with the madness of the world. We may have rationalized that in our extremes we were embracing richer, fuller lives. If someone had one foot in a bucket of ice and the other foot in a bucket of boiling water, would they be perfectly comfortable? No—we can't combat one extreme with an opposite extreme. Actuarial calculations might give the thumbs up to a rich, full life, averaging out these two extremes, but in real life we are neither fulfilled nor comfortable. Opposite extremes beget unmanageability and lives of constant upheaval.

Early in recovery we may face resistance and temptation from enablers. We won't likely have placed real trust in our new recovery friends. A new spiritual life in a material world may look out of place if chaos is still all around us.

How well do I maintain my equilibrium in a mad, mad world?

# April 8

*"I thought how unpleasant it was to be locked out;*
*and I thought how it is worse, perhaps, to be locked in."*

*Virginia Woolf (1882–1941)*

---

Step Nine unlocks us from a final state of emotional solitary confinement. Freeing ourselves from regret, shame and guilt happens by degrees from Step to Step. In Step One, we resisted admitting who and what we were. We were selective about what we revealed to others, and that included confiding in people about our addictions. We were "locked in," ashamed and isolating behind a façade.

Many of us were still phonies in meetings and the truth revealed in Step Four was a hard pill to swallow. The risk of exposing the truth in Step Five, saying our secrets out loud to another human being, has to be experienced to be understood. In a very big way, the door behind which we had locked ourself was opened and our fate rested on how we were received. Right-sizing of our wrongs occurred in reflecting on these truths in the months that followed Step Five. In solitude, the severity of our worst secrets had been over-blown. The light of day showed that we were flawed, not evil. Other shortcomings that we had minimized had to be faced. We took responsibility. Steps Six and Seven helped us become authentic.

When we face the victims of our misdeeds we have new clarity and personal responsibility. We still risk ridicule, rejection or being "locked out." No one is obligated to accept our apologies. But we are right with the world, whatever the consequences. We are not hiding behind a wall of excuses and blame. Taking responsibility makes us feel better about ourselves and increased self-worth helps us feel more connected to others. We can look the world in the eye, maybe for the first time in our lives. It is hard to describe to someone who hasn't experienced it first-hand what living without shame is like.

Have I experienced this new freedom and a new happiness? Am I no longer locked in?

# April 9

*"If I leave this Twelve Step meeting and get hit
by a bus, don't take me to another Twelve Step
meeting—take me to a hospital."*

Father Joe Martin (1924–2009)

Recovery programs do solve a lot of problems in life. The Twelve Steps have been defined as a toolbox of wrenches that can fit any nut. Many of us come here to conquer one problem and get on with life. To our surprise, working the Steps has more far-reaching value. We read our program literature over and over again not because this is pleasure reading or because the Twelve Steps are a cure-all. Reading is one of the rituals that some of us incorporate into a recovery lifestyle.

But as pointed out above, not every problem calls for a Twelve Step remedy. Many problems need professional and/or expert help, help we can't expect to find in meetings. We may need a guidance counselor, relationship therapist, psychiatrist, trainer or medical doctor. Because the program has helped in more ways than we bargained for, we run the risk of putting the program of recovery on a fix-all pedestal. Self-help fellowships are people sharing their experience with each other—no less and no more.

Most of us have problems other than addiction. Some of us are candid about what ails us and what we are taking for it. Some of us keep those cards close to our chest. Addicts tend to need help in other mental health areas. The National Institute on Alcohol Abuse and Alcoholism reports that alcoholics are two to three times more likely to have anxiety disorders or other (concurrent) psychiatric disorders than members of the general population.[40]

Do I have right-sized expectations about my program and fellowship? Have I ever caught myself talking about Twelve Step recovery as a cure-all or a one-stop shop?

# April 10

*"Each group should be autonomous except in matters affecting other groups or A.A. as a whole."*

Tradition Four[41]

---

With all this autonomy, it is remarkable how meetings of the same fellowship can look so similar when compared to each other. On the other hand, members who recover in one place and move to another town are often uncomfortable or put off by the subtle variances of meeting style in the new town—the meetings feel different. We may think that the new town has it wrong. The practices in our home group seem sacred—as if there was a *right* way of doing things. We resist change and we crave familiarity. Each meeting can conduct itself the way the members choose and, ultimately, it must be responsible for itself. If one meeting can't afford to keep its doors open, it closes—other groups don't pitch in to keep it afloat, although individual members may attend a struggling meeting to show support.

Some meetings are just for men, or women, or run by members based on age, creed or sexual orientation. Some meetings are designed for new members. The only rules are rules that each group's members agree on. What is read, written, said or believed at one meeting is of no concern to anyone else. Service works in an upside-down triangle: the service structure does the bidding of groups. It doesn't dictate or police what goes on inside each group's walls. If we don't like what a group is doing we ask what's behind our intolerance or strong feelings. Natural selection or *God's will,* if you like, takes care of any group that is so far out of line they have distorted the program's principles.

Do I encourage autonomy within my group and with others? Do I show interest in issues that affect the fellowship as a whole? Do I do my share of the work? I may consider myself a steward of our fellowship's future. Many who hold our fellowship as dearly as I do don't see eye-to-eye with me. Can I remember "Vive la différence"?

# April 11

*"Scepticism is ... a form of belief. Dogma cannot be abandoned;*
*it can only be revised in view of some*
*more elementary dogma which it has not yet*
*occurred to the sceptic to doubt."*

*George Santayana (1863–1952)*

---

This uncongenial pragmatist who studied under both William James and John Dewey didn't accept anything as *Gospel*. Santayana invites us to doubt our own skepticism. Doubt is healthy, natural and a sure way to keep an open mind. But any habit can start showing signs of being a schema. There is a difference between skepticism and cynicism. A logical disposition and constant need for evidence can limit as well as enhance our lives. What we believe can get stale.

To navigate through life, some of us use our gut feelings, the Steps or our wits. If we are true to the process, no matter what our leanings, counter-intuitive skills can become complementary skills, as we learn new ways to perceive both our world and our condition. If we keep exercising our thinking and feeling, in time, our coping and observation skills will evolve.

We shouldn't cling too tightly to our assumptions or ways of seeing. Do we really want to think exactly the same way we do today, a year or a decade from now? The risk of only travelling in circles of people who think, act and talk like us is that we reinforce tunnel vision. More of the same creates a consensus on more of the same. Not being able to learn from those who think differently from us is like only eating protein, only vegetables or only carbohydrates. We need a rich idea-diet to keep life from being made unmanageable by our overconfidence. Not being married to our beliefs can be even more peaceful than being absolutely sure. It can reduce the chances of becoming drunk on our own dogma.

Do I clutch my beliefs with white knuckles? Am I open to new ways of seeing?

## April 12

*"We must be the change we wish to see in the world."*

*Mohandas Gandhi (1869–1948)*

Have our lives transformed from being self-destructive to being productive? We hear it said that gratitude is a behavior as much as it is a feeling. Gratitude may be a feeling about our satisfaction for the way life is; alternatively, it could be an action or our duty to make a positive difference in the lives of others. If we want our meetings, our homes or workplaces to be better, we lead by example. Standing up against discrimination or making our community more just or more environmentally sound would be applying Step Twelve to our lives.

In time, we will know the difference between bandwagon bitching and constructively making a difference in the world. We will intuitively know the difference between doing something for accolades and doing something for altruistic reasons. We can draw the line between enabling and being helpful. We'll never be perfect but a desire to "be the change we wish to see in the world" is healing. Choosing a cause requires consideration. Our houses have to be in order—charity begins at home. We worked so hard to get well; why not keep it by giving it away? Empathy as an action rewires self-centered habitual impulses. Service, in or out of the fellowship, renews our energy where being self-absorbed can drain us. For some of us, service starts in our fellowship, but there's a bigger world out there if and when we want to lend a hand.

Like so many others, I came here as a taker, a parasite and a needy addict. Today, what can I do to make the world a better place?

# April 13

*"A dream you dream alone is only a dream.*
*A dream you dream together is reality."*

*John Lennon (1940–1980)*

---

We addicts dreamed and talked of turning our lives around, without recovery materializing on our own. In fellowship "we can do together what we could not do by ourselves." This is a socially constructed reality in Twelve Step life—a dream we dream together. Addiction as a disease is another widely held construct that gives order and structure to our worldviews. Consensus doesn't make a belief true, just popular. The world's most popular *truths* are Abrahamic faiths (obedience to one deity by name, being either Allah or God.) To half the world this is a truth/dream shared with likeminded people. The other half of the world would call such beliefs mythology. Speaking of our beliefs as universal truths will always make us look foolish to someone.

Families each have their own dreams/truths. Some psychologists look at the cohesiveness and functionality of family systems in what they call a Circumplex Model.[42] Imagine a compass with *Enmeshed* as North and *Disengaged* as South, measuring relative cohesion. *Rigid* as East and *Chaotic* as West will measure family adaptability. Perfectly healthy would be right in the middle. Some social challenges come from being stretched between two of these poles. The Enmeshed/Rigid (NE) home demands obedience and produces malcontent, irritable children. Enmeshed/Chaotic (NW) homes have kids running the show when small and acting rebellious, bossy and unmotivated by the time they leave. Disengaged/Rigid (SE) kids feel uncared for, with rules that are random or unfair. Stunted maturity leads to psychological problems. Parents in Disengaged/Chaotic (SW) homes don't care what the kids do as long as it doesn't put the parent(s) out. This is a breeding ground for underachieving loners. Dysfunctional homes stretch family dynamics to unpredictable extremes. For kids, that's a nightmare, not a dream. When we look back we find that many of the "realities" in childhood can be changed.

Do I feel that I have shared dreams with my family and fellowship? Consensus is a constructed reality, not the truth. Do I get dogmatic about my "realities," insisting they are universal truths for everyone?

## April 14

*"One act of beneficence, one act of real usefulness,
is worth all the abstract sentiment in the world."*

*Ann Radcliffe (1762–1823)*

---

Radcliffe's well-crafted gothic novels lent respectability to the genre. At a time when traditional moralization and superstition were the order of the day, reason drove Radcliffe's life. Women's rights would prevail and much that was considered supernatural would be scientifically articulated, but such developments occurred many years after her death. She was a freethinker and a realist before such terms were in vogue. She was inspired by such painters as Claude Lorrain and Salvator Rosa and, in turn, she inspired such writers as Edgar Allan Poe and the Marquis de Sade. Radcliffe serves as an example of how works and deeds can inspire other great works and deeds.

The mere intention to do a good deed inspires few. Action teaches us integrity as we move step by step from promise to realization, and action inspires others, too. Recovery inspires us to do good—what is good for us and what is good for others. We don't simply talk about, read about or plan for it.

Like this author, we have lists of those to whom we owe a debt of gratitude. Having been spared from addiction's finale, we may be tempted to canonize those who helped us. We may get the service bug and welcome more responsibility. We may get preoccupied by the rearview mirror of recovery and want to reify the good old days for generations to come. Noble as our tributes may be, let's maintain focus on the road ahead. We do our part to ensure the program's principles are preserved and that the message is attractive and relevant to the next generation whom we help to find salvation.

When I *pass it on*, do I honor our founders by practicing what they taught us? Is my gratitude paid forward?

# April 15

*"A lot of people in the academic world think, 'No sacred cows.'*
*We shouldn't sacralize anything. But they sacralize reason*
*itself, as though reason is this noble attribute, reason is our*
*highest nature. And if we could just reason, we will solve our*
*problems. All right, that sounds good on paper. But given all*
*the stuff psychologists have discovered about reason, reasoning*
*is not good at finding the truth. Conscious verbal reasoning is*
*really good at confirming."*

Jonathan Haidt (Born 1963)

---

Haidt, a political and positive psychologist, wrote *The Righteous Mind: Why Good People Are Divided by Politics and Religion*. Reason has its shortcomings as a prospector for truth. Confirmation bias is a trap we fall into when nursing pet theories. We claim open-mindedness but dwell on facts that favor our biases. The political left gets its information about the right from other leftist members and vice versa. Each side sees themselves as logical and reasonable while the other side is demonized and considered insane. Our side has the one truth and we are virtuous. We decry their position and behavior as dangerous, corrupt and a force that must be stopped by any means. When this polarization happens, our reason will betray us, directing us toward justification, instead of truth and cooperation.

Bill Wilson wrote essays as he formulated the Traditions in the 1940s. They can be found in the pamphlet, "AA Tradition, How it Developed."[43] He writes about the Pharisee, noted for strict observance of ceremony and rules, self-righteous and with a tendency to be hypocritical. On the other side, the Recalcitrant is resistant to authority, disobedient and hard to manage. In "Concept XII," Bill states that AA will never govern members or groups (Warranty Six) and that, "No penalties are to be inflicted for nonconformity, no member can be expelled … each A.A. group shall conduct its internal affairs as it wishes … care will be observed to respect and protect all minorities …"

Do I make villains out of others inside or outside of my fellowship? Do I see my way as righteous and others' ways as depraved? Should I walk a mile in another's shoes and try to understand them?

## April 16

*"Sought through mindful inquiry and meditation to improve our spiritual awareness, seeking only for knowledge of our rightful path in life and the power to carry that out."*

*Step Eleven (aaagnostica.org)*

---

No two Hindus, Humanists, Christians, Jews, Buddhists or Atheists have identical spiritual definitions, experiences and practices. Who am I? What am I doing here? Who are these others? This trilogy of spiritual conundrums is as practical as it is philosophical. Mindful inquiry devoted to these three questions is as spiritual as it is material and as obvious as it is unanswerable. Knowledge isn't to comfort our souls; it is to enhance awareness—that's an awakening. Some things have to be *believed* to be *seen*. Feelings articulate truth in ways that our brains cannot. We may have a sense about who we are, what our purpose is and how we relate to the rest of the world even without the vocabulary to articulate it. Recovery is visceral as much as it is intellectual. The Eleventh Step is our spiritual barometer, feeding back sensations, feelings and thoughts as we observe.

Step Eleven isn't just something done simply while kneeling in solitude. Our recovery isn't our "gift" to our family or loved ones; why make virtue out of necessity? Seeing others as individuals and not as spokes branching out from the hub of our ego-centric self helps us to be present, patient and empathetic. Lingering narcissism transforms into self-actualization. When we practice Step Eleven we recognize our potential.

The dark side of self is a self-absorbed, parasitic state, which is manifested in the desperateness of addiction. Early in recovery, friends and members of our communities see us finding our rightful path. We are thoughtful—entertaining hunches without jumping to conclusions. We think before reacting.

Are meditation and mindfulness about finding comfort? Are they about self-awareness?

# April 17

*"If you have learned how to disagree without being disagreeable, then you have discovered the secret of getting along—whether it be business, family relations, or life itself."*

Bernard Meltzer (1916–1998)

---

We can agree to disagree. If we are controversial in Step meetings, no one should balk. Being agreeable is not the key to maintaining sobriety. The fighters might have an advantage over the amiable ones in the recovery arena. The pain in the neck—the person who questions, doubts and asks for evidence—isn't fighting sobriety. Rather, he or she is fighting *for* sobriety. We have all seen members who answer any challenge with "Yes, I know," or "You are probably right," and "Yes I should," and then fall off the wagon without warning, eighty meetings into a ninety in ninety regimen. On the other hand, the restless and irritable newcomer whom you expect will never come back, considering the mood they left in, stays clean and the program takes hold. What looks like aversion may just be authenticity.

Being disagreeable out of reflex is cynicism—a barrier to recovery. Treating the Twelve Step fellowship as a popularity contest is dangerous business, too. As the quote above suggests, sticking to our guns and having some tact is the best of both worlds. If our personal bottom line varies from group-think, that might be a concern, but not a deal breaker. This century, methadone and buprenorphine patients are being treated for opiate addiction through harm reduction clinics.44 Disclosing this fact in our abstinence-based Step meetings could be met with unsolicited advice. Evidence suggests that for opiate-dependent patients, prospects for relapse-prevention are much greater with a medically supervised regulation of blood and brain chemistry. There is no shortage of quackery out there but many newcomers are enjoying far more cutting edge treatment than was available when our "traditional wisdom" was forged. Can old-timers be as open-minded as newcomers are asked to be?

Have I exercised my right to work the program based on my beliefs, bottom line and timing?

*"Ego tells us that our defenses will make us feel secure, yet
all that results in increased feelings of isolation and fear. It is
impossible to feel secure while we are building high walls behind
which we hide. Safety and security are by-products of peace of
mind. In laying down our defenses and adopting an attitude of
acceptance, our world changes."*

Healing the Addictive Mind *by Lee Jampolsky*

---

If we subscribe to the idea that the addict's brain is wired differently from the *normie's* brain, we will jump to rash conclusions on a regular basis. Egotism is over-compensation. Behind the bravado and sense of entitlement we fear that we are worthless. We feel ashamed deep down inside. Because we suspect we are unworthy, we feel vulnerable to attack. We protect ourselves by building defenses—humor, pride, delusion and isolation to name a few. If we don't have bricks for a wall, a smokescreen will make a fine hiding place. If that doesn't work, there is always perpetual motion to help us steer clear of being discovered or unmasked.

Acceptance is life minus the struggle; we accept ourselves and the world, faults and all. Hey—let's not forget that we label ourselves and the world as flawed, which might be just how we see it. What if we remove the walls and reveal to others that we feel inadequate and unsure? *Healing the Addictive Mind* contends that, by making peace with our imperfection, we feel *good enough*, which is more spiritually sound than acting perfect. We won't feel threatened by our vulnerability. In fact, we are candid about it. Saying "I am imperfect and I accept this about me" is more empowering and takes less energy than hiding or overcompensating. Longtime members remember that being a *power of example* is about how we deal with misfortune and imperfection. It isn't about being flawless and all-knowing.

Am I aware of when I am putting up walls or barriers? If I can't stop doing it entirely, am I at least taking inventory of what triggers my flight, freeze or fight instincts?

# April 19

*"There is always something ridiculous about the emotions of people whom one has ceased to love."*

Oscar Wilde (1854–1900)

---

When we hear others talk about their past lives being full of villains who are described as "bitches" or "assholes," we take what they say with a grain of salt, knowing that each of the demonized characters in these sad stories were once part of a promise of a new day for the narrators. What was "playfulness" can now be re-written as "childishness," "sexy" can become "slutty" and "proactive" is now "manipulative." These are all the same characteristics but new, soured opinions can lead us to rewrite the entire history of relationships. We had expectations going into them. Expectations are premeditated resentments.

Identifying rationalization in others is so much easier than taking ownership of our own rationalizations. Blaming others, even those we love or loved, is easy. Maybe that's why in the early directions for doing a Step Four in Chapter Five of *Alcoholics Anonymous* they played to our natural tendencies. We write down resentments, fears and our sexual conduct, starting with resentments. They flow so easily because we can describe the shortcomings of others with articulate candor. But then we are asked to look back at our lives and review our role in these situations. We look at our insecurities, shame and fear and at how these people triggered us. We see our true nature and patterns, maybe for the first time.

Do I still feel superior to, or victimized by, people and/or life? How can I accept them for who they are (or were) and make peace with the facts and the infinite unknowns of life?

## April 20

*"One's suffering disappears when one lets oneself go,
when one yields—even to sadness."*

Antoine de Saint-Exupéry (1900–1944)

---

Labeling our experiences as misfortune triggers suffering. We associate feelings with our experiences. Feeling loss is normal. Expressing feelings doesn't cause suffering either. Fighting or fleeing fear, sadness, grief or anger is what escalates the experience of feeling into unworkable suffering. Avoidance is an old defense for addicts. Maybe in our formative years we had to cope with unstable, non-supportive or hostile environments. Avoidance was the best we could do as children. We had few choices about our environment or our caregivers. We are older now, with more choices, yet we still follow engrained habits of repressing and avoiding undesirable feelings.

Some of us try to intellectualize our emotional pain by labeling and quantifying. Thinking isn't the right tool for the job when it comes to feelings—no matter how smart we are. The only healthy way to manage feelings is to experience them, under safe circumstances that do not cause us or anyone else undue harm. Facing our grief, shame, fear and anger won't overwhelm us. On the contrary, it will heal us if we let our emotions pass through us like waves, waxing and then waning. In the same way we will never start laughing and not be able to stop, feelings run their course. Crying doesn't last forever, nor does anger. We addicts make bogeymen out of uncomfortable feelings when they come our way. Fight or flight instinct doesn't save us. It compounds the problem for another day and it may invite depression or anxiety today. With practice, we gain insight, courage and confidence. Pain becomes our beacon and we move toward it. It's rare that strong feelings last more than a few minutes. If we stay with it we will make it through to the other side. If we run, we run forever.

Pain in life is unavoidable. The next time I feel, can I put out the welcome mat, let go and experience the feeling? If I judge feelings, that's me doing the judging and I can stop if I want to.

## April 21

*"Forgiveness is giving up the hope that the past
could have been any different."*

*Oprah Winfrey (born 1954)*

---

In the rooms we hear, "Live and let live" or "Forgiveness is a gift you give yourself." Even universal truths have an exception or two. The deeper recovery gets, the more binary thinking gives way to pluralism. Our internal, existential lives are rarely made up of absolutes, of rights and wrongs so clearly defined in black and white. We have a range of feelings and it is folly to deny any of them. There is healing power in justice as there is in reconciliation but we might not be clear or consistent in what we want or how we feel. Obligatory forgiveness as part of the therapeutic process is anything but freeing. Sexual abuse victims, for instance, may feel empowered to be given permission to never forgive. For some of us, certain violations are unforgivable. The appeal of forgiveness is that with it, the victim regains control: "I decide if and when you are forgiven. I have the power, not you."

We look at each deed from many vantage points—as many as we can. We may feel an act was malicious and intentional. The offender may feel falsely accused or justified. To them, nothing inappropriate occurred and no contract was either entered into or broken. We may resist moving beyond our victimhood, which we may use to define ourselves. Conversely, we may rush to forgiveness as a seemingly noble or mature gesture. We may use what psychologists call "causal attribution": "Hurt people hurt people." We don't take the inevitable act personally. Turning the other cheek could be a reflexive, avoidant coping technique. One might hear at a meeting that there are steps to forgiveness. In a criminal proceeding the pardon doesn't come first; first there is the trial, then there is the sentencing, later comes the pardon.

Forgiving myself and others is a complex matter. Will I honor my pain by feeling my pain? Will I look at the deed, the perpetrator and their circumstances? Is my perpetrator a victim as well? Do I have to forgive to heal? Does the perpetrator have to admit fault to be forgiven?

## April 22

*"The difficulty lies not so much in developing new ideas as in escaping from old ones."*

*John Maynard Keynes (1883–1946)*

By August 2012, over 31 million copies of *Alcoholics Anonymous* had been circulated and the Big Book had been recognized as one of the most influential books to shape American culture.[45] The first 164 pages have been preserved, as is, despite the fact that we knew so much more about alcoholism and recovery in the years of later editions—1955, 1976 and 2001. "We realize we know only a little," concludes the final chapter of the Big Book, "A Vision for You." The founders' humility is ignored by followers who have chosen instead to make the text sacred. Dogma ends the discussion, forfeiting the input of the next generation. Instead of treating the text as anecdotal experiences we treat it as though it has been divinely inspired. We can see why this reverence appears cult-like to on-lookers.

If Bob and Bill were Buddhists who met in the 1930s, halfway around the world, they would likely have come up with an equally effective answer to alcoholism, although written in quite a different voice. Bill's favorite number might have been eight, not twelve. His approach may have been based on noble truths instead of Christian tenets. The program would work. It would be somewhat different. Stewards of our program may have still canonized founders and reified the message. Once we deem a passage sacred we are blind to new evidence or more contemporary ways of expressing the kernels of truth in the message. The Twelve Steps, as expressed in 1939, are the medium, not the message. The message is the life-restoring force of those words, which can be articulated in many thoughtful ways.

Do I honor the wisdom of our founders without being rigid about the message? Is it the principles or verbatim text that holds the secret of my recovery? Am I firm on principle and flexible on method?

# April 23

*"Every one of us is sort of a figment of our own imaginations."*
*Kris Kristofferson (born June 1936)*

---

Yesterday we imagined what the differences and similarities of our movement would have been by altering geographic or historical facts. Kristofferson reminds us, in "The Pilgrim, Chapter 33," that how we see ourselves and our world is "partly truth and partly fiction." Individually, the inventory process keeps us aware of the space between who we are and how we perceive ourselves. This is a worthwhile exercise to practice when considering our collective history, too.

Today we will look at Big Book mythology—the space between what the founders were saying and the figments of our imagination that we call the message. What would AA founders have to say to zealots today who decry, "There is 'A' solution—not multiple choices, and if you want freedom from this merciless obsession you must follow these instructions, exactly as laid out, exactly as each of the first one hundred members did"? How comical to imagine one hundred gathered together as one saying, "The third thing I did was to abandon dependence on self-will, then I did an inventory, making a list of three things—resentments, fears and sex conduct." Then a chorus starts around the room, "Me too," "Wow, same with me, and then I admitted to God, myself and another human being, the exact nature of my wrongs." "Really, so did I." "Me too," "Me too," "Same here, except at some of these I balked, I thought I could find an easier softer way." "OMG, so did I, so did I!" etc.

I know that not one of the founders did the steps exactly this way, in this exact order. These were general ideas explored in a general way. Do I ever get carried away with Twelve Step lore? Do I remember that my history and the history of my fellowship is a perception—"partly truth and partly fiction"?

## April 24

*"I know of no society in human history that ever suffered because its people became too desirous of evidence in support of their core beliefs."*

Sam Harris (born 1967)

---

The Twelve Step community is a society. Our fellowship offers an empowering freedom in that we are encouraged to accept what we want, dismiss what we want and explore what works. Our whole culture was borne of challenging core beliefs and if we hadn't, we would all be members of the Oxford Group.

Founders took what they liked from the Oxford Group's core beliefs and the psychology of the day, purging dogmatic beliefs and practices that couldn't be supported by evidence. The Four Absolutes of Honesty, Purity, Unselfishness and Love were great principles but the absolute expectation was discouraging and they were replaced by the notion of "progress, not perfection." Early drafts from our recently recovered founders put our own core beliefs up for scrutiny. The Big Book originally included more rigid "you must" statements than we see today. Both our professional friends of the day and our early membership didn't have evidence that a list of rules and barking orders was the best ways to appeal to drunks. Many *musts* were replaced with suggestions. Buddhist AA members who didn't share the Western belief in God adapted the Steps to work without God—and this won the blessings of AA.[46]

Fellowships that followed have adapted again, looking at evidence from their experiences to dictate what to keep and what to let go of. Along with a theistic view of Higher Power, new fellowships removed the patriarchal bias of the original literature and other antiquated language.

The inventory process forces me to challenge my core beliefs. Am I still rigorous about continuing to challenge my beliefs when I do my daily inventory?

# April 25

*"In our country we are pretty good at responding to crisis.
We are not very good at avoiding it."*

*Albert A. Bartlett (born 1923)*

---

As addicts we know all about this. No matter how much worse life got when we were using, we lowered our expectations instead of curing the problem. We could have quit, we could have avoided hurting ourselves and hurting others, but we kept spiraling down, into rationalization and cognitive dissonance.

Media, government and the stock market prefer to respond to symptoms rather than to confront the cause. Today's author, a physics professor, applies arithmetic to the contradiction of sustainable growth and he tries to impress on students that modest growth of 5% per annum will turn every billion people into eight billion within fifty years. How is that sustainable? Environmental decline, peak oil and peak everything are examples of how people in the plural are even more disinclined to face the truth than people in the singular.

James Joyce wrote in the early twentieth century, "History is a nightmare from which I am trying to awake." What Joyce was sharing with addicts like us is that history will be a nightmare today if we are repeating the mistakes of our past. To be trapped in monotony is a nightmare. Even if we are fully cognizant of our misdeeds, we will repeat the cycle if we don't awaken from the denial about the futility of the paths we trudge.

In our hearts, we know when we are being self-destructive. The nightmare is the repetitive history of our addictive cycles. In despair, we find the support of others and we feel a glimmer of hope that the cycle will end. We can avoid the tragic end of untreated addiction. Instead of reconciling ourselves to crisis management, we take steps to arrest our addictions. We begin to see our own potential.

Integrity is one of the byproducts of living well. Free from the enslavement of insatiable needs we begin looking after ourselves, contributing to family and community and becoming mindful and responsible stewards of planet earth.

Do I still live in the nightmare of repetitive cycles? How do I now avoid hardship which I used to grin and bear? Do I endure consequences that I can avoid?

## April 26

*"When we take the actions to complete one vision, another one may emerge. For instance, our original vision of being solvent may expand to include returning to school, opening our own business, going abroad, etc."*

*"Visions," Debtors Anonymous*

It is sometimes said in the rooms that "if I made a wish-list when I got here, I would have sold myself short." We come to recovery reluctantly. We might expect no more than a life of white-knuckled sobriety. We see only two limited choices once we accept being defeated by addiction: the purgatory of recovery or continuing down a dead-end path of escalating addiction all the way to hell.

Changing our attitudes in recovery is two-fold. On one hand, we may find we are unlocking a Pandora's Box of personal issues that reach greater depths than we could have foreseen through the foggy, reactive state we arrived in. We may have more work than we first bargained for and our bottom line behaviors are likely going to be adjusted as our minds and our expectations unclog.

But on the other hand, our new lifestyles, which we expected to be big limitations, opened doors for us and we often see these new opportunities as being beyond our hopes or imaginations.

Material possessions may be unexpected benefits. New attitudes and outlooks may emerge. We have new values that guide us. Our hindered feelings of self-worth begin to blossom. Creativity that we didn't know we had is likely to surprise us.

How is life today, compared to what I expected? How have my goals and values changed since I started my recovery?

# April 27

*"Everything that Hitler did was 'legal.' It was 'illegal' to aid and comfort a Jew in Hitler's Germany. But I am sure that if I had lived in Germany during that time I would have aided and comforted my Jewish brothers even though it was illegal."*

*Martin Luther King, Jr. (1929–1968)*

---

One day doing the right thing will make us unpopular and put us at risk of being judged or persecuted. So much of our new lives involve getting along, going with the flow, improving ourselves, focusing on what's wrong on our side of the street and accepting the rest. Is there ever a time to be the vigilante or defy an unjust law or speak out about harassment or discrimination? Absolutely—what's the point of finding our values if we aren't willing to put them on the line? That said, those of us who have been around for a few twenty-four hours have been on at least one crusade of self-will that we had mistaken for a mission from God. When we look back on it now, we find it laughable that we thought we found the universe no longer unfolding as it should and ourselves being charged with righting this wrong.

The THINK test looks at five caveats: Is it True and am I being Honest? Is it Important, Necessary and Kind? Sometimes we hear something we are predisposed to believe. Let's do our research and be sure what we put our necks out for is true. Rigorous honesty demands the question "Is my ego/pride on the line?" Narcissism can be lurking behind feigned altruism. How important is this? If this is a turning point in history, how will our children and grandchildren view our involvement in this cause? A good night's sleep can help evaluate each situation's relevance. Is it necessary? Even when we are right about something, do we have to be publicly vindicated? A bad loser is one thing but a self-righteous winner is hard to take. A pause for thought can stop us from gloating. Fantasies of vindication have to be curbed before we pull the trigger on *inflicting* justice. "Is it kind?" reminds us that, when it comes to the truth, few things are black and white. More important than being right is doing the right thing.

If I stand to be counted, am I doing it with humility and compassion?

# April 28

*"The writer operates at a peculiar crossroads*
*where time and place and eternity somehow meet.*
*His problem is to find that location."*

Flannery O'Connor (1925–1964)

---

Creativity can seem elusive; it doesn't come when we summon it. We cannot simply set a GPS to the creativity crossroads. Like the writing greats, we put pen to paper (or characters on a screen) to help us find what we are searching for. We journal, we write inventories, and maybe we write poems or songs, as well. For much of our lives we have been like screenwriters, crafting scripts and roles of whom we should be. We each cast ourselves as the story's hero. When the world we lived in became unbearable, we rewrote our scripts, recasting new co-stars and scouting out new geographical settings.

The same creative skills we employed to deny and delude can help us find our way back to reality, too. The Twelve Steps have writing exercises built right in to help us face the facts. Journaling can become part of the meditation and reflection process, or it may simply be a way to filter the useless crap out of our heads. Ruminating and regretting can be purged onto the paper or screen so we can get on with the day, less encumbered.

Even doodling can be like meditative breathing, scribbling as we negotiate through our *mind–field*. Searching our hearts can be like an emotional minefield. We tread lightly, afraid of tripping up a memory or repressed feeling that might blow up in our face. Sometimes we are afraid for good reason. Other times we are anxious, merely suffering from fear of the unknown. Writing can be a way of discovering. It can also help defuse potentially explosive memories or feelings that we might disturb along the way. Seeking is a commitment, not a prison sentence—we come and go as we please.

Am I a writer? Do I use my creative power to escape, create or discover?

# April 29

This is an old-school card used to trump *Live and Let Live*. Sometimes kindness kills. Late last century, formal, guided interventions became popular for the first time. Staged by families and a professional, addicts/ alcoholics got an unexpected emotional shock treatment. Everyone was prepared to rub the subject the wrong way, getting in their face with (a) how much it hurt to see them self-destruct (how much they were loved) and (b) what the ultimatum would be, should the targeted problem-case not go to treatment. Was this conditional love or tough love?

These organized interventions were facilitated by a *treatment professional* whose two-year community college certificate and finder's fee from the treatment center raised questions from critics. But this professional assured the family that "interventions save lives." She or he went on to assure the addict or alcoholic that everyone gathered together loved them and, consequently, would not sit quietly by and let them die.

There are successful interventions that have saved lives. In early AA, taking each other's inventory was called "telling a drunk how it is." There were a lot of rocks thrown by a lot of glass house renters but unsolicited advice came free with membership back in the day. It's not as if this style of sponsorship is unheard of now. Some targets of interventions left in disgust, calling it interference. Others got the wakeup call they needed. Some of us are not cut out for confrontational sponsorship and some of us get a rush out of it.

Do I remember that I am no expert and nobody's keeper? Would I speak out if I thought it would help someone? How do I feel when someone is cruel to be kind with me or offers a "loving appraisal?"

# April 30

*"Help people reach their full potential—catch them doing something right."*

The One Minute Manager
*by Kenneth Blanchard, PhD, Spencer Johnson, MD*

---

Be a rebel. If pointing out the failings of others is the norm, we can choose to be different. We can ignore shortcomings, smile through mishaps and not raise our voices until friends or children around us get it right. None of us are motivated by the reverse of an idea. "Don't do _____ that way!" This only lowers someone's self-image without improving their performance. Somehow, our brains don't remember the little words like "never" and "don't," just the dramatic words said with passion, like "you idiot," "failure" and "wrong." In fact, maybe we don't remember the words at all—we might just remember how we felt after hearing them. If our mistakes inspire the day's most enthusiastic outpouring from onlookers, then that negative behavior gets locked into the memory.

Who works best when they are tense and who works best relaxed? Stop a kid in his or her tracks, point a finger, and say, "Don't think I didn't see you put your dishes away. Do you have any idea how proud I feel when I see you being responsible? Do you? Just let me catch you getting it right again and you'll get another ear full. Do you hear me?" Are we not happier ourselves, when we catch people doing something right?

We can try it for just one day. We bite our tongues when we would usually criticize and we express ourselves when we are impressed, proud or happy as a result of the actions of others. This exercise may make us feel great. When we are focused on the good things going on it affects how we feel. Also, the way people will warm to us when we are considerate of others, will improve how we feel about ourselves. "Instant Karma's going to get you!" as John Lennon would say.

Can I try pointing out the good in others, just for today?

# May 1

*"Religion without science is blind and
science without religion is lame."*

Albert Einstein (1879–1955)

---

Albert Einstein grew uncomfortable with the Jewish dogma with which he was raised, such as the idea that they were the chosen people of God: "For me the Jewish religion like all others is an incarnation of the most childish superstitions. And the Jewish people to whom I gladly belong and with whose mentality I have a deep affinity have no different quality for me than all other people."

Einstein is known the world round as a man of science, with an affinity for the known, quantifiable, material world. But even as he worshipped science, he never discounted the mystery and relevance of the unknown and the immeasurable. Einstein mastered the material world but was never threatened by, in denial of or at odds with the mystical unknown. Our program teaches us the humility we need to not be at odds with our fellows. We tolerate, or, where we can, we embrace perspectives that are contrary to our own. We are comfortable with our beliefs but we don't present them as the be-all and end-all because we see no need for permanent attachment to them. Where surrounding ourselves with like-minded people provides a comfortable confirmation of our biases, enlightenment and new awakening can only come from contrary stimulation. Great scientists invite the prospect of being proven wrong. It is science, not their pet theories, which they revere.

Do I get defensive in the presence of opposing views or can I learn from everyone? If I can only learn from people who believe and think as I do, how open will I be to a world of possibilities? I never know when I am judging someone who will one day be my unlikely teacher.

## May 2

*"When you find peace within yourself, you become the kind of person who can live at peace with others."*

*Mildred Lisette Norman (1908–1981)*

---

The words of "Peace Pilgrim," an anti-war activist most of her adult life, have special meaning for us in recovery. There is a time in our recovery to be rigorous, thorough and vigilant. Reversing the self-destructive ways we learned as addicts required relentless effort. But what is gained and what is lost when we are so hard on ourselves? Being hard on ourselves makes it difficult to escape being hard on those around us. A critical double-edged sword cuts both ways. There comes a time to be more gentle.

Letting go is most often associated with shedding surface worries, fears and tensions. But letting go can be letting that which is repressed come up to the surface. Think of the tension we can release if we have nothing to hide, no shame, no fear that we are avoiding. In letting things go in this way we feel no need to overcompensate. Authenticity brings peace with self and we naturally make peace with our surroundings, too.

Think of the people in our circle—who is easy-going with those around them and who is more critical? With few exceptions, those who give themselves a break can easily find understanding for others. As for those who look for fault like there's a reward for it, chances are they are projecting how hyper-critical they are of themselves. Let's learn to make peace with ourselves. Those around us will be better off and they deserve a break today.

Today, can I commit to being more at peace, knowing I am just fine the way I am? So are those around me. With whom can I make an extra effort to be peaceful with today?

## May 3

*"The moment we decide to stop and look at what is going on
(like a swimmer suddenly changing course to swim upstream
instead of downstream), we find ourselves battered by powerful
currents we had never even suspected—precisely because until
that moment we were largely living at their command."*

*Stephen Batchelor (born 1953)*

---

Today's author illustrates why we often hear, "Stopping is easy, I quit all the time. Staying stopped—can't seem to do that." Like the swimmer, we were enslaved by environmental forces. We thought we were in control because our arms and legs were moving. But when we stopped and went against the current we could see that we had previously been pulled along by more than our will. Going up against addiction seemed insurmountable. The shock of struggling against the current motivated us to seek power beyond our resources to counter the overwhelming pressure. We needed help. No matter what we conceive this power to be, we don't passively "get saved." Step Three is like pushing upstream, tired, uncertain, but with faith that the strength we need will be there. We see others who have done it. This power of example gets us through those moments when we think, "I can't make it."

Later, in Steps Six and Seven, we again find the same dilemma of uncertainty. In taking inventory, we identify rationalizations, habits, deeds and excuses that don't really fit our value systems. Now, with willingness, humility and effort, we try right-living on for size. New behaviors and new thinking help us develop new swimming muscles to resist the current all over again. We are reminded that "going with the flow" isn't always living rightly.

In sobriety, do I go with the flow or fight the current? Do I recognize that, like learning to swim, working the Steps takes time and discipline as I gradually develop new muscles?

# May 4

*"We realized that resources were available to help us
win our freedom, if we were willing to use them."*

Step Two, The Pagan (Nine) Steps, ninesteppagans.faithweb.com

---

The addictive or dysfunctional mind has a defiant edge that *protects* our illness from the force of reason or love. Twelve Step recovery doesn't work *on* us, but it can work *for* us, if we make a commitment. Generally, others saw we needed help before we did. In the denial of addiction how did we respond to loving intervention or criticism of any kind? We isolated ourselves from loved ones, institutions or movements that suggested that we had a problem. Or we were defeatist, saying, "What's the use?" Many play both sides of the fence, declaring we are fine and don't need help on one hand and then that we are victims of circumstances on the other hand. "I am not an alcoholic," one stubborn drunk insists, "I am a heavy social drinker with bad luck."

In the addiction world, many of us die in defiance rather than recover. For those of us who recover and prosper, admitting and accepting we need help is a key to the Second Step. Facing the fact that we do not have the means to combat the *merciless obsession* solely on our own, we now (i) consider that maybe we don't have all the answers and we aren't all powerful; (ii) have the vulnerability to welcome the love, experience and guidance of others (letting other people love us takes a surprising amount of effort); and (iii) take the plunge, or immerse ourselves in the recovery community. Changing our scenery and influences goes a long way toward changing our attitudes.

Have I learned to let other people love me? Can I call people or ask for help? If I am reluctant, what is that about? Is it pride, shyness, procrastination or something else? Real change requires willingness and effort. Once the effort is made, it won't feel uncomfortable for long.

## May 5

*"The terms spiritual experience and spiritual awakening
are used many times in this book which, upon careful reading,
shows that the personality change sufficient to
bring about recovery from alcoholism has manifested
itself among us in many different forms."*
Alcoholics Anonymous, Appendix II, 569

---

Who hasn't heard that "our program is an adjustable wrench that can work on any nut"? Regardless of our beliefs, practices or culture, addiction shows little bias. It's widely agreed that addiction affects our minds, our bodies and spirits. Recovery *by The Book* is also three-fold— mental, physical and spiritual. It doesn't matter whether we are deeply religious or secular. We might believe we have an addiction or disease or just an obsession, habit or a craving. We might think we're possessed by an evil spirit. For some of us, "spiritual" describes a connectedness to a higher or inner power. For others, "spiritual" is a catch-all phrase to describe abstract or intuitive aspects of recovery that are neither mental nor physical.

Our opening position is willingness; an understanding comes later. No two people have identical experiences with either addiction or recovery. The Steps almost always affect us differently than we expected. Our thoughts and attitudes will be challenged along the way and we welcome these challenges. Addiction flourishes in closed-mindedness. In recovery we expect that our beliefs, preferences and attitudes will change. When faced with something that doesn't make sense to us, do we consider our ways of seeing as dynamic and likely to change ten years from now?

Today, in my own words, how do I describe addiction and the recovery process? Does the idea of a threefold recovery—physical, mental and spiritual—fit with my beliefs? Do I respect matters of both the physical and metaphysical world?

## May 6

*"In blindly pursuing progress, our civilization has, in effect, institutionalized frustration. For in seeking to accentuate the positive and eliminate the negative, we have forgotten entirely that the positive is defined only in terms of the negative. The opposites might indeed be as different as night and day, but the essential point is that without night we would not even be able to recognize something called day."*

*Ken Wilber (born 1949)*

---

If we were to take the Twelve Steps literally we would expect each of us to look like a slice of Swiss cheese—our character defects would be removed and nothing would remain but the yummy us. In *No Boundaries,* Wilber looks at our tendency to define ourselves by the boundaries we create between us and others, us and our things, and even us and own bodies. Our boundaries aren't just between us and the outside world. We draw lines between our good sides and our shadow selves, too. Our self-worth is defined by our progress: "I am not the person I use to be," "That's not like me," etc. Greed and manipulation may be part of the dark sides of our personalities that will continue to act up while we strive for more righteous values. This frustrates us but that's what daily inventory is for.

This is a time for examination, not condemnation. Why are we acting or feeling this way? Greed might signal a feeling of lacking. If we find ourselves manipulating, do we feel oppressed or out of control? These feelings may be accurate assessments and they may be way off. The goal is to keep searching, to understand more. With understanding, we can act more consciously and less reactively—if we can cut ourselves some slack. In western culture, never being satisfied is encouraged. Even in our meetings we can be pretty hard on ourselves and receive nothing but understanding nods in response.

Do I subscribe to the "accentuate the positive/eliminate the negative" program? If that's frustrating me, why stay with a program that isn't working? Can I steal a page from the Jungian play book, borrowed from Eastern philosophy, which encourages integrating the yin and the yang?

*"You feel strong and weak at the same time. You feel excited and at the same time, terrified. The truth is you don't know the way you feel, except you know the kind of man you want to be. It's as if you've reached the unreachable and you weren't ready for it."*

Peter Parker, Spider-Man (2002)

___

If only all spiritual guidance could come from comic book heroes or their alter egos. Clues to right living can come from almost anywhere, even the most commercial of art forms. We take our inspiration where we can get it. In this instance, Peter Parker is talking. Spider-Man is the alter ego who enjoys unwavering confidence, not Parker. We admire the superhero and identify with the more human persona of Peter, who questions what's right and wrong and whose indecisiveness means he never gets the girl. Peter Parker is nothing if not ambivalent.

Dr. Patrick Carnes, who authored such books as *Don't Call it Love*, *Out of the Shadows* and *The Gentle Path Through the Twelve Steps*, has been heard in seminars likening recovery to the plight of the hobbit from *The Lord of The Rings*, Frodo Baggins: "I take the ring though I know not the way." Both Frodo and Peter Parker are reluctant messiahs—they never asked for their lots in life, but they accept responsibility. They'll figure it out along the way. Didn't Peter Parker's uncle tell him, "With great power, comes great responsibility"? Every life has great power; Uncle Ben's message is for all of us.

Do I take responsibility—for myself and others in whose lives I play a role? Can I accept responsibility without reservation or recognition? If I have doubt, can I press on, one day at a time?

## May 8

It sounds irrational, but think about it: what if mistakes were good? We would never have to lie about one again. They would not cause us shame or doubt. We wouldn't have fear about erring today or later this year. No longer would we be critical of others who make mistakes—not our kids, our parents or our friends. If mistakes weren't wrong, we wouldn't give up. If we think about it for a while, this simple way of seeing changes everything.

Edison was working for Westinghouse and had not yet invented the incandescent light bulb when interviewed by a young reporter who asked him how it felt to try variations of an experiment 10,000 times and have nothing but failure to show for it. Edison said, "I have not failed. I've just found 10,000 ways that won't work." It may have taken this stubborn man another 4,000 tries, but he did invent the light bulb.

Think for a moment—what are the biggest mistakes we have ever made in our lives? OK, now take time to consider what we learned from them. Did our ways of seeing get altered for the better because of what each mistake taught us?

Can I think of the smallest or most recent mistakes I made? Did getting it wrong mean the end of the world? Was I embarrassed? Have I or do I expect that I will learn something from the results that followed my effort? Could I rethink the automatic reflex that pours regret on my mistakes? I can if I want to. Thomas Edison said so. I say so, too.

## May 9

*"Until you value yourself, you won't value your time. Until you value your time, you will not do anything with it."*

M. Scott Peck (1936–2005)

---

Self-worth wanes and shame remains when we fall short of our values—or are they someone else's values? When we say "I should" it is worth exploring whose values we are measuring ourselves by. *shoulds* that we live with or claim to live with might be consolations for not knowing what we stand for. Do we feel we have a right to our own values? That's what a healthy self-image is about. Finding our true values makes living by them easier than seeking approval or sucking up to someone else's standards. How does one muster the integrity to live up to someone else's values? We were people-pleasing, hoping that the approval of others would rub off in terms of how we felt. Some of us resent having others' expectations imposed on us. "You're not the boss of me!" was our childish knee-jerk reaction.

When other people's needs come before our own, we don't value our time in the way that we do when we feel equal to others. We give ourselves away and have little to show for it. We may resent others or fall into a passive-aggressive trap and find ourselves being snappy or feeling hurt.

Time is one area we can take responsibility for, right now. We get some important benefits from respecting time. Time, like money, can seem scarce. Too much time on our hands can spook us; we run around creating drama to avoid spare time. Our attitudes about time teach us a lot about our core beliefs. Peck talks about valuing ourselves first and then respecting our time. We have found that we can act our way into good thinking at least as well as we can think our way into good acting. Respecting our time and others' time will make us feel differently about ourselves. It also sets the tone for how others treat us.

What am I prepared to say "no" to? What am I going to show up for? Showing up for myself (emotionally) is part of self-care or what Adult Children of Alcoholics (ACA) oriented therapy calls self-parenting.

## May 10

*"Each group has but one primary purpose—to carry its message to other codependents who still suffer."*

*coda.org.*

---

Bill Wilson said we should rejoice in the fact that drunks are getting sober any way at all. George Vaillant, a Harvard doctor, joined AA as a non-alcoholic Trustee in 1998 and estimated that 40% of sober people are so because of AA.[47] AA is not everything to everyone, which means that it doesn't profess to have found a cure for every problem or even the one and only solution for alcoholics. AA is for people who want to stop drinking, but can't on their own. Understanding the limitations of our recovery programs can keep us from developing unreasonable expectations. People are at liberty to take or leave our help. We don't know what is best for people. Tradition Five helps us, the newcomer and the public stay clear on what the fellowship has to offer.

A diverse membership improves the odds that the newcomer can relate to and/or be inspired by someone. It also gives us all a greater tapestry of experience and perspective to draw upon. Looking around at our home groups, do we see that they reflect the general population just outside our doors? What might there be about our groups that frustrates carrying the message to sufferers? Habits and rituals may make one group feel welcoming and comfortable while different habits and rituals may make another group feel uncomfortable. If our population doesn't accurately reflect our community, is there more our groups could do to adapt to gender, racial and cultural differences? Our primary purpose is to make all who suffer feel welcome. We feel welcome and comfortable at our meetings. Is there anything we do that would discourage potential members from other cultural backgrounds?

How is a primary purpose different from a single purpose? Do I follow the crowd or take the lead in tabling ideas to make my group better for everyone?

*"Using reality as your higher power, you will have to bend the steps from their current and now canonical wording. You can't pray to reality, but you can form and express your intention to live by its rules. And you can meditate in order to cultivate mindfulness of what's real. This won't necessarily please all those orthodox 12 Steppers, but then it's unrealistic to expect literalists to be open-minded. And getting real is the whole idea here."*

Thailo, An Atheist's Guide to Twelve-Step Recovery

---

The blog *An Atheist's Guide to Twelve-Step Recovery from Substance Addiction* relates to the doubters' conundrum of finding a workable secular interpretation of the classic Twelve Steps.[48] Yesterday's discussion talked about our primary purpose of carrying the message. The message is always that each person can find his or her own salvation, without having to subscribe to set ideas about salvation. Part of carrying the message is to further widen the gateway.

What *we* know to be true is just *opinion* to another. Many of us rely on our thinking skills to make sense of the world. We find evidence to corroborate our hypotheses. In other areas, we may feel strongly about issues without having the facts, and with the support of intuition we have the same conviction as someone with the soundest arguments. It only stands to reason that in meetings, at work, at home and at play we won't always agree with others. How do we get along? How do we relate?

Practicing love and tolerance involves more than putting up with others; it requires a sincere desire to understand, respect and empathize. Attitude is felt by others and is hard to hide from them. No matter how sincerely we frame our words, even a child can hear through a condescending attitude.

Do I consciously nurture an attitude of tolerance and love? When I reach out to help another am I mindful to help them find their own salvation, not *the* salvation? Is reality a power or principle that I can build sane, healthy recovery around? Is living in accordance with reality a goal of mine?

# May 12

*"A man must make up his mind to do everything in his power
to cooperate in such work as there is to be done. Halfway
measures are of no avail. Even if the patient is interviewed
every day, it is obvious that one hour of instruction,
analysis and persuasion could not be effective
should a man have an adverse or indifferent state of mind
during the other twenty-three."*

The Common Sense of Drinking
*by Richard R. Peabody (1892–1936)*

---

"Half measures are of no avail" was one of many ideas Bill (and Bob) adopted from the 1931 book, *The Common Sense of Drinking* by alcoholic and alcohol treatment facilitator R. Peabody. He was the first quasi-professional to promote the idea of alcoholism as an incurable disease. Peabody lost his family and fortune to drinking, and found himself at the psychologically-based healing center of the Emmanuel Movement in Boston. He would later council chronic upscale alcoholics in New York with the secular system of recovery outlined in his best-selling book.

Down the road, the Oxford Group was sobering up Ebby Thacher at this time in history. Bellevue Hospital in NYC and other facilities in Boston and Philadelphia adopted the Peabody method, while Bill and Lois Wilson read it with interest, as did many of the original members. Raymond G. McCarthy, a Peabody-trained therapist, started The Yale Center of Alcohol Studies in 1944, and it was the first free clinic devoted solely to treating alcoholism. Followers continued his work until the 1950s.

Some AAs said Peabody died intoxicated. The medical report said heart failure. Was there a rift over the religious/spiritual factions of recovery that disapproved of his secular approach? Come to think of it, is there still some tribal rivalry inside our culture now? One thing that is for sure is that Peabody's work, book and experiences are still heard in modern attitudes about addiction and recovery.

Do I keep in mind that many contributors had a hand in Twelve Step philosophy, practices and creed? How much impact does the idea that "halfway measures are of no avail" impact my beliefs now?

*"When I think of what liquor does to me and how much it
makes me suffer, I sometimes feel as if I didn't know why I
drank, as if any reason sounded too foolish to bother with. Then
again when I concentrate on the problem it seems as if there
were reasons or impulses, some of which are obvious, and some
of which are vague and hence hard to explain."*

The Common Sense of Drinking
*by Richard R. Peabody (1892–1936)*

---

Yesterday we read that a good deal of the recovery community attitude about alcoholism and treatment came from the best-selling Peabody book, *The Common Sense of Drinking.*[49] At $20 an hour, five times a week, not many drunks were sitting in Peabody's waiting room in the aftermath of the Great Depression. The fact that AA was a free fellowship is one reason it was able to run with the best of these ideas and soon eclipsed its predecessor. AA was also influenced by the Oxford Group, which offered Four Absolutes, which were Christ's message of God's will—Honesty, Purity, Unselfishness and Love. AA broke away from the Oxford Group because founders disagreed with absolutes, but their concepts are still found in Twelve Step lore.

Peabody found many earnest practitioners trying to make gentlemen drinkers out of drunkards with 0% success. Peabody was convinced that recovery from addiction required personal commitment to relieve an addict from their fate. He also felt that the experience of addiction, of losing one's self to compulsion, had to be articulated—to tell the fellow addict that someone understood and, additionally, to help the medical world know that addiction is not a moral or discipline issue.

As I read the passage above, do I appreciate the timeless commonality of addiction? Relapse is so easy to judge and hypothesize about. Do I know what causes relapse and what it takes to stay in recovery? We will never be all-knowing. Humility and gratitude can go a long way to getting and staying sober, even without offering crystal clear answers.

## May 14

*"When he not only lied to himself, but himself believed
the lie and lied back again to those lying factions,
among whom was not even their own honour. There was
not even a consistent basis to his self-deception."*

*Malcolm Lowry (1909–1957)*

---

Malcolm Lowry's *Under the Volcano* is a portrait of an alcoholic. Today's quote illustrates how self-destructive behavior and self-deception are inseparable. Everything gets distorted. We abdicate personal responsibility in some areas of life while we take the blame for facts and events that we have no power over in other instances. Insanity and/or distorted reality and substance or process addiction and/or codependency need each other. This interdependence is not very subtle.

When called on our bullshit by others, how do we react? Do we rationalize or go on the offensive? Just as a rolling stone collects no moss, we know that we can avoid confrontation when we keep moving. Our fabrications are convincing to others, but only for a time. We develop an impeccable sense of timing for "getting out of Dodge" before we are found out. Some members joke now that, "I lied when it was unnecessary, just to stay sharp." Delegating blame is part of our fraud too—we don't have the right life partners, bipolar disorder is to blame, we are under-employed or misunderstood. Every fact brings limits but we can forget that we still have choices within those limits. People sometimes blame their circumstances for their moods. We may win over the targets of our affection, the absence of which was making us unhappy. Soon they become the problem and with equal conviction we declare that all will be fine with us, once we are rid of this vitality-sucking dead-wood.

Self-deception may be a trait of the *addict's mind*. "That's my addict talking," I might say. What does my *recovery mind* have to say? What does "to thine own self be true" mean to me today? What do I tend to kid or deceive myself about? Why?

## May 15

*"Worry does not empty tomorrow of its sorrow; it
empties today of its strength."*

*Corrie ten Boom (1892–1983)*

---

How do we react when someone calls us on excessive worry? Do we dig in our heels and declare that we are just being responsible? Do we argue that a sense of impending doom now will mitigate future suffering? Today's worry only sucks the energy and enjoyment out of the here and now. Planning isn't worrying; worrying isn't planning.

Planning relieves anxiety. We just can't plan the outcome. It might be our struggle with control, or the lack thereof, which is pouring gas on this fire of worry. Are we overinvested in a certain outcome? All the stress in the world won't give us control over either the results of our efforts or the efforts of others. In our addictive and/or codependent ways we were the consummate manipulators who wrote scripts for everything and everyone to live by. If only everyone could save time and see it our way, wouldn't everyone be happier?

The "one day at a time" mantra can lessen our propensity to resist being controlled as well as our desire to be in control. If our efforts are focused on today's tasks and *what if* thinking kicks in, we can remember to think about our effort, not the outcome. If all else fails to free us from worry, putting ourselves in the service of others is a sure thing. When we give to others with pure intention it doesn't cost us energy—it replenishes our energy. With the outcome ball in someone else's court we can hope for the best without being obsessed.

Yoga, deep breathing, prayer or meditation are more ways people find peace from regret for the past or dread of what tomorrow may bring.

Do I have a routine or system to help me when my thoughts are focused on what Richard Walker referred to, in *Twenty-Four Hours A Day*, as "those two awful eternities—yesterday and tomorrow"?

## May 16

*"There are no greater adversaries than yin and yang, because
nothing in Heaven or on Earth escapes them. But it is not yin
and yang that do this, it is your heart that makes it so."*

*Chuang Tzu (c.360 BC–c. 275 BC)*

---

Enslavement to excesses isn't cured by a life of deprivation. Healthy living is focused more on the middle of our lives and less on opposite extremes. Being true to our bottom lines as addicts will not demand rigidity in all areas of life. To hit a ball with a bat well, you make contact in the bat's sweet-spot, not at either end. Let's keep from categorizing the rest of the world and every behavior as all good or evil. A life well lived has give and take in it. Peacefulness is felt in the middle of the merry-go-round, not at the edge where we feel centrifugal force spinning us out of control.

Jung criticized Christian mythology for separating good and evil, the righteous and the wicked, salvation and damnation. He posited that we were born integrated and that separateness of our ego selves from our shadow selves was the cause of a lot of humanity's psychic and/or spiritual damage. When we accept doubt, fear, rage and grief without hiding, over-compensating or self-destructing, we can integrate our dark and light selves. Jung referred to this integration as "individuation."

We exercise courage while honoring our fear. Both serve us well. We can disagree with another and honor their alternate viewpoint. Our wasted lives become immensely valuable as we identify with other addicts without judging them or ourselves. Our greatest shame becomes a gift when we show another that they are not alone. When we introduce ourselves to a newcomer, look them in the eye and say "tell me how you are doing," our effectiveness stems from having made peace with our duality.

Am I grounded today? When I feel that all-or-nothing trap, do I know I am doing it to myself? Do I know that life isn't black *or* white? Can I see that it's black *and* white with lots of shades in between?

## May 17

*"Nothing is more dangerous than an idea
when it is the only one you have."*

*Emile Chartier (1868–1951)*

---

The alcoholic may not recall the question, but the answer was to have a drink and take it from there. Ask an addict in the throes of compulsive spending, eating, gambling or romantic intrigue if acting out is really such a good idea. Who knows what they will tell you but you can rest assured that acting out is the only idea they are thinking about right now. If we hit bottom and we contemplate suicide, that idea is extremely dangerous if no other idea comes to mind.

"I had no choice" is still a knee-jerk rationalization in recovery. For impulsive people, it takes practice to learn thoughtful action instead of immediate reaction as a reflex. We get triggered. Our internal comfort-seeking, confrontation-avoidant auto-pilots kick into gear before our rational brains can weigh the pros and cons of a given dilemma. We get angry, offended, fearful and/or aggressive before we have time to think things through. For early AA members, "Easy Does It," "First Things First" and "Think, Think, Think" were slogans or mantras used to retrain their compulsive natures.

When we are very sure and feel compelled to act, why not take a few minutes to consider, "What else could this mean?" Artists and inventors will train themselves to not get married to their first good idea. They keep digging for ideas. Maybe they have stumbled upon a gold-mine of good ideas and something better might be overlooked. There is nothing sacred about our first inspiration.

A group conscience that voted rashly because they felt a sense of urgency might end up revisiting the same issue over and over again, using up time that could be better spent. If there is time to do it over, then there is time to improve the chances of getting it right the first time.

On a scale of one to ten, how impulsive am I? At certain times or in certain circumstances do I tend to react instead of considering what the best alternative is, given all the options?

## May 18

*"Nothing is more important than reconnecting with your bliss. Nothing is as rich. Nothing is more real."*

*Deepak Chopra (born 1946)*

---

Facing life clean and sober is no easy task. Consequences of our pasts loom; a sense of impending doom sometimes hangs over us. Then someone says, "So, are you feeling the bliss of recovery now?" Chaos lite might be achievable, but bliss? Many of us are cynical and we liken being blissful to being not so sharp or living in la-la land.

Chopra argues that bliss is rooted in reality, not fantasy. Bliss is natural and distress is unnatural. Is that true for addicts? For addicts, *disease* is normal, not bliss. Even after vigilant Step work or other therapy, we can be uncomfortable when all is calm. Bliss may be real, but it seems unnatural for many of us. Making a gratitude list is medicine prescribed by senior members for changing moods from grumpy to happy.

Can we remember a time as children when we felt entitled to joy? Bliss is natural in a healthy childhood. Children don't work on being happy; they feel it unabashedly. We are allowed to be blissful. Do we have memories of organic joyfulness? If not, it's never too late to have a happy childhood. We aren't obligated to be happy all the time. We aren't failing when we are sad. The point is that if happiness is unfamiliar or uncomfortable for us, that is bound to mean something. It is worth thinking about from time to time.

What are my attitudes about happiness? Do I feel entitled to it? What about today—how do I expect to feel today? Do I feel useful? Do I have a sense of purpose? Does being useful make me feel better? To what extent does my attitude dictate my feelings? Can I change my attitude?

## May 19

*"For a long time it had seemed to me that life was about to begin—real-life. But there was always some obstacle in the way. Something to be got through first, some unfinished business, time still to be served, a debt to be paid. Then life would begin. At last it dawned on me that these obstacles were my life."*

*Fr. Alfred D'Souza*

---

Life's value comes from our struggles and suffering. What would a novel or movie be without the conflict? We marvel at our heroes because they don't always win each conflict, they don't always have the confidence that they will overcome, yet they persist with grace. We care how we are perceived by our children, parents, coworkers and friends in the fellowship. How we are coping with today's struggle, be it a crisis or monotony, will impact how they feel about us.

Some days we will feel that we are not yet ready, worthy or complete. We can get trapped in thinking that we will have all the love, all the time, all the rewards in life once we are prepared, once the Twelve Steps are finished. Then life will begin to be fun, we will start to feel accomplished and we won't have to make any more excuses. But tomorrow never comes. Life is fair enough and we are good enough, right now. Regardless of how much unfinished business we have, this is life, obstacles and all. These are the good ol' days.

Today I can lay out the welcome mat for my dilemmas and say, "Hello life—I was expecting you and I am ready." Can I do this with an engaging smile and playful expectation?

## May 20

*"It's okay to make mistakes. Mistakes are our*
*teachers—they help us to learn."*

*John Bradshaw (born 1933)*

---

The National Institution of Drug Addiction (NIDA) treats addiction as a disease of the brain. In the 1930s, acting out was seen as a moral or behavioral issue. Slips are often treated as a failure to work the program. Like the rest of the recovery community we are well served to reevaluate our attitudes. Science suggests that relapse is not automatically our fault. Heredity and remission are factors in any diseases, as is recurrence, or as we call it—relapse. Addicts demonstrate patterns of relapse that are similar to those of other patients with chronic conditions such asthma, hypertension or diabetes.

Relapses, or mistakes, can teach. If someone is clean and sober for a considerable amount of time and then relapses, some of us will discount the previous clean-time. Maybe total time in the fellowship is as important a measure as our consecutive days of abstinence. The more "mistakes" we've made and the more "teachers" we've had, the wiser we are—right? If we glorify our programs of recovery as being flawless, we blame the victim for relapse. Maybe we do that to make us feel we have more control over our own destinies—"That will never happen to me. I got an 'A' in the Twelve Steps!"

Who knows why or how we got sober or why we relapse? Our explanations are narratives, not scientific fact. According to NIDA reports early this century, the part of the brain that controls mood and memory is disturbed in addicts (and maybe in all people with obsessive-compulsive disorders).[50] The anterior cingulated cortex of the brain is responsible for reward anticipation, rational cognitive function, decision-making, empathy and emotion. When fully functional, if we eat something that makes us sick this part of the brain will warn us about eating it again. The addict's brain's wiring may be short-circuiting. With this part of the brain malfunctioning, one of us can be "off the wagon" before we can say, "my name is _____ and I am a recovered _____."

Do I treat my mistakes as failures? Can I see how they can be teachers?

## May 21

*"Whether you think you can or whether you think
you can't, you're right."*

*Henry Ford (1863–1947)*

---

Limits—they exist. Some are physical, some mental, some perceived and others are facts of life. It's worth remembering the flatness of our planet was once a fact. Then the *impossible* four-minute mile was accomplished. Legend has it that the race to be the first barefoot water-skier came down to two Florida competitors. One heard that the other skier had just achieved successful barefoot skiing and this compelled the man not to be outdone. Before the day was over he, too, could barefoot ski. But as the story goes, the original tale of his adversary's achievement was a fabrication. The moral of the story is that being convinced that we can succeed improves the odds over doubting it can be done.

When do determination and tenacity cross the line and become self-will run riot? How many addicts have died trying to achieve self-control, one more time? Each challenge has to be put to the Serenity Prayer test: Courage to change, serenity to accept—where does the wisdom to know the difference come from? Twelve Step recovery includes meditation, self-appraisal and, for many, prayer. Confidence and caution need not be adversaries. Sober second thoughts give our lofty goals and our quandaries perspective. Ultimately, we decide for ourselves where to draw the line between worthy ambition and an insane undertaking. After thoughtful reflection it is time for action. Still, limits are best viewed as opinions and not facts. Keeping a playful attitude keeps mistakes from feeling like failures. Some of us do a periodic spot-check inventory on our limits just to keep real and perceived limits separate in our minds.

Are my limits based on my values, my limited experience or inevitable facts of life? Is there something in my life that is "impossible" only because I have labeled it as so?

# May 22

*"There is often a vast difference between group conscience and group opinion, as dictated by powerful personalities or popularity. Some of our most painful growing experiences have come as a result of decisions made in the name of group conscience. True spiritual principles are never in conflict; they complement each other."*

Narcotics Anonymous 5th Edition

---

"Principles before personalities" need not stifle our personalities. Personalities are what draw people to the fellowship. It wasn't the principles that gave us hope so much as relating to others who seemed to reach us in how they identified. Different personalities and the liberal expression of these are good for our culture. Even conflict and criticism aren't unhealthy. So *vive la différence*, but let's not have egos controlling the agenda. In AA circles we have heard, for decades, "All you need to start a new meeting is a resentment and a coffee pot." What's the net result? More newcomers are reached and, a year later, who knows or cares about the rift that started it? Most problems self-correct; they don't need policing.

If we start to talk of rules, who's going to police them? What will we do with nonconformists?

"Firm on principle, flexible on method" reminds us that another way is different, not inferior. The "narcissism of small differences," a phrase that was coined by Freud in the early twentieth century, blinds us to what bonds us. British anthropologist Ernest Crawley observed that we reserve our most virulent emotions (aggression and envy), for those most like us. Those with whom we share little in common are no real threat.[51] Sometimes we bicker about what outside issues are permitted topics or why we should be identifying as recovered, not recovering, or the other way around. Fascinating topics as they may be, the bigger issues are sometimes lost. Instead, we should be asking, "How do we appeal to those who are still suffering from addiction?"

Is it enough that I have my say, without always get my way? Do I make *informed* decisions? Do I see that group conscience is about doing the right thing, not choosing the most popular option?

# May 23

*"If I give this, what is there left for me? Thinking of oneself—*
*the way of evil ghosts. If I keep this, what is there left to give?*
*Concern for others is the way of Gods."*

*Master Shantideva (687–763)*

---

Some of history's wealthiest people died trying to acquire more. Stuff, people or escapism make us feel good, temporarily. Being in the service of our fellows frees us from our otherwise restless states of longing, loathing and/or ruminating. Working with new members, we learn that service work isn't sacrificing our well-being—service begets well-being. Freedom from the bondage of self doesn't make us door mats, taking on the burdens of others. Twelve Step work teaches us and we help others empower themselves. They may or may not express gratitude for our giving but we don't expect gratitude, anyway. Our reward isn't tied to accolades. Carl Jung would tell inebriated patients in his care, "Spiritus Contra Spiritum"—"A spiritual quest cures a thirst for spirits."

Yin and yang—the sickness (addiction) and the healthy spiritual quest—are not oppositional so much as they are interdependent. Our pain is our gift to others. Taking an interest in another's suffering transcends our ego-centric cycle, making room for a new sense of value and usefulness. Two addicts sharing with each other transform despair into hope for both of them.

In Christian talk, we do for others what we wish others would do for us. In Buddhist language, we erase our egos by emptying ourselves. An empty life finds context through engaging and giving to others. In recovery terms, "no matter how far down the scale we have gone, we will see how our experience can benefit others."

Did my addiction start out as being too much of a good thing or was there an emptiness I tried to fill that couldn't be satisfied? Do I feel more whole when I am in the service of others?

## May 24

*"Games are a compromise between intimacy
and keeping intimacy away."*

Eric Berne (1910–1970)

We play games to be included while feeling deep down inside that we are unworthy. We want to belong but we dare not be authentic and risk being rejected. Here's a list of games, or roles, most of us are familiar with: the cynic, the clown, the seductress, the braggart, the dominator, the submissive, the gossip, the snob, the lovable loser, wonder-woman, the chronic slipper, the concurrent disorder double-winner, the believer, the skeptic, the power of example. These could be excuses or badges of honor. It doesn't matter so much if other people labeled us or if we branded ourselves. Masks put the kibosh on intimacy because attention we attract isn't ours to enjoy when we aren't being ourselves. We may replay our pet roles, change the cast and act out the same drama, never seeing others for who they are or letting people love us for who we are. If we are actors, where do the scripts come from?

Even introductions at meetings such as "My name is _____ and I am a _____ " label us as what we are, more that who we are. Admitting powerlessness is good. Letting this malady define us for life isn't beneficial.

Steps One through Eight help us understand who we are, how we cope and the games we play. Step Nine requires great discretion and empathy as we connect to how we impact others. Step Nine—not acting it out but being honest and authentic—is another test. In Steps Ten and Eleven, we review and meditate on the games we play and reflect on what we protect and portray.

Do I remember how uncomfortable I felt at my first meeting? In order to keep growing, am I still prepared to be uncomfortable, vulnerable, imperfect and uncertain? After all, who am I trying to impress?

# May 25

*"It's always hard to figure out to what extent global economic change is planned and strategized and to what extent it emerges as a trend that we, who do economics, impose on the chaos. Honestly, although it's more frightening, there's no one driving the train."*

*Max Fraad Wolff*[32]

---

In sobriety, a life without preoccupation and constant self-imposed chaos presents an opportunity, maybe even a responsibility, to apply our sanity and our second chance in life to a greater purpose. The economist quoted above could easily be talking about climate change, economic crisis, overpopulation, peak oil or any other issue that we may have placed on the "serenity to accept the things I cannot change" side of the ledger.

When we are new and when we are still shoulder-deep in drama, what good are we to planet earth? We can't even pay our taxes or arrive at a meeting on time! But there comes a time when we ask ourselves, where larger matters are concerned, "If not me then who?" Having faith that someone else can look after this is wishful thinking. As the author quoted today points out, in a mad, mad world, why would we think, "Someone smart and thoughtful is already anticipating and dealing with the big picture"? In many areas of life we are passengers on a runaway train. And in our group and fellowship, who is looking after this stewardship? Of course we don't take on every burden that presents itself. We do our part, or at least invest the time to think things through. We have been given a rare and fortunate second chance at life. How shall we show our gratitude?

What's my relationship to the bigger issues and causes in life? Am I overwhelmed, too busy, or do I love to bitch about how it should be and what others should do to fix things?

## May 26

*"How great in number are the little minded men."*

*Titus Maccius Plautus (254 BCE–184 BCE)*

---

Step One is the beginning of a journey from sickness to wellness. Admitting powerlessness over addiction opens us up, making us less small-minded. Closed mindedness isn't restricted to addicts. Both humbling and enlightening is the realization that we are not as unique and complicated as we hypothesized. Addiction begets *little mindedness.* Contrary to the elaborate narratives of our labyrinth-like lives, we were quite predictable. Our wits were used in the simplest of ways—lying, cheating and maintaining self-justified, self-absorbed states. What's profound about self-pity or self-loathing? Did we think we were great artists or geniuses? The truth hurts and heals. We had been Humpty Dumpty, sitting on the wall; we come to terms with how far our fall (from grace) was. We doubt that all the king's horses and all the king's men can ever put us back together again. Well, they can't. We have to make something new out of the building blocks of our broken lives. There is no going back.

Self-righteousness is a powerful intoxicant to the *little minded.* The more we crave certainty or affirmation, the more *little minded* we stay. If Step One is about looking at life from new angles, then this isn't a one-time-only Step. It is easy to grow complacent. Like getting a regular oil change for a car, checking our own *little mindedness* requires periodic maintenance. We don't have to control things and be right all the time.

Do I love being right? What are the signs I have too tight a grip on petty things? Being less small-minded and reactive doesn't ensure I will be a genius but being open is surely more enriching than the limits of *little mindedness.*

## May 27

*"Take risks. Success comes from lucky accidents. Don't be afraid to fail. Only by putting yourself in new and uncomfortable positions can you grow."*

*Bob Lefsetz*

---

In the chaos of addicted living, we may have rationalized our problems as a series of bad breaks and serious misunderstandings. Recovery may be a lucky accident, a chance encounter, the result of taking someone else to a meeting or reading a book about addiction just to get the person who loaned it to us off our back. Recovery from addiction can be post-traumatic as we see with sober eyes the risks we shrugged off and the damage we sustained while living in addiction. Becoming risk-averse in sobriety is a common countermeasure. Trauma can leave us gun-shy about getting back into life. Books are written and seminars are presented about the formula for success. Authors look back at a number of successes, find the commonality and sell audiences on this *winning* formula. Some success does come from following a strategy. Cover tunes are popular because nothing succeeds like past success. The Twelve Steps aren't hit songs, great literature or particularly original, but as a guide for living, they have a track record. Change doesn't come from reading and understanding the Steps. They are a successful formula that can be loosely or strictly adhered to. But the recovery is in the action—the doing. Having worked the Steps, we set our sights on goals beyond getting through the day sober. Do we want to be gun shy in all areas of our lives?

Talent, timing, preparation, persistence, inspiration and momentum all have to align to make history out of our efforts. Success requires risk-taking and the seemingly illogical following of our instincts. In sobriety, this isn't recklessness but courage. Courage to try and the confidence to make mistakes without being disheartened by failure is evidence that the trauma of our past isn't an anchor.

Wanting to succeed is no crime. I don't have the power to dictate outcomes, but will I do my best?

*"Go on a hunt for any areas of incompletion, large or small, and you will not be disappointed. A burst of creativity will often follow the completion of some long-left issue. Clearing up an incompletion gives you a feeling of aliveness that you can get nowhere else."*

Conscious Loving
*by Gay Hendricks, PhD & Kathlyn Hendricks, PhD*

---

The Twelve Steps are a series of mental and emotional challenges. In rewiring our short-circuited selves, we identify and meet our needs, break down walls and clear away blockages. Inventories uncover faulty coping techniques, the hurt we felt and the hurt we caused. Steps Six and Seven are a time to be open to bursts of creativity. We have discovered areas of incompleteness. An opportunity exists now—what can we do to feel more alive? Step Eight explores our deeds and we revisit what it means to us to be accountable to others. Blame and shame have been triggers in our relationships. The way we saw our impact on others is often overstated or understated. Seeing all humans as incomplete and trying to see how we affect them, through their eyes, gives us both compassion and perspective.

Some of us report that when we clear out the rationalizations and misperceptions we had about ourselves and the world, we unearth a host of feelings that have been repressed. These buried feelings are still very much alive. We persevere through the pain, seeking understanding instead of running and hiding. Do we need help? Maybe we seek out a therapist. Maybe we need to journal or talk to others. There's no shame or time limit. Keeping up appearances is not our priority. Renewal doesn't involve assigning blame; it's a way to understand more deeply. We ask the same question we would ask upon accepting we were in bad physical shape: what are we going to do about it? It is never too late to deal with our emotional incompleteness. A new freedom and new happiness can be a reality but, as with physical fitness, we have to accept certain limitations and take some responsibility.

How do I look at self-help? Is it a chore, self-indulgence, a preoccupation or simply part of life?

## May 29

*"In AA's first years, I all but ruined the whole undertaking with this sort of unconscious arrogance. God as I understood Him had to be for everybody. Sometimes my aggression was subtle and sometimes it was crude. But either way it was damaging— perhaps fatally so—to numbers of nonbelievers ... . Even now, I catch myself chanting same old barrier-building refrain: 'Do as I do, believe as I do—or else!'"*

*Bill W. A.A. Grapevine, April 1961*[53]

---

A bigot is defined by Merriam-Webster as "a person who is obstinately or intolerantly devoted to his or her own opinions and prejudices." In 1961, Bill Wilson's "The Dilemma of No Faith" was, in part, his coming to terms with his own binary thinking. Bill wondered how atheists were to find recovery in AA. How could AA be more accommodating? There are more recovering atheists today than there were members of AA when he wrote this passage. Herb Silverman, President of the Secular Coalition of America, says, "Most people adopt the religion of their parents and the dominant religion in the country where they live. Religion is more about geography than theology."[54] AA is more global than back in the day of Bill's realization, so more people are joining the Twelve Step community from non-Christian perspectives.

Some sincerely try the creator of the universe theory. After a good ol' college try, letting go *of God* becomes as freeing as letting go and *letting God* is for others. It's about being true to ourselves. What works now might not work later. Let's not get married to our current worldviews, because the only constant is change. Apostates are people whose beliefs shift. It could be from atheistic to theistic or it could go the other way. A true seeker is always ready to shed their beliefs like worn out clothes.

What Bill calls *unconscious* (arrogance), Freud called *subconscious*. This discrepancy is an example of the "narcissism of small differences."[55] When we doubt, we may feel vulnerable and anxious. Sometimes we project our anxiety onto others, scapegoating them and their beliefs, which may make us feel better.

In what way am I contemptuous or arrogant today? When I feel elitist is it because I am so sure or because I am anxious or uncertain?

## May 30

*"A year from now you may wish you had started today."*
*Karen Lamb (born 1960)*

Procrastination is a coping technique more often than an act of laziness. An easier life is not a tardy life; there is nothing easy about being late. Sometimes we are being childish. Either we overextend ourselves and are thus unrealistic or, like children, we are resistant to being controlled. Kids say things like, "You're not the boss of me" or "Who's going to make me?" How often are we dealing with adult issues with an eleven-year-old mentality? Maturity and tenacity are muscles that we exercise. Vigilance is one way we show up for ourselves, today.

If we have to *do* something, who are we doing it for? A passive-aggressive reaction to someone's perceived control over us may trigger avoidance or delay. Do we want the positive outcome from our effort, or does someone else? Regardless of whose needs we are serving, doing a given task might still be the best choice for us, given all the alternatives. Maybe we said we would do something to gain approval. Do we agree to do things because we think something is expected of us?

We need to examine our goals. What do we wish we had started a year ago? Let's say we were thinking about going back to school. Would this give us control or take it away? Is being a starving student going to affect our status or reputation? If so, how important is that? Even when a goal is a calling in life, there will be obstacles to overcome; it won't be a free ride. When we are sure we want something or want to do something we have to be ready for setbacks, avoid our impulse reactions and, most importantly, we have to get started.

Instead of *should*-ing all over myself, today I will consider whether or not I feel frozen in my tracks about something. What have I learned so far in recovery about action? Does action conquer fear?

## May 31

*"At least two thirds of our miseries spring from human stupidity, human malice and those great motivators and justifiers of malice and stupidity, dogmatism and proselytizing zeal on behalf of religious or political idols."*

*Aldous Huxley (1894–1963)*

---

Huxley referred to Bill Wilson as "the greatest social architect of the twentieth century" but Bill and the rest of the founders never touted themselves as experts.[56] When we attempt to represent founders or their words as something more than peer-to-peer dialogue we get into that idealistic, dogmatic, proselytizing trap. We look cult-like if we always talk in recovery jargon. It is one thing to share how, inspired by the program, we applied the principles and they transformed our lives. It is quite another matter to cite chapter-and-verse as if we are parroting the authoritative word of gurus.

What if one hundred people from any fellowship were charged with the duty of starting from scratch—writing a new text to describe the steps we took which are suggested as a program of recovery? Chances are the new book would be just as good. It may be better. It wouldn't be perfect, all-encompassing or the final word. Chances are it would be an improvement. These hundred random people know so much more than those who came before them.

Traditions come from experience. They're a chronicle of missteps from our past—not rules that must be adhered to and enforced. We need not become rigid about how a meeting must be run. During a group inventory let's ask ourselves how our rituals look to new people. Do the things we say, read and do coerce conformity? Here's where the feedback from newcomers is most helpful.

Do I quote literature to look like an authority? Do I stick to my experience and refrain from advice or opinions? How do I do with those who have different worldviews? Do I ever proselytize to others who see the world differently?

# June 1

*"We learn to accept that we may never know. When we question we learn to accept that there may be no answer. When we shout our doubt out into the universe we learn to accept that we may be met with a silence that we do not know how to read."*

Waiting: A Nonbeliever's Higher Power
*by Marya Hornbacher (born 1974)*

---

Knowledge isn't always power. Nut-bars, warmongers and religious zealots all *know*. They know their roles, what's best for everyone and the will of God (or whatever they call their muses). We are not like them; we doubt and hope and maybe act as if, but we do not *know*.

Step Three invites us to say, "OK then, not my terms. What then?" We are vulnerable. Nowhere are we asked to understand the consequences of letting go. For all the time that some of us spent in meetings defining this higher power that we will invest our hopes in, we never know—we just let go. What we do know is the alternative to making this Step Three decision. We know the price we paid for closed-mindedness and the pursuit of artificial hope. Wilfulness or the assertion of being in control is a form of overcompensation. Taken to an extreme, overcompensation starts to look like playing God.

A long-time member may say, "Here at meetings, suggestions are free. The only advice we pay for is the advice we refuse." "This is what I suggest" essentially means "This worked for me." None of us are instructors. We have experience, but no expertise. Step Three is about willingness to work with the unknown—to take life as it comes. Willingness may include seemingly absurd and unlikely suggestions that we try on for size, like a hat, recommended by a friend, that we would never choose for ourselves. "My way or the highway" thinking brought us to this crossroads. The simple act of humility—being willing to doubt and admitting that we don't know—may be as life-saving as all the will we can muster.

In Step Three, do I get caught up in the idea that understanding is the key? Isn't demanding answers more of life-on-my-terms? Can I surrender my need to have it my way?

# June 2

*"Art is life's dream interpretation."*

Otto Rank (1884–1939)

---

Psychoanalyst Rank was surrounded by neurotics and artists. Some of us identify as both. While the observer interprets art, art interprets our lives, bonding artists and observers "with a cosmos floating in mystic vapors in which present, past, and future are dissolved."[57] Artistic expression is a positive escape from reality. Addiction is another means of escaping from reality. Psychologists want to understand the nature of the dread addicts wish to escape from and the coping techniques employed to divert it.

Rank studied under Sigmund Freud, who placed the cause of escapism at the feet of our egos.[58] Rationally, we may see ourselves as a link in a chain or a blip in an infinite universe, here for an infinitesimal visit. We get it—we are not that significant. Try telling that to our egos! Our egos think we are god-like. The truth is untenable to a self-idolizing, narcissistic subconscious, but we are not immortal. Death is inevitable. To our egos, mortality is unimaginable and we will deny this reality. Substance or process addiction assuages this reality, but has consequences.

Some say that the neurotic isn't disconnected from reality but, rather, is hyper-aware. The anxiety caused by life's uncertainty can't be escaped so the neurotic acts out compulsively and is often out of step with society. While the neurotic suffers, the artist thrives.

Art is another coping technique—creating it or enjoying it. We all need to escape reality sometimes. The lines between reality and the dream world are the artist's canvas. If art is life's dream interpretation, Otto Rank would concur that the art gallery is a cheap and fun alternative to another appointment with a therapist. Painting or poetry can be as good for self-discovery as one more personal inventory would be.

To deny we have fear is a dangerous proposition. We know how powerful denial is. It nearly killed us. If we don't own up to our insecurities, we will be oblivious to our delusions.

What are the healthy and unhealthy ways that I process anxiety? How important is art to me? Do I make time for art for both pleasure and mental health?

# June 3

*"The explicit awareness that you are a breathing piece of defecating meat, destined to die and ultimately no more significant than, let's say, a lizard or a potato, is not especially uplifting."*

Sheldon Solomon

---

Yesterday we explored how we process life's uncertainties personally. Today we look at how fear affects us socially. Cognitive dissonance is an uncomfortable feeling arising from holding conflicting beliefs or values.[59] Knowing that humans are remarkable and that life's potential is infinite, while also realizing that death is inevitable, can be anxiety-provoking. Much of human activity is an attempt to ignore or avoid our untenable finitude. Culture, religion and procreation suggest continuity and are symbols of our immortality. We can engage in such immortality projects to feel as though we're leaving a lasting impression; to say "I was here."

Terror Management theorists (TMT) study the ways people avoid confronting the reality of the Grim Reaper. This theory piggybacks on the work of cultural anthropologist Ernest Becker. *Denial of Death*, his Pulitzer Prize-winning book, explores how death-anxiety subconsciously triggers some of the worst aspects of human nature as we fight to cope with or deny inevitability.[60]

Culture and society reduce anxiety by means of consensus. Worldviews tell us, "Don't worry, everything will be OK." Surrounding ourselves with like-minded people reinforces our beliefs. Exhorting our country, religion, recovery program, sports team or political party as *the best* also reinforces our denial of death. This works for us just fine, until we are confronted with people who hold alternative worldviews. Social psychologists like Solomon find that when our death-denying illusion is shaken, fear is the result and we up the ante, demonizing others to prop up our own feeble brands of denial. When escalated, denying our denial can be responsible for many of mankind's greatest atrocities—defending one symbol by vilifying and destroying another, compensating for a lack of power by bullying another.[61]

Recovery has taught me to cope with seemingly untenable facts of life—I didn't invent denial but I sure am familiar with it. Do I ever prop up my beliefs, culture, fellowship or home group by putting down another?

# June 4

*"Keep your faith in all beautiful things; in the sun
when it is hidden, in the spring when it is gone."*

*Roy R. Gilson*

---

Everything ends. Each day ends for us while it is just starting for someone else. Yesterday we challenged ourselves to get a grip on our own finitude. We won't live forever, nor will the people we love. We humans have the capacity to imagine days, years or centuries into the future. We can imagine a cure for a disease and we might even fanaticize about how we can contribute to that cure. But we also know we die, no matter how many cures we find.

Not accepting limitations is a cornerstone of insanity. What we refuse to accept can kill us. Alcoholics accept that they can never again drink socially. Codependents see that they have become addicted to the drama of their addicts. Lacking control—of our own addictions or someone else's—can seem intolerable and we can become irrational and dangerous if we refuse to come to terms with our limits.

Today's quote infers that if it was always sunny and always spring, there would be no beauty. The philosophy "Enjoy it while it lasts" is a *celebration of* finitude. We would take fair weather for granted if it lasted forever. Yesterday we talked about the terror of death. Is life futile because life is finite? Au contraire; the shortness and unpredictability of life are what make it priceless. The universe that created us may be indifferent to us and our welfare. Meaning in life is created—not discovered. The length of life is finite, but the depth with which we engage each moment is endless. How deeply we enjoy life is within our influence. With sober thought we resign ourselves to the knowledge that fear of death will never be conquered. Rather, we own up to our fears. We take note of how our base fears impact our policies, beliefs and reflexes each time life pokes us in our bellies. We take responsibility. If we don't enjoy our lives while they last, who will?

If I was to live forever, would that increase or diminish the meaning of life? If I could see it all and do it all would anything matter? Limits and finitude are not enemies to spirituality or happiness. Facing life on life's terms—does that limit me or free me?

# June 5

*"The habit of categorizing and judging our experiences locks us into mechanical reactions that we are not even aware of and that often have no objective basis at all. These judgments tend to dominate our minds, making it difficult for us ever to find any peace."*

*Jon Kabat-Zinn (born 1944)*

---

Longing and loathing and labeling are "mechanical reactions." We respond to situations and people in ways that are subjective and that we think will make or keep us happy. We long for what we presume to be advantageous and loathe what we expect to be undesirable. When looking at today's tasks, do we loathe what is in store for us and long for another lot in life? Is being single attractive while being in a relationship seems like a downer, or is it the other way around? Is that grass we see over there actually greener or this just a perception? We can stop longing and loathing and labeling when we resist the urge to place value judgments on things, tasks and people—"This job will make me happy"; "This illness is a great injustice."

We often recite a descriptive narrative about our lives, our circumstances and the characters in our lives. Villains, heroes, injustices and misfortune "prove" that life is unfair, or that we live a charmed life, if that is how we describe it. We say that we are telling it like it is, but are we? In the spiritual kindergarten of early recovery we shift from defending to demonizing our addictive ways. This replaces one reaction with another. As we graduate from this kindergarten, we gain humility; we know less and judge less as we mature. Kabat-Zinn invites us to try out a beginner's mind or apply childlike awe to situations we had been reactively judging as clearly good or bad. Judging is a coping mechanism. Thinking fast certainly saved our asses before. That's what made us good in emergencies. Sobriety teaches us to excel at the everyday experience—not just at crises.

Does contentment elude me? Can I spend a few days keeping an eye on how I judge and articulate my experiences? Peace and contentment might be attained by simply letting go of preconceived ideas.

# June 6

*"Be yourself. Especially do not feign affection. Neither be cynical about love, for in the face of all aridity and disenchantment, it is as perennial as the grass."*

*Max Ehrmann (1872–1945)*

---

"Desiderata" is Latin for "things that are desirable." What is more desirable than to love and be loved? The poem "Desiderata" is a lesson in love, which includes avoiding being cynical or phony. We can't have love or be loved if we are inauthentic. As phonies, we may long for, but feel undeserving of, love. If we don't love ourselves, no one's love can reach us. If it did, we would reject it, anyway.

No one wins if we fake love. Even in recovery we still want approval. What's different now is that we won't go to any lengths to get it. There was a time when we would say or do almost anything to get what we wanted. Offering love to improve the chances of reciprocation isn't sincere. Today, we look at the Steps, or any code that we live by in recovery, and see that we are to be kind and wish others well. Accepting love from others is its own challenge for us, too. Unconditional acts, given and received, can be habit forming.

Many of us felt ashamed and unworthy of love. We went through life acting, always afraid that people would discover we were frauds. Boundary issues are just a given when we don't respect ourselves. We hear, "People who need love the most deserve it the least." We might remember not being easy to love when we were new, but people reached out to help us anyway. By following the examples of others, we learn to love. We meet our own needs because we deserve to have our needs met. We show up and are present to those around us; they deserve love, too.

Am I cynical about love? In what kinds of situations do I feel natural? When do I fake it?

# June 7

*"Resistance to historical truth is a function of group identity: nations and people weave their sense of themselves into narcissistic narratives that strenuously resist correction. Similarly, regimes depend for their legitimacy on historical myths that are armored against the truth."*

The Warrior's Honor *by Michael Ignatieff (born 1947)*

---

Ignatieff shares his firsthand account of the carnage resulting from ideological clashes between the Hutus and Tutsis as well as Serbs and Croatians. Brothers and sisters became enemies, sworn to kill each other to preserve a way of life that was ostensibly under attack. During such clashes, mythical attributes can be created to differentiate one side from the other. Some societies attach heroic qualities to warriors and atrocity. To outsiders, the differences that people are willing to kill for may seem indiscernible.

The Twelve Traditions attempt to unify and preserve fellowships from conflict. Our wisdom comes not so much from wise ideas but from bad experiences. Neither our flawed but earnest founders nor "the good ol' days" should be painted with mythological qualities. Bill Wilson saw personal responsibility as a sign of maturity for members, and the fellowship. Groups and members are each autonomous. We are free to leave, but we can't be kicked out. Forty-year members get one vote, as do forty-day members, when making decisions about their groups' futures. Affiliation and controversy are discouraged. We don't lobby or advocate and we barely defend criticism.

Grandiose visions of what the future should hold can be divisive, too. AA history includes dreams of property, treatment and banking. One such project had 61 rules. Bill Wilson's support was sought. Bill recommended against it but affirmed his lack of authority to stop it. The project imploded and the promoter lived through the failure. He sent Bill rule # 62: "We best never take ourselves so damn seriously."[62] AA bent but didn't break. The member has the autonomy to pursue his idea, no matter how unpopular. We all have the right to be wrong. His intent was noble. The promoter had the humility to see his application was flawed.

Do I have an impression of our fellowship that could be described as a "narcissistic [narrative] that strenuously resist[s] correction"? When have I had to apply Rule # 62?

## June 8

*"There should be a period of grieving. However, if grieving is prolonged more than necessary, it results in a perpetual lamentation, culminating into an unforgiving vendetta passed on to generations."*

*Fr. Ephraim Mensah (born 1949)*

---

Sobriety has taught us that there is value in all of life's experiences, even suffering. Many of us avoided pain; this escapism was a primer for addiction. Then, the cure for pain (drowning our sorrows) became the new infliction. Pain can be the touchstone to spiritual growth—from post-traumatic stress, to heightened self-awareness to *post-traumatic gain*. Loss, abuse and injustice bring suffering. Recovery teaches us better ways to grieve, express anger and cope with chaos. What overwhelmed us then is still difficult, but manageable now.

Depression and anxiety are not feelings in and of themselves, but are widely considered coping techniques. Negative emotional states that we repress grow and spread into long-term conditions. Like a fit of hysterical laughter, emotions take over our bodies, build, run their courses, and then subside. With practice, we face our feelings with dignity and courage. We don't avoid because we aren't afraid.

While we honor our feelings and experience them fully, we don't glorify suffering, nor are we defined by it. With maturity, we see struggle as par for the course—not being off-course. Perspective comes in time. We put out the welcome mat to greet life; we don't lock the door and hide under the bed.

I know people who are defined by their suffering. Am I more inclined to dwell on my misery or do I try to avoid my feelings altogether? Have I ever had misfortune fester and grow into a vendetta or bitterness? Do I over-manage my feelings? When do I need to let go and experience grief? Then, when is it time to let grief go?

# June 9

*"The whole problem with the world is that fools
and fanatics are always so certain of themselves,
but wiser people so full of doubts."*

Bertrand Russell (1872–1970)

---

Are we the fools boasting of our certainty or more like the wise, waffling doubters? How many times have we been absolutely certain, yet 100% wrong? Remember when we insisted that we had addiction under control? We were just as certain that recovery would result in a boring life not worth living. We're not automatically wrong when we are certain, but sober second thought suggests that there is always cause to both think and feel our way through life. Can we be at peace with uncertainty, or do we only feel in control when we can say, "No worries, I have this situation all figured out"?

Certainty is revered and doubt has a bad name. Don't we always vote for someone with confidence? Maybe leaders plagued by doubt could make more thoughtful decisions. Humility, in part, involves accepting that we are only human; we know only a little and our conclusions may be flawed. Maybe there is a quiet confidence that comes with not needing to be right. We can be confident that we will do the best we can and be willing to alter our course as need be—without regret or shame. Not knowing does not make us incomplete or inadequate. Learning is a life-long project. Some of the time, it includes reevaluating what we think is true. A dependency on being right marries us to ideas which may stunt our growth. For some of us, unabashedly doubting is a higher state of consciousness than certainty. Doubt and uncertainty can be spiritual states. Being wrong isn't wrong—overcompensating is wrong.

What am I so sure about? How attached do I feel to my version of the truth? How much intuitive know-how do I have? What are my blind spots? Do I feel inadequate if I don't know? Do I feel like I failed if I get it wrong?

# June 10

*"Few rich men own their property; their property owns them."*
*Robert Ingersoll (1833–1899)*

Tradition Six cautions us that we "ought never endorse, finance or lend the A.A. name to any related facility or outside enterprise, lest problems of money, property and prestige divert us from our primary purpose."[63] Good ideas and good causes tease us to make exceptions to a sound code of conduct. Tradition Six has been bent and even broken in the past—every tradition is being broken somewhere right now. We are a fellowship of flawed people, not perfect people. Traditions guide us, but we have no rules or authority. This Tradition of non-affiliation has kept groups and fellowships from the unintended consequences of what might seem to be shrewd and widely accepted business practices. We could ride on the coattails of brand loyalty under the guise of reaching more still-suffering addicts. Mergers, acquisitions, co-branding and trendy practices that serve businesses, non-profit or public sector agencies might help Twelve & Twelve groups, but that's not how we roll.

From treatment centers to coffee shops, club houses to pharmaceutical companies, a relationship with outside interests may look like a perfect marriage but the cost is unknown. This hyper-vigilance might seem outdated. Is it worth it? Every time we see brands throw their reputations behind superstar athletes that get caught in a sex or doping scandal, we see that short term gain can be punished by unforeseeable forces that do irreparable harm. Any fellowship would be vulnerable to such bad publicity.

Do I keep my mind on the primary purpose—carrying the message to those who still suffer? Am I predisposed to ideas of grandeur, pomp and ceremony? Can I let these ideas be without acting on them?

# June 11

*"We cannot discover new oceans until we have the
courage to lose sight of the shore."*

*Muriel Chen*

---

Let go, and then what? Do we outsource problems to a higher power?
Do we believe there is nothing but chaotic universe out there? Can we
let go and *not know*? The comfort of the familiar is hard to relinquish.
Even a maladaptive coping technique has the familiar feeling of home.
We admit our modus operandi sucks but we put off changing for the
better: "This isn't working for me. Tomorrow I will definitely give it
up." But how is *letting go* different from *reckless abandon*? Refusing
challenges and diving in without looking are not the only two options
here.

Why is learning to walk so difficult for toddlers? Every new step
requires a willingness to enter that in-between state of imbalance. We
feel grounded, with our weight on two feet. We step forward and, before
we are grounded again, we lose our balance. We are essentially falling
between each step. As adults, much like during our time as toddlers, we
march forward with awe and courage one day and then fall on our asses
the next day. Years pass and these risky steps go unnoticed.

Starting our drug of choice came with some resistance and/or
trepidation. Giving them up came with still more resistance. We had
to let go absolutely and abandon "the shore" to find recovery. All the
reading, learning and talking in the world couldn't assure us or cure us.
So what do we do? We make peace with the discomfort of not knowing.
This test will repeat itself throughout life. In time, the unknown will
seem more familiar and less frightening.

Muscular atrophy comes to me when I stay frozen in my tracks.
Emotional atrophy comes with avoiding risk. How white are my
knuckles? Am I holding on to the safe and familiar too tightly?

# June 12

*"Meditation brings wisdom; lack of meditation leaves ignorance. Know well what leads you forward and what holds you back, and choose the path that leads to wisdom."*

Prince Gautama Siddhartha (563–483 B.C.E.)

---

Peace and balance are the rewards for practicing Step Eleven. For the young at heart, the exercise of meditation might seem dull or unimaginative—peace and balance may be synonymous with boring. How about living life to the fullest? Try going days without boring old sleep, taking in maximum stimulation—live *extreme sobriety*! So, how's that working out so far? Is it rewarding or is the net result somewhat unfulfilling?

No matter how much lust for life we have, the art of living well is to live in balance. There's no rule against overdoing it periodically and living through the consequences. We don't want to live rigidly. But we value the HALT warning—don't get too Hungry, Angry, Lonely or Tired. Over-stimulation leads to exhaustion, leaving us susceptible to all-or-nothing thinking. This may lead to acting out and then remorse.

We think of meditation as a path to discovering the secret to how we tick. Peacefulness comes from self-knowledge. Jung said that those who look outside themselves will dream and those who search inside will awaken. If our answer to the dream-turned-nightmare that addiction was is to find a better dream—fine. But to awaken, we don't seek *out there* for wisdom. We find it *in here*.

After exercising mindfulness in our routines we see that reckless abandon was not much of a lifestyle choice. The truth turned out to be that we were not living life to the fullest; we were escaping it—on the run with nowhere in particular to go.

A little bit of letting our hair down, self-indulgence and even overdoing it periodically, is vital to a rich and spontaneous life. Rigidity is not sobriety. We learn to trust our instincts and we can tell when we are living life to the fullest or hiding out in plain view.

What is my attitude toward balance, serenity and peace? Do I entertain fears about recovery making me boring? Does sobriety ever seem lame?

*"Some of us think holding on makes us strong,
but sometimes it is letting go."*

*Herman Hesse (1877–1962)*

---

For theists, "Let go and let God" doesn't come easily at first, but then it becomes a way of life. So convinced that faith was the turning point in addiction, an overly zealous believer will attempt to persuade atheists that belief in God is a prerequisite for sobriety. Without it, they say, we are lost at sea.

Atheists see trading dependency on intoxication for belief in what they perceive to be a myth as pure folly. Many nonbelievers connect with an inner power for guidance. Some argue that self-will has a bad rap. It's self-will run riot that ruins us. Recovery depends on a healthy self-will. The overly zealous atheist may see his or her worldview as more evolved and chirp at the believer that reality is better than fiction.

An apostate is someone who reaches a turning point in faith. It may be the result of a dramatic crisis or it may be a quiet realization. Some of us forsake customs and beliefs that worked for us at one point in recovery but don't sit right with our evolving worldviews. Step Three becomes letting go *of* God. A layer of skin that once protected us is replaced, sometimes with only the eerie unknown. Recovery is a continuum. Some come to believe and never look back. Some try faith and find it lacking. Reality can be a power greater than false hope. Just as there are none so righteous as the recently converted, the recently freed might think their brands of sobriety would be liberating for everyone.

Whatever we believe, we don't have to defend. Proselytizing or putting others down doesn't signal strength. Preaching or evangelizing signals a lack of confidence in one's beliefs.

How married am I to my current worldview? When I work with others do I help them find their salvation—not my own brand of recovery?

## June 14

*"Most drinking alcoholics don't want to be helped. They are sick, unable to think rationally, and incapable of giving up alcohol by themselves. Most recovered alcoholics were forced into treatment against their will. Self-motivation usually occurs during treatment, not before."*

*James R. Milam, PhD & Katherine Ketcham*

---

There is a pervasive myth that we have to reach rock-bottom before we can find recovery. The truth is that most of us came to our first meetings for reasons other than conceding defeat. Still, we break the ice with others like us and that builds a foundation. Coming to meetings is phase one; "coming to" is next. Some old ideas fall by the wayside. Ideas we would have never swallowed become ideas that give us hope, even if we still don't understand them.

Then we *come to believe*. We get a few consecutive days of recovery under our belts, and we can see how, one day at a time, this is worth a try. Not long ago this seemed impossible. Many things we first thought we could never accept are still unacceptable after the passage of time. But many of our ideas and practices have changed.

Buddhism teaches about the five hindrances to enlightenment: (i) sensual desire, (ii) ill-will/aversion, (iii) sloth and torpor, (iv) restlessness and remorse, and (v) avoidance. In treatment-talk these hindrances translate as (i) craving, (ii) resentment and revenge, (iii) growing fat and apathetic, (iv) dreading the future and shame about the past, and (v) denial. None of these states have to be eradicated in order to go to meetings. Some honesty, willingness and open-mindedness are needed eventually, but we can come to our first meetings completely unwilling to change.

Some of us talk a good talk in the early days but we are more uncommitted than gung-ho. Many of us stay sober today, harboring secret fantasies of falling off the wagon at some time in the future. We are sober "just for today."

Is my sobriety a process or an event? Was I ready for sobriety when I first got it, or was I reluctantly coaxed into recovery, only working for it later? Do these five hindrances challenge me daily?

# June 15

*"The greatest dangers to liberty lurk in the insidious
encroachment by men of zeal, well meaning
but without understanding."*

*Justice Louis D. Brandeis (1856–1941)*

---

The experiences of "men of zeal, well meaning but without
understanding," helped to form our Traditions. Rules may seem like
a solution for Twelve & Twelve disobedience, but who enforces or
interprets them? We have no membership requirement except for a
desire to change. Each group is free from scrutiny. Bill Wilson believed
in "radical inclusion." In the days of early AA, professional onlookers
and some members feared that this anarchy would corrupt, confuse and
destroy what was felt to be a life-saving fellowship, so groups restricted
membership. When they collected the membership requirements from
each group and added them all onto one list of prerequisites, not one
could meet all the requirements.

No one diagnoses newcomers, checks homework or takes
attendance. In the same anarchistic way, groups read what they wish
and say what they want, so long as they don't significantly affect other
groups or their fellowship. Fellowship central offices do the bidding of
the groups; they don't dictate terms or enforce rules. Well-intentioned
fault-finders might find themselves gathering the support of others to
correct or discipline a wayward group or member. The *missionaries*
may ask themselves, "Do I sing eloquently but lack an understanding
of the words and music?" Diversity requires accommodation. Tolerance
doesn't require liking everyone or every group, but we love them like
family.

Am I mindful about preserving our principles while respecting
the autonomy of groups and members? It's my side of the street that
warrants inventory—not theirs. When I think I have found something
*out of order*, do I carefully weigh my evidence and consider all sides?
"What else could this mean?" is a good question to ask myself when I
feel certain, before I start flapping my gums in self-righteousness.

## June 16

*"Feeling gratitude and not expressing it is like wrapping a gift and not giving it."*

*Heard around the rooms*

An "attitude of gratitude" is a winning formula during our first days of wrestling with recovery and throughout life. We have troubles when we arrive here. If the only gratitude we can muster is a list of how it could be worse, that's a start. There must be something we have not yet lost. We may be clinically depressed or out of sorts, thanks to a concurrent disorder or two—that's the norm around here, not the exception. At times when we are anxious, depressed or angry, making a gratitude list may seem like faking it. Isn't this an honest program? We can be unhappy and grateful at the same time. We may feel sorrow, grief or rage. It isn't inauthentic to speak of what we have to be grateful for even during the most appalling of circumstances. This isn't delusion or avoidance; it is a matter of perspective and balance.

Expressing gratitude is no magic pill. Perspective is altered by what we focus on. Positive expectation feels better than impending doom, even if the outcome is no different. When our thoughts and reactions to life are focused on what's wrong, it can be healing to take a break and make a written or mental list of what's right. Why not pick up the phone and tell a relative how important a role model they were to us, or just say that we were thinking of them. We can spend one hour a week doing charity work if we currently do none at all. It's a start and it flexes our gratitude muscles, making them stronger. If we can find a way to express our gratitude we take time to do so. If not, we tell someone why we are grateful. Acting and speaking positively improve our moods.

Gratitude is like one-a-day medicine. If I take it, I won't get sick—not as sick, anyway. Can I list five things I am grateful for? How do I act when I am grateful? Do I see the value in making this a ritual?

## June 17

*"I would much rather have regrets about not
doing what people said, than regretting not doing
what my heart led me to and wondering what life would
have been like if I'd just been myself."*

*Brittany Renée (born 1986)*

---

In addiction, certain people co-signed our bullshit; we counted on them to help rationalize that we weren't all that bad. A lot of us recall admitting powerlessness as a superficial gesture at first. We weren't willing to go to any lengths; we just wanted to get the heat off. Saying "uncle" was often an act to tell loved ones what they wanted to hear. We were not only conning our loved ones; we were also kidding ourselves.

Some of us get a rare flash of introspection—a candid voice inside that knows we are beaten and cannot afford to be prideful. Some call this a spiritual awakening, a moment of clarity or a postcard from our subconscious. In such instances we don't listen to others; we follow our hearts.

The longer we are clean and sober, the more twists and turns our lives take. We care what others have to say. We can take advice but we have our own unique paths and we follow our own muses. We have self-worth now and we aren't afraid to try and fail. We don't blame ourselves or others for mistakes; they are an intrinsic result of trying new things. When we are unsure, sometimes the best thing to do is to try something. Then we can back off if that turns out not to sit well with us.

What do I see when I look in the mirror today? Am I being true to myself? Am I following my heart or just playing it safe?

# June 18

*"To have faith is to trust yourself to the water. When you swim you don't grab hold of the water, because if you do you will sink and drown. Instead you relax, and float."*

*Alan Watts (1915–1973)*

---

An old-timer asks a newcomer, "Do you believe the program works or do you have faith the program works?" "I thought we had to resign from the debating society when we got here," replies the newcomer, "Are we playing the semantics game? What's the difference between *belief* and *faith*?"

"If I told you that I could tie a rope from the roof of one 40-storey building to another and wheel a wheelbarrow across the rope you might say, 'OK, fine, I believe you,'" explains the old-timer. "But if you had *faith*, sight unseen, you would sit in the wheelbarrow. Now I ask you again, do you *believe* the program works or do you have *faith*?" That's a good question. Are we sitting in the wheelbarrow of recovery or evaluating the program from the sidelines?

Living sober is like swimming—it requires an act of faith. It requires jumping in and trusting in the process. It takes faith to stay sober. Another member may say, "It gets better. Maybe not right away, maybe not today, but it does." But it is us, not them, who have to play our cards and take our chances.

Many of us are waiting for proof from a program that doesn't feel a need to impress us. It is by facing fear of the unknown that we find courage and it is by taking an extraordinary leap of faith that we expand our comfort zone. As is the case when learning to swim, being preoccupied with the "what ifs" makes us anxious and stifles us. We can *expect* the best, or if that's too controlling for us, *welcome* the best.

Do I have positive expectations about my sobriety today? Reluctance is something I have to face some days. Each Step along the way requires preparation, but eventually I have to dive into the unknown one more time and do it.

# June 19

*"Most men pursue pleasure with such
breathless haste that they hurry past it."*

Søren Kierkegaard (1813–1855)

---

The original directions for Fourth Step inventory include listing resentments, fears and sex conduct. When the Big Book was written, sex was not considered its own addiction. Founders presented the illness angle and busted the myth that drinking was a moral failing. Sexual misconduct was still treated as a character flaw. Any endorphin-boosting activity, such as fantasy, risky behavior, masturbation or watching porn, can become obsessive-compulsive.

Many addicts have intimacy issues. The addiction premise argues that sex addiction or aversion is a progressive, mental and physical illness or disorder. Some of us found sexual preoccupation became more unmanageable after arresting a primary addiction. "Everyone needs a hobby" or a "good man's folly" might rationalize misbehavior. The addict's or codependent's cycle sometimes involves binging and purging; we go from sexual anorexia to indiscriminant acting out. When we are *on the wagon* we may speak very moralistically; when we are acting out we might isolate in shame.

Even if we have rejected the moral rigidity of religion or society, it takes time to articulate our true values and bring our behavior in line with these values. Our sexual boundaries say a lot about who we are. We owe it to ourselves to be authentic and integral. Even for the emotionally healthiest of us, romance and sexuality are fraught with insecurities, judgments and cat-and-mouse reactions.

Do I know that real intimacy demands a level of honesty and maturity that will challenge me? Am I learning about patterns and triggers when I look at my sex conduct and fantasy? Are binging and purging part of my addiction modus operandi? Do I play the victim, perpetrator and/or rescuer roles in my relations with others? Am I loveable? Do I feel there is enough love in the world for me?

## June 20

*"Admitted to ourselves and to another human being,
the exact nature of our wrongs."*

*Step Five, secular version
from aatorontoagnostics.com*

---

A lot is made of the importance of doing this epic step. In Step Five, blind faith is required in order to share, out loud, things that have never been shared.[64] We have to overcome a classic fear: "What if I am rejected for my deeds or for who I am?" Sponsors will sometimes say, "You have one thing that you still aren't sure if you're going to disclose today. Tell me that one thing first and all the rest will be easy."

Some members report that after Step Five they feel like authentic members of the fellowship and planet earth for the first time. Masks, fears and compartmentalization kept us isolated while we were out there and can continue to do so in recovery. Some of us expected so much from Step Five that we feel let down when a white light experience doesn't follow it.

A Twelve Step room is a place where we can easily get by behind a façade of being serious about our recovery chores. Most members won't hold us accountable for what we say we are going to do. Shame is a triggering part of our addiction cycles and Step Five gives us a chance to be accepted for who we are. The feeling of being bad or unworthy may be completely lifted. But it won't last. Through Steps Six and Seven we will evaluate how we think and feel about ourselves and train ourselves to act accordingly toward others and view ourselves with respect.

When I am doing this Step as the teller or listener, can I remember that every experience is different? Can I avoid expectations? Can I be open, willing and present?

# June 21

*"Let no one be slow to seek wisdom when he is young, nor weary in the search thereof when he is grown old. For no age is too early or too late for the health of the soul."*

*Epictetus (AD 55–135)*

---

Seeking is in style, no matter what the season. Maybe old dogs can't learn new tricks, but we're not dogs, we're homo sapiens with 85 cubic inch brains. When we were getting sober, few of us expected to hang around with this *group of losers* any longer than we had to. When we'd been around for a few months and noticed other members still going to meetings every week after years in the fellowship, we wondered if they lacked imagination or got some sick satisfaction from watching the younger members vibrating in discomfort.

For some, Twelve & Twelve meeting attendance is a finite commitment until we get our bearings. For others, recovery is a way of life, a life-long learning program. Those who quit meetings are not closed-minded and have not stopped growing. This is an individual journey and where our roads take us and how we manage is so unique, it could take a lifetime to find someone working the program exactly the way we do. Many of us may mimic someone in one aspect of their program but are worlds apart in another aspect of recovery.

Relapse can happen—how many times will it take to get this thing? Relapse is a characteristic of the disease more than a statement about how willing or hard-working we are. They don't tell a cancer patient to come back when they are serious about getting well after they fall out of remission. Sobriety, like life, is something we just keep working at. If sobriety comes quickly we can't forget that there will be other challenges ahead.

Did I think I would get this thing in a few months at most? The great thing about having more to learn is it keeps me engaged. Do I fancy myself the teacher or student?

# June 22

*"Vizzini: 'Inconceivable!' Inigo Montoya: 'You keep using this word. I do not think it means what you think it means.'"*

*The Princess Bride (1987)*

---

"This is a spiritual program, not a religious one." Does this mean what we think it means? Is *Twelve-Steppery* a religion? At the core of religion is the recognition that humans are flawed. Christianity says we are damned because we sin. Buddhism says we lack enlightenment. But religions offer a cure—Jesus and Buddhism can save us. Advertising exploits our propensity to feel incomplete with similar flaw/solution gimmicks: "You are flawed—our product will make you feel complete." The Twelve Step model has some of this flaw/solution dogma. We repeatedly admit we are powerless, immoral and insane. Addiction as a disease is a premise but it's far from a proven fact. The American Medical Association concurs with the illness model which gives them license to treat us. Even medicine comes with faith and dogma.

Our harshest critics keep using the word cult, but we do not think it means what they think it means. The Merriam-Webster dictionary defines a health-cult as a system for the cure of a disease based on dogma set forth by the promulgator. In AA's case, the cultish beliefs include the conviction that alcoholics can never drink socially again and must attend meetings. These are tenets AA members follow. However, no one has to accept anyone else's beliefs or deny their own. Reification and dogma raise ye olde *cult-barometer*. Weekends with "self-help Twelve Step specialists" interpreting the Big Book for followers promulgate the idea of *charismatic leaders*. Intensive weekends are fine when they are fellowship-based—but not when they're based on leaders and followers. The existence of leaders and followers signals a program of learned dependency.

What does "spiritual, not religious" mean to me? Do I ever label others as priests, cardinals, teachers or gurus? Do I ever treat the literature as sacred or assign magical qualities to the fellowship?

## June 23

*"Know that although in the eternal scheme of things you are small, you are also unique and irreplaceable, as are all your fellow humans everywhere in the world."*

*Margaret Laurence (1926–1987)*

Gaining perspective, or right-sizing our capacity and our role in the universe, is a big part of Twelve & Twelve recovery. Recovery can be a lifestyle more than a project. Each Step along the way allows us to see more of who we are and how we fit in. "We seek spiritual progress rather than spiritual perfection" is what Bill Wilson wrote in the fifth chapter of *Alcoholics Anonymous*. We keep seeking progress. We learn to see ourselves and our growth through the eyes of a best friend. Best friends appreciate us just the way we are. Sure we have some work to do. However, we are already worthy, based on who we are now, not on what we do or on the conditions of self-improvement and attaining certain goals. So, we all have damage; that doesn't make us unworthy.

We are part of a universe but not the center of it. We notice those around us and we are concerned for their welfare. There is training built into peer-to-peer recovery to help us think of our fellows. We need their perspective and some of our healing comes from helping them. We soon learn how much richer our lives are when we give a damn about others. To matter in the lives of others evokes a feeling that money can't buy and intoxicants can't replicate.

Can I enjoy myself today, just the way I am? Can I enjoy the others in my life? Everyone in this world is unique and significant. I don't have to like everyone, but why not cultivate compassion for them anyway? How I feel about myself and how I treat others are connected. It works both ways. If I am gentle and forgiving with myself, I cut others some slack; when I am hard on myself, am I not the perfectionist, and hyper-critical of everyone else?

# June 24

*"To move an emotion, move a muscle."*

*Heard around the rooms*

---

Action brings about healing in a way that reading, talking, thinking and promising cannot. Sticking to our bottom lines one day at a time turns hope into confidence. Study and meditation, counseling or regular check-ins with a sponsor make it possible for healthy patterns to replace bad habits. By *making a list and checking it twice*, in Steps Four through Nine, we alter how we feel about ourselves and the world. If we feel nervous, let's get involved in service. That's the action of Step Twelve. Doing can free our minds from nagging insecurity or uncertainty. We can be immobilized by a seemingly overwhelming to-do list. A friend may say, "Stop ruminating on the whole list and do just one thing on the list." We move a muscle and it defuses the catatonic state of our feelings. Exercise or travel can help to heal us. It doesn't solve our problems, but moving muscles relieves the tension, turning an unworkable situation into a manageable one.

Doing can also be avoiding. Just ask our friends from Online Gaming Anonymous. In 2011, 72% of USA citizens between six and forty-four years of age played video games. Extreme gamers (people who play more than 50 hours per week) make up 4% of users. Extreme gamers could build 48 Empire State Buildings a week if they were all engineering instead of gaming. Eight to twelve year old boys gamed sixteen hours a week. Girls played ten hours a week. After the age of thirteen, boys increased game time, while girls decreased their gaming hours per week. Is this a serious trend? One Farmville player shook her baby to death for interrupting her game, an Ohio teen shot his parents for taking away Halo and a Korean child starved while the parents raised a virtual child in an Internet Café.[65]

There aren't right and wrong hobbies and activities. We get enthusiastic about what we do, too—no problem. The key for addicts is to check in about how we are doing and how it is making us feel. The clues will be oblivious to us if we are getting out of hand.

Doing is a great cure for ruminating. However, avoiding feelings that need to be faced keeps me sick. Do I keep a balance? Who do I check in with for a second opinion?

# June 25

*"Snobbery? But it's only a form of despair."*
*Joseph Brodsky (1940–1996)*

"Do You Think You're Different?" was an AA pamphlet compiled by Barry L. and published in 1976. In this pamphlet, feeling superior and feeling inferior are described as being two sides of the same ego-driven coin. Chronic uniqueness (being the best or the worst) leads to isolation and despair. Do we see an "us-vs.-them" fellowship of literalists vs. realists, people with concurrent disorders vs. pure addicts, bleeding deacons vs. youth or members vs. earth-people? Focusing on differences in cultures, creeds, family histories or astrological signs is a game we play called, "Look how unique I am!" Even in sports, fans can get carried away, viewing their favored teams as *the team* of destiny and vilifying the opponent. But chronically feeling unique can lead to a distorted belief in a hierarchy of people.

We may implode if we have a negative self-image, destroying ourselves because we are uniquely flawed and unworthy. The opposite is personal megalomania which is a delusional concept of the significance of one's self or one's race. This can be seen when one faction in a home group storms off to start their own group or, in extreme cases, this human characteristic can explode into violent, destructive atrocities that shape history, as in wars that are the result of religious conflicts. Anthropologist Ernest Becker wrote *Escape from Evil* to comment on mankind at its worst, describing the tendency of societies in support of certain worldviews to make pre-emptive strikes to wipe out differing worldviews.[66] This highest form of snobbery is still rooted in despair. Even if we feel superior, we still won't live forever. Our power is limited and our time is finite. Becker said, "To live fully is to live with an awareness of the rumble of terror that underlies everything." Nothing assuages our own insecurities and anxieties like power over another.

The higher road or spiritual way is to own up to our insecurities and to humbly be in accordance with our fears and egotistical tendencies. Personal inventory and checking in with our closest confidants helps to keep us each level-headed.

Do I see that my snobbery (superiority) is no more than fear and insecurity? Or do I tend to get off on being uniquely inferior? In truth we are all slightly different, and we all have a right to be here.

# June 26

*"Vision without action is a daydream.*
*Action without vision is a nightmare."*

Japanese Proverb

---

So we've been pretty good in this text at focusing on *our* misgivings and the Steps *we* need to take to move forward. Just for the guilty pleasure of it, if only for a paragraph, let's pick on those around us in meetings. We have all heard people in meetings say, "When I do my Step Four, then..." They said the same thing twelve weeks earlier in the last Step Four meeting we were in. Some people might recover by osmosis, by simply putting their asses in chairs—or what we might call *ass-mosis*. Staying clean and sober is good enough for many, but the benefits of the Twelve Steps can only be realized by doing them. The nightmare (for us) of action without vision can come in the form of a member who seems to speak just to hear her/his own voice. They have no point; they simply put their lips into action. Hearing others theorize about the Steps, devoid of firsthand experience, is a "nightmare" for the rest of us.

OK, so how did that feel? What's more exhilarating than talking about the shortcomings of others? Getting back to introspection, we see that we may be throwing stones at others while we live in glass houses ourselves. Have we not talked big in meetings and then not followed through? Have we shared at meetings or done service work just looking for kudos? We are responsible for our own recovery. If we have an issue with any of the Twelve Steps, we struggle through or replace these exercises with something more authentic—the Steps are only suggestions. There has never been one right way to do them. The reflection in the mirror can tell us if our vision is pure and if our actions are integral.

So, today, am I going through the motions or am I working with a vision? What project that I have been talking about doing will I roll up my sleeves and get to work on today?

# June 27

*"A good scare is worth more to a man than good advice."*

*Ed Howe (1858–1929)*

---

When we look back on our *days of wine and roses*, many of us recall that someone cared enough to confront or warn us early in our addiction. But many of us either rejected the advice emphatically or told the person that we agreed and we were committed to change—some day, but not today. So what precipitated making the move to seriously consider recovery? Was it a "good scare?"

In recovery, a more contented life would include more proactive and less reactive motivation. We don't want to stay in the habit of waiting on everything until it's an emergency. Do we file our taxes on time or wait for a foreboding letter? If we own a car do we get the brakes done at the first sound of wear or not until the car skids to a halt, barely averting an accident? There is a cost to procrastination. With taxes and bills, there can be penalties. With car or home repair the costs of neglect may be more substantial than a financial slap on the wrist. What is the emotional toll of ruminating about these things without taking action and what self-talk do we inflict upon ourselves? Do we *should* all over ourselves? Are we rebelling against routine or authority like a child does? Are we over-extended, neglecting or avoiding our own or someone else's "good advice?"

Persistent unmanageability that follows us through recovery could be a symptom of emotional problems in the same way liver enlargement could be a sign that someone is drinking too much. A chaotic life is a tiring life. It's more work than living with order. Is this unmanageability a smokescreen masking repressed hurt, regret or grief—things we'd rather not think about at all? We write these things off as lazy when, in truth, they are way more work. So it's worth asking the question of what's going on if unmanageability persists in recovery.

How manageable is my life today? What are the underlying issues? What's one thing I can commit to doing that will help make my life more manageable? Am I waiting for a good scare? Do I feel integral when I do what needs to be done every day?

# June 28

*"The harder you fight to hold on to specific assumptions, the more likely there's gold in letting go of them."*

John Seely Brown

---

The author of today's quote devoted much of his life to innovation. Assumptions are barriers to innovation because they blind us to opportunities. In some rooms we hear "I had a thinking problem." Twelve & Twelve philosophy didn't invent the cognitive dissonance paradigm. Sigmund Freud and then later his daughter, Anna (1895–1982), studied defense mechanisms like denial that play havoc with untenable truths. In *The Ecologist*, Pat Thomas expressed how these ideas are transferable in his article on climate change denial—one more way we sidestep an inconvenient truth.[67] Thomas's article, "How to beat denial—a 12-step plan" identified the following: *Simple Denial* is a digging in of our heels, refusing to bend to any facts or reason; *Minimizing* makes the problem less serious; *Rationalizing* crafts excuses; *Intellectualizing* sidesteps emotional engagement by theorizing; *Blaming* insists fault is elsewhere; *Diversion* points to "bigger" problems; *Bargaining* sees us negotiating deals that we won't be able to follow through with; *Passivity* has us surrendering to the futility or impossibility of problems; and *Hostility* uses "the best defense is a good offense" approach—like a porcupine, we hope they will find us too unpleasant to confront again.

Self-deception is old-hat to any addict. Maybe it's a function of the human condition to deny unpleasant truths. As addicts we have overcome denial before. This skill can be taken from the meetings to many outside battlefields. It would be a stubborn assumption indeed if we declared that our denial-busting capacity is to arrest our addiction only and take no responsibility to take this skill outside the rooms if and when it may do some good. A spiritual life takes effort and doesn't always agree with the crowd. Wouldn't it be karmic to spend the rest of our lives wrestling with other people's denial?

How familiar do these denial traps sound to me now? Of these rackets above, what's my favorite for avoiding unpleasant truths? Do I have skills learned in the rooms that could be a good example out in the community?

## June 29

*"Compassion literally means to feel with, to suffer with. Everyone is capable of compassion, and yet everyone tends to avoid it because it's uncomfortable. And the avoidance produces psychic numbing—resistance to experiencing our pain for the world and other beings."*

Joanna Macy (born 1929)

---

Narcissism is the antithesis of compassion. Healing from addiction involves breaking out of our parasitic, self-absorbed ways. Getting honest is hardest if we think of ourselves as people-pleasers. It takes rescuers longer to understand how the role they play is self-serving. We are "psychically numb" and feigning love. We may think of ourselves as loving and caring, misunderstood souls when we arrive in the rooms. As we explore more thoroughly, we see that the loneliness and self-abuse caused by our addiction-cycles reduced us to desperate, self-absorbed, manipulative and unauthentic people. Survival mode gave us provisional lives marred by shame and the rescuer role was a form of over-compensation. Our needs were met by being needed and appreciated.

Self-compassion is where it starts. We forgive ourselves for being emotionally immature or naïve. We work through our own feelings in a gentle way. Feelings of any kind are rough on the system when we are white-knuckling through the early days. "Feelings—I don't do feelings" is a common refrain in twenty-eight day programs. We get encouragement. We make healthy choices for ourselves. Effective compassion for others only follows freeing ourselves from our own self-abuse. Can we love another if we don't love ourselves?

It is true that anyone can help another, no matter how down and out they are. But when it comes to relating to others on a deep level, how can we help others if we still habitually repress our feelings? To be of the most service to others we have to do the work ourselves as far as healing, Step work or therapy is concerned.

Do I feel compassion? Am I still overwhelmed and numbed out? Do I enjoy listening to others or is it a chore?

*"We worked at a comfortable pace and rest before we get
tired. To remind ourselves, we check our level of energy before
proceeding to our next activity. We do not get
'wound up' in our work so we do not have to unwind."*

*W.A. Tools of Recovery*, Workaholics Anonymous

---

Pace, prioritizing and perfectionism are words that any addict can use as a focus for a spot inventory when life starts to feel like it is too much. Prioritizing ensures a time for rest, work and play. When new activities are added, something has to go; we don't overextend ourselves. We can't say "yes" to everything. Under-scheduling allows ample time for each task, for travel time and for relaxation, which means not pressuring others or getting pressured. When we feel tense or off stride, we take a few deep breaths to get grounded.

Perfectionism and impatience sidetrack sober, balanced living and they are worth understanding. Do we ever forget we are human? Do we ever forget to ask for help? Some of us are workaholics and all of us have workaholics who impact our lives. Some of us are doubly blessed or double-losers, depending on how you look at concurrent disorders. Imbalance in work can lead to other addictions. There is no making up for lost time—that's an illusion. Impatience may be part of a chaotic life that kept things way too busy for touchy-feely time. Sometimes we are rushing for arbitrary self-imposed deadlines. What's that about? If we don't have time to do it right, how do we always find time to do it over? If perfectionism or impatience pesters us in recovery or, worse yet, if we self-righteously wear our impatience or perfectionism as badges of honor, why not check in with someone about this?

What makes me susceptible to work imbalance may be avoidance; busy-busy is a great place to hide in plain view. Do I come from a chaotic or dysfunctional background? Have I inherited naïve or unrealistic expectations? Is my pace good or am I impatient? Have I prioritized my day and left time for spontaneity? Am I a perfectionist? What does this tell me about my stage of recovery?

# July 1

*"Cautious, careful people, always casting about to
preserve their reputation and social standing
never can bring about reform."*

Susan B. Anthony, (1820–1906)

---

Anthony was a suffragette and her likeness had been burned in effigy by angry, resistant mobs. Society owes suffragettes a debt of gratitude for shattering the status quo and advancing civilization. We hear "all you have to do to get criticized in the fellowship is to do something—anything." By the second edition of the Big Book in 1955, Bill Wilson delighted in the fact that in regions of the globe dominated by various faiths (Judaism, Hinduism, Buddhism) AA's doctrine was being adapted to local worldviews. Like today's author, the change championed by General Service Office of the day met with resistance from members who thought that unchecked adaptation was reckless.

Twenty-three million addicts are in recovery in the USA alone.[68] The text *Alcoholics Anonymous* was available in over 40 languages by the 2010 World Conference of Alcoholics Anonymous. The American Medical Association (AMA) was presented with the thirty-millionth copy of the Big Book to commemorate, as AA General Service Board Chair Ward Ewing put it, "[The AMAs] helped A.A. erase stereotypes and spread the message of sobriety." Twelve & Twelve culture has had success in adapting to the needs of many addicts in new fellowships and through ever-changing times. Growth will always be celebrated in hindsight while resisted during implementation. It seems to be the human way. Critics wonder if more couldn't be done to reach out to those who don't know us and to accommodate minorities who don't all feel comfortable once they are inside our rooms. We must always strive to be better. Each of us will confront apathy, corruption, discrimination and abuse inside and outside of Twelve & Twelve fellowships. Will we ignore the need to adapt for fear of what change will bring? Will we be concerned about reputation and popularity or the needs of others?

Do I stand up for what I believe in or do I stand where I gain the most attention and approval?

# July 2

*"If you have to talk to more than three people about the same problem, you don't want help, you want attention."*

*Heard around the rooms*

---

Checking in with other members is a key to mitigating *stinking thinking*. Ideas sound different when we say them out loud. In some fellowship circles, this is called "getting current." More often than not, we determine our best course of action just by hearing ourselves articulate the problem out loud. It feels good to relieve the tension. "A problem shared is a problem halved" is a reminder given at the end of some meetings, encouraging newcomers to talk to someone. Sometimes, someone we never suspected would be helpful to us has a relevant experience that gives us insight.

Lone wolves who get to meetings just as they start and dart away the moment they end can expand their comfort zones by finding running mates in the rooms. Like us, they are going to meetings, focusing on getting well and learning sober strategies for living. It's good to be authentic with these people. Engaging with the fellowship helps many of us get and stay clean and sober.

Today's quip reminds us that sharing a problem doesn't solve the problem—it just relieves the tension. We should be honest with ourselves about why we are opening our mouths. Do we want to understand, solve a problem, self-justify, elicit sympathy or hear ourselves talk? Sharing is one tool in the recovery toolbox. There is also Step work and/or therapy, reading, solitary time, journaling and/or meditating. Some of us love to share and some of us don't. Some of us can grow by passing once in a while, even when we have an urge to be heard; sharing the time is a form of sharing, too. For some of us, learning to be vulnerable by letting others know us better helps us feel worthy. Those of us who are reluctant to speak up can remember that we never know who we might help by sharing.

What does "living in the solution" mean to me when it comes to sharing with others?

# July 3

*"You only live twice: Once when you are born. And once when you look death in the face."*

*Ian Fleming (1908–1964)*

---

Just twice, you say ol' boy? How many of us have had several close calls? Lots of Twelve Step members treat their dry-date as a second chance at life. Some of us think that recovery is for quitters—living on the edge ends when recovery begins. If we harbor romantic notions of returning to the glory days, abstinence looks like purgatory, or death.

But wait—maybe there are *many* times in recovery when we "look death in the face." Every ego-shedding stage of recovery is another small death of our narcissistic selves. Shame and guilt dissipate a little more with each Step. With each demon we face, we become a little more courageous and authentic. Self-disgust is just the flip-side of grandiosity; both are distortions of a healthy self-image. We may struggle with our self-image for the rest of our lives. As we gain perspective, the two-headed dragon of self-loathing and overcompensation has less power over us.

James Bond is the epitome of courage, never shirking his responsibility or giving in to his fear. Even when faced with insurmountable odds, his duty trumps his impulse for self-preservation. We live vicariously through him as he lives his life to the fullest. If only we could show such composure. But like 007 we had no say in our lives. Addiction was unknown, chaotic and traumatic. Recovery continues to be unpredictable. We face change—stranger than fiction some of the time. Are we going to live twice or wither away? Denial, resignation, self-justification and blame-shifting will all look us in the eyes. They threaten our lives as barriers to our potential and our usefulness. Bond's duty was to queen and country—ours is to fulfill our potential.

At the end of life will I regret not doing something that I should have given an honest try? Is there something I could stand to apply some *double-oh* bravado to?

# July 4

*"In the grip of addiction or obsessive behavior, life becomes chaotic and crisis-filled. Addicts and coaddicts live in excess and on the edge. Because they do not complete things, they have much unfinished business. They lack boundaries, so they often do not use good judgment. Others see them as irresponsible and lacking in common sense."*

A Gentle Path through the 12 Steps *by Patrick Carnes,*

---

A "disease of perception" is how the book *Alcoholics Anonymous* describes addiction. Behavior, including risk-taking, adrenaline dependency and establishing poor boundaries, has resulted in impulsive undertakings, incomplete projects and being late for appointments. Havoc in our lives impacts those we love, in addition to ourselves. Being realistic, responsible and sensible sounds so simple, but sometimes in recovery sober-mindedness seems elusive. With sober second thought, we sit with every good idea for a minute before acting. Impulse is a reflex. Careful consideration of our options is a new way to operate.

When we unravel the cause and effect of the calamity of our lives we wonder why we have acted so self-destructively. Some say chaos is a smokescreen that protects us or hides us from our feelings. We fear that our own guilt, shame and anger, if faced, will be so overwhelming that we will be consumed or destroyed by these fang-bearing emotions. Is this realistic? If we face repressed feelings are they likely to grow into demons three times our size, suck out our guts and spit out the shells of our corpses? No, but who ever accused us of being realistic?

What chaos do I keep in my life? Am I ready to let go and see what might be hidden behind it? Am I the type of person who is at home with peace and quiet?

## July 5

*"Then, without realizing it, you try to improve yourself at the start of each new day; of course, you achieve quite a lot in the course of time. Anyone can do this; it costs nothing and is certainly very helpful. Whoever doesn't know it must learn and find by experience that a quiet conscience makes one strong."*

*Anne Frank (1929–1945)*

---

Who doesn't sometimes look at the task of recovery and feel overwhelmed? Anne Frank reminds us that life is lived a day at a time and if we make small progress each day great strides happen over time. When we are new, just staying clean and sober until the next meeting can be all we can muster and, before we know it, a month of continuous sobriety has passed and we have new hope. The quiet conscience that makes us strong, referred to above, comes from accumulated days of right living.

Through our imperfections we grow to be better members of society. Personal inventory in Step Ten isn't about shaming and persecuting ourselves. It's about learning and improving. We look at how we handled situations, consider what improvements we can make, correct what we can, and chalk the rest up to learning. We forgive our mistakes and practice being less harsh in our judgment of others.

Do I welcome my setbacks as life lessons and know that they are part of the human experience? Goals are worthy beacons to follow but do I appreciate each day's progress, including the back and forth? Do I have the strength that comes from a quiet conscience? A purpose in my life makes me happy and it takes wisdom to know that searching and striving—in other words, the struggle—are what gives vitality to our time on Earth. Life is the journey, not the destination.

# July 6

*"We must believe in free will, we have no choice."*

*Isaac Bashevis Singer, (1904–1991)*

---

Contemporary sage Hal Lee Luyah has expressed the same conundrum in saying "Man was predestined to have free will." In purely scientific terms the idea of free will is an illusion. A physicist and a philosopher will draw very different conclusions on the topic of human will. We can imagine that a theologian and a cosmologist could both agree on much of determinism. It's just the "why?" that would be the stumbling block. Is destiny determined by the momentum of the most recent billion years or is it a divine plan? Incalculable variables landed us in meetings, talking to each other about the merciless obsession of addiction. Like dominos in a line, here we are. So what now? Are we driven by a sophisticated set of circumstances that render our thoughts and decisions inevitable in the same way our hearts pump blood without our consent—or are we masters of our own destiny?

In recovery terms, self-will vs. the higher power's will is about moral, disciplined behavior altering choices we make—to pick up a drink or not, go to the casino vs. a meeting, buy cake or broccoli or both. Even the most determined of determinists will concede that many life choices are evitable. We can avoid hardship, we can choose noble paths, we can stop to help someone in need, we can drive over the speed limit or follow the rules. Every choice has consequences. For theists, there is a distinction between the addict's will and God's will. One is a path to ruin. Some say we are at fault and some blame the booze or the drug of choice. On the other path, we accept our limits. We ask for help and we restructure our behaviors or rewire our thinking (depending on how we look at it). Twelve & Twelve rooms don't have a uniform position on the issue of will. Some love the semantics debate and some of us aren't caught up in wording.

George H. Mead (1863–1931) said, "Society is unity in diversity" which is very true in our meetings. We don't need a consensus on the nature of human will to share our experiences with each other.

How do I feel about will today? Am I accountable for my choices?

# July 7

*"I was angry with my friend—I told my wrath,*
*my wrath did end. I was angry with my foe—I told it not,*
*my wrath did grow."*

William Blake (1757–1827)

---

Resentment is what we call wrath that grows. The author suggests that anger is different with loved ones than it is with foes. How many enemies could be befriended if we had the capacity for honest discourse, if we could work to express our anger in healthy ways? We don't have to be enemy-free to be successful in recovery. In fact, our rightful paths may rattle the foundation, which may lead to more adversaries. Understanding anger is essential for sustained recovery, and personal inventory plays an important role in mapping out the cause and effect of our conflicts. Today we look at Step Four.

First-time Fourth Steppers are cautioned that this list is no magic pill; it is a step in the right direction to honest self-appraisal. Many of us do Step Four more than once just as some businesses do a complete inventory every year or two. Each new inventory isn't an admission of failure of the previous stocktaking. Rather, it is a new balance sheet on a new day to quantify progress and circumstances.

Some inventories look at the good and bad: shameful acts vs. great accomplishments, healthy expressions of fear and anger vs. unhealthy expressions of fear and anger and our histories of deception and avoidance vs. examples of bravery and honesty. Mismanaged feelings are addiction triggers. Step Four uncovers the emotional triggers that set off the freeze, fight and flight reflexes. Like a blueprint, Step Four shows us how we're wired, opening the door to change.

If I am awaiting my first or tenth Step Four, are my expectations in check and do I have a plan—a timeline for starting and completing it? Are anger and other triggering feelings still a mystery to me?

# July 8

*"We relax and take it easy. We don't struggle. We are often surprised how the right answers come after we have tried this for a while. What used to be the hunch or the occasional inspiration gradually becomes a working part of the mind."*

Alcoholics Anonymous, 86–87

---

This extravagant promise is offered at the end of discussion in the Big Book on Step Eleven, the art of meditation, consciousness and finding our rightful paths in life. When we are feeling psychically and emotionally bankrupt, this is one of many claims that seem unrealistic or like cheesy salesmanship. In "Into Action," this claim follows a promise that alcohol will not tempt the recovered alcoholic. A drink will look no more attractive than poison. In early stage abstinence and/or recovery, we hardly dare dream of such carefree living.

Time away from our addictive patterns doesn't turn us into model citizens automatically. What we do with our clean time determines how transforming our recovery becomes. The promises of recovery unfold, sometimes quickly, sometimes gradually, but not in a straight line. Sometimes we are on the path and sometimes we stumble or nap for a while. Thoughts, sensations and feelings come and go. Some will overwhelm or derail us. Sometimes we are inspired or we feel carried through the day. We are ensured progress but denied perfection. A seeker's work is never done. We aren't slaves to the recovery regimen but seeking is better than stagnating. If we are cerebral addicts we slowly learn to take cues from our intuition. If we are deeply feeling members we exercise our rational capacities, without betraying our creativity.

I can learn meditation. It may feel unusual, but not for long. Can I see how it can become a working part of my routine, just like sleeping, eating or exercising?

# July 9

*"It is not a sign of good health
to be well adjusted to a sick society."*

*Jiddu Krishnamurti (1895–1986)*

---

Krishnamurti was an Indian-born Hindu thinker and lecturer who influenced education and politics in Great Britain, the USA and India. This quote suggests that being well-adjusted and fitting in are not necessarily synonymous.

Subjective Well-Being (SWB) is a term psychologists use to measure how individuals and whole societies are doing.[69] Happiness comes to us from the pursuit of worthy goals and activities of right living. SWB does not come from more and more of a good thing. From our knowledge of personal addiction, we see this same greedy craziness in groups. In a world seemingly gone mad, copious consumption creates a feeding frenzy. Everyone wants some because everyone wants some. How are we to behave when supply is finite? Do we panic, hoard or adjust our consumption and behaviors to conserve supply?

Throughout our lives we find new applications for lessons learned as newcomers. We remember "First things first," "The best things in life are free" or "It's more important to want what we have than have what we want." Society and government both mortgage the future and deny today's realities. We see the addict's rationalizations in so many news stories. Our continued recovery is a priority and we have to remember this any time we feel the crazy-making from the outside world pulling us in. When we feel strong we have unique insights that can help us be part of the solution. We were certainly part of the problem at one time. As addicts we were takers, borrowers and chaos makers.

Perspective and attitude make all the difference. Do I keep my tasks, my abilities and my needs right-sized? What does healthy living mean? How has my definition of a rich, full life changed over time?

# July 10

*"It means giving up searching for a home, becoming a refugee, a lonely person who must depend on himself ... . Fundamentally, no one can help us. If we seek to relieve our loneliness, we will be distracted from the path. Instead, we must make a relationship with loneliness until it becomes aloneness."*

*Chögyam Trungpa Rinpoche (1939–1987)*

---

In his book *The Myth of Freedom and the Way of Meditation*, this contemporary Tibetan Buddhist author opens our eyes to a way of seeing self-support. Twelve & Twelve fellowships avoid owning property, decline outside contributions and promote the tenet of self-support throughout the fellowship.[70] We write the agendas for our meetings, pay for our rent and literature and forward what we have left for fellowship-wide services. We each take turns supporting outreach, service meetings or running retreats or conferences. The illusion that acquiring assets will make us feel secure is baseless for both individuals and fellowships. Each generation of members is accountable to themselves and they pass on the idea of independence and personal responsibility to the next generation of members.

What does it mean to make a relationship with loneliness? As a spiritual principle we don't seek "outside contributions" to cure us, make us whole or reassure us. The Seventh Tradition means we are alone in our financial affairs. We may have sponsors but we are in charge of recovery—it isn't done to us or given to us. We may feel connected to our groups but not dependent on them for every decision. We grow beyond being dependent or enabling others. Some of us have families but we don't *need* them to be complete. We ought never depend on treatment centers to bring us newcomers, the media to speak well of us or expect that someone else will assume stewardship of our fellowship's legacy.

Am I "fully self supporting, declining outside contributions" as a spiritual daily practice?

# July 11

*"You cannot change anything in your life with intention alone, which can become a watered-down, occasional hope that you'll get to tomorrow. Intention without action is useless."*

*Caroline Myss (born 1952)*

---

"I am going to: stop smoking, eat better, work the Steps harder, stop criticizing myself, start working out, get active in service..." We make declarations of our intentions. With conviction that would fool a polygraph, we have said that tomorrow we are going to change, only to wake up with a story about why it just isn't right to begin today, but tomorrow for sure we'll get started.

Ours is a program of action. Yes, we do learn from reading program literature and a myriad of other great works on recovery. The experiences and examples of our peers at meetings also encourage us, and socializing after meetings fosters new and deeper relationships. But lasting recovery comes from action—writing, meditating, altering our behaviors and systematically making amends. This is where lasting change comes from.

The FEAR acronym—False Evidence Appearing Real—only gets worse when we ruminate. Action dispels fear and brings integrity to our intentions. Once in motion we often wonder what we were waiting for. Many feared outcomes that take our thoughts hostage never materialize.

Is fear holding me back? What does "integrity" mean to me? Do I still have self-improvement projects that I keep putting off? What about promises I have made to others? Just for today, can I commit to taking action whenever worries stop me cold in my tracks? Tomorrow I can return to worry, in place of action, if I prefer. Today I take action with everything I said I would or should do.

# July 12

*"There is no truth sure enough to justify persecution."*
*John Milton (1604–1674)*

---

If we fall prey to the seductiveness of moral disgust, all humility is lost. If we take the extra step of verbally or physically persecuting others, we will be known as people to keep a distance from. AA members enjoy rallying behind "Appendix II" in the AA Big Book: "There is a principle which is a bar against all information, which is proof against all argument and which cannot fail to keep a man in everlasting ignorance—that principle is contempt prior to investigation" (This has been erroneously credited to Herbert Spencer). The acid test when we rhyme off chapter and verse is this: Are we speaking of *our* closed-mindedness or are we pointing the finger at *someone else*, calling on The Big Book as our witness to a crime? Gossip and judgment are tempting when we reek of self-justification. Offering a *loving appraisal* rationalizes blatant inventory-taking of someone else. Many of us have institutional rage. Governments, banks, utilities and all of their inefficiencies and injustices are justified targets of our wrath. It seems like a victimless crime. But it is we who are the victims, bent out of shape and suffering from our rage.

We all live in glass houses in recovery, and who are we to criticize the choices, behaviors or paths of anyone else? If we feel justified in our feelings we may soon feel justified in retaliation. Let's get some perspective. Perspective will help deter us from acting on our fantasies. History tends to be contemptible of the persecutor. Think of how we look now at parents who spanked their kids. Today that seems as odd as breastfeeding while smoking. The truth is that there is a seemingly normal activity we are doing today that the next generation will despise us for.

When am I most self-righteous? When am I intolerant? When I hate intolerant people, am I not then a hypocrite as well?

## July 13

*"Everyone has his own specific vocation or mission in life; everyone must carry out a concrete assignment that demands fulfillment. Therein he cannot be replaced, nor can his life be repeated, thus, everyone's task is unique as his specific opportunity to implement it."*

*Viktor Frankl (1905–1997)*

---

Without Leonardo da Vinci there would be no Mona Lisa. In her absence, what would the world's most famous work of art be? Without Frankl we would not have logotherapy/existential analysis.[71] Borrowing ideas from Sigmund Freud and Alfred Adler and using his personal experience in an Auschwitz death camp, Frankl found value in moving away from asking, "What is the meaning of my life?" He worked it backward by determining to do something meaningful with his life.

We don't have meaningful lives; we bring meaning to what we do. Even the most persecuted of us have choices within our limits. There are things we can do and these volitions can bring satisfaction. Inside Twelve Step rooms we are taught to act our way into good thinking, not think our way into good actions. From right living a calling may be found, inside the rooms or in another noble endeavor. A pleasant life is no good for addicts, wired for more-is-better. This predisposition renders the gift of modest indulgences a letdown. Purposefulness gives meaning in a way that indulgence can't.

Why the Mona Lisa is the world's most recognized masterpiece makes for great debate. What we see today is not what was created. The art has degraded so we cannot accurately picture the tones and colors of the masterpiece on the day of completion. We can only enjoy what has, and why it has, endured. The works of Bill Wilson and Viktor Frankl have also faded against new perspectives and discovery. Still, we see their contributions in the relay race of life. It is just as important to find our own purposes.

Have I discovered my unique purpose? Am I yearning for more meaning or more pleasure?

# July 14

*"The meaning of the Prajñāpāramitā is not to be looked for elsewhere: It exists within yourself."*

Master Aryadeva (Third Century AD)

---

"Prajñāpāramitā" translates as "the perfection of wisdom." The problem with *The Truth,* if we are seeking it from an outside source, is that there are so many versions of it. Looking for guidance is wiser than going it alone, but to expect the answers of life to be granted from an outside source is folly. Like pursuing substances or processes to fill our void, the idea that the truth is "out there" is never more than partly true. Clues and direction can come from outside sources but our journey in life involves finding our own truths. *The Truth* may be a moving target because, like the world around us, we are changing.

Buddhism differs from many other philosophies in that there is no deity to plead with for direction. Truth is an inside job—cultivated by an inner (rather than a higher) power. In meditation, the journey is the destination. Like perfection, meditation is a direction and not a place we hope to get to. Even the objective of living a noble life without desire is—in itself—a desire, so a sense of humor about our journey is essential to keep extremism at bay.

We hear in the fellowship that it's a "we" program, not an "I" program—we don't have to do this alone. But the reason the program works only for those who want it, not for all who need it, is that each person has to do the work: write the lists, muster the courage and face the truth about him or herself. No one will check to see if we've done our Twelve Step homework. If we do the work, we find enlightenment. Suffering is met with perspective instead of avoidance. We gain wisdom—it isn't granted. We accept the world as it is. We have power to help ourselves and others but not unlimited power.

With freedom comes responsibility. Am I waiting for something or someone? Do I take responsibility or do I delegate blame and wait for direction?

## July 15

*"Since nothing else has worked for them, many believe that the Steps are mystical and magical and as a result, these same persons fail to search for and identify the underlying principles that make them work. Working the Steps can create the miracle of sobriety but the miracle isn't magic. The miracle occurs because working the Twelve Steps allows people to use powerful principles of recovery. Those who are willing to dig beneath the surface and truly understand the principles upon which the Steps are based are better able to use the principles in their lives."*

Understanding the Twelve Steps, *by Terence T. Gorski*

---

Doing the Steps with blind faith will work. Let's consider the advantage of understanding the processes we are engaged in and the cognitive-behavioral transformations we go through. Doctors generally prefer patients who take an active role in health care instead of passively asking what pill to take and for how long. Active patients have better health and the reasons for this should be easy to see.

Turning it over and awaiting divine intervention has a proud heritage, but if we seek more freedom and more control then let's take an active interest in the process, inside the program and outside. No therapist should balk at us working with a sponsor and no sponsor should discourage new members seeking therapy; it is all part of a holistic, self-actualizing effort for those of us who need recovery-extra.

Bill Wilson jokingly referred to his own talk as "the bed-time story" because it comforted others to hear the story of how AA's founder got sober. But his story did not offer a gateway to Shangri-La; Wilson constantly sought medical and spiritual help for a better understanding of the recovery process and for outside issues as well. To think that Wilson saw a flash of light and never struggled again would be magical thinking. He was also quick to say that many were better examples of spiritual living than he was.

Do I apply magical qualities to phenomena that I can't explain? Can I explain "how it works" in my own words?

# July 16

*"Confront the dark parts of yourself, and work to banish them*
*with illumination and forgiveness. Your willingness to wrestle*
*with your demons will cause your angels to sing.*
*Use the pain as fuel, as a reminder of your strength."*

August Wilson (1945–2005)

---

"Searching and fearless moral inventory" is the original verbiage of *Twelve Steppery*. Many workbooks, articles and new-look inventory approaches have been adapted over the years to make the process more holistic and useful. Also of note: there are enough choices to stall us indefinitely. A good thing to remember for a first-time Step Four adventurer: it won't be perfect. It will be a good start at honest self-appraisal. Most of us will find it so useful we will do it again sometime. Life is never a final draft; each day involves a new edit and a new balance sheet.

Perfectionism can lead to *analysis paralysis*, stalling us from getting started. Preparation is important. However, there comes a point when getting started is more important than more preparation. The other stall factor is that we are very likely afraid. We may feel like kids facing a real-life Dracula. The shame we feel will be silenced with greater self-awareness and self-forgiveness. Our fears and deeds will not be the end of us.

Am I suffering from procrastination on Step Four or any other crucial tasks? If so, is it possible I am making too big a deal out of it? Step Four is an inventory that helps me gain perspective on what might be exaggerated strengths and weaknesses. I have to right-size the importance of this process, too.

## July 17

*"As the blessings of health and fortune have a beginning,
so they must also find an end. Everything rises but to fall,
and increases but to decay."*

*Sallust (86–34 BCE)*

---

The twenty-first century kicked off with a curious decline in AA population. AA still sells one million Big Books a year, and in the USA alone (2012), 12,000 treatment centers send a fresh batch of newcomers to AA every month. Court-ordered meeting attendance still happens, as do referrals and direct enquiries to AA hotlines. AA's 2011 census showed 2,133,842 members, 88,086 less than a decade previous.[72] So where are the newcomers going, and why aren't they staying? Or is it one old-timer trading his 2.6 meetings a week for each newcomer that arrives? Either way: no growth, according to AA's census. Over half of all groups and members are in the USA, whose population increased from 250 million to 312 million over 20 years ending with 2012. That's a 25% increase in population, so as a percentage of the population, AA membership in the USA has dropped 25% in twenty years.

The 1941 Jack Alexander article in *The Saturday Evening Post* caused a spike in membership following that printing. *Readers Digest* followed with glowing reports, as did other sources. In 1963 the first impactful criticism came from *Harper's*, in Dr. Cain's article, "Alcoholics Anonymous: Cult or Cure?" in which he said the AA dogma was a hindrance to research and enslaved alcoholics to AA itself (learned dependency). A lot of members wrote nasty letters to the magazine but Bill W. said the article was partly right and encouraged AA to pay attention to its critics.[73] Is AA preaching or listening today?

A January 2011 *Harper's* member's-eye view article was called "The Drunk's Club: A.A., The Cult That Cures." Some of the sentiment shows it's the same flawed but functional dogmatic AA of 1963. Even sacred cows will one day be dead cows. Will AA's 100th anniversary count twice or half the population of the 75th anniversary? That's a good question.

AA's future will be watched by all fellowships. What do I hope for our future? Complacency is costly—but so is panic. Can I think of ways I rest on my laurels? Do I get drunk on dogma?

*"Accept your backsliding as normal—as something that happens to almost all people who at first improve emotionally and then fall back. See it as part of your human fallibility. Don't make yourself feel ashamed when some of your old symptoms return, and don't think you have to handle them entirely by yourself and that it is weak for you to seek some additional help."*

*"How To Deal With Back Slide,"* SMART Recovery

---

Slips or setbacks are not the result of not working hard enough at recovery. We can see them as bad decisions without persecuting ourselves. It's better to see slips as indicators that adjustments may be needed. If we feel ashamed or humiliated we compound the problem by hiding the facts from others or staying away from meetings. Also, although it's reasonable to feel proud of our sobriety it's best not to see the accumulating months or years as a status symbol. Otherwise, it's harder to own up to slipping and starting over. We influence our bottom line adherence with our choices but there will always be forces and factors we can't prepare for. Some of us will maintain sobriety in one addiction and innocently cross that invisible line with a new obsessive-compulsive disorder. Is this the result of not working the program rigorously? Maybe we could have done better but shit happens, so there could be many reasons why we slip. Perhaps we will find ourselves in a new fellowship that deals with our new preoccupations. Maybe we want to try therapy. None of these personal choices signal failure.

As we progress, what it means to be clean and sober changes for us. Some of us take a good look at our caffeine intake or our smoking or our rationalizations about cash-register honesty, physical fitness, short-cut-seeking or imbalances in our work, health or home lives. "To err is human" is the point that today's quote makes. Recovery is not a competition; it's a journey.

Do I believe that effort, not just results, is what matters? Do I hold pernicious ideas about addiction resulting from a lack of character or do I see it like any other illness? Am I judgmental about relapse?

# July 19

*"Do not value either your children or your life
or anything else more than goodness."*

Socrates (469–399 BCE)

---

A bit of folk wisdom heard around the rooms is "anything you make more important than your recovery, you will lose." Work and family are part of our recovery, not an either/or proposition. None of these need be held above the others. There is nothing unhealthy about duty to family, employer or country. Duty is good. Socrates suggests that our commitment to goodness should be non-negotiable. What are we willing to take a bullet for? Are our values negotiable at gunpoint? We may have responsible positions, but the jobs, the roles and/or the trappings are not more important than our values. Goodness lifts us above the primal instinct to hoard, possess and control.

Being right, or seeking oblivion, comfort or numbness, as we learned in Step One, can be obsessions that form a power greater than us. Many of us planned on stopping tomorrow, or being good tomorrow. But when the rubber hit the road we clung to the familiar, sought relief and put off the right action for another day.

Do I put people, places and things in front of being good for goodness's sake? Is being good more righteous than getting good rewards?

# July 20

*"Life isn't about waiting for the storm to pass ...
It's about learning to dance in the rain."*

*Vivian Greene*

---

"If only" this, "if only" that. Bitch, bitch, bitch! Sometimes our moods are such that we could brighten up a whole room—by leaving it. "If only" is a popular way to start conversations in the world of sports, politics, entertainment or any other armchair activity. "If only" is a copout if it stands between us and the start of a spiritual (or some would say *natural*) journey. Our lives are here and now. We are good enough right now, the world is fair enough and we have enough to get by for today.

Perfectionism is customary among addicts. There is a Twelve Step trap some addicts fall into: approval and the need for it. We will overcompensate, we will act as if, we will set unrealistic goals and we will feel ashamed for not meeting them. A thirst for approval interferes with our abilities to accept life as it is. It gets worse with time if we fancy ourselves powers of example. In a peer-to-peer fellowship we may never get called on our perfectionism by others. Everyone's working their own program. Also, flogging ourselves about how we have fallen short will be applauded by fellow perfectionists. We hear, "It gets better. Try a little harder and stay a little longer." Unconditional self-approval can start now. We are imperfect. Life is chaotic. The future is uncertain. This is here, this is now and this is as good as it gets.

It's raining, I am dancing and life is fine! Can I see myself being happy no matter what the circumstances?

# July 21

*"Judgment is given to men that they may use it. Because it may be used erroneously, are men to be told that they ought not to use it at all?"*

*John Stuart Mill (1806–1873)*

---

Being wrong isn't wrong. We generally get things wrong before we get them right. Reveling in the failings of others is unimaginative and may be overcompensation for anxiety we feel about our own misgivings. Mistakes are part of life. Ideas begin as concepts, are tested by trial and error, and eventually some become facts. In time rock-solid facts fade and are replaced by others. Everything evolves, or should. Here are the Twelve Steps in the late 1930s as penned by Bill Wilson:

1. We admitted we were licked.
2. Got honest with ourselves.
3. Got honest with someone else.
4. Made amends.
5. Gave without asking for anything in return.
6. Prayed to whatever God we understood for the power to do these steps.[74]

This was prior to the first printing of *Alcoholics Anonymous*, a text that claimed to be only a beginning and that more would be revealed. The devil is in the details—what do you leave in and what do you take out? As Six or Twelve Steps, noble truths or commandments, we employ a system that aids us in self-awareness and empathy. None of us do it exactly the same way and most won't do it just once. We err and we try again. Our program is effective, not flawless. It can't be absorbed by observation or study. It has to be lived, buggered up and tried again. Fellow members are neither our students nor our professors; we gain perspective, ideas and road-tested testimony that we can take or leave.

Do I see my recovery as a work in progress? Do I expect flawlessness from myself and others?

## July 22

*"When love and hate are both absent everything becomes clear and undisguised. Make the smallest distinction, however and heaven and earth are set infinitely apart. If you wish to see the truth, then hold no opinion for or against anything. To set up what you like against what you dislike is the disease of the mind."*

Seng-ts'an (?–606)

---

Holy crap, can this be true? If we harbor a preference, have an agenda or feel strongly about something then we can't see the truth? What a mind bender! Mindfulness invites us to be open to our sensations and feelings, our thoughts and intuitions without judging, labeling or steering. This state of letting go may be experienced for a moment, but like holding our breath, the clarity of dispassion is, at best, fleeting. We don't get life 100% right 100% of the time. The point is to play with the idea of non-judgment and improve our minds' fitness. When we do judge, let's not blame ourselves. Rather, let's observe our judgment without labels.

If we begin to do cardiovascular exercise, on day one we might only be able to run a single block, but on day two we do one block, plus one driveway. Some days we don't do as well as the day before. Some days we don't get out the door. Eventually, after a regimen that's included progression and regression, we can run a 10-k run or a marathon. Maybe just being, non-judgmentally, doesn't seem practical while "swimming with the sharks" at work. That's fine; we can apply different rules of engagement throughout the day. We can be Twelve Step Buddhists and nine-to-five capitalists. During the big game we don't have to be open to a world of possibilities. We can root for our team, bitch at the officials when they don't rule in our favor and revel in our opponent's misfortune.

How do I feel about these exercises to seek truth? Is this a way of life for me or something to try out to keep life interesting? Is this relevant, an impossible ideal or something I wish I was better at? If I want to be more non-judgmental, maybe I can try doing it for two minutes at a time.

# July 23

*"The only time you have too much fuel is when you're on fire."*

*Unknown*

---

"Too much is just enough" was our battle cry during active addiction. Today's quip  might get us thinking seriously about how many of us indulged until we were "on fire" and it was too late to eject to safety. The rationalization is that it is only painful to fly with the crows when we are being shot at. Some of us spend with this mind-set, gamble this way, date this way, eat this way, work this way. Denial, shame and pride keep our acting out as secret as possible. This leads to isolation. Sometimes we don't seem to be able to assess risk and make good choices. We portray ourselves in public one way but we still have forbidden pleasures that we aren't so proud of.

There's the joke about a European pharmaceutical company that came up with a pill that will allow alcoholics to control their drinking. "No thanks," said the alcoholics, "come back when you have a pill that lets us overindulge without consequences; that's the pill for us." In recovery, the wish to keep indulging without consequence doesn't vanish suddenly. How many of us hoard, ruminate, fidget or pump ourselves full of coffee or nicotine, or go the other way with exercise and rigid dieting? Old habits die hard, you say? Consider that quitting may not end our problems—some say quitting exposes our problems. Putting the plug in the jug is something many an alcoholic has done more than twice. Living sober is hard when the feelings and consequences we were avoiding show up unabated. One member says, "I thought that sobriety was a punishment for admitting I was an alcoholic. Dying drunk looked more romantic to me than living sober."

What are the problems that my addiction was hiding? Do I handle or avoid them now? Do I still overindulge in certain behaviour? What consequences do I face when I overindulge?

# July 24

*"Being healthy is a natural state and the means for achieving
it is in the grasp of each one of us. I believe that a judicious
mixture of hard work, clear thinking, humor and self-confidence
are the ingredients of effective living."*

Your Erroneous Zone *by Dr. Wayne Dyer*

---

Restless, irritable, discontented—isn't this the *natural state* of an addict's mental health? If there was only one promise it might be that working the Twelve Steps will make us less miserable. Positive Psychology moves away from dysfunction to focus on accentuating our positive, functional selves. Dyer's book and concepts inadvertently describe the value of working the program. Hard-working, clear-thinking, humorous and self-confident—are these not the qualities of those who we admire?

If we are slothful, confused, morose and hypercritical as a *natural state*, we find we are not alone in Twelve & Twelve circles, but steps Six and Seven help us reinvent ourselves. We took inventory and talked frankly about the poorly functioning aspects of our natures. Next, we incorporated "a judicious mixture of hard work, clear thinking, humor and self-confidence." The fact is that if we have gotten through the first five Steps we have certainly demonstrated better work habits. We have more clarity and we don't take ourselves as seriously as we once did. Life is not a vacuum. Do we tend to attract conflict or harmony from those around us? This is worth noting before we size up our treatment of others in Steps Eight and Nine. If we are still reactive and blaming, are we in the right frame of mind to engage effectively with those we have hurt? Life is a mirror—if we rub people the wrong way, we get friction back. Likewise, if we exude self-respect and compassion for others, the world around us seems like a nice place to be. Steps Ten and Eleven help us take inventory of how we are doing all by ourselves. How well do we deal with calm? We can deal with a crisis but are we alright without it?

Is mental and physical health a natural state for me? If not, do I see how it can be cultivated?

# July 25

*"Meditation is very effective when one sits close to a window so that the outer world of nature can be observed. This provides a means for reflection, for it helps us to realize that there is a much larger but less complicated, more normal life out there, a life not riddled with arguments, fights about money, worries about mundane things. It is a world of order and harmony. There is the dependability of the moon rising and the sun setting."*

*Jean Kirkpatrick, PhD*

---

Meditation is part of the cure outlined in the literature but we often have to go outside the program to learn to meditate. Nature has an enriching and often calming effect on us. If we can't find it, we can imagine it. Getting beyond our worries, fears and dissatisfactions by focusing on the breeze, the sun and the life force around us can ground us. Need more? Take a look at images from the Hubble space telescope and that will give our petty concerns some perspective. The universe has been here for 13.5 billion years and the worries we have today won't have much of an impact on the next 13.5 billion years. Maybe our worries are largely caused by how we interpret what is happening around us. What else could this mean?

Back to Earth for now. We are reminded today to consciously breathe the air and enjoy the beauty. If we live in a city, how long has it been since we felt grass, rocks or sand on our bare feet? Just taking our shoes off on a warm day and stepping mindfully on the grass and feeling the sun on our skin can help open our minds and lower our heart rates. No matter what our meditation and/or prayer routines are, it pays to mix it up a bit. A yoga class or a day-long hike can be as healing as making lists and going to more meetings.

No one said I have to wait until after Step Ten to meditate. Mindful enquiry can help through each and every Step. Do I have a routine for meditation? Could it use a little shaking up?

# July 26

*"Because I'm not perfect looking, I get to play better roles."*

Juliette Lewis (born 1973)

---

For seekers, the following three questions have philosophical and psychological relevance: Who am I? What am I doing here? Who are these others? In recovery, we reassess these three pivotal questions about our identities.

Actors follow scripts that include action and dialogue designed by the director and writer. All characters in a story stay consistent with their identities, their roles in the story and the way they fit in with the rest of their environment. We have life-scripts that we follow for cues. Some roles were crafted by *directors* we worked under in childhood. In adolescence we began to craft our own identities, taking over the roles of writer, director and actor. We craft roles and scripts for those around us, too. We have an idea of how they *should* be fitting in. In finding or forging our roles in life we try to answer these three nagging questions about identity, purpose and how we interact within our setting.

Role models have a lasting impact on us too. We see ourselves as autonomous decision makers and that is partly true. Parents will consciously resist the scripts imposed by previous generations, but it is hard work not to react to what we lived. Some actions/reactions happen like muscular reflexes. We are slaves to some persistent life-scripts that prompt our reactions before free will is in play. It's like we are *in character* even when we are off the set. Heritage and culture impose values upon us about who we are, what activities are important and how we differ from others. Advertisers give their products appeal by preying on deep-rooted scripts of ours that their products will appeal to. Our programs of recovery train us in new scripts and counter-scripts that help us fit in, giving us new language and behavior for life. Some of these roles become authentically us; some of the recovery jargon becomes *auto-speak* we use to fit in. Over three days we'll explore these existential questions more thoroughly.

Am I in the midst of an identity crisis or do I know who I am, what my role is and where and how I fit in?

# July 27

*"The final mystery is oneself."*

Oscar Wilde (1854–1900)

---

So: "Who am I?" We are seekers. We look for answers in art, the zodiac, our heritage, by gazing in the mirror or staring at the stars. We have core beliefs that present themselves as facts of life: "You are just like your father," "You are a natural leader," "You are so selfish" and "You're so funny" are examples. Core beliefs come with scripted dialogue and actions. Taking inventory of internal and external messages helps differentiate facts from opinions and we would be wise to scrutinize the sources of the messages. "I am Australian," "I am a Libra," "I am a daughter" and "I am diabetic" may be facts but we can still choose what bearing they have on our identities. We apply meaning to the facts. Some opinions we treat as facts: "I am a bum," "I am a winner," "I am unworthy," "I am smart" or "I am a natural athlete." Even the "addict" label can be argued as an opinion or fact. Opinions color our beliefs and define or redefine our realities. We construct reality—we don't discover it. It helps to know what building materials we are employing. If we have treated fact and fiction equally as building materials, we may have faulty houses that come crashing down one day.

How do we feel about who we are? Counter-scripts and self-visualization rebrand our self-concepts or worldviews. These new scripts may help bandage destructive scripts but they can't sustain the pressure unless we alter our core beliefs. "I am black and I am proud" would be symbolic of someone who is proud of their identity. But if a core belief is "I am inferior" the counter-script will buckle under pressure. Inadequacy is epidemic among addicts. Our scripts are of resignation or over-compensation. A good start is to create a counter-script portraying us as rights-bearing equals.

What is my narrative about who I am? Is that my own voice answering this question or am I following someone else's script?

*"Live a good life. If there are gods and they are just, then they will not care how devout you have been, but will welcome you based on the virtues you have lived by. If there are gods, but unjust, then you should not want to worship them. If there are no gods, then you will be gone, but will have lived a noble life that will live on in the memories of your loved ones.*
*I am not afraid."*

*Marcus Aurelius (121–180)*

---

Our man Marc would be called an *apatheist* today. Proof that God is either a myth or a reality would not change his deeds or behavior. Apathetic to the answer, he lived righteously. If the big question is irrelevant, why spend so much time on it? So with that issue out of the way, next question…

"What am I doing here?" Psychologists suggest that a sense of purpose or self-worth comes from feeling that we add value to a world of meaning. More than economic or social stature, a purpose enhances our self-esteem. Life-scripts and role play come with built-in definitions. Transactional Analysis scripts like persecutor (disciplinarian), victim and rescuer are interchangeable roles that most of us act out at home, school, work and in meetings. Taking inventory of the hats we wear and the triggers and rationalizations that support these roles enhances self-awareness. A weekend inventory or a check-list meditation while standing in line can help us review how these roles play out in our lives. "I keep the peace here," "I attend the 'Keep It Simple' group," "I relapse a lot" and "I write songs" are scripts that define and defend what we do. With greater understanding we start living more consciously and less reactively. With more choice and less reaction we find we are doing good and doing good feels good. Working with others frees us from the bondage of self—a surefire way to keep existential angst at bay, one day at a time. Right action makes right thinking easier.

"What am I doing here?" Looking at the script I follow today, to what extent is my life determined by environment or habits? Do I feel trapped by my social caste, or free to do as I please?

*"Nearly all human activity is programmed by an ongoing script dating from early childhood, so that the feeling of autonomy is nearly always an illusion—an illusion which is the greatest affliction of the human race because it makes awareness, honesty, creativity and intimacy possible for only a few fortunate individuals. For the rest of humanity, other people are seen mainly as objects to be manipulated, persuaded, seduced, bribed or forced into playing the proper roles to reinforce the protagonist's position and fulfill his/her script."*

*Eric Berne (1910–1970)*

---

"Who are these others?" Narcissism and addiction are often synonymous with each other. Seeing others as individuals separate from our needs and our agendas is essential for contentment. When we are in a healthy mental state, our parents, children, siblings, lovers, coworkers and fellow members are separate individuals. A healthy understanding of their roles in our lives and our role in theirs guides our interdependent relationships. We see the boundaries. Some lines we created and we are mindful of what these lines symbolize. Other lines are boundaries drawn by others, which we respect. Either way, we don't look at people as things to control or avoid being controlled by, to use or be used by, etc.

They say that the AA meeting is where all the laughing happens and that the Al-Anon meeting is where the crying happens. The addict has the illness, but loved ones show the symptoms. Codependents are encouraged to go to AA meetings (or others) once a week to understand addiction. Addicts are well-served to go to the co-addict meetings from time to time to understand the damage done to others.

Have I been seeking love and happiness with neither a sense of my own identity nor healthy boundaries between myself and those around me? Can I see the futility of chasing control? Do I harbor hidden agendas when I'm with the people closest to me? Can I now relate to these people with healthy inclusion and separation? How has my illness made other people suffer? How can I be more mindful in how I treat others, today?

# July 30

*"I prayed for twenty years but received no answer
until I prayed with my legs."*

Frederick Douglass (1817–1895)

---

Some of us pray, some meditate, some practice mindful inquiry. Some of us make lists, plans and inventories. This is all *working the program*. When we find our meditating or mindfulness has degraded to ruminating, we share with another and see if this gives us more clarity. But there comes a time when action is the only cure for our troubles. Sometimes it seems that there is too much to do and too little time. "One day at a time" is sometimes twenty-three hours and fifty minutes too much for us. We have things to do! We pick one of our tasks and devote ten minutes to it. It is amazing how many problems can be tackled with only three to ten minutes of attention: the call we dread, the mess that needs cleaning. We might not get months of disorganization turned around in ten minutes, but we feel better getting it started. Maybe we just keep going once we start. During times of stress, a little footwork can dissipate our angst better than calling a dozen sponsors or dwelling and dreading all day long.

"Easy does it—but do it" and "First Things First" both make sense. A thousand mile journey starts with one step. Perfectionism can be cured by committing to an average effort for the next ten minutes.

When the Big Book was edited in the late 1930s, a lot of "you must" statements were purged and replaced with suggestions and "our experience" statements. One of the absolute statements remained: "*Do not* be discouraged." Unrealistic expectations easily disguise themselves as rigorous efforts and can stop us in our tracks. Today any *must magnet* members can comb through the Big Book and find anywhere from fifty-five to twice that number of "must" messages still remaining. Find them all—win a prize. It makes a great party game for sober friends.

"Faith without works is dead." That means what to me? Can I resolve to work on something that is upsetting me by spending just ten minutes of time on it? Do I find more solutions to my problems when I put some leg work into it?

# July 31

*"The method of averting one's attention from evil,*
*and living simply in the light of good, is splendid as long as it*
*will work ... . But ... there is no doubt that healthy-mindedness is*
*inadequate as a positive philosophical*
*doctrine, because the evil facts which it refuses to account*
*for, are genuine; and may be the best key to life's significance,*
*and possibly the openers to the deepest levels of truth."*

*William James (1842–1910)*

---

We move from the "evil" of addiction, clear the wreckage of the past and live in the light—nice! Who wouldn't want to leave it at that? We put on sunglasses and bask in recovery's peace and happiness, not regretting the past nor wishing to shut the door on it—sweet!

Some of us don't know much about that. Why? We are seekers, and when we find peace, we just can't stop seeking; we seek truth, not pleasure, and as we peel away layers we discover it's not all pretty underneath. Some of us will get shit on. Cornered and blindsided, our happy, joyous and free passes are snatched away without consent. We did not sign up for more abuse. But if we are faced with evil and we find the courage to move forward, we may find (or create) meaning from suffering. Dignity and integrity constantly get tested. There may be no end in sight but we will make it through, gradually. At some point, we will be asked to show up for a loved one facing some kind of unthinkable evil. A problem shared is a problem halved. Good listeners can bear witness to great truths, too.

Our program, at its core, involves words and witnessing. We talk, we listen, we heal and we help. The phrase "advice-giving" is not often found in Twelve & Twelve literature. We find our own answers by voicing our troubles; others listen and identify. Our experience—not our advice—is why peer-to-peer works. Doing it solo or blockading ourselves with books sometimes fails where sharing does not.

Do I know that recovery promises a life—not a good one or an easy one—but one to make my own?

## August 1

*"I swore never to be silent whenever and wherever human beings endure suffering and humiliation. We must always take sides. Neutrality helps the oppressor, never the victim. Silence encourages the tormentor, never the tormented."*

*Elie Wiesel (born 1928)*

---

We have heard it said that the program is circular—Steps One to Twelve, back to One and so on. Also true is that Step Twelve is a springboard to the study and practice of the Traditions. From there we seek opportunities for service and stewardship, in and beyond our fellowship. All anonymous fellowships have done a great deal to convert predatory, narcissistic, self-destructive addicts into useful contributors to society—not to say that there aren't other means of recovery equal to the task. Once we become whole we become useful again. If we are grateful, we will easily find a chance to pay it forward.

Causes and injustices will present themselves to us and encourage us to get our heads out of our own asses and engage in lives of service. Recovery brings a humble, clear-thinking approach to life's woes. We may intuitively know what the right thing to do is. Like the Nobel Peace Prize winner and holocaust survivor quoted above, we will know what side to take and when to speak up. Our fellowship ought never be drawn into controversy but there is a time and place for us as individuals to stand and be counted. In developing the habit of being compassionate, we become more aware of our surroundings. Resignation is the greatest adversary to usefulness. We should never say "What's the use?" or "It's not my battle" or "What good could I do?" when we know in our hearts that it would be wrong to turn away and say nothing.

Looking at my progress in recovery, can I see where I have become more of a giver than a taker? Do I see how my own special traits and principles bring value to the world around me? Do I know what I am prepared to stand up for in and out of the fellowship?

## August 2

*"The hero is the one who comes to participate in life courageously and decently, in the way of nature, not in the way of personal rancor, disappointment or revenge."*

*Joseph Campbell (1904–1987)*

Some mythologies point to the earth as being the bearer of all things sinful—every natural instinct is a sin. Some mythologies speak of the Great Spirit as being in all things natural—the sun, the trees, the earth. Myths are fictions that can have power over people as though they were facts. We have *voices in our heads*. Do we tend to give them mythological power over us? Much of the fight to recover involves our own internal struggles—rewiring programmed messages about what was demanded and/or forbidden. Wrestling our demons doesn't make us heroes. We have to fight decently, with no personal rancor or revenge.

Do we confuse having chips on our shoulders with being heroic? Are we clamoring for attention or control? Are we overcompensating for negative self-images? Are we playing the roles of martyrs, rescuers or saviors? In our addictions, we raped, plundered and pillaged, calling it taking our comfort. Are we now the keepers of our brothers and sisters? We must always be mindful of our intentions. Even if we want to be good in the world and make up for our parasitical pasts, we think about Campbell's quote to ensure that what we might see as "heroic" is truly decent.

We learn the type of giving that asks nothing in return, and how the spirit of anonymity can help us do the right thing without fanfare or direct reward. We can start at home, too. Custody disputes, sorting our garbage, reaching an informed group conscience or being a kind neighbor—there is room for a noble hero in whatever we do.

Today I meditate on my values and consider what I stand for. What would I like to be remembered for? What do I admire most in others? Who are my heroes and why?

## August 3

*"A smile is a curve that sets everything straight."*

*Phyllis Diller (1917–2012)*

---

The Big Book describes the alcoholic as "restless, irritable and discontent." It makes no mention of circumstances—just the seeming difficulty with sustaining a feeling of well-being. Neither winning or losing nor being a *have* or a *have not* determine our moods. After a while, happy, joyous and free may become normal.

When we are new, finding pleasure in life may be nearly impossible. Anhedionia is the inability to feel pleasure or happiness in response to experiences that are ordinarily pleasurable. Anhedionia is a symptom of depression and schizophrenia, so sometimes sullen addicts in withdrawal are misdiagnosed with suffering from a far more serious chronic condition. When our brains dry out in the first few months of recovery, dopamine levels usually reach equilibrium. Our brains produce dopamine in several areas and our brains each have five receptors. It makes sense that it can take a few months for levels to moderate and for our receptivity to joy and fun to go back to normal, naturally. Anhedionia can trigger relapse if we don't understand it as a temporary stage; this early case of the blues isn't what sobriety will always look like.

In recovery we are mindful of what feeds malcontent. Two common killjoys are *longing* and *loathing*; unquenchable wanting and aversion leave no room for contentment. We feel incomplete. Of course it was the drug of choice that we once used to dissipate this feeling of incompleteness. Smiling at these nagging thoughts can defuse their joy-killing effects. By recognizing our wanting, we can laugh and say to our feelings, "You're not the boss of me." If we need stronger medicine, we can call up a friend and watch something funny together. At home or in a theater we can smile and laugh away sullenness.

William James is credited with saying, "We do not sing because we are happy; we are happy because we sing." Just for today, can I smile, sing or laugh when the blues threaten to ruin my day?

## August 4

*"Desperado, oh, you ain't gettin' no younger. Your pain and
your hunger, they're drivin' you home. And freedom,
oh freedom well, that's just some people talkin.'
Your prison is walking through this world all alone."*

Don Henley and Glenn Frey (The Eagles)

---

Solitude is a lifestyle choice; isolation is a defense. "Desperado" certainly isn't describing someone who is content in their solitude. Isolation occurs when human connection feels impossible. Foisting ourselves onto others to have our needs met is no solution to this problem. *How to bag the partner you need* books sell us the idea that we can't have what we want and deserve until we make peace with relationships from the past. We may say we forgive, but if we still talk of that "bitch" or "bastard" from the past, clearly we still stand in judgment or feel hard done by. What if everything that happened to us was unavoidable? What if everyone acted the only way they could? Would that feel different? If blame is part of our narratives, we are tragically predisposed to change the cast and replay the same scripts again and again.

There is no step in the Twelve Steps on domestic or romantic bliss. Being able to play nice is one of the secondary benefits of recovery. Step Eight reveals how we are, in part, the architects of our own romantic misfortune. Forgiving ourselves and forgiving others opens the door to harmony in a relationship or in solitude. In Step Nine we express the regret we uncover for how our needs made us selfish, manipulative and cruel. Our pain and our hunger are not excuses. We aren't negotiating forgiveness. We are coming clean and acknowledging the harm we have done.

We come to value solitude. Partnership becomes more than a cure for loneliness. Many will not make it this far into the amends Steps because it is so demanding. Risk and reward are both beyond our control. Who could fault anyone for rationalizing that it is enough to no longer be part of the problem?

Do the lyrics "come to your senses... let somebody love you, before it's too late" resonate with me?

## August 5

*"We're probably wondering where, precisely, our character defects end and our character begins within the complex structure of our personality. Why do we do the things we do? Is it someone's fault? When did we first feel this way?"*

The Narcotics Anonymous Step Working Guide

---

This excerpt from the *Guide* discusses becoming entirely ready, in Step Six, to remove our "defects of character." The word "defect" may grate on our nerves if we don't subscribe to the presumption that we are inherently bad or flawed. Some have changed the term "defects" to "defenses" because lying, compartmentalizing, rationalizing, angry outbursts, self-pity, avoidance and self-sufficiency were techniques for coping with unmet needs. Our needs weren't met so we adapted with resourceful, albeit limited, coping methods. These defenses may be detrimental to our new way of life but they don't have to be demonized. The language of the Steps might not sit well with our worldviews. Skipping steps won't give us the inherent pay-off, so what to do? Adapt—we can take what we like and rewrite the rest. Roadblocks didn't halt our self-destructiveness—we adapted. The same creativity we applied during our acting out days can be applied to personalizing our programs. If changing a word makes the process palatable, we do it. We can check with another trusted member if we fear that our translation is a lazy shortcut.

The questions above are prompts to gain self-understanding. By accepting our incompleteness, we will be less inclined to overcompensate or isolate. What will it take to achieve the results we want from each Step? Substituting "defenses" for "defects" is an example of how we can adapt rather than quit. Like modernizing or customizing the literature we read, we can make an acronym for GOD such as Great OutDoors, Group of Drunks or Good Orderly Direction—anything we need to do to speak these Steps in our language is fair game. If the word "God" offends, we replace it. The word won't mind.

What roadblocks are holding me back right now? Would a little customization solve these problems? How would I define the Twelve Step process in my own words?

# August 6

*"There are no facts, only interpretations."*

*Friedrich Nietzsche (1844–1900)*

---

The only problem with speaking the truth is that there are so many versions of it. We all have truths that are near and dear to us but it is best not to declare that our interpretations are universal laws or that we have some higher level of insight. Like life itself, truth is best worn as a loose garment. An open mind isn't an empty mind; rather, it is a willingness to reconsider. Scientists who are certain are hard to come by. They remain skeptical even of their own theories. Recovery reveals that being certain doesn't improve our chances of being right about an idea. There may have been a time when we thought the program had too many inconsistencies to be true. Then we thought it was too good to be true. Looking back, we can see how each fact we leaned on was merely an interpretation.

In recovery, we are a fellowship of people with little in common; we have our inflictions, but they played out differently for each of us. Our commitments to better living are unique, based on our individual designs for living or what our bottom line recovery is defined as. In addition to that, we each have styles, attitudes and convictions that differ from one other. We aren't threatened by alternative perspectives. We learn from each other. We accept what people say because it is true for them. We take what we like and leave the rest. We are careful not to discard contrary views rashly, and we try not to be quick to judge.

My truth doesn't trump anyone else's. Does remembering "vive la différence" keep my mind open to the wisdom of others? In fact, not that long ago, I lived by *facts of life* that I don't even consider sound interpretations now. Today, do I take what I speak of as the truth with a grain of salt?

*"Be yourself. There is something that you can do better than any other. Listen to the inward voice and bravely obey that."*

Author unknown

---

The *disease of perception* isn't a clinical diagnosis. This disease does come with cognitive dissonance and a peculiar brand of self-deception. So being ourselves isn't as easy and automatic as it sounds. Authenticity is buried under layers. We'll get to it when we can. Recovery has some perception challenges, too. One such distortion is that self-acceptance or self-reliance may stall progress or lead to relapse. If we accept ourselves just the way we are, might we become self-satisfied and stagnate? A good start for us is to work the program in our own ways.

Some members seek recovery from sages or Step Study guides. In 1977, AA was inundated with requests to quote literature for Step Study guides from outside agencies, which prompted study of the idea of AA creating its own guide. In a report called "Big Book Study Guides: Reviewing a Position Paper," the General Service Board concludes, "A.A. is a program of self-diagnosis, self-motivation and self-action— and that the use of study guides, courses, classes or interpretations is therefore not generally appropriate. The program is spiritual rather than academic. There are no authorities in A.A. and even a self-appointed 'teacher' has feet of clay. Hence, it is preferable that the individual member or prospect interpret the literature according to his/her own point of view."[75] As always, AA neither endorses nor opposes the use of study guides by members or groups.

Do I feel worthy and authentic? Do I trust my inner voice? Do I connect with an inner power through meditation, or a higher power through prayer, to guide my life? What does "a self-appointed teacher has feet of clay" mean to me?

# August 8

*"Those who eat too much or eat too little, who sleep too much
or sleep too little, will not succeed in meditation.
But those who are temperate in eating and sleeping,
work and recreation, will come to the end of
sorrow through meditation."*

*Bhagavad Gita*

---

What do addicts know about balance? We know excess. We took excess to the extreme. It was such an integral part of our makeup that many of us fear at some level that without our excesses, there will be no fun left in life. Will we be dull and lifeless without extremes? We might believe that excesses engage us with the outside world and that they are part of our charm. Excess leads to isolation, not engagement—who eats a whole tub of ice cream in plain view? Do we still entertain the idea that binging and purging is living life to the fullest? Maybe we think opposite extremes can be a form of balance. If we stay up all night reading books about balance are we not missing the point? Our true natures still exude personality; we don't have to rely on extreme or exaggerated behavior.

Meditation breeds balance and peace. Extreme living has made serenity uncomfortable or at least unfamiliar. We adjust to balanced living. It takes an open mind. If the first few days of practice cannot quiet the clamor from the *committees in our heads*, we try again. How many of us have tried for a whole week to become experts at meditation only to say, "What's the use?" We are not very realistic, are we? And let's consider what the end result will look like. Many of us have learning disabilities, emotional disturbances and trauma that plague our attempts to focus. That is all the more reason to dig in because we have the most to gain from even a small improvement in concentration or relaxation. Let's not compare ourselves or strive for unreachable standards. Let's just see how our progress goes.

Do I believe, in my heart-of-hearts, that I am a hopeless case when it comes to meditation? If balance and happiness don't come naturally, can I celebrate progress rather than perfection?

## August 9

*"A peacefulness follows any decision, even the wrong one."*

*Rita Mae Brown (born 1944)*

---

In the heat of the moment, even false hope feels better than despair. We hear in the rooms, "Often wrong but never in doubt" and "Don't believe everything you think." We are reminded not to take ourselves so seriously. We aren't always right. We aren't supposed to be, nor are we expected to be. For some, being wrong is good exercise. We arrive at the door of recovery with warped perceptions. It takes time for our faculties to calibrate. The jury is still out on the prospect of a full cognitive recovery for any of us. Did we ever have a legitimate state of sanity that we can be restored to?

We try to embrace our limits and imperfections, treating *doing our best* as good enough. While today's quote is another reminder to not be overly confident even when we are sure we are right, it also speaks to the importance of making decisions, even if we don't have all the facts we would like. Our expectations have to recover from addiction, too. We can make decisions imperfectly. We live with our humanity and the imperfection of the world around us. That is how right-mindedness looks. Humility is a process, a value we live by, not an accomplishment marked by a celebration. We gain peace when we make decisions. We may be wrong, but we weren't wrong to make a decision. We couldn't have known the outcome. Rewarding the effort, we give ourselves credit for trying. The courage is in doing within, when we are without— without proof, without experience and sometimes, without courage. We do it.

Let's imagine a golf tournament. All the pros are meticulously preparing. They bear down at the driving range, concentrating and hitting the ball with all the skill they can muster. One pro is lazily dropping one ball after another and slapping it down the range with his club. Someone asks, "My God, how will that help you prepare for today's round?" The pro says, "I am practicing not caring about the outcome."

Am I rigid about plans or decisions today? "Just doing it" is about my effort—not the result.

## August 10

*"If such work was abdicated by Alcoholics Anonymous to professionals, what happened to the program? What happened to the fellowship itself, to which 'carrying the message' was so essential? What to do when ordinary people prefer the 'cheap grace' offered by experts has been a constant and characteristic problem for expressions of Evangelically Pietist religion."*

Not God: A History of Alcoholics Anonymous *by Ernest Kurtz*

---

Tradition Eight states that our fellowship is to "remain forever non-professional but our service centers may employ special workers." Administration we can delegate, but carrying the message always involves one addict with nothing to gain financially talking to another, perplexed by addiction. Even two newcomers have the power to help each other stay sober. We don't have cardinals and bishops in Twelve & Twelve groups. Some members may have a flock of sponsees but they still rely on experience and not expertise. In a business meeting they have one vote like everyone else. This is the tell-tale sign of the peer-to-peer recovery model. If people want professionally-led group therapy or religious leadership it is readily available in the community but that's not how we roll in meetings.

To understand how "special workers" have played a role in our fellowship, we can look into our fellowship's archives or read annual reports. We can read *Pass it On: The Story of Bill Wilson and How the A.A. Message Reached the World* or some of the historical books on early AA. There we will read about Bill Wilson's ethical struggle with the invitation offered him to become a professional Twelve-stepper. He needed the money but said, "Thanks but no thanks." These stories are significant for all of us.

Am I careful never to think of myself as an expert or quasi-professional when it comes to recovery or mental health? Do I understand the scope of what it takes to run the administration of this fellowship— to answer calls and emails, print and distribute literature and maintain a central office? Do I do what I can to support these efforts?

## August 11

*"Correct me if I am wrong, but hasn't the line between sanity and madness gotten finer?"*

George Price (1901–1995)

---

In *Empire of Illusion: The End of Literacy and the Triumph of Spectacle*, Chris Hedges expands on cartoonist Price's notion when writing that cultures that cannot distinguish between reality and illusion die. Humans and our society need sanity to thrive. In the world around us politics, consumerism, sports and entertainment have become mythical. Sometimes we nurture a false intimacy with TV personalities. We feel a kindred David vs. Goliath struggle with politicians or sports heroes but we don't know these people. They don't go to bed thinking about us. We sometimes blur the lines between actors' roles and their personal exploits. Look at professional wrestling—what is scripted and what is spontaneous? Movies are shot like documentaries. Still images are easily manipulated. Our leaders try to connect with us by appearing on talk shows or YouTube posts. Advertisers tie their products to our unmet needs by grossly simplifying our lives into stereotypes.

Our Steps teach us to understand more deeply and to look at ourselves and others both critically and compassionately. We can use these tools to maintain a fairly even temperament in a world gone mad. We avoid complacency by periodically reviewing our own beliefs and convictions. Twelve & Twelve culture has its own brand of mythology and fellowships come with their own magical thinking. This isn't to say there isn't value to be found, but we don't take anything for granted. This principle helps us maintain a playful curiosity about what is concrete and what is anecdotal. In a sane world it's natural to be wrong; to err is human. To expect perfection would be a wee bit nuts.

What are my own blurred lines between reality and wish-upon-a-star thinking?

*"Worry is spiritual near-sightedness, a fumbling way of looking at little things and magnifying their value."*

*Anna Robertson Brown Lindsay (1864–1948)*

---

The crazy thing about ruminating on our problems is that we think we would be worse off if we didn't. Some of us sit down to meditate and we start worrying, dreading imagined outcomes. What a surprise that we don't find this to be at all refreshing or relaxing. A great deal of creative energy is devoted to worrying about things that might happen and never do. A lot of the rest is inevitable. So why worry?

In *The Mindful Way through Depression*, authors Williams et al invite us to make peace with our feelings—to befriend them. Worry is a manifestation of fear. Fear is not our enemy. So often our daily meditations pit us against our thoughts and feelings. Hey, we're on the same team! Let's learn to work together! We are encouraged to guard against "here I go again" thinking. It is true that if we react in the same manner as we always have we can't hope for a new outcome. But we have some control over worry and sadness and this control is within our imagination. We may see our thoughts as facts—"This is hopeless!"; "I will never be loved"; "I am such a loser." Thoughts are made up. Our imaginations created them like the worry described above. If we created them we can change them. The facts don't change but we have assigned meaning to the facts; we have biases and we even have expectations of what all this will mean in the future. What *else* could all this mean? *The Mindful Way Through Depression* also discusses how mindfulness isn't an event and it doesn't take place somewhere else. We can be mindful now. When we feel impulsive or overwhelmed we can breathe and contemplate instead of reacting and regretting.

Do I "major in minors?" Does focusing on minutia make me think I can control outcomes? Am I magnifying the value of my worries now?

*"So long as there is the slightest interest in sobriety, the most unmoral, the most anti-social, the most critical alcoholic may gather about him a few kindred spirits and announce to us that a new Alcoholics Anonymous Group has been formed. Anti-God, anti-medicine, anti-our recovery program, even anti-each other—these rampant individuals are still an A.A. Group if they think so!"*[76]

*Bill W. A.A. Grapevine, July 1946*

---

Before the Traditions were adopted by AA, Bill was writing about what he called them then, Twelve Principles. In "The Individual in Relation to A.A. as a Group" Bill Wilson wrote about inclusion. Specialty meetings can cater to young people, specific professions, LGBT (queer culture), agnostics and atheists, men only, women only and can be conducted in any language. Most groups wouldn't turn away a newcomer, no matter what team colors they wear. If we ever find ourselves debating another group or member's legitimacy, we are suffering from binary thinking—the belief that there is one right way and other ways are wrong. If one member successfully works *every step as directed*, that doesn't make *taking what we like and leaving the rest* inferior. Ours is a pluralist society, not a binary one. We are equal, not the same. Minority voices and unpopular practices have the right of inclusion.

Anarchy is not a perfect system but would Twelve & Twelve culture flourish better with rules? There is no freedom without responsibility. We are free as individuals from addiction or codependency due largely to taking responsibility for ourselves. Others helped, maybe the time was right, but without applying our wills, recovery could not have happened. Each group has a responsibility to conduct itself rightly and resolve internal differences. The only authority in groups is their own collective conscience. Spiritually, this is more than popular opinion—it has to be fair and it has to be true.

Do I think people should save time and see it my way? Do I find contrarian worldviews threatening to me or my fellowship? Even if my group or another group gets it wrong, am I inclined to trust self-correction to take hold organically or do I think I have to intervene?

# August 14

*"A poem records emotions and moods that lie beyond*
*normal language that can only be patched*
*together and hinted at metaphorically."*
Diane Ackerman (born 1948)

---

Language can be a second-rate means of communication. Cosmologists prefer mathematics to express the truth and musicians say it in notes and chords. A poem has a greater capacity than a well-crafted theory to bring enemies to tears and to encourage them to embrace their foes. Feelings are so much more provocative than thoughts. Art can reach us where sound arguments may not. So when we are seeking answers, let's not make assumptions about where our clues will be found. Let's put the psychology book down and reserve tickets for the opera, gallery or symphony. Or we could revisit the classic rhymes and stories of our youth.

Balanced living is recovery's *sweet spot*—where we get the most impact and best results. We learn to take in the subtle, which is often missed in a life of extremes. Realizations can come when having a laugh or during restful times. Enlightenment can take us by surprise just as it can come to us through deep concentration. Music, movies or theater aren't always merely escapism. Who knows what truth might be uncovered while laughing or crying or singing along?

Today I can open myself to awe and imagination, employing a playful curiosity about where life will lead. Am I ready for a breakthrough to come from anywhere at any time? Do I understand that, just as recuperation is a vital part of physical fitness, play and rest are as important as Steps and therapy? Work, rest and play are all life skills. If I am cerebral by nature can I make it a habit to indulge in the lighter side of life and appreciate the value of art and culture?

## August 15

*"Every defeat, every heartbreak, every loss, contains*
*its own seed, its own lesson on how to improve*
*your performance the next time."*

Og Mandino (1923–1996)

---

Having a slip seems tragic. Some of us are reticent to take our own recovery for granted, never looking past more than a day or so. While it's true that every relapse is potentially fatal, every lesson we live through can be a meaningful experience. We tend to feel humiliated if we thought we were above failure. Pride and shame can haunt us if we felt others depended on us. We can feel quite defeated at times like this and we are prone to latch on to handy clichés to give our experiences meaning for ourselves or to offer explanations to others.

When we understand powerlessness and the surface and inner complexities of unmanageability, we need not be ashamed. Recovery is a process, not an event. The slip can be a barometer that alerts us to a mental or spiritual blind spot. If we can come to terms with our humanity and trade humiliation in for humility, we can acknowledge the complexities and insidiousness of addiction. Some of us have to build defenses against relapse. Were our acts premeditated, passive-aggressive or the result of a chain of events? Automatic feelings and thoughts can lead to impulsive acting when we don't assess risks or options.

Can we imagine having the type of sobriety whereby we would be no more tempted by our drug of choice than by a bowl of rat poison? Only if we are honest and candid will we get the help and compassion we need from the rooms and our other communities.

Do I have preconceived ideas and judgments about slips? Are slips a question of integrity or a reality of addiction and disease? If relapse is the furthest thing from my mind, I'm lucky. Are there other challenges that get me down and that I beat myself up over? Instead, can these challenges help me to learn and improve?

# August 16

*"By and large, language is a tool for concealing the truth."*

George Carlin (1937–2008)

---

Yesterday we talked about slipping back into our primary addictions. Another *slip* of sorts is into replacement addictions. We are adhering to our bottom lines—keeping our noses clean, being examples of how this program works and saying all the things a power of example would say. We may even feel obligated to talk a good talk but our language, while still amusing to others, conceals a quiet desperation below. All of us have bad habits and there is a difference between pesky defects and destructive behaviors. This is a highly personal issue—we mind our side of the street. A drug addict may justify smoking because she or he doesn't steal or lie to do it. It's not healthy but it's a choice. An Al-Anon member might justify a romantic affair as taking one's comfort, in light of the suffering endured with an alcoholic loved one. We could become hypochondriacs or hyper-vigilant about every behavior. On the other hand, we may be too liberal in what we define as good clean fun.

Checking in about these behaviors with another, we articulate how they make us feel. Do our new vices come with the same denial and deception that our original drug of choice led to? Do we feel powerless or ashamed? Coming to terms with our imperfection is part of maturity. On the other hand, if we feel ashamed, this could isolate us in our own rationalizations and/or self-loathing. In meetings, others may interfere with us when we share, playing the *outside issue* card. We stand our ground or we go where we are welcome. The NA member may find gambling is good clean fun but internet addiction is a problem. An Al-Anon member may concede that their alcoholic isn't the only addict in the house and google GA or OA in search of perspective on their own obsessive-compulsiveness.

Do I talk like a power of example and feel like a phony? How do I differentiate overdoing it once in a while from having a serious problem? Do I have trouble showing weakness at meetings and admitting that I feel on shaky ground?

## August 17

*"Instant Karma's gonna get you, gonna look you
right in the face. You better get yourself together
darling, join the human race."*

*John Lennon (1940–1980)*

---

Today we consider the emotional sobriety slip—the dry drunk or dry high. Today, "Instant Karma" is a metaphor for a wake-up-call or the universe calling us on our bullshit. Do we sometimes inflate our places in the human race? Ego trips are a big cause of dry drunks. Right-sizing our egos or getting ourselves together takes commitment and practice. If we practice not thinking about ourselves 24/7, keeping our egos in check will become second nature.

Emotional slips happen. Some are sudden and some are built up over time. Just as serious as ego trips are self-pity and resentment—these are *red flags* in our daily reflection and meditation during Steps Ten and Eleven. Feelings aren't the enemy of the addict; repressing our feelings is our danger. Denial and procrastination are what lead to "bad karma" for us.

Over the past two days we looked at slips as relapses and as newly discovered self-destructive patterns that require renewal in the form of inventory, amends, etc. Maybe we will need a few meetings at another Twelve & Twelve fellowship. Meditation isn't formally discussed in the program until Step Eleven, but it is never too early to be mindful in our Step work. Even Step One deserves mindful inquiry and reflection. Questioning our motives and balancing our thoughts against our gut feelings is one way to measure our progress. We do this in daily meditation to guard against a date with "Instant Karma."

Some fellowships measure sobriety in absolutes—if I maintained a bottom line, I am OK today. Other fellowships measure sobriety by more day-to-day standards—am I present in my work and with loved ones? Am I distracted by intrigue, craving or fantasizing about revenge? Today, am I either rationalizing misguided behavior or rigidly setting impossible goals? I don't want to have a *wet slip* but I don't want to get so dry I am a fire hazard either.

## August 18

*"Enlightenment seems like a complicated concept,*
*but it is very simple. When you understand the nature*
*of your own mind, which is boundless and compassionate,*
*the layers of confusion begin to thin out. It's not that*
*you achieve enlightenment—rather that slowly and*
*gradually you become less deluded."*

*Jane Hope*

---

Media watchdogs measure content with what is called a "signal-to-noise ratio." They evaluate how much relevant, informative or enjoyable content gets through compared to the clamor and pointless tripe. Our brains are similar—there is an abundance of quality content. We just have to clear out the BS that clouds our heads or hearts. In the commercialized, consumption-based world we live in, there is a lot of clutter, so we filter out the empty calories and tune in to the high-fiber signal.

This isn't to say we can will our way to clarity, compassion and reason. We consider that for addicts, noise, confusion, chaos and drama are sometimes coping techniques. If we are chronically late, broke, worried, angry or overwhelmed, might these be symptoms of avoidance? What are we avoiding? On the other hand, it may be Attention Deficit Disorder—addicts tend to score moderate to high on tests for this disorder. Calm and balanced living might not be a reasonable expectation for all of us. Living within our limitations, we keep it real in terms of self-image, self-importance and self-sufficiency.

If we don't get enlightened, at least we get less deluded. We can keep trying new things and see how they feel. We don't need to be heart specialists to have a good sense of what is healthy exercise and what is overdoing it. We practice, learn and observe, and we can apply the same to meditation. We aren't in an enlightenment competition. The journey is inward. There's no race and no map.

First I meditate and then I find answers. It doesn't need to be the other way around, does it?

*"It makes no sense to take my broken television set to a washing machine repair shop, and then grow outraged when the people there refuse to try to repair it. And it does not matter that 'they both work on electricity.' Repairing television sets is a different kind of job from repairing washing machines, and requires a different kind of tool kit and body of knowledge gained from long experience in repairing those particular items."*

The Psychology of Alcoholism
*by William E. Swegan with Glenn F. Chestnut, PhD.*

---

Swegan's mother died when he was young. As a young man, he dodged bombs and machine gun fire in the Pearl Harbor attack. In his search for the meaning of life, Swegan found more answers in the practical world than the mystical world. His Twelve Step approach was more psychological than theistic. He explains his approach to the Steps as involving (1) insight; (2) surrender; (3) establishing positive goals; (4) introspection; (5) confession; (6) a more complete submission to the positive power of the healing process; (7) humility; (8) amendment; (9) restitution; (10) reorganization; (11) spirituality; and (12) learning to love others in a fuller and less selfish way.[77]

Swegan and Chestnut suggest that if we are powerless over drugs, overeating or drinking, we shouldn't be surprised that they don't have the answers at the Gamblers Anonymous meeting. And if any of us find secondary addictions emerging, we can try applying the principles from our fellowship-of-choice but it is reasonable to expect that the experience that we really need can only be found in a new Twelve & Twelve group or from its literature. Step One help comes in languages and experiences that are very specific to each fellowship. Sharing a commonality is how we find it easier to separate what we need to take control of from what we need to let go of. Many more issues will require professional help. There is no more shame in seeking out psychotherapy than in consulting an accountant, plumber or nutritionist.

Do I admit powerlessness without reservation? I can't solve all my problems alone.

# August 20

*"Asking the right questions takes as much skill
as giving the right answers."*

Robert Half (born 1918)

---

Even before our personal recovery is assured we find ourselves being asked for help or advice from those who are even greener than we are. "Oh my dog, I want to say what she needs to hear, but I just don't know what to say." The truth is that people need to feel heard more than they need to be told. Some of us wag fingers and tell the new person how it is and what to do. Some of us liken having a domineering sponsor to being loved: "They care about me enough to tell me off." This type of dynamic doesn't work forever. Newcomers mature quickly and as they outgrow this dominant/submissive role-play it will put strain on the relationship if not an end to it.

Self-evaluation won't uncover all the answers until we uncover the right questions. We are looking in 360 degrees for answers. Helping others can be more about listening than knowing what to say. "How does that make you feel?" and "What else do you think this could mean?" are good questions to ask because, firstly, we don't know the answers—they do. Secondly, what is true for us might not be true for someone else. Thirdly, nobody likes to be controlled—well, not all of the time, that is. The Big Book is still quite theatrical but it went through a rigorous toning down. Professionals were asked to review the first draft of *Alcoholics Anonymous* and encouraged the fellowship to take out many of the "you must" statements and replace them with "these suggestions" and "our experience." It is helpful to frame what we hear as experience rather than expertise.

When tempted to say, "Face it, your life is unmanageable," can I try "How are you managing?" Instead of saying "Turn it over" can I say "I was a control freak and it didn't help me much—how about you?" Questions help me help others find their own answers.

*"I don't see ultimate reality as God's kingdom.
That language is exactly what stops some would-be
recoverers flat in their tracks. It's not that they're unwilling.
But the God stuff they hear in meetings creates an
aversion to the whole idea of 12-Step recovery."*
The 12-Step Buddhist *by Darren Littlejohn*

---

Fellowships wax and wane in popularity in part because of how adaptive they are to changing times and how open they are to new possibilities. We can embrace God-consciousness, justify it, dismiss it as irrelevant or abandon the mystical component of recovery and put our faith in a more scientific version of "how it works." Autonomy isn't new to Twelve Step membership. Neither is disagreement between members. Just as every generation thinks it discovered sex, we might think we are more evolved than our forefathers. More has been revealed—that's for sure. Will history record that we are the wiser? There's great fodder for coffee shop debate.

Bill Wilson is quoted in Ernest Kurtz's *Not God* as having said, in a February 6, 1961 letter to Howard E.: "As time passes our book literature has a tendency to get more and more frozen, a tendency for conversion into something like dogma, a human trait I am afraid we can do little about. We may as well face the fact that AA will always have its fundamentalists, its absolutists and its relativists."[78] Wilson seems to side with Littlejohn—there is no *one right way* to put Twelve & Twelve solutions to work. If we are Christian or Muslim we will work recovery in accordance with our theistic beliefs. Hindu adherents have 330 deities being worshiped throughout the faith. Buddhism, as Littlejohn points out in his book, isn't considered a religion by all practitioners. "Mind-science" is how Littlejohn describes this Eastern philosophy. Materialists have success with or without our Steps, yet with no reliance on spiritual concepts. The world is awe-inspiring enough and needs no *collective consciousness* to explain what holds us all together. No worldview is incompatible with the Steps as a means to overcoming addiction.

Do I do my part to encourage people who are earnest about recovery, no matter what they believe?

## August 22

*"No matter how lovesick a woman is, she shouldn't take the first pill that comes along."*

Joyce Brothers (born 1927)

---

The escape artist meets the quick fix—this may have been our history, but are we condemned to continually repeat it? In early AA days a distinction was made between sober and dry. Dry is like the lovesick one, white-knuckling it to stay away from "the pill." Sober is the lovesick *becoming love-healthy* and not needing another's approval to feel worthy. She or he has transformed from "a seemingly hopeless state of mind and body," as blogging Bill W. would post if he were alive today.

When hardship rains on our recovery parades, do we reflexively point ourselves toward a quick fix? Can we suck it up and manage life's fickle turns without making a run for it? It seems at times that a committee of voices in our heads is crying out to be heard. There is the impulsive voice, the disciplined one, the runner, the courageous one, the crybaby and the stoic one. Of all the voices in our heads why does the *addict's* voice scream the loudest? One member says, "I love *the addict* like a traumatized child. When she screams for attention I am like the meeting chair. I give the addict her due and say, 'thanks for sharing, Ms. Addict. Who else has something to add?' My brain is a democracy. Every voice gets their say, but they can't all get their way. Someone's got to decide and I do."

Boundaries and relationships are a bit theoretical and mostly practical. We learn by engaging—not by just reading and talking about it. If stopping our drug of choice leads to acting out in a different form, we should be on the lookout for intimacy issues that are off-kilter. Abstinence is a sound counter-measure for mind altering chemicals. For sex, food and work, moderation is needed. Would you ever hear a sponsor say, "We recommend you don't eat during your first year of recovery"?

Lovesick goes around. How do I cope when I feel a hole in my heart? Am I a good leaning post for others who need to talk their way through their heartache? Do I ever get preachy about what I think is good for others?

## August 23

*"The advantages found in history seem to be of three kinds,
as it amuses the fancy, as it improves the
understanding, and as it strengthens virtue."*

David Hume (1711–1776)

---

This Scottish skeptic would love Twelve Step meetings. All three advantages are found as we discuss "in a general way, what it was like, what happened and what it's like now."[79] Once we have enough distance from the drama of our addictions we see considerable humor. We learn so much about ourselves through the tales of others. We interpret the Steps together and share our failures and triumphs, doubts and beliefs. What were once vices have indeed become virtues as we share around the table or in online discussion. Hume suggests that understanding where we come from will find us wiser, well-humored and living with principles that we can each call our own.

After a while, we may get involved in service. With drama no longer hijacking our day-to-day lives, we can take time to understand the history of our fellowship. In service, application of the Twelve Traditions gives us greater perspective. We each have a voice and a say in the future of our fellowship. Like good parents who prepare and protect their children, stewardship is not strictly a matter of preserving how it's always been. Survival of individuals and societies demands adaptation. Preparation comes from the experience and guidance of those who came before us.

Our collective history shows that founders encouraged us to not fear change; to preserve the principles but be flexible in the method. Change can break down barriers. No matter how uncomfortable it first feels, change is worth trying. Everything was and still is accomplished by trial and error. When working with newcomers or our fellows in business meetings, our humor, wisdom and the strength of our virtues will all be tested.

On a scale from one to ten, how do I do with humor today? How about wisdom and virtue?

## August 24

*"We run, not because we think it is doing us good, but because we enjoy it and cannot help ourselves. It also does us good because it helps us to do other things better. It gives a man or woman the chance to bring out power that might otherwise remain locked away inside.*
*The urge to struggle lies latent in everyone."*

Sir Roger Bannister (born 1929)

---

Life contains struggle—batteries and meaning not included. Enduring pain can be futile, cathartic, inspiring or a gateway to freedom beyond our imaginations. Suffering may yield clarity about our purpose and/or forge or identify our values. Running can either be synonymous with pain or with pain-avoidance. As we mature in recovery, we neither overindulge nor shy away from challenge or pain.

We do not define ourselves by our suffering. That is to become a martyr—one whose burden is carried for the benefit of others—"Don't worry about me, you enjoy yourself while I am left here on fire to smolder away. I am sure the flames will go out by the time you get back. You just go have fun without me." That's us at our self-pitying best; we are acting out martyrdom as the tragic Greek character, *Poor-me-theus*. How do we break the cycle of self-pity? We follow the clues to see what's eating us. If we dig underneath the surface we could find bitterness, unmet needs, shame, anger or guilt are the root-system that feeds our surface self-pity. Depression can be a coping mechanism to dull feelings that are otherwise overwhelming. When did we first start acting like martyrs? It takes work to get to the root of these issues. Bannister says "the urge to struggle lies latent in everyone." Struggle tests our limits—maybe it increases them. Maybe we feel most alive when we are struggling, engaged in the game of life.

Do I feel like I carry the burden of the world? Do I feel sorry for myself because others don't understand my burden? Am I bitter about the expectations I feel others impose on me? What are my earliest memories of what was expected of me? Did I learn the *Poor-me-theus* role from someone? Does my struggle define me? Who would I be without it?

# August 25

*"The Buddha preached a doctrine which demands an in-depth
analysis of suffering and its causes as a means of bringing
about suffering's end and, therefore, of ushering in a new and
lasting peace, tranquility and insightfulness."*

*Jan Willis (born 1948)*

---

Professor Willis teaches and writes about religion and Buddhism at Wesleyan University. Buddhism encourages "in-depth analysis" of our suffering. For Buddhists, the flipside of the suffering coin is enlightenment—not happiness. Wisdom, perspective and context convert suffering into insight. Is a fearless personal inventory needed to prevent relapse? Firstly, no—many people suffer through sobriety. Secondly, doing Step Four to avoid relapse is a fearful inventory. Think of how much more we can learn if we search fearlessly. Step Four (or Ten), done fearlessly, ends our suffering and replaces it with insight.

Longing (likes) and loathing (dislikes) color our experiences: they are entered in either the good or bad side of the ledger. Longing for something, no matter how petty or virtuous, or wishing for an outcome, be it righting an injustice or getting public approval, deprives us of serenity. Longing always brings suffering. Loathing brings equal suffering. Judging experiences through the ego-based lens of wants attaches us to favorable circumstances and helps us avoid adversity. Our egos write us shopping lists of what we deserve and how we expect others should respond to us. Life doesn't follow our bidding. The universe unfolds without concern for us.

The Serenity Prayer invites us to accept what comes, take responsibility for our contributions to the world and to focus on the difference between intention and outcome. Acceptance is not resignation; it is acknowledging that we can't control everything. Accepting is love with a healthy detachment. Even with the things in life we feel that we must muster the courage to change, by first accepting our challenge and our own lack of omnipotence, we can gain understanding that will greatly aid our courageous efforts.

Do I frustrate myself by placing expectations on myself and others?

## August 26

*"No finite point has meaning without*
*an infinite reference point."*

Jean-Paul Sartre (1905–1980)

---

For fun, let's join today's existentialist by reflecting on what we will call *recovery relativity*. We seek an ever-increasing approximation of the truth. What we know compared to what there is still to know can make our experience of earth seem futile. "We can never learn it all, so what's the use?" This sullen resignation is self-defeating. Isn't it better to embrace the wonder of the infinite unknown? One more productive way to look at knowledge is from a collectivist perspective; we take the baton from those who came before us, accept the challenge to absorb what we can learn during our lap around life, making any slight improvements or adjustments that we can, and pass the baton on to the next generation or the next student in line. So if we believe truth and knowledge to be infinite, the best we can do in our lives and also our recovery is to point ourselves in the right direction, making honesty, open-mindedness and willingness like three basic food groups that we need to nourish our minds and our hearts.

From a Zen perspective, enlightenment is attained by embracing emptiness—"being" and "nothingness." In this respect, wisdom comes from letting go, not from seeking. While one looks to the god of the heavens to be filled with serenity, courage and wisdom, another merely divests themselves of chaos, fear and biases. Both goals have no finish line. As recovery is about balance, we are going to get more done each day if we monitor our serenity, courage and wisdom. This way we are content in the process and not anticipating an end or a goal.

Our recovery is easy to take for granted. As a finite point, sobriety has meaning when measured against the many who are suffering from addiction right now and the infinite disastrous outcomes that could have been the story of our addiction.

My recovery is relative. What do I use to measure my troubles and triumphs against? How do I keep perspective?

*"The biggest challenge seemed to revolve around how to characterize the spiritual transformation, which was at the heart of the program. Even when the total membership was made up of just forty sober alcoholics, their views on the subject ranged from fervent belief that the entire program was divinely inspired to adamant agnosticism or atheism."*

Bill W.: A Biography of Alcoholics Anonymous
Cofounder Bill Wilson
*by Francis Hartigan*

---

Sounds like coffee shop chatter that could have taken place after yesterday's meeting, doesn't it? We have literalists who treat our texts as sacred and we have just as many who think that revising them bi-annually wouldn't be often enough. Founders were forward-thinkers who overcame their biases to welcome gays, people of color, women and young people despite their fears that inclusion could dilute the program, impact reputation or spell its demise. Quite the opposite happened. Vive la différence!

The openness of interpretation, the "take what you like, leave the rest" structure of Twelve & Twelve meetings, the invitation to define spiritual transformation or dismiss it—all these freedoms of choice are ensconced in our Traditions. Oh, we will meet people whom we find disagreeable and we will find conflict with some of the suggestions and assumptions laid out in the program of recovery. This is a way of life that invites questioning and trying new things on for size. We are equal but not the same. We each trudge a unique path of happy destiny, a pattern that is as individual as our thumb prints. We are likely to identify with many, yet unlikely to ever meet our identical recovery twins.

After the *Alcoholics Anonymous* text had been in circulation for a while, Bill W. and the founders felt they didn't quite articulate the spiritual aspect of recovery so they added "Appendix II" which reported that while transformations of a religious nature were not uncommon, educational-variety awakenings happened over time with the same good effect as any white-light experience.

Am I trying to hear from everyone? Some people's experiences with recovery, were I to duplicate them, would take me outside of my comfort zone. Do I try on new things and keep an open mind?

## August 28

*"People genuinely happy in their choices seem less often
tempted to force them on other people than those who
feel martyred and broken by their lives."*

*Jane Rule (1931–2007)*

---

We "live and let live." Looking around at others, we see that people
who *live* freely, satisfied in their choices, naturally *let live*. Conversely,
those who are judgmental of other people's beliefs, behavior and choices
may well feel enslaved in their own lives. Are their lives a series of
limits—"I have to," "I must," "I should"? We will find people who feel
trapped, martyred and as though they're living lives they didn't choose.
If we felt trapped or limited, would we be happy for, or resentful of,
others who get to do their own thing?

There is a subtler form of overcompensating—outrage. Reading,
listening to or watching the news, don't we love to get outraged about
so-and-so saying such-and-such? How could they? What a demon!
Don't they care about anyone but themselves? Whether we're left or
right leaning in our politics, we watch the other side say and do as they
ought to say and do, and we can't believe it. They are in character, acting
predictably and we are shocked. How could they? Really now—if we
were peaceful in our philosophies and worldviews, why would it matter
if they felt differently? So what?

What's going on with both the proselytizer and the condemner is
this: their lives aren't perfect. Committed to a worldview, we are loyal
but not completely satisfied. If we feel anxious about the shortcomings
of our views we can be open to new ways of seeing. Alternatively, we
can call contrarian views inferior and scapegoat their brand of all-for-
one, one-for-all as having an apocalyptic future. There, now don't we
feel better? "I suck, but that guy sucks more!"

OK, guilty as charged—I do that. Just for today can I impose a
moratorium on putting others down?

*"Happiness is not a goal; it is a by-product."*

*Eleanor Roosevelt (1884–1962)*

---

The pursuit of happiness is culturally encouraged. Who doesn't want more happiness? That depends on how we were raised and how we reacted to our upbringings. Aaron C. Ahuvia of the University of Michigan has authored academic papers on factors affecting subjective well-being (SWB), exploring individualism vs. collectivism, cultural influence and socio-economic conditions.[80] Ahuvia explores Kasser and Ryan's (1996) Table of Intrinsic vs. Extrinsic Goals.

Intrinsic goals are internal objectives like self-acceptance, autonomy, enjoying our relationships, improving the world, etc. Extrinsic goals include financial success, fame, body image and career advancement. Attaining either type of goal could make us happy. Our happiness depends on our motivations. There are intrinsic and extrinsic factors driving us. Intrinsic motivation is natural, internal self-motivation—we want to do it. But if positive or negative external motivators suggest that we "ought" to do it, others will not approve of us if we don't do it, or we get an incentive for doing it—these are extrinsic (external) motivators. SWB is rooted in *why*, not *what*, we do.

Not only do we need the right goals, we need the right motivation. Values aren't goals; learning might be a value and getting a degree might be a goal. The value doesn't end when the goal is either achieved or abandoned. Values, like favorite colors, don't have to be justified; they are unique to us. If we live by our values SWB is a byproduct. Authentic values may be a mystery to addicts, especially for those with a history of trauma. We have acted as if, people-pleased, hidden our feelings and reacted to life so much that we often don't know what we really stand for. It is worth exploring and may require assistance. The Twelve Steps or therapy can work for us, but as we've read today, why we do them matters.

Is recovery a value or a status symbol for me? What do I value more than getting happy?

## August 30

*"You can live a perfectly normal life if you accept that
your life will never be perfectly normal."*

*Heard around the rooms*

---

OK, we admit that we have been behaving insanely and our lives have become unmanageable. This is something we learn early on in Twelve Step recovery. But admitting fault does not make us poster children for sane and manageable living. For many of us, there was no sanity to return to once we owned up to the Step Two proposition of being and/or acting insane.

Sobriety can become the new normal and addictive behavior abnormal. Instead of "returning" to sanity, we can just start living more sanely. We don't expect care-free lives or a perfect record of decision-making. Associated with the Steps are promises—not unattainable carrots but the actual experiences of members who have done some Step work. How *normal* will look will be unique to each of us. *Normal* will involve the promises unfolding as well as regression and setbacks. We master old situations that once set us off, but now, new poor choices will be fumbled through. Let's not demand a refund from recovery the first time we fear for our financial security.

Shame is at the core of many addicts. If we feel vulnerable, inadequate and unworthy it seems normal to seek the refuge of intoxication. Acting out postponed our troubles—it didn't cure them. In therapy or in the rooms, we are able to differentiate guilt (doing a bad thing) from shame (being a bad person). Love from others can't get through if we don't feel worthy. Taking small steps by being considerate to others (doing good things) chips away at shame. We slowly feel better about ourselves, and consider the possibility that we are worthy of love, too. As others care for us, we learn to care for ourselves and think more of others. Insanity is isolating. We drive others away and become paranoid. Recovery requires engaging with others.

Can I define "recovery," "manageable," or "sanity" in my own words? What is my new normal?

*"He argued strongly with the early group in New York that it needed to tone down what he called the 'God bit.' This resulted in the much more inclusive 'Higher Power' and 'God as we understand him' concepts that are now so closely associated with Alcoholics Anonymous. This compromise was crucial— without it, AA would probably not have survived at all, much less have reached the number of people it has worldwide today. Jim B's contribution to Alcoholics Anonymous is considered second only to that of AA's two co-founders."*

*wikipedia.org*

---

This quote is referring to the story and impact of James Burwell (1898–1974), author of "The Vicious Cycle" in the Second to Fourth editions of the Big Book. Bill Wilson explained Tradition Three, "The only requirement for membership is a desire to stop drinking," by telling a story loosely based on Jim B. The tale credits Ed's (Jim's) atheism as one of the many weighty issues responsible for the elimination of the membership rules that groups had established to fortify AA. Jim helped AA to grow by helping to orchestrate The Jack Alexander article in the *Saturday Night Post*, and by starting meetings in two additional cities.[81] God was never more than a man-made myth to Jim B. He didn't have a leg up on theists, nor was he at any disadvantage in getting sober. We all do it in our own ways, based on our own beliefs. Twelve & Twelve unity does not require uniformity. When we think our programs would be better without so-and-so, maybe we should think again. We might have no obvious use for the person's contributions but someone will. It may be our closed minds that restrict our abilities to learn and gain from those we feel opposed to.

People don't have to agree to get along. We may know members whose opinions and practices differ greatly from our own. They may get under our skin; that's our issue, not theirs. They deserve our love and respect, even when agreement is impossible. Everyone's contribution is important in a fellowship.

Can I say, "You know, you may be right," when I really want to say, "I think you're absurd"?

## September 1

*"A human being is a single being. Unique and unrepeatable."*

*Eileen Caddy (1917–2006)*

---

We are all unique. We each use this book differently; some of us make it a daily ritual, some of us pick it up every now and then and some of us leave it on the bookshelf and only own it because a friend gave it to us at a meeting. Some of us talk to each other about it, some of us shout at the book in disagreement. Some of us read it and say, "You know who should be reading this?"

Our boundaries are different. Some hug and chant at meetings, while others don't. Some people are conference junkies; for others, the idea of attending two meetings in a day shows a lack of imagination. We get along with each other. That does not mean we assimilate into one school of thought. Tolerance means more than humoring opposing views. Welcoming differences puts us in a better mind than putting up with each other. Just as we can't solve a problem with the same attitude that created it, if we only listen to people we get along with, we reinforce our own bullshit instead of challenging it. Every unique being has something different to teach us just as we each have a unique gift to share with others.

We also come to appreciate others as we grow more comfortable in our own skin. Self-actualization as a psychological concept became part of the popular psychology vernacular with Abraham Maslow's needs hierarchy. Simply put, in becoming self-actualized, we accept the reality of ourselves and our world; we are self-aware but not self-absorbed. We are present and involved with the world around us. Recovery is an ascending journey from barely being able to meet our physiological and safety needs to a feeling of belonging, confidence and the respect of others. We find our uniqueness, and we aren't ashamed of who we are. Morality, creativity and a sense of mastery eventually come from the work we do in recovery. We feel a right to be here and see that we can have a positive role in the lives of others.

Addicts have a hard time being natural. Can I celebrate my uniqueness without saying "I should be this" or "I should do that"? Am I afraid to let people know who I really am?

## September 2

*"My grandfather rode a camel, my father rode a camel, I drive a Mercedes, my son drives a Land Rover, his son will drive a Land Rover, but his son will ride a camel."*

Sheikh Rashid bin Saeed Al Maktoum (1912–1990)

---

Impermanence impacts everything, including social values, trends and family dynamics. In North America, the family-life mythology of the happy Christmas greeting-card nuclear family turns out to be a hoax. By 1970, just 40% of us were members of a household including one married couple and at least one child living at home. By the turn of the millennium, married couples with biological children in the home accounted for 26% of households.[82] What our culture portrays as normal isn't normal anymore—if it ever was. Discussion about family life may trigger very different emotional reactions in two different people.

We all come to the rooms feeling something worse than different—we feel abnormal. Many of us grew up in dysfunctional homes as defined by Adult Children of Alcoholic Syndrome—we grew up with rigidity, excess, boundary issues, unclear roles, neglect, violence and mixed messages. What mode of transportation our parents took is the least of our concerns. Any of us that did come from functional nuclear families are the true odd-balls, according to statistics.

We felt *less than* and expended energy trying to right perceived inadequacies. Meditation and healthier self-talk reinforces a sense that we are not inadequate; we are OK already and the goal is not perfection. Willingness to change ourselves is a positive characteristic but we are already worthy. We feel different, which of course is true, but we are rights-bearing equals, be it a camel, a Mercedes Benz or public transit that gets us to meetings.

Who is the last person I compared myself to? Do I compare how I feel with how others appear? If I feel like I am not good enough, where did I get such an idea?

# September 3

*"Some of us have never known social joy or honest intimacy or emotional reciprocity. We have no sense of these things. Faced with getting our needs met we are baffled because we can't even name these needs."*

*From "Anorexia—Sexual, social and emotional,"*
*Sex and Love Addicts Anonymous*

---

Anorexia is an eating disorder, and sufferers deny themselves nutrition and pleasure from food. In sex and love addiction, anorexia refers to intimacy deprivation. In the most obvious sense, the anorexic is withdrawing from all physical intimacy, but even among the sexually active, we can find emotional anorexia. Promiscuity may signal avoidance of deeper emotional, intimate contact with anyone. Just as it is not the amount of alcohol consumed that defines alcoholism, frequency and choice of vice does not determine sex and love addiction. Is our behavior consistent with our values?

Many addicts and codependents have love-life imbalances. The origin of our intimacy disorders is thought to go back to our formative experiences with needs, expectations and boundaries. In the original Big Book Step Four directions, we focus on three areas: fear, resentments and sex conduct. Frustration from an inability to sustain intimate connections with people drove many a Twelve Stepper, unsatisfied with peer-to-peer support, into therapy.

Hundreds of Twelve Step programs are available for a variety of obsessions or dysfunctions. Attending six meetings or so isn't a big commitment to make in order to see how our peers deal with addiction and find clarity. Abstinence is a healthy option for substance abuse yet for other obsessive-compulsive disorders, finding equilibrium through trial and error is the path to healthy living.

Falling prey to a new addiction isn't failure. To blame the addict denies the power of addiction. That said, once we've confronted a problem, no one else is going to solve it for us. We recognize unmanageability, modify our behavior, seek help and take the Steps. We know this—we've been here before.

Do my relationships mirror my values? Am I clear on my needs and values? Do I have social joy and intimacy in my life?

## September 4

*"If The Phone Doesn't Ring, It's Me."*

Jimmy Buffet (born 1946)

---

An AA member said at a conference, "If you want to know my true intentions don't follow my thinking, follow my feet." Someone who really wants to stop drinking doesn't kill time in a bar; they go to a meeting, stay home or go for coffee.

If we seek to understand people, intentions that are emphatically stated won't provide the same clues as one's deeds do. Do they deliver in marriage what they promised in courtship? What people say can be colored by any number of factors. They may be avoiding confrontation by saying what we want to hear and their *white lies* may be well-intentioned to spare us or others from an unflattering fact or opinion.

If someone didn't call, it's not because they were busy or lost their phone or worked overtime or forgot. They didn't call because it wasn't an all-out priority. Think of a time when we meant to call, or promised we would call, but didn't. Why not? We wanted to avoid confrontation, we didn't want to offend or hurt another, or we had information we weren't ready to share. Maybe we were not realistic about our own time. For whatever reason, people tend not to say exactly what they mean, leaving the rest of us to read between the lines.

When I feel confused about someone's intentions is the message from their actions more revealing? Today, can I state my intentions and then summon the integrity to be true to my word? What is my bottom line about rigorous honesty? When is it alright for me to lie (just this once)? Do I extend this artistic liberty to others? Do I impose my values on others?

## September 5

*"Most conversations are simply monologues
delivered in the presence of a witness."*

*Margaret Millar (1915–1994)*

---

Millar created compelling and detailed characters. No doubt she is able to tell us a lot about her characters by how they communicate. Talking serves a number of purposes at different times during parts of the recovery process. Twelve & Twelve therapies are often described as a *words and witness* formula. We hear that this is a selfish program. Most everything that we say is said, first and foremost, for our own benefit. "How can I tell you how I feel until I hear what I say?" is a funny truism. Often through talking it out, we find our own answers.

Speaking in a meeting may release tension, allow us to articulate our thoughts, or make us feel valuable—a *power of example*, as it is often put. Sometimes we simply purge the annoyances or anxieties of the day. This isn't wrong, selfish or self-absorbed. It is how we take responsibility for our lives.

This isn't to say that we don't engage in deeper conversation with one another. We can be present, vulnerable and empathetic with others. In and out of the program we find that deeper connections with people are one of recovery's benefits. We do have something valuable to share when we speak and we sometimes hear just what we needed to hear. But the fickle law of unintended consequences suggests that there is more going on in the peer-to-peer recovery process than we can quantify. One reason skeptics dismiss Twelve & Twelve programs is that *how it works* is still a mystery.

If I ever feel that I am not getting my needs met by a meeting, is it worth considering what I have to give, instead of what I need to get? Sometimes, just being there and listening can make a difference. Sharing the time is as thoughtful, at times, as sharing my thoughts.

# September 6

*"If we could read the secret history of our enemies, we should find in each man's life sorrow and suffering enough to disarm all hostility."*

Henry Wadsworth Longfellow (1807–1882)

---

Attribution theories in social psychology explain how we attribute causes to behaviors. Being late can be caused by either unforeseen traffic or thoughtlessness; one is a circumstance, the other is a personality trait. How we feel about the person who was late will influence what we attribute the cause to. When we place too much weight on personality characteristics as a cause for other people's behaviors and don't pay enough attention to their circumstances, this is called a fundamental attribution error. When we are late, we blame the traffic. We may not be as understanding or empathetic to others—a foe for instance. We attribute his or her behavior to negative personality traits—"She is a selfish egomaniac," "He is a careless pecker-head," "They are such narcissists."

When we are heavily invested in relationships, we generally assign causal attribution to unavoidable circumstances. If the relationship sours, our biases shift, and we may blame their lack of character for the same behaviors that we forgave before. Knowing the particular secret lives of our enemies—their circumstances—could render us less critical of them. If we truly understand another, how could we not be sympathetic? To understand fully is to forgive fully. That said, forgiveness is a choice—not an obligation.

What if we want to be more understanding but we reactively judge our *foes* as being morally reprehensible? We know about writing an inventory and attributing causes to effects. We can do this for our *foes*, too. We dug up the exact nature of our wrongs, writing and/or meditating to gain better understanding. We can apply the same method to our adversaries, viewing them as the victims of circumstance. Even if we don't know everything about them we empathize, putting ourselves in their shoes. Could we not see their deeds as forgivable, if not unavoidable? We can understand that they, too, are doing the best they can.

For me, carrying grudges or justifiable resentment is like carrying a ticking time bomb—I'm the one in danger. Do I have a means to disarm resentments before they blow up in my face?

# September 7

*"Just as it is wrong to enable or support any alcoholic to become re-addicted to any drug, it's equally wrong to deprive any alcoholic of medication which can alleviate or control other disabling physical and/or emotional problems."*

Living Sober, 88

---

*Living Sober* is the great secular sourcebook for people new to AA. Any newcomer from any Twelve Step fellowship could find some value in its practical advice. The appendix in *Living Sober* is written by doctors who are sober members. They speak to issues of physical and mental problems most members will face and explain how we can be honest with ourselves and our doctors regarding mental health. Members freely give their own experience, strength and help on issues of depression, mood disorders, syndromes and surgeries that require painkillers. No member should play doctor. We avoid expressing our views as widely held or strongly recommended.

If we are faced with our own mental, emotional or physical issues we have a number of tests ahead of us. We may be predisposed to seeking chemical relief for physical or emotional pain. On the other hand, we may be long-timers with heads full of Twelve Step dogma and hearts full of do-it-myself pride. We keep our minds open; we don't rely strictly on what we know and think.

When I am ambivalent about a life choice, why not ask myself what I would say to someone else in my situation? Maybe I already know the best course of action for myself. Who else can I consult?

## September 8

*"Kindness is more important than wisdom and the recognition of this is the beginning of wisdom."*

Theodore Isaac Rubin, MD (born 1923)

---

This New York psychoanalyst blended Tibetan Buddhism with western psychology. These words are applied daily in our program in at least two ways. First, before we formally sort through the wreckage of our past and our current imperfections, we can treat ourselves with the compassion we would offer a troubled child. Even when looking at our dark side, we can be gentle and kind with ourselves. Healing comes from self-acceptance, not self-condemnation. Taking 100% responsibility for our roles in relationships is paramount to recovery. We may not be the cause of all of our trouble, but who else will correct our problems? To be overly harsh undermines this work in the same way that rationalizing away accountability does. Let's be gentle with ourselves.

Second, by being kind to ourselves, we are less disappointed in, or critical of, others—"I'm OK, you're OK" vs. "I'm not good enough, what the hell's wrong with you?" Once again the adage "when we smile, the whole world smiles back at us" reminds us that in many ways the world reflects back the attitudes we project.

When a newcomer talks with us it isn't our knowledge of the literature or our way with words that moves them. It is our attitude that reaches them, our sincere kindness. A love that asks nothing in return is not dramatic and can often be a part of a daily routine—it includes showing up on time, pitching in to help and/or listening intently.

Just for today, can I lead the way with kindness and let the day unfold as it will?

# September 9

*"Advice is what you ask for when you already know
the answer but wish you didn't."*

*Erica Jong (born 1942)*

---

Ouch, that hurts! According to Buddhist teachings, our enlightenment is to be mined from within—not inserted from outside. How often does a guru answer a question with a question? They don't provide answers; they provide broader ways to frame our situations and different ways to look at them. We are helped to see beyond our blind spots.

When we are new it is sometimes hard to sort out automatic thoughts (the addictive cycle) and our inherent truths (what many experience as the guidance of a higher power). Inside our heads it isn't one cross-legged skinny guru on the top of a mountain; it's a committee of lobbyists pleading for our attention. What voice do we focus on? ("Yes," "no," "hurry," "wait," "do it," "don't do it," "don't be stupid," "don't be such a sissy!")

When we are new a regular day is one of dread, impulse, uncertainty and chaos. Maybe that's where a sponsor isn't such a bad idea. If we don't have sponsors we check in with our running mates or best friends. Most decisions don't have to be rushed and most wrong decisions can be corrected. Creating melodrama only makes our predicaments worse.

As sponsors, we don't always tell others what we know. Our job is to listen with compassion and let them find their own way. We encourage inquiry instead of impulse. We don't give someone a fish and feed them for a day; we teach them to fish, feeding them for a lifetime.

How good am I at waiting out the truth for myself? How am I at letting others find their own truth?

## September 10

*"A.A. as such, ought never be organized;*
*but we may create service boards or committees*
*directly responsible to those they serve."*
Tradition Nine[83]

Oh, how some of us love to take liberties with how we ought never be organized. It relieves the tension as we fumble through the formalities of our meetings. But it is refreshing indeed that seeming ego-maniacs like us can learn to wear life like a loose garment. We have as little organization and structure as we can get away with while efficiently carrying out our primary purpose, as a group. The functionality of our fellowship is puzzling to newcomers and outsiders. It seems too simple to be true.

In service work, as one position becomes comfortable we are rotated out of it to let someone else benefit from service. With other ventures, like regional or world conferences, committees are formed and we work together, sometimes years in advance. Dealing with the media, professionals and creating our literature requires staff and members to respond to emails and calls. But committees and head office staff work for the groups—they don't dictate to us, instruct us or resolve local disputes.

Am I patient, willing and humble with service work? Do I avoid back-room politics and do I encourage all decisions to be made with transparency and due consideration? Will special attention be given to the voice of the minority? A well heard minority is our best defense against a confident, yet careless majority. When I let my name stand for a service position is my interest in serving others or furthering my own image of how things should be run?

## September 11

*"A man practices the art of adventure when he breaks the chain of routine and renews his life through reading new books, traveling to new places, making new friends, taking up new hobbies and adopting new viewpoints."*

*Wilfred Peterson (1900–1995)*

---

Some evidence suggests that Alzheimer's disease can be delayed, mitigated and maybe even prevented by ensuring that the elderly continue to learn new things. This can be fun, of course. Learning to dance for the first time, learning a wind instrument if you've only ever played stringed instruments, learning a language—these are all activities that stimulate the brain and can mitigate the deterioration associated with aging. No doubt, new challenges can help young people keep their brains and bodies resilient, too.

Recovery can be enhanced by avoiding complacency and *hardening of the attitudes*. Just going to new meetings and sharing with new people can shake up our routines a little. Getting away from meetings if we are going out of habit or finding new activities could do as much to positively stir our recovery as doubling our efforts, which can sometimes burn us out. If we have always thought we might qualify for another Twelve & Twelve fellowship, we can go to some meetings and see if the message resonates or not. We will surely meet some new people, be exposed to some new literature and gain a fresh perspective on addiction and recovery.

A new book is a good idea. If we always read non-fiction we try something adventurous. If we read nothing but program literature, we try a psychology or philosophy book, or maybe history or poetry—why not? How many books a year would be just right?

Am I open to new viewpoints? Do I expose myself to new ways of seeing? Can I and should I shake up my routine today? Change is as good as a rest.

*"What makes these platitudes so hurtful is that they're usually delivered by caring people with the best intentions. Ironically, some of these little beauties actually may be true, but I think that the biggest problem with them is that their timing is all wrong."*

*Greg Harvey, PhD*

---

*Grieving for Dummies* identifies the top-ten consoling clichés. These are the wrong things to say at a time when people really need to be heard—not told. Grievers don't need us to *see through them* with x-ray, best friend vision. They just need us to *see them through* a difficult experience. People aren't crazy to feel what they feel. We will lose loved ones one day; other times we will be looked to for support by families that lose loved ones. Meetings are places where we encounter people who are suffering losses. Here are the ten clichés to bite our tongue on: (1) "I know how you feel," (2) You're never given anything that you can't deal with," (3) "Time heals all wounds," (4) "Don't dwell on it," (5) "Don't feel bad," (6) "It's time for you to move on," (7) "It's probably for the best," (8) "It's in the natural order of things," (9) "He lived a good life" and (10) "Be grateful you had him with you for so long."[84]

Meditating on empathy prepares us to be compassionate. "I don't know what to say, but I can listen" is sometimes enough from us. Maybe we have our own experiences to draw on in terms of what comforted or annoyed us during a loss. There are great books on grief and grieving that will help prepare us for our inevitable sorrow, as well as make us better friends.

If I don't know what to say, do I know it's OK to say "I don't know what to say"? Can I ask my friend what they want and need instead of thinking I am expected to know? I don't have to be an expert to be a good friend. If I am not great with words, what else can I do? Can I make a meal or do some chores?

## September 13

*"I do not believe that sheer suffering teaches. If suffering alone taught, all the world would be wise, since everyone suffers. To suffering must be added mourning, understanding, patience, love, openness and the willingness to remain vulnerable."*

Anne Morrow Lindbergh (1906–2001)

---

Suffering, processing, learning and growing are healthy human experiences. What stunts emotional growth are coping techniques designed to do the impossible—avoid pain. Three impediments to growing through pain are resignation, escapism and overcompensation. These shortcuts dull the pain and deflect attention from core issues until we are ready for them. Today, let's look at resignation.

Resignation is not the healthy process of accepting what we cannot change. When we *resign* ourselves to suffering we are giving in, playing victim to our plight as if nothing can be changed. We become our labels—I am bipolar, an addict or HIV+; I have a learning disability or "That's just the way it is." The classic addict's cop-out is "I didn't want to let you down but I can't help it."

In recovery, healing starts with an admission of limits. Chronic conditions and deadly illnesses are no laughing matter and when confronted with them we may be forced to accept a lot. Accepting the truth, incorporating limits into life and framing a way to make the most of circumstances is quite different from using our limitations as excuses—"I can't quit smoking because I am an addict," "I can't learn to organize because I am dyslexic." These are self-imposed limits. Maybe our resignation assuages guilt or shame. "I am an addict" can be a crutch if we don't take responsibility for it. Resignation can be debilitating. We could be stuck for life.

Wallowing in my pity doesn't feel good for long. What are the circumstances in my life that I can do nothing about? Is there something I have resigned myself to that maybe I can work through?

# September 14

*"If you can't be a good example then you'll just have to be a horrible warning."*

Catherine Aird (born 1930)

---

Escapism is a coping technique that doesn't cure anything, but it is second nature to the self-respecting addict or codependent. Most of us nearly killed ourselves drowning our sorrows in mood-altering substances, by risk-taking or by engaging in unhealthy relationships and/or violating boundaries. Recovery from one addiction won't assure us that other behaviors don't get out of hand. Avoiding domestic dissatisfaction is easy with workaholism. Escaping can look noble. Hiding in a meeting can be an escape when we should be solving a problem or working the next Step.

Good examples in recovery are candid about never being *cured* of their escape artist tendencies. Like diabetes, coping techniques can be controlled, not eliminated. We need not be discouraged when escapism flares up. Our own escapist yearnings can be treated as a barometric reading instead of a failure. We can be examples by how we respond to our escape artist tendencies or we may be terrible warnings about what happens if we deny our idiosyncrasies.

We are drawn to what we long for and we avoid what we loathe. Addiction was a way to delay or avoid feelings that we found to be unbearable. Today, do we know what our avoidance tendencies are? If we are avoiding, what are we avoiding? Is there a feeling of being repressed or a responsibility that we are trying to put off? A "good man's folly" is a term used by AA's cofounders that makes for a good rationalization from an authoritative source. Bill W. was a forefather of peer-to-peer recovery and he died of emphysema that was the result of an untreated nicotine addiction. He was no better or worse than any of us. He had his maladaptive coping techniques too. How fitting that an entire society's original good example left us with a terrible warning.

Am I aware of my tendencies toward escapism and resignation? What would I rather escape than face today?

# September 15

*"Emotion turning back on itself, and not leading on to thought or action, is the element of madness."*

John Sterling (1806–1844)

---

Twelve & Twelve fellowships don't hold the franchise on madness; repressed feelings can cause mental health issues for anyone. Addiction brought us to a turning point, yet it may have been only a symptom of an underlying issue. Overcompensating, the third of three avoidance techniques, inspires a false sense of self-sufficiency when help is what's needed. In some cases, this cycle of maladjusted coping has origins that go way back. Some coping techniques were learned before we had the language to describe them. We didn't learn healthy reactions; we escaped, by resigning and overcompensating. A typical overcompensation learned in a hostile, chaotic or unsupportive family is adoption of the attitude, "I don't need you. I can get along fine without you." This tough-talk can come from a jilted lover or a fired employee. When we hear ourselves or others overcompensating with tough-talk, the bravado may be smoke and mirrors that hide grief, anger, self-doubt and/or fear.

Cognitive Behavioral Therapy helps us analyze situations where we act badly, laugh it off or go catatonic. What are we feeling? What events and assumptions or reasoning led to these feelings? Are we feeling trapped or disgusted? What else could these facts, thoughts and feelings mean? If we have an emotional slip today, maybe we can learn something from it that will help us next time.

How and when do I overcompensate? Resignation, escapism and overcompensation result from a narrative about me, my world and the others in it. As always, I should ask, "What else could this mean?" Coping techniques are impulsive reactions. Coping strategies are a trail or a doorway that says to me, "Pay attention: inner truth found here!" Am I figuring out more about how I tick?

## September 16

*"The possibility of stepping into a higher plane is quite real for everyone. It requires no force or effort or sacrifice. It involves little more than changing our ideas about what is normal."*

Deepak Chopra (born 1946)

---

What is our immediate reaction to this statement? If recovery feels hard, if life seems relentlessly burdensome, we might cynically think D-Man (Deepak, can we call you D-Man?) is trying to sell more books by telling us what we want to hear. For others, this idea is a matter of fact: we were using and abusing one day and then we were transformed from hopeless people to powers of example. Why would we think that we have any limits? A caution for Twelve Steppers is that we need to check our expectations periodically with someone we trust: We can be so negative we could brighten a room just by leaving it, plus any of us can get recurring flare-ups of magical thinking from time to time, too.

Magnetic resonance imaging reveals how some addict's brains are impaired in their ability to identify and avoid risk. Our members are notorious for getting caught up in get-rich-quick schemes or get-enlightened-quick workshops that do little more than part another fool from their money. Having a higher power comes highly recommended in these parts but some of us get carried away in assigning magical qualities to that power or our special relationship with it. There is a lot of liberty in Twelve & Twelve culture and individuals set the terms for their own recovery, including determining what is and is not healthy living and how to define sane thinking. What is supernatural hogwash for one of us is evidence-based living for another.

Dr. Chopra also suggests that self-identifying as an addict chains us down. By stating "I am an alcoholic" or a "gambler" or "codependent" or "I am powerless over_____," we focus on the negative, repeatedly reminding ourselves that we are sick. He would recommend: "My name is _____ and I am a field of limitless potential."

It pays to dream big and why wouldn't I open my mind to endless possibilities? Even if I err, it isn't the end of the world. Can I dream big dreams without placing both feet firmly in mid-air?

*"The future remains uncertain. There is no event. In reality,
probability merely forms the starting point in our judgement of
likelihood, in our degree of belief concerning the future.
We then use logic, reason and even intuition to argue our case.
And this arguing is largely done with ourselves—
making our belief in what will happen, heavily subjective."*

Dr. Strangelove's Game: A Brief History of Economic Genius
by Paul Strathern (born 1940)

---

In his book, Strathern describes the theory and philosophy of economist John Keynes (pronounced "Canes"), a British architect of monetary policy through two world wars and the Great Depression.

Economists, like addicts, tend to fixate on the future. The price paid for ruminating about what might happen offers little improvement on the long odds of accurate predictions. But the longer we invest in our predictions, the stronger we defend them. In recovery, the present should offer all we can handle. We practice letting go of the idea of trying to will the future to our design.

For some of us the principle behind Step Three isn't so off-putting. It's the wording. So, we change the wording. Each of us has more at our disposal to define the recovery process than the original architects of the Twelve Steps did—not the least of which is decades of experience of what works and what doesn't. The wording isn't sacred. The original literature referred to adherence to spiritual principles, not rigid wording. However, a mastery of words will not give us the power to control the outcomes in our lives.

T.H. Huxley invented the word "agnostic" in the 1800s to describe the impossibility of knowing how and why we exist, or what guides us. Agnosticism simply means "without knowledge." When we are at peace with being vulnerable to outcomes we can't completely control, we are living Step Three.

Do I get invested in my own expectations and theories? When I do, am I open to new ways of seeing or do I vigorously defend my point of view? "There is no event." Do I live as if my life will begin for real following some "event," or once I am good enough, or ready? Can I remember this is here, this is now?

*"Do not judge your neighbor until you walk two moons in his moccasins. Our first teacher is our own heart. Judge not by the eye but by the heart."*

*Cheyenne teaching*

---

Who are we and how are we to judge another? Our individual addictions played out like nobody else's and our recoveries are one of a kind, too. It's silly to read our literature and imagine all of us working the Steps the same way, enjoying a universal experience. By medical definition, we have a disease. Cynics scoff and say that this definition is more about the medical infrastructure claiming a monopoly on addiction care than a scientific description of our experience. Maybe there's truth to that, but there is still value in considering the disease concept metaphorically. Substance abuse has led to medical handicaps, some of which people can't fully recover from, so the medical impact of addiction is undeniable.[85] Again, we all have our own unique damage.

"Double-winners" is a fun term that describes concurrent mental/emotional disorders (comorbidity) or multiple addictions.[86] Recovery characteristics are likely going to differ dramatically, depending on the wide variety of "isms" that we sport. Relapse susceptibility will vary also, along with our psychological make-ups. Medically, relapse has no bearing on our characters or moral fortitude; relapse is about the nature of addiction as much as it speaks to the quality of our recovery. Some of us who "keep our noses clean" on our primary addiction will demonstrate new bad habits elsewhere. We are each unique in our struggles and our skills. Nietzsche said, "At the bottom every man knows well enough that he is a unique being, only once on this earth; and by no extraordinary chance will such a marvelous picturesque piece of diversity in unity as he is, ever be put together a second time."

Comparing or competing is folly. I will never be putting apples up against apples so what's the point? Do I think I am different? I win, I am right and tied for first place—we're all unique. I can identify with others but I need not judge myself or others harshly.

## September 19

*"Alcoholics who continue to be depressed, anxious, irritable,
and unhappy after they stop drinking are actually suffering
from a phenomenon called the 'protracted withdrawal
syndrome.' The physical damage caused by years of excessive
drinking has not been completely reversed; they are, in fact, still
sick and in need of more effective therapy."*

Under the Influence
*by James Robert Milam, PhD & Katherine Ketcham*

---

Anhedionia is a common symptom of withdrawal, and it means that we can't appreciate normally joyful experiences such as a sunny day or playing with our kids. This dulling of the senses is common for newcomers and drives a lot of people back to addiction, or into new addictive patterns for escape. Our substance or process of choice may kill us eventually but they end the malcontented state right now. Many of us were self-medicating underlying mental health problems. Taking away our crutches didn't solve our problems, it exposed them.

Some of us exhibit serious psychiatric disorders in early recovery that will pass naturally when our brains dry out and recovery takes hold. While seeking help, we shouldn't rashly embrace every label put on us. Professionals can mistake our withdrawal symptoms for permanent or chronic conditions that may clear up as our heads clear. Still, getting medical or psychological attention early in recovery isn't being melodramatic. The following is a shopping list of symptoms to look for after our first year. If these symptoms persist after we have some sobriety, help could be needed: impaired interpersonal skills, pessimism, obsessive tendencies, shame or guilt, low energy, memory problems, craving, over-reacting or feeling numb when facing conflict, panic, stress, coordination problems, suicidal thoughts or anxiety attacks. We will identify with all or most, but it's ye olde question of degrees.

Am I feeling like a hypochondriac now? Seriously, if these factors are present, what am I doing about it?

## September 20

*"I believe that we are solely responsible for our choices,
and we have to accept the consequences of every deed,
word, and thought throughout our lifetime."*

Elisabeth Kubler-Ross (1926–2004)

---

What if our Traditions concluded with "Personal responsibility is the spiritual foundation of our Traditions..."? Not to discount the cherished reminder of humility that the principle of anonymity offers us, but personal responsibility is also a spiritual principle that weaves throughout the program of recovery. Every Step is an exercise in taking responsibility. In Step One we stop blaming others and stop making excuses for ourselves. Admitting our unmanageability may be taking the most personal responsibility we have accepted in a long time. This theme continues throughout the Twelve Steps and we are encouraged to own up to responsibility for ourselves and to the extent that we impact others. When anyone, anywhere, reaches out for help, we will not complacently hope that someone else will help; rather, we commit ourselves to putting the needs of the still suffering ahead of our own. "And for that I am responsible."

The opposite of bedeviled self-will run riot is not passivity, but personal responsibility. Responsibility is not an ego-feeding proposition, but rather a sign of maturity. The above quote could be a mantra for living the program and said in accordance with every Step. Even Step Three. For the most theistic of us, it is our decision that puts this new attitude into action; we are not completely abdicating responsibility to a guiding force. The stewardship throughout the Traditions is about integrity, a call to duty to "let it begin with me." Of course humility, unity and the spirit of rotation are the other legs of the stool upon which the future of our fellowship sits. But how can we take pride in our spiritual progress without taking responsibility?

Do I believe that opening the door to responsibility is the only way to the freedom that recovery promises?

# September 21

Some people are doing what they feel that they were meant to do. They may have troubles and obstacles but fulfilling their purpose comes naturally. Boundaries between work and play are often lost.

Some of us have to search for our talents. Envy of others may offer clues to what we want—we want what *they* have; can't we just do what *they did*? If we want the success that comes from someone else's talent and/or good fortune, we follow their path back far enough and we will see where they were before we became envious of them. Their story is our road map—if we understand what it takes to have what they have. Before we cast out envy as a deadly sin, let's see what it tells us about ourselves. Possibly, this journey will change our minds about what we want.

When approaching our purpose, be it destiny or design, a playful curiosity can guide us. Suspending expectation helps keep us present to the experience. Goals that are too narrowly defined become obstacles. Setting ourselves up for what we *think* fulfillment will look like isn't nearly as useful as trying new things until we find a fit. Today's quote talks of following our talent to dark places. We have to leave our comfort zones and go into the unknown to achieve our potential. That could mean going back to school, changing jobs or expressing ourselves through art. Change is scary and that's why few of us go all the way. To settle for *good enough* isn't necessarily a cop-out. It is everyone's prerogative to play it safe or take a leap of faith to follow a muse.

What would I do if I didn't want the approval of others? Does fear hold me back? At the end of my life will I wish I hadn't been so scared? Alternatively, what's wrong with the simple life? To right-size my expectations and self-image is a sign of maturity, too.

## September 22

*"The question 'Who am I?' really asks, 'Where do I belong or fit?' We get the sense of that 'direction'—the sense of moving toward the place where we fit, or of shaping the place toward which we are moving so that it will fit us—from hearing how others have handled or are attempting to handle similar (but never exactly the same) situations. We learn by listening to their stories, by hearing how they came (or failed) to belong or fit."*

*Ernest Kurtz & Katherine Ketcham*

---

Parting with dependency is a double-edged sword; we belonged together. Many of us were secretive about the extent of our addictions or how we felt about ourselves. Addiction, both foe and companion, was the leaning post we depended on most. Metaphorically, our substances or processes of choice were our best friends, but all the while they were plotting our demise. It may be normal to mourn the loss of our "old friends." Some will demonize their pre-recovery days with statements like "I wouldn't give up my worst day sober for my best day drunk." Some of us may prefer a balanced perspective; we acknowledge that there were good times in our past and that a part of us that we will miss was left behind on day one of sobriety.

At one time addiction helped us fit in, but this solution turned out to be the fool's gold of cure-alls. We invested a good deal of our hopes and lives into attempts to curb addiction on our own, which proved hopeless. Despite the harmful consequences, we may mourn the loss of our old friends—our addictions. Without going so far as to romanticize our pasts, it may be healthy to pay respect to our old selves. This makes us more approachable to newcomers, as we have compassion for the dilemmas they are about to face.

Now that I am no longer a figment of my addiction, who am I? Am I still defined by my addiction in recovery? "My name's _____ and I am a(n) _____"? Do I fit into the fellowship? Is that the only place I fit or has recovery given me the courage to spread my wings? Can addiction and recovery be part of my life without being the focus of my life?

# September 23

*"Be who you are and say what you feel, because those who mind don't matter and those who matter don't mind."*

*Dr. Seuss (1904–1991)*

---

According to this advice from the good doctor, we are fine just the way we are. Whether we change dramatically or stay the same, we need not be ashamed of today's thoughts, feelings and actions. Dr. Seuss tells us that while it may be prudent to hear out our critics, our self-image need not be swayed by their vantage points. Our best friends are not waiting for us to be better; they appreciate us completely—just the way we are.

How long can we sustain belief in ourselves without becoming critical of ourselves? It will likely take practice. Somewhere along the line we became conditioned to never be satisfied. Where did that get us? Did we turn to pills, booze, bad relationships, gambling, spending, eating and/or self-abuse? The doctor has prescribed a new medicine for the mind. Can we accept the remedy? Let's look at ourselves through the eyes of those who consider us fine—right now, just like this. Why not start loving ourselves the way we are right now? When we hear the internal critic, how about showing that voice some compassion too?

In being fair with myself I will avoid judging others. Bill W. said, "The way our 'worthy' alcoholics have sometimes tried to judge the 'less worthy' is, as we look back on it, rather comical. Imagine, if you can, one alcoholic judging another!" Now imagine needing the approval of another addict to feel worthy. We may hear in meetings, "Once I needed your approval and I would do anything to get it; today I appreciate your approval, but I am not willing to do anything to get it."

What situations challenge my ability to be authentic? How many minutes can I go without criticizing myself? Do I feel desperate for the approval of others?

## September 24

*"A man who as a physical being is always turned toward the outside, thinking that his happiness lies outside him, finally turns inward and discovers that the source is within him."*

*Søren Kierkegaard (1813–1855)*

---

Happiness is an inside job and maintaining peace requires regular spring cleaning. We are only as sick as our secrets, they tell us. Our public and private selves—what we present and what we hide from others—may look different from one another. We may be candid about deep, dark secrets in one environment and zipper-lipped in another. Self-deception and unconscious biases are unavoidable. It takes years to understand the triggers that impact us emotionally and cause us to act or react. These reactions are not always conscious or premeditated. For the purposes of today's musing we look at outer and inner unmanageability and how the road of happy destiny is navigated.

In the midst of our addictions, we looked to the outside world for something to lean on, to relieve inner discomfort. In Step One we look at the unmanageable fact of being powerless over our cravings. There is other surface damage, too. There may have been bankruptcy, illness, legal trouble and blows to our image and reputation. As we learn more about ourselves, we find distorted perceptions, fear, greed, desperation and maybe neurotic or psychotic symptoms. We have codependent predispositions stemming from irrational beliefs that drive us into ever-escalating, risky and reckless dramas and ambushes with the people we hook up with in life. No wonder we want to outsource our salvation.

Until I understand triggers, compulsions and automatic thinking I will feed my needs with people, places and things—just like the old days. History will haunt me until I take the time to identify and face my exact nature. Does internal turmoil stop me from being happy? If this is not my first look at Step One, is there more to my dependency than meets the eye?

# September 25

*"Never reach out your hand
unless you're willing to extend an arm."*

Pope Paul VI (1897–1978)

A statistic bandied around is that seven lives are deeply affected by each addict. If we believe in karma, there's our payback. We have seven addicts to help. Service to others will come with both demands and rewards and rarely will it be what we bargained for. The AA Responsibility Declaration states that we are all responsible to extend a hand of help whenever and where ever. We get involved in the lives of others as part of our ongoing recovery. The great balancing act in reaching out our hands and being willing to go to any lengths, when saving the drowning, involves not being pulled in ourselves.

When a youth is brought into treatment an invitation is extended to the adult(s). Addiction is a family disease. Addiction is often borne of communication and bonding issues. Because the symptoms are obvious in one family member, it's a bit rash to scapegoat the addict as the only family problem. Sometimes symptoms of narcissism are first detected in those affected by the narcissist. Some mental disorders are like viral infections—the carrier is asymptomatic while others suffer the outbreaks. Family treatment takes a holistic approach to causes and effects in family dynamics.

Recovery and relapse prevention improve when everyone takes responsibility for their roles in the problem and in the solution. Twelve & Twelve fellowships have plenty of adolescent and adult children of substance or process addicts who make do without extensive family treatments. For members with offspring, part of their amends can be to encourage discussion on family dynamics, making it OK to talk about such things. The sobering addict need not be pampered. We can be overbearing when we say, "You need help." Saying "I am here to help if you need me" is a better way to reach out to those who are ready.

Do I remember that charity begins at home? Am I mindful of others at home and in my home group?

*"The feeling is often the deeper truth,
the opinion the more superficial one."*

*Augustus William Hare (1792–1834)*

---

More than being an intellectual decision, our commitment to recovery is visceral. Who among us was not told, warned or reasoned with? Most of us articulated one or two convincing pledges about how we could see the error of our ways and how things would be different. Then, we disappointed ourselves and those who loved us. Conceding defeat wasn't enough. How we feel may be more prophetic than all the reason in the world when it comes to Step One finally taking hold in our lives.

Feeling remorse can be crippling. We may concede, intellectually, that addiction is a disease and we need not feel guilt for the harm we caused to our children, our parents, our partners or our best friends. We didn't hurt them out of malice. Feeling powerless over addiction is more profound than intellectualizing addiction. Flight, fight and freeze are natural reactions to feelings. *Feeling* that recovery is worth fighting for packs a greater punch than any opinion does.

Pundits debate the rationale of addiction being classified as a disease. They often have no skin in the game. Twelve Step treatments may look like quackery if we see them as mere intellectual exercises. Instead of consulting outsiders, we observe those who have practiced a Twelve & Twelve way of life. We were invited to try it first and judge the results. The opinions turned out to be superficial truths. The experiences shared with us and the way others in recovery made us feel turned out to be the deeper truth.

Do I tend to trust my intuition or my thoughts more? Can I relate to the power of feelings?

# September 27

*"We can let circumstances rule us—or we can take charge and rule our lives from within."*

*Earl Nightingale (1921–1989)*

---

The possibilities of this quip can be enticing—intoxicatingly enticing. In the thrill of the moment, words like this can have us close the book with a pop and say to ourselves, "Why yes, things will be different now!" The adrenalin we feel could be confused with a life-altering force. Our "diseases of perception" can befuddle good intentions. This quote could lead us to greatness just as surely as it could lead us to self-willed madness. Sober second thought gives insight into our ruling circumstances. Nightingale is talking of the self-actualization of sane, reasoning people. Is that us? Maybe. Consider the alcoholic who took this missive as a sign that he or she could and should train themselves to be social drinkers. Intuition helps us differentiate the trustworthy voice from within, from cunning self-will run riot. The above quote could easily articulate our own personal transformations from hopeless to recovering. On the other hand, it could be an epitaph.

When Bill Wilson first heard the Serenity Prayer, he said that never had so much of AA philosophy been put into so few words. It is frustrating at first to differentiate the circumstances that deserve our unyielding determination from those that need our humble acceptance. Practice, mediation and consultation are how we learn. We have already changed our lives from within in remarkable ways. We have also had to let go of a lot, which we at one time refused to do. We are promised "a new freedom and a new happiness." Progress, regression and more progress is our lot, but never perfection.

Today, how do I keep my passion in check so stubbornness is not disguised as persistence, closed-mindedness is not rationalized as determination and my goals don't become obsessions? Now isn't that the wisdom to know the difference?

## September 28

*"In the meditation practice we intentionally put aside the tendency to elevate some aspects of our experience and to reject others. Instead we just let our experience be what it is and practice observing it from moment to moment. Letting go is a way of letting things be, of accepting things as they are."*

Jon Kabat-Zinn (born 1944)

In his book *Full Catastrophe Living*, Kabat-Zinn outlines the attitudinal foundations of mindfulness practice: non-judging, patience, nurturing a beginner's mind, trusting in one's inner voice, non-striving, acceptance and letting go.

To illustrate the importance of letting go, Kabat-Zinn shares a story of how hunters in India capture monkeys. Hunters tie a coconut to the base of a tree, drill a hole just big enough for a monkey's hand to reach into, and they put a banana in the hollowed out coconut. The monkey's open hand easily reaches into the hole, he grabs the banana and he won't let go. Monkeys are easy prey. All they have to do to be free is to let go, but they rather stubbornly won't do it.[87]

What do we hold onto every day in the same way? Sometimes our banana is a maladaptive coping-technique that is sabotaging our growth. Sometimes we cling to arguments because we have already invested so much in them. In our own moments of clarity we can see the futility, but we press on, trying to give credence to our fevered insanity.

Letting go in recovery is not resignation. Experiencing feelings, thoughts and sensations without labeling is to achieve sobriety in consciousness. What am I holding onto that I can consider letting go of? Is there something in my life I have labeled unacceptable? If so, what is another way to look at it? Am I awake to the reality of my world or trapped in a dream?

# September 29

*"It is another thing to set myself up as judge of your delusions.
This is playing God. I must not try to be the guarantor of your
integrity and honesty: that is your work. I can only hope that
my honesty with and about myself will empower
you to be honest with and about yourself."*

*John Powell (1925–2009)*

---

In our pluralistic fellowship, finding salvation is an individual process. The further away we are from our fellowships when we look at them, the more uniformity we see. The closer we get the more individuality we see. In our work with others we aren't strong-arming anyone to see it our way or to submit to *by the book* salvation. We help them find *their* salvation.

The Twelve & Twelve legacies are recovery, unity and service. Unity is not short for uniformity. Uniformity would mean our recovery processes would be identical. Unity means combining diverse parts into one. Our purpose unifies us; our processes are unique. We were each treating our own problems when we fell into addiction. Each of our individual journeys is different from one another. Still, we can feel connected. We can treat each other as equals. Our experience is our only currency. We don't have expertise, because what works for one would result in failure for another.

When we judge, evaluate and compare we are playing the *intellectual*. Recovery isn't an intellectual process. It is a visceral, emotional experience. Maybe it is fun to play savior or recovery guru, but let's get real. Even our own stories are just that—narratives. The mystery of addiction, our own psyches and the unknowns of the universe are experiences we are having, not lectures we're giving. We tell our truths candidly, and others can interpret them liberally. Each of us must muster our own reasons for recovery.

Do I have enough on my plate with managing my own delusions? Do I wish people would save time and see it my way?

## September 30

*"I have been one acquainted with the night.*
*I have walked out in the rain—and back in rain.*
*I have outwalked the furthest city light."*

Robert Frost (1874–1963)

---

In art, night is sometimes a metaphor for our fear of the unknown. Rain is a popular symbol for turmoil and hardship. Rain is also a metaphor for renewal—like "April showers bring May flowers." Frost's city light can refer to the path most traveled, the familiar, safe and the comfortable.

We have darkness in our history. Blotting it out with behavior and stimulants drove us to or near insanity. The insanity we speak of is, in part, our own self-deception. We were the architects of an altered or recreated reality. We have built sandcastles in the sky and booked a moving truck. Our poet, on the other hand, faces life as it comes (the rain and the dark). He is not beaten, hiding or complaining.

Letting go can include consciously loosening our grip on self-will or shortcomings. It can also represent letting our internal darkness be free to come to the surface. When we are ashamed, we expend a lot of energy camouflaging. Truths that we are repressing or denying can eat away at us. Instead of struggling we let go of what's inside and permit the truth to flow to the surface. In recovery we are challenged many times to walk beyond the comforting light or to fearlessly venture into the rain or darkness. When we walk through the rain and in and out of the darkness we may find a new peace and strength. We are vulnerable and authentic now and the consequences of coming clean, if there are any, can be endured. We will be free. It's only rain, not acid. It's only darkness, not death.

Do I have a confirmation bias in the way I *seek the truth*? In what ways are the things I do and the way I talk a bid for approval? Do I differentiate between having the conviction of my conscience and being intellectually stubborn?

# October 1

*"Intolerant you say? Well we were frightened.*
*Naturally, we began to act like most everybody*
*does when afraid. After all, isn't fear the true basis of*
*intolerance? Yes we were intolerant. How could we*
*guess that all those fears were to prove groundless?*
*How could we know that thousands of these sometimes*
*frightening people were to make astonishing recoveries*
*and become our greatest workers and intimate friends?"*

Twelve Steps and Twelve Traditions, 140

---

Has anyone ever tried showing up early at a meeting and setting up the chairs facing a different way or in a different configuration? Are our home groups likely to adapt to the new environment or rush to make it the way it should be, the way it must be, to start the meeting on time? How many of us have moved after a few years of sobriety, only to find the brand of fellowship is different from the home town that gave us our recovery? This new way of doing things isn't easy to take for a typical member, easily set in their ways. If we remember how foreign the behavior of our fellowship seemed to us when we arrived, we can reconnect with the sensations these unnatural customs stir. Changing rituals doesn't upset any natural order, though it may stir hostility from people who are change-resistant. Fearless stewardship demands perspective. Change is risky and threatens our survival—but so does stagnation. Our forefathers stumbled with every new issue. Do we ever speak of vigilance and duty when irrational fear is pushing us toward rigidity? Instead of reification of our programs, orderly stewardship demands adaptation. Bill W. was a fan of Toucherville who, along with Mills, speaks of zeitgeist, or what he called "the spirit of the age." How would founders write "How It Works" if written for the first time, today?

Can I stay firm on principle and flexible on method? Do I believe that the needs of today's and tomorrow's newcomer are more important than preserving what is familiar to me? Do I find myself intolerant of ideas about change, be it in my fellowship, work, home or community?

# October 2

*"You, as an addict, are like a light switch that is either totally on or totally off. Life, however, requires a rheostat, a switch mechanism in which there are various degrees of middle ground. Mental health involves a disciplined balance that relies on self-limits and boundaries. Nowhere is that more evident than in the two core issues... intimacy and dependency."*

*Patrick Carnes*

---

Social/emotional anorexia is the avoidance of either physical closeness or emotional connection. Someone who is promiscuous may judge their partner's or their own indiscretions harshly, and this may drive a wedge between the two of them, preventing intimacy. Some of us might be self-righteous about holding out on sex when we are, in truth, being emotionally rigid. For sex addicts in recovery, a period of abstaining from all sexual expression is part of withdrawal in early recovery. That doesn't make abstinence a healthy new way of life, permanently. Even those of us who choose solitude over union learn to take emotional risks and to build intimate boundaries where we are vulnerable in inter-dependent relationships. Risk avoidance, judgment, perfectionism or deprivation may be rationalized as the antithesis of chaotic living but life is lived in the middle, not at the extremes. Recovery involves taking chances and risks within limits. This is true for substance abusers, codependents and process addicts, like gamblers, internet addicts or sex addicts.

Am I moralistic about my behavior? Do I see sexual or emotional health in extreme terms? Have I practiced binging and purging in any area of life and if so, how have I affected others in my life? How do I feel about myself as a sexual, sensual being? Am I respecting my boundaries, needs and imperfections? Am I judgmental of others?

## October 3

*"There is no freedom like seeing myself as
I am and not losing heart."*

*Elizabeth J. Canham*

How much of our lives in recovery do we spend longing to be better? In this righteous journey toward our potential, can we pause to love ourselves, just the way we are? Can this—the here and now—be good enough? At first, being happy with how we are might seem like falling from the rigorous path, or resting on our laurels. But it's not. If we are on the right path we are living rightly. It isn't about arriving at any destination; it is about the direction we are moving in. Crafting or adopting values and objectives for our physical, emotional, mental and spiritual well-being is living the program. We are already there, not at the destination but on a wholesome path.

All human beings need "strokes" for emotional well-being. We crave love. Let's start by expressing love and acceptance for ourselves right now. We don't have to be perfect to be worthy of love. Parenting involves showing up for our children and embracing them with all the love we possess. There is still much to learn and so much more for children to achieve in life. But a parent's love holds back nothing because the parent appreciates kids just the way they are. Children thrive in this unconditional environment. They don't rest on their laurels and get lazy—rather, they strive forward with a gritty enthusiasm. We can love ourselves in the same way. What are we waiting for?

Self-love and compassion can overwrite old repeated messages. I can start today. When I look at myself and assess how I feel about myself, what are the words that come to mind? Am I withholding love from myself? How about trying unconditional self-talk and seeing if it makes me feel and act differently?

# October 4

*"Reading makes a full man, meditation a
profound man, discourse a clear man."*

Benjamin Franklin (1706–1790)

---

Just like honesty, open-mindedness and willingness are keys to starting us on the path of recovery, study, meditation and sharing are keys to personal growth. All three are needed to have a rounded recovery and life. If we get by on fellowship and sharing, time may pass without us ever picking up new books or learning new skills. Is that the type of recovery we seek? Maybe yes, maybe no—we decide how deep we go. By the same token, if we read one book and start another one as soon as the first is finished without reflecting on, sharing or applying what we've learned, have we truly learned a new life-skill? Or have we just incorporated some new vocabulary?

One aim of meditation is to still our minds, explore past our automatic, surface thoughts/chatter and engage our authentic voice—we might call this our gut instinct, intestinal fortitude or the voice that speaks from the heart. In reflection we find our unabashed truths, direction and purpose. A lot of people think of addiction recovery as something that takes twenty-eight days or ninety meetings. Most of us see it like diabetes or HIV—we have an illness that commands a process of healing from the symptoms, followed by a lifetime of managing the condition. Reading is one way we can keep recovering and of course keep growing as people. Reading, for an addict, is one way to introduce new thinking and programming.

No one of these disciplines—reading, meditating and sharing—can make me whole. Am I balanced in my practices of recovery? Do I have my recovery in balance with my life?

# October 5

*"Start where you are."*

*Edgar Cayce (1877–1945)*

---

The secret to happiness in recovery isn't a problem-free life. Rather it is the habit of dealing with life as it comes—life is now and this is the place where our lives are happening. Three mental traps can impose conditions or distort reality, nullifying the capacity to start where we are. These three thinking-traps can cause procrastination and impede joy in our lives:

*If only*: If only I was with the right partner, had a different job, had more money, worked the Steps better, etc. "If only" messages lead to self-blame, envy and self-pity.

*When _____ then _____ thinking*: When I win the lottery *then* …; *when* my coworkers see it my way, *then*…; *when* I am appreciated…; *when* I die… When _____ then _____ thinking is a pity trap that finds us praying for a magic bullet or a rescuer. The silver lining on this mental trap is that it is full of clues about our values. If what we write down in *then* is so important, we can make it so without the *when* occurring. Right now we can complete a "When/Then" sentence. "When I am rich, then I will help the homeless." The *then* may be specific but it gives a general clue about our real values. We can honor these values now even if our conditional *when* never happens.

*What if*: What if I get sick, I start drinking, I go broke, I get found out, I fail, I hurt myself? Living with a crisis is one thing, but fantasizing about it is something else entirely.

Whatever my challenges are today, can I see that the place to start is right here, the time to start is now, and the priorities to start with are of my choosing?

# October 6

*"It is the highest form of self-respect to admit our errors and mistakes and make amends for them. To make a mistake is only an error in judgment, but to adhere to it when it is discovered shows infirmity of character."*

*Dale Turner*

---

Self-correction and making amends is healing, humbling and freeing. The Narcotics Anonymous workbook tells us that making direct amends except when to do so would injure them or others (Step Nine) is the stage in which we get to look the world in the eye.

The amends Step is the first time we are invited to use discretion. Up until now, the language has been absolute—*fearless, exact* nature of our wrongs, *entirely* ready, *all* these defects, *all* the persons we had harmed—there isn't room for creative interpretation here; the Steps are extreme. We mature in our recovery. This Step isn't about us—the victims of a merciless malady. It's about (innocent) people that we have wronged. The Steps are in an order and there is a reason that making amends isn't at the beginning. We aren't in the spotlight here. This Step can't be about the drama of the lengths we are going to. These people are not the audience or a bit part in our "recovery" play. Step Nine is about their needs and our willingness to understand. Our old modus operandi would make this Step about our journey. Now we need to live the humility as learned in Step Seven. We consider the impact of the deeds we listed in Step Eight. We imagine how the harm we've done feels to our victims. Step Nine requires prudence more than eagerness. It can't be launched into because we need or want the pay-off. Maybe we should ad lib and maybe we should rehearse with a sponsor, friend or therapist.

I am a better person but am I ready to make amends? I don't want to procrastinate, but I don't want to do more harm. How should I prepare?

## October 7

*"Fear is a question: What are you afraid of, and why? Just as the seed of health is in illness, because illness contains information, your fears are a treasure house of self-knowledge if you explore them."*

*Marilyn Ferguson (1938–2008)*

---

What some of us think of as meditation is what a therapist would call rumination. Obsessive preoccupation is not Step Eleven. Ruminating could possibly be associated with post-traumatic stress disorder, depression and/or anxiety. Let's look at this process: (i) I feel bad, (ii) I shouldn't feel or think this, (iii) I am wrong to feel or think this way and (iv) Am I damaged and unfixable? Like someone struggling in quicksand, the more we struggle to fix ourselves, the more we suffer. We may have the best of intentions and still find ourselves losing ground. So finding our way in meditation and finding guidance involves a degree of experimentation. We explore feelings. There is no need to mask or force them. Confronted by our fear, anger and sorrow, we "explore" instead of judge.

Meditative focus can be internal or external. Concentrating on external focal points like a candle flame or a peaceful sound may be a preferred starting place for those of us with deep psychic damage not ready to be stirred. Focusing helps still our thoughts, helps us sleep at night and manage stress by day. Inward focus can lead to the "what" and "why" of our feelings. We welcome a myriad of thoughts, sensations and feelings and engage with them with curiosity. Instead of wrestling our way into mental health we apply loving kindness to the most difficult-to-treat conditions.

A clinical instructor of psychology at Harvard Medical School, Dr. Christopher Germer does just that. He incorporates mindfulness with stress reduction and cognitive therapies and *Acceptance and Commitment* therapy to treat depression, chronic pain and borderline personality disorder. The doctor finds *radical acceptance* goes down smoother with compassion, love and tenderness. We can honor and make peace with our feelings and experiences.[88]

Can I treat my thoughts and feelings as welcome guests—not intruders? Do I see unpleasant feelings as helpful clues rather than punishments to be avoided? What am I feeling now? Why?

# October 8

*"Sobriety is like a merry-go-round. It's easy to stay on when you're in the middle. You can fly off when you're on the edge."*

*Heard around the rooms*

---

Some of us loners isolate and feel apart from the recovery community. No wonder we are tempted to quit recovery when we stay on the perimeter—all the centrifugal force is encouraging us to bolt out the door. If we want recovery, we push through the resistance and work our way into the middle of the merry-go-round. We get contact information from three or four or five members who will welcome our calls/texts/emails when we are panicking, need to unload or talk though our difficulties. We might not be comfortable with contacting strangers so we can make test calls—we reach out even if we are feeling good, just to break the ice: "Hey, just calling to touch base." This expands our comfort zone and prepares us for when the shit hits the fan, which will happen in sobriety. Some can make it without a network, but we are social beings. To engage with others and participate in the process is to be in the middle of the merry-go-round. Jumping in improves our chances of not flying off the edge. Steps One, Two and Three involve surrendering to the fact that recovery won't happen strictly on our terms, by doing it how we've always done it.

Getting active improves our chances of long-term recovery. We can find a group that needs a greeter, someone to set up, clean up or help with some kind of behind-the-scenes work. *Feeling nervous? Do service.* Feeling *a part of* significantly improves our chances of avoiding relapse. Arriving at meetings last, being the first to leave and skipping the socializing may be natural. Relapse is also natural for addicts. It's worth thinking about how natural we can afford to feel or be.

What does willingness mean to me? Do I take my addiction seriously? Am I still willing to go to any lengths to enhance my recovery?

## October 9

*"Umbrella, light, landscape, sky—there is no language
of the holy. The sacred lies in the ordinary."*

*Deng Ming-Dao (born 1954)*

---

Learning to chew good food slowly and consciously in silence seems beneath us or beyond us in early recovery. However, this is an example of how we exercise and strengthen our spirits. Addicts crave lives of excitement and extremes—too much is just enough. The lines between self-indulgence and self-destruction get blurred. Mindfulness and meditation with all electronic devices turned off, or a quiet evening and an early bed-time are about as attractive to us intensity junkies as eating plain oatmeal for breakfast, lunch and dinner. This dependence on intensity we seem to fall back on is not simply our nature—it is a coping mechanism. In the same way a movie can help us forget about our troubles for two hours, melodrama can help us avoid reality almost indefinitely. That is why we are ever mindful of substitute addictions. While it makes sense to know the difference between bad habits and deadly addiction, we can still see our avoidance techniques at work in all of our habits.

At the end of our lives, if we were to see that instead of living them, we had been distracted by illusion and drama, wouldn't we feel robbed or short-changed? When we are in constant search for the spectacular and we miss the nuances of the ordinary, our lives are passing us by. A real life hero changes diapers, sets up chairs in a meeting and calls a friend whom they haven't seen for a while to say "hello." Heroes show up on time but nobody notices. Heroes make mistakes and learn from them. The "sacred," referred to above, is connected with gods or goodness. We find connection to the ordinary and it enriches our lives in a way that escapism and indulgence cannot.

Today, can I find profundity in the simple? Just for today, can I find the happy moments in my own peace and quiet?

# October 10

*"Bill C. was a 'guest' of the Wilsons for nearly a year. He was a lawyer and a professional bridge player—that is, a respectable attorney by day and a gambler by night … .*
*Bill Wilson returned home first. The minute he opened the front door he smelled gas. Rushing upstairs, he found Bill C.'s body; the man had committed suicide by running a tube from a gas jet into his mouth."*

Pass It On: The Story of Bill Wilson
and How the A.A. Message Reached the World 165, 166

---

How do we view *outside issues* in our fellowship? Both Bill W. and Dr. Bob took in seemingly well-intentioned drunks to help them get their lives straightened out in the first days or months of their sobriety. Wilson was over his head with this double winner (dually addicted). In describing the events leading up to the new member's death, nothing suggested he died drunk. It's reasonable to conclude that gambling killed the man, or a concurrent mental disorder that had gone undiagnosed. It was later revealed that this compulsive gambler was stealing and selling the Wilsons's evening wear to pay off his gambling debt. Bill C. "sold every stitch of clothing in the house and turned on the gas in remorse." The shock and sadness of such occurrences had Bob and Bill reevaluating the wisdom of *carrying the body* along with carrying the message. "Bill referred to the suicide as an example of literally 'killing people with kindness.'"[89] Something was learned from this tragedy. What may have been missed by these alcohol-centric crusaders was the seriousness of other addictions. "A good man's folly" is how the Big Book describes one way we justify problems other than alcoholism. Rightly or wrongly, AA stays singular in its targeted problem and solution, and many groups turn away addicts strictly suffering from other killer addictions. It was 1953 before a group of AAs formed NA and 1957 before GA followed suit in California.

I understand that Tradition Ten discourages an official opinion on outside issues or associating the fellowship's name with public controversy.[90] As an individual, what is my opinion on *outside issues*? Do I impose my opinion about such things on others? Am I receptive to how others deal with mental health issues and/or other addictions? I am no expert; experience is my only currency.

*"We toss around the concepts of 'god' and 'country' quite easily, without giving much thought to how they got started. Both ideas have been fairly significant throughout human history. For centuries, people have believed that to serve god or country—or both—was a noble calling. But few of us may realize that Egypt—land of the pharaohs, sphinxes, and mummies—essentially invented both concepts."*

*Kenneth C. Davis*

---

In his book, *Don't Know Much about Mythology*, Davis points out that 5,000 years ago Egypt was the original nation and original theocracy. State and religious lines were not differentiated; pharaohs were thought to be personified gods. In Davis's interpretation of this early civilization, Egyptians had a sophisticated value system that lent itself to a compassionate, spiritual and responsible community, seemingly free of slavery or oppressive policing.

Today, "god" and "country" are rally-cry words that create a perceived brotherhood of shared values and priorities. We feel an intimate connection to *our* side—those who worship the same idols that we do. There are perceived barriers between us and *them*—those with a differing ideology. In Freudian language, the "narcissism of small differences" focuses us on the 1% that separates us from the *foreigner*. In truth, when we distill the core values of even the most seemingly hostile of tribes, we find that their society is strikingly similar to our own. In our meetings we may perceive great differences between us and the outside world, suggesting that we of Twelve & Twelve lore are culturally different from *earth-people*. Are we so different because we are addicts in recovery? Don't we have the same foibles and attributes as anyone else?

What tribal standards do I use to differentiate *my people* from *them*? Do I put some on a pedestal and scapegoat others?

## October 12

*"A man should not strive to eliminate his complexes
but to get into accord with them: they are legitimately
what directs his conduct in the world."*

Sigmund Freud (1856–1939)

---

It is tempting to take the promises and Steps literally, thinking that we are going to be free of our baggage—never tripping over our foibles again. We don't turn our wills over never to have selfish or self-destructive behavior rear its ugly head again. We become entirely ready to have these character defects removed yet we don't have that new-car-smell from that moment forward. Will the first time we feel financial security mark the end of money troubles? Can we mark the end of doubt in our lives as the first time we intuitively know how to handle situations that used to baffle us? The Steps in Chapter Five of the Big Book were an anecdotal account of a process taken by a group of drunks. They don't claim to be scientific. The first time a promise buckles under pressure we may feel ripped off. The Steps offer sobriety—not Shangri-La. We can be satisfied that although our "complexes" won't be eliminated, we will understand them and identify how they work in our lives. We don't eliminate defects of character; rather, we "get into accord" with our idiosyncrasies and grow more and more mindful of and responsible for our conduct. From the *book of Freud* to the *book on recovery*, "Progress—not perfection" is our credo.

New unmanageability or substitute addictions may signal that we aren't in accord with our complexes. Common substitutes in recovery are workaholism, internet addiction, extreme exercising, an insatiable spiritual search, sex and fantasy preoccupation, and comfort eating. Substitute addictions stunt our growth in that they tend to come with renewed rituals of shame, denial and obsession.

I am learning to accept myself as imperfect, aren't I? I don't actually expect that I can pull out the rotten bits of me like pruning a plant, do I?

# October 13

*"How pathetically scanty my self-knowledge is compared with, say, my knowledge of my room. There is no such thing as observation of the inner world, as there is of the outer world."*

*Franz Kafka (1883–1924)*

---

Daily reflection reveals that much of the behavior that causes grief is in being reactive. To what extent we are at the mercy of the subconscious is, by its very nature, impossible to say. We look to the results for clues. Why do we have knee-jerk reactions to people and situations? Is it based on programming? Transactional Analysis (TA) is a school of psychology that charts how we trigger and are triggered by others.[91] We each have three *ego-states* called *Parent*, *Adult* and *Child*. Our *Adult* ego-state is our resting state—logical, reasoning and functional. In *Child* ego-state, we feel unabashedly—we cry when we are sad, scream when mad, and laugh when we are happy. *Parent* ego-state finds us nurturing, pampering and protecting and/or critical, judgmental and controlling. These three states (*Parent, Adult, Child*), have nothing to do with our roles in life. A seven-year-old can be in a *Parent* or *Adult* ego state, just as an eighty-year-old can be a *Child*. For the next few days we will look at how we operate in each of these ego-states and how other people's ego-states trigger us.

In the *Adult* ego-state we are free of triggers/reaction and we work through problems systematically. Then someone says, "You *should* do it this way" (*Critical Parent* ego-state), and we react without thinking, saying, "Who asked for your opinion? I am doing just fine." Perceived criticism triggers our *Rebellious Child* ego-state. If we aren't triggered, we stay in *Adult* Ego-state and say, "You may be right. I will consider every option." We can't ever be in two ego-states at the same time. By identifying triggers, we can lessen the tendency to react and develop the habits and skills to consider alternate, less reactive ways of responding.

Who are the people who trigger me or make me reactive? What situations get me off my game?

# October 14

*"Habits are first cobwebs, then cables."*

*Spanish Proverb*

---

Habits develop either consciously or reactively. We are strongly influenced by interpretations of our environment and biases we assign to people, places and things. Learning more about Transactional Analysis (TA), which is how our *Adult, Child and Parent* ego-states interact with other people's three ego-states, is going to give us a broader understanding of our addictions and our relationships. Yesterday we gave a brief example of how we react to our environment from the *Parent, Adult* or *Child* ego-states. Environment can trigger a change from one ego-state to another, before we consciously engage in the transaction. Today, let's look at the *Child* ego-state's three sub-categories: *Free Child, Adaptive Child* and *Rebellious Child.*

*Free Child*, sometimes called *Natural Child*, is a state in which we authentically feel anger, bliss, fear and pleasure without judgment. A baby never considers whether it is appropriate to cry or laugh or take a dump. They just do. None of us could achieve orgasm in any ego-state other than *Free Child*. Analyzing as *Adult* or judging as *Parent*, we can't achieve orgasm—we have to let go and be present to our feelings. As *Rebellious Child* we dig our heels in. This ego-state can protect us from danger or keep us sober out of spite. It can also create a deadlock in negotiations or resistance in our recovery. *Adaptive Child*, sometimes called *Little Professor*, is the most misunderstood ego-state subtype. Here we examine our environment and develop life-long coping skills. Maladaptive coping skills can form when adequate guidance is unavailable or personal insight is underdeveloped. The *Adaptive Child* does the best he/she can. Some of these early crafted coping methods are automatic today. Laughter or exhilaration, refusing to be subordinated or becoming speechless during an argument are all *Child* ego-state reactions. Tomorrow we look at *Parent* and how *Child* and *Parent* ego states trigger each other.

Can I point to a recent interaction that triggered my stubbornness? Do I sometimes feel free of inhibitions? What is one of the *child-like* coping techniques I use when I feel stress?

# October 15

*"Great wisdom is generous; petty wisdom is contentious."*

*Chuang Tzu (369–286 BCE)*

---

We've looked at *Adult* and *Child* ego-states from a Transactional Analysis point of view over the last two days. Today we explore our *Parent* ego-state, which brings out either our nurturing or judgmental side. *Nurturing Parent* makes others feel protected and sympathized with, as a counselor or sponsor might. *Critical Parent* is often associated with controlling or judgmental "You should" messages: "If you don't go to meetings...," "If you don't do your homework...," "If you don't meet your quota..." are what we hear or say in the voice of *Critical Parent*. These same messages can be delivered in *Adult* ego-state (non-judging, non-controlling). "It's suggested to go to meetings," "Consider the benefit of doing homework each day" and "There are targets and standards in this job" say the same things but in logical, generous and non-contentious ways.

Tone is everything. If someone tries to hide a *Critical Parent* message behind *Adult* words, people will see right through it and react to the tone instead of the words. The most common unconscious reaction to *Critical Parent* is to respond as *Rebellious Child*. The second most likely way would be by fighting fire with fire as another *Critical Parent*, pointing the finger the other way. *Nurturing Parent* will often trigger *Natural Child*. When nurtured we feel safe and react authentically. The Adult Children of Alcoholics messages about being our own loving parents incorporate this idea of self-care—by being more nurturing and less critical. We cannot be in two ego-states at the same time. Mindfulness helps us be more aware and less reactive. If someone talks to us in *Critical Parent* ego-state, we can resist reacting rebelliously and reply instead as *Adult,* with "Thanks for your input." Ideally, this takes the other party off their high-horse. Even self-talk comes from an ego-state. *Adult* is the ego-state we operate from most of the time but there is a time and place for *Child* and *Parent* ego-states, too.

Do I understand my triggers? Do I see how taking time to breathe and think can make me less reactive?

# October 16

*"Human history is not a battle of good struggling to overcome evil. It is a battle fought by a great evil, struggling to crush a small kernel of human kindness. But if what is human in human beings has not been destroyed even now, then evil will never conquer."*

Vasily Grossman (1905–1964)

---

In *Life and Fate*, Grossman challenges the defeatist idea that good is impotent and evil is powerful. Like fire, evil always burns out. Fire destroys and can't even conserve itself for its own survival. Fire, like evil, runs out of resources. Kindness, love and even sentimental hope are self-sustaining. These virtues don't feed off themselves so they can only be overcome by willing surrender. Such atrocities as a death camp or killing field darken our history, leaving lifeless bodies in its wake. Yet human spirit has survived. Oppression has never sustained itself indefinitely.

Addiction wages its battle between good and evil in our hearts—the seemingly endless rationalization and temptation vs. a flicker of hope and integrity. Coming to terms with our personal capacities for evil and good is a humbling, sometimes shame-inducing, journey. As the expression goes, "Shit happens." The fickle finger of fate will have us feeling that the wrath of evildoers is besieging us once again. *Practicing these principles* in all areas of our lives requires honest inventory at these times. Are we unfairly vilifying others and/or playing the victim? Is this really a time to stand up and be counted, and put our values to the test? Sometimes *these principles* are to forgive and forget. Sometimes we must take a stand, maybe even by putting ourselves in harm's way. Either way, *these principles* of spiritual living are rarely the easier softer way. The greatest rewards come not so much from good fortune as from right living.

When worldly concerns of good vs. evil get me down, can I remember to be part of the solution and not the problem if even in a small way? I am responsible for my actions, not the outcomes.

## October 17

*"We cannot let another person into our hearts or minds unless we empty ourselves. We can truly listen to him or truly hear her only out of emptiness."*

*M. Scott Peck, (1936–2005)*

---

As we approach Steps Eight and Nine, we review lists of persons we have harmed, our deeds and omissions, our neglect and manipulations. Empty of our own selfish perspectives, we face and feel the impact we have on others. With empathy, we look at ourselves through their eyes. We see our deeds without hiding behind our excuses. We will let others vent while we resist the urge to rationalize. Empathic attention to others will reprogram our self-centeredness. Narcissism is a self-protecting coping technique, often borne of shame. Feeling unworthy tends to make us overcompensate. We become *full of ourselves* and this is why we need to deflate to a right-sized self image. The Step process helps us think of ourselves less without thinking less of ourselves.

Empathy muscles get more exercise in Step Twelve as we work with others. Obviously, selfishness can't be resolved by being self-absorbed; rather, we act our way into better thinking. What helps people is the sense that they are finally being heard (rather than being told). Sharing may break through resistance in ways that lecturing just can't. To apply this M. Scott Peck idea, we don't need to fill them up. We empty ourselves of our need to be heard or recognized and let them purge. If we invite newcomers to talk about themselves they feel more comfortable. New members won't remember what we said—not exactly—but they will remember how we made them feel.

With kids, parents, siblings, friends, partners or coworkers, I am more, not less, when I empty myself. Emptiness is openness; I have room, I have time and I have an open mind. If I empty myself am I better prepared to help others find their salvation—not mine? Can I be less *full of myself?*

# October 18

*"It were far better never to think of investigating truth at all than to do so without a method."*

*Rene Descartes (1596–1650)*

---

Descartes balked at authority, conventional wisdom and group-think. He believed we should all think for ourselves. This philosopher advocated that we all scrutinize our own thought processes. Addicts, like everyone else, have to examine their reasoning. "Stinking thinking" or "my best thinking got me here" are amusing phrases that shine a light on the folly of denial and delusion. Early in recovery, we favor guidance and experience over our intuition or *bright ideas*. What's wrong with an addict's grey matter? Is vilifying our thinking going too far?

MRI brain scans reveal that addicts' brains look different than *normal* noggins. Brains have a "Go" and a "Stop" system. The brain's reward ("Go") function is basic to human evolution; it helped us pursue the necessities of survival. All human advancement has come from this system. The caution ("Stop") system evaluates risk and weighs the pros and cons of every situation. Thinking twice about going inside a cave with a growling animal ensured the survival of our ancestors. Consequences from something like excessive drug use would deter a recreational user, but how about addicts?

Intoxicants (and maybe compulsive, escapist behavior) dull the "Stop" system so it no longer works symbiotically with "Go." Relapse can happen because "Go" is triggered well before a conscious defense can be mounted. Addicts feel they have failed when they fall off the wagon, but our wiring is fried and reprogramming takes longer than twenty-eight day programs last. (For more on National Institute on Alcohol Abuse and Alcoholism study of Go/Reward and Stop/Risk system see endnote 31).

As addicts, we have to use whatever added defenses we can muster—fellowship, a sponsor, education or therapy. Descartes would have been a good addictions counselor.

My brain is my instrument to evaluate the world. Is it in tune? Do I maintain it and treat it right?

# October 19

*"Great bodies of people are never responsible
for what they do."*

*Virginia Woolf (1882–1941)*

---

There will always be evil forces to be conquered or managed. History books sometimes simplify good and evil with clear-cut villains and victims. When we read about World War II, we read about Hitler as the persecutor, concentration camp hostages as the victims and the Allied forces as the rescuers (see endnote 11). The "great bodies of people [who] are never responsible" are the many that were complicit or passive, engaging in systemic discrimination and who could have, or should have, risen up against fascism. In the case of the rise of Hitler, some religious Westerners were quick to side with Nazis because of a common disdain for godless communists. The truth is complicated. We have allies and we have foes. We tend to fall in line on one side or the other of an issue, depending on where our allegiances lie. It has been said that morality is doing what's right regardless of what we are told; obedience is doing what we are told, regardless of what is right.

The *Responsibility Declaration* was unveiled at AA's world conference in Toronto in 1965: "I am responsible, when anyone, anywhere, reaches out for help, I want the hand of A.A. always to be there. And for that: I am responsible." In our recovery program we don't rely on *someone else's* system to carry the message and ensure the stewardship of our fellowship. We avoid complacency and do our part. How easy it is to be part of an apathetic majority and shirk responsibility.

Do I "let it begin with me?" Am I part of the problem or part of the solution? Can I bring sanity, humility and responsibility to the dilemmas of the world I live in?

## October 20

*"If you were to ask me what is the greatest danger facing*
*A.A. today, I would have to answer: the growing rigidity—*
*the increasing demand for absolute answers to nit-picking*
*questions; pressure for G.S.O. to 'enforce' our Traditions;*
*screening alcoholics at closed meetings; prohibiting non-*
*Conference-approved literature, i.e., 'banning books'; laying*
*more and more rules on groups and members."*

Bob P. (1917–2008), Thirty-Sixth General Service Conference of
Alcoholics Anonymous 1986

---

Bob P.'s story is in the third and fourth editions of the Big Book, and is entitled "A.A. Taught Him to Handle Sobriety." This 1986 quote was part of a farewell speech he gave as a senior advisor to the General Service Office (GSO). In one capacity or another Bob was active in service at eighteen General Service assemblies. He didn't see his fellowship suffering risks from what critics, treatment centers or public policy makers do or say. Rather, he worried that decay would happen as with a potato fallen prey to ring rot, from the inside out. Stewardship of the fellowship requires love and tolerance and, most of all, open-mindedness. We don't know what's right for everyone—we barely have a grasp on what's right for ourselves. We may be in so much awe of the process that saved our souls/asses that we become evangelical about our personal brand of fellowship or program. We want to preserve this *winning formula* for generations to come.

The future of our fellowship will be fraught with challenges and ambiguity. Other people may have radically different views but that doesn't mean they love our fellowship less. Rigidity can be prevented by constant trial and error, and the introduction of new ideas. Adaptability has a future. Reification—taking a fluid idea and making it rigid—can lead to extinction.

I can be flexible and welcoming. If I can be an example in my group, this can have a contagious impact throughout the whole fellowship. Am I receptive to foreign ways of seeing or do I dismiss different opinions as being dangerous or inferior?

# October 21

*"People respond to incentives, although not necessarily in ways that are predictable or manifest. Therefore, one of the most powerful laws in the universe is the law of unintended consequences. This applies to schoolteachers, and Realtors and crack dealers as well as expectant mothers, sumo wrestlers, bagel salesman and the Ku Klux Klan."*

Super Freakonomics *by S. Levitt & S. Dubner*

---

In their two books of freaky facts, these authors look at why things aren't always as they appear. Results are rarely what we expect from a given set of causes. Addicts know all about unexpected and unintended consequences. Before recovery, many of us triggered tragic and unintended events by miscalculating the use of our drug of choice. In recovery, we find that the results of our efforts are quite different from anything we imagined—sometimes greater than expected. A lot is said and written about the power of intention and the importance of goals. A modicum of truth is at the root of this notion. A ton of hype has made *self-actualization* a self-help consumer industry but *Freakonomics* research reveals what John Lennon told us years ago: "Life is what happens while you're busy making other plans."

We, and those who love us, are relieved to discover that, having worked the Steps, we have gained the power to adapt to life, and we do it without being control freaks. We wear life like a loose garment.

What are some of the unintended consequences in my life so far? Am I ready to face today with curiosity and grace?

*"From this initial willingness comes more willingness. Step Two tells us that a power greater than ourselves can restore us to sanity. This power can be God, Higher Power, the Universe, the W.A. group—whatever is our source of strength."*

"The Solution," Workaholics Anonymous

---

"The wording was, of course, quite optional so long as we expressed the idea, voicing it without reservation," was how the Big Book assured people that they could discover what worked for themselves rather than adhere to a singular dogma.[92] Almost every conceivable Twelve & Twelve fellowship has since followed their lead, including new millennium programs for twenty-first century problems like online gaming. Along with new addictions to apply our solution to, variations on how to administer the medicine grow with each generation of addicts. Today's quote looks at how personal objection to theology need not be a barrier to applying the Steps. The Oxford Group was cutting edge by being non-denominational. That was still too restrictive for AA, which presented itself as *not religious*. Our world has gotten smaller and our peripheral vision has grown to include more faiths as well as those of us who get along fine with a humanist worldview. Teen Addicts Anonymous, formed in 2003, omitted the word "God" as well as the religious morality found in AA's Twelve Steps.

WA literature is more current than AA literature. Each new fellowship speaks the language of the day. Traditions ensure autonomy for new generations but orthodoxy can bog down each fellowship as it ages—if we aren't vigilant. Through time, the spirit of Step Two remains universal—self-sufficiency is put aside for humility, paving the way for recovery from addiction.

Am I tempted to dance the semantics dance or have I found an understanding of Step Two that works for me? What is Step Two in my own words?

# October 23

*"Children are natural Zen masters; their world is*
*brand new in each and every moment."*

John Bradshaw (born 1933)

---

Growing up seems to be the theme of Twelve Step work, right? The irony is that as we become more enlightened we learn to be more present, more aware and more spiritual. An adjective oft used to describe many spiritual leaders is *child-like*—awe, playfulness and a total immersion in the *here and now* seem to come with guru culture.

The purpose of clearing out the wreckage of our past isn't to move back there—it's to move on. Living life to the fullest is the ultimate goal of recovery. As responsible people we prepare for the future, but we don't dwell on a tomorrow that never comes. A good measure of the quality of our recovery is how well we live in the moment. When we are working do we wish we could be somewhere else? When we are with family do we worry about work? When trying to relax, do obsessive thoughts make us tense? For all the energy expended in worrying about the future and feeling regret for the past, the net result is that we rob ourselves of the *here and now*. Being present is being in a state of recovery.

I can't be a Zen master all the time. I don't choose my thoughts. I am not failing when I suddenly become preoccupied with Yesterday or Tomorrow. There is a time for reflection and a time for planning. But what can I do to help focus on today? Today, can I treat my life as brand new and fascinating?

# October 24

*"I am not a strict vegan, because I'm a hedonist pig. If I see a big chocolate cake that is made with eggs, I'll have it."*

*Grace Slick (born 1939)*

---

Freedom within limits is important in a rich, balanced life. As addicts we have bottom lines. Abstinence is prudent for a drug addict. But if we apply the same absolutes to every area of living we may explode or fade away. If we work but don't play, are so disciplined that we can't be spontaneous, we haven't reached a higher plane. If we are so hard on ourselves that we are hyper-critical of ourselves and loved ones, chances are we need to loosen up on our definition of sobriety (living in the solution).

Healthy boundaries are moving targets. Can a vegan have a chocolate bar without feeling like a fraud? Only the individual can judge. If we are compulsive spenders can we go for an unscheduled lunch at a nice restaurant with an old friend we have unexpectedly bumped into? That depends on our individual bottom lines. There are a myriad of choices for this situation. Within our values there are both restrictions and freedoms. Sobriety isn't a punishment for admitting we are addicts. "Rules are meant to be broken" is a slogan to live by.

*Metarules* are rules about rules—when and how they should be used as well as who can break them and when. For example, after being told by a parent never to lie, a child witnesses the parent saying "I don't have any money" to a panhandler. Outside the home, lying to the homeless is an exception to the rigorous honesty that is expected of one another in the home. In time, we intuitively know when it's no "biggie" to break a rule. A vegan drug addict having dairy is a far cry from a heroin slip. However, we can't expect or demand that others adhere to our interpretation of what rules are sacred and when and how other rules can be broken. We may feel we've done nothing wrong, yet never be trusted by another.

Do I have rules and limits in my life? Are they good for me? What happens when I adapt them? What happens when I break them? How do I feel? How do I react? What are the consequences?

# October 25

*"We are quick enough at perceiving and weighing
what we suffer from others, but we mind not
what others suffer from us."*

*Thomas à Kempis (1380–1471)*

---

This is how one Catholic monk put it but this theme is heard around the rooms as, "When you point a finger at another, three fingers point back at you." Some of us find fault in others like there's a reward for it. Despite our sharp appraisal skills, our own foibles remain a mystery or if we see them we rationalize them.

Maybe this is why, in the original Fourth Step instructions in the text *Alcoholics Anonymous*, we are asked to write down our resentments toward people, institutions and the laws of nature. This is playing to our strengths. It is only after this list is exhausted that we are directed to record what our role was in these conflicts. Seeing these dramas in this way opens the door to clear self-appraisal and healthier living. We are mindful of our constant inclination to criticize. That which we are most critical of reveals our own emotional or behavioral handicaps. Funny, in Step Four, the people who hurt and annoy us the most help us to understand aspects of our nature that we might have missed.

Who was the last person, place or thing to piss me off? What can I learn about myself and my nature from that experience? Did I have retaliation fantasies for this injustice? What sensations, feelings and thoughts come with my anger or judgment?

## October 26

*"We share experience, strength and hope with each other. What we don't do, and should not do, is to share one another's burdens, whether financial or emotional."*

One Day at a Time in Al-Anon

---

"Live and let live" is harder when we perceive that a loved one is suffering. The Al-Anon program teaches loving-detachment. We carry the message—not the body. For one thing, we may deprive others of the enriching first-hand lessons of self-reliance if we hastily jump to alleviate their plights.

The "rescuer" role looks and feels noble. But not only might we cripple others by making life too easy for them, getting absorbed into another life might be a codependent means of avoiding our own things-to-do list—"Oh yes, I meant to get my taxes done, but I have been busy rescuing hurricane victims." There are those too who are hard to love. Sometimes people who need love the most deserve it the least. Developing healthy boundaries is a process that takes practice and requires adjustment as we go along.

Raising kids is about protecting and preparing. We gradually increase freedoms within limits with children. Fellow members are peers, not our kids, so let's remember that smother-love is not being a good friend or parent. Controlling or fostering dependence meets our needs—not the needs of others.

Am I overly invested in some of my relationships? Do I find some relationships in my life burdensome? Do I feel that other people's needs come before my own? Do I feel indispensable to anyone?

# October 27

*"There is a wonderful mythical law of nature
that the three things we crave most in life—happiness,
freedom, and peace of mind—are always
attained by giving them to someone else."*

*Peyton Conway March (1864–1955)*

Yesterday we warned of a tendency to be codependent, to have our well-being enmeshed with the outcomes in another's life, or being too invested in how seriously they take our advice. Today we are all about freedom from the bondage of self. That comes from being in the service of others.

Right living has its subtleties. We can cripple people by making life too easy for them. A good rule of thumb is to be the type of friend that we would like to have. For that matter, we can practice being better, kinder and more loving to ourselves. Sometimes we treat ourselves in ways we would never treat a friend. Getting back to our boundaries with others—how do we be the friends we would like to have?

We all like to feel heard, needed and wanted. We don't trample on anyone's boundaries by listening to and valuing them. Peace, happiness and freedom are all futile as goals. They find us when we are looking away from our needs and our wants. They are byproducts of right living. Doing the next right thing in life, be it for family, work, community or our home group might just make us happy, joyous and free faster than self-seeking or the pursuit of pleasure.

Have I gained interest in my fellows and lost interest in selfish things? In being there for others can I remember that I don't have to see through them to anticipate what they need and want? I just have to help see them through.

# October 28

*"I didn't come here to save my soul; I came here to save my ass. It wasn't until much later that I learned they were connected."*

*Heard around the rooms*

---

We look to telescopes and microscopes to reveal secrets of the universe, yet the profundity that makes addiction and recovery make sense may come from the nut-bar sitting across from us every week at our home group, the one who can't keep track of her or his phone and keys. We could debate the anatomical accuracy or literary quality of today's aphorism but there is a message that should not be passed over: as addicts and codependents, we jump to conclusions that we think are rock-solid, inescapable truths on which we build our lives. A healthy skepticism about our assumptions will reveal that things are not always as they appear to be.

Ask anyone who has been in recovery for two to five years if sobriety is what they expected. The majority will tell you that life isn't at all what they imagined. Having miscalculated outcomes before, we might think this humbling experience would lead to second-guessing future conclusions. Some of us identify with being *often wrong but never in doubt*.

A Yiddish saying is "Man plans and God laughs." It is good to make plans. But we have all expected true happiness to finally be ours as the result of a new job, home or relationship, only to find new circumstances don't change how we feel. Also, like today's quote says, some of us have had the experience of feigning sincerity about wanting to change, but were in fact transformed, quite accidentally, just by going through the actions. Some will say you have to want it (recovery) for treatment to take. Yet some of us find that by bringing the body, the heart and mind will follow.

Where did I think I would be at this stage in my life? How much do I believe in destiny, self-determination and/or a chaotic, fickle world of chance?

# October 29

*"Self-pity in its early stages is as snug as a feather mattress.
Only when it hardens does it become uncomfortable."*

*Maya Angelou (born 1928)*

---

Angelou, a writer, dancer and civil rights activist, poetically reminds us that feeling sorry for ourselves can be a trap. A self-pity party can lead to a self-destructive cycle. In AA circles, it's "Poor me, poor me, pour me a drink." We will be mistreated in life. Feeling hard done by is unavoidable. But indulging in these guilty pleasures is something we can take some responsibility for.

The balancing act for us is to mitigate our self-pity while facing a life that will include hardships, abuses and misfortune. To counter over-reaction by repressing grief and anger isn't what we're talking about. When we suppress feelings we don't kill them; we bury them alive. They will resurface again and again until we let them breathe and run their course. The idea that our feelings will consume and destroy us if we let them out is generally backward. Repressing feelings is toxic— experiencing them relieves the poison.

Meditation can help sort out whether we are over-indulging in pity or honoring our feelings. If, after reflection, we need more feedback about our motives, we can consult a sponsor, counselor or close confidant.

It has been said that self-pity is like kicking the thing that stubbed your toe. Am I in a pity-party over anything right now? When was the last one? Can I learn something about myself by looking at what triggers this behavior?

# October 30

*"You don't have to control your thoughts;*
*you just have to stop letting them control you."*

*Dan Millman (born 1946)*

---

When we arrive in the rooms, we may be defiant, closed-minded or poster children for self-will run riot. Automatic thoughts control our lives. Conscious thinking and mindfulness, where impulsivity once dominated us, are benefits we can expect to gain, at least some of the time, from meditation and the practice of the slogan, "Think, think, think." We all fall prey to our own biases and coping techniques. The more self-aware we are the less we give up our control to these tendencies.

MRI technology reveals, in the brains of chronic addicts, an impaired ability to assess risk and perceive reality. Neurotransmissions that inform and protect normal people at critical times misfire in our brains. It is no stretch to consider that our perception has been compromised. Pain-avoidant coping techniques kick into auto-pilot before our rational, cognitive capacity is engaged. Self-deceit about how we feel, the incapacity to identify or express feelings, and what amounts to addictive brain damage frustrate our liberation over our thoughts. Meditation helps slow our impulses and lets us act more consciously. In the early days, just counting to ten might help us avoid regretful statements or actions.

Steps One to Four make us aware of our blind spots. In Steps Five through Eight, understanding and acceptance help to unshackle us from the impulsiveness that sabotages our lives. In Steps Nine to Twelve, we live what we have learned. We don't choose our thoughts, feelings and sensations, but we take responsibility for them. "Think, think, think" helps us transform our lives, enabling us to go from living reactively to living proactively. In time, we learn to live and love more consciously.

Am I still overwhelmed by thoughts and feelings?

## October 31

*"I claim to be a simple individual liable to err like any other fellow mortal. I own, however, that I have humility enough to confess my errors and to retrace my steps."*

*Mohandas Gandhi (1869–1948)*

A member once said that if there was one step to describe the whole program, Step Ten was it. Spot inventories of our motives and expectations, righting a situation when we have wronged someone—this is living the program. Nothing does more to trap us in an unproductive, catatonic state than perfectionism. The first nine Steps are expressions of new values in sober life—not perfection. Step Ten is for slight adjustments when needed. It is healing and freeing to realize we don't have to be perfect. Doing our best is doing it right.

To err is human. Perfectionism is an overcompensating façade. We cultivate humility and learn to catch ourselves when we are judgmental. "Should" messages in our daily meditation such as "I should this" or "I shouldn't do that" trigger thoughts, feelings and sensations. Those who practice mindfulness will review the day's thoughts, feelings and encounters with a beginner's mind. We may have been triggered to label during the day but this isn't the heat of moment anymore. We review. Are these "should" messages *our* values or are we feigning an allegiance to *someone else's* values? How much energy have we wasted on feeling guilty about values that are not our own? We cultivate compassion for ourselves and others. Letting go of our perfectionism leads to treating ourselves and others better. Catching ourselves getting it right is good for our morale, too. We don't need to *admit* to others when we get it right yet we can still take time to reflect on the big and small victories during the daily inventory process, enjoying our growth with gratitude.

Am I realistic when I evaluate my progress? Do I give myself credit for the things I do well and take pride in my willingness to right my wrongs?

# November 1

*"For fast-acting relief try slowing down."*
*Lily Tomlin (born 1939)*

---

Feeling "in a panic" does not always indicate a real emergency is occurring; rather, this feeling can be the result of a perception. Distress may be a coping technique. Some of the stress and distress throughout the day is a smokescreen. A child getting caught with a hand in the cookie jar may create a diversion to draw the attention of others away from the crime. Stirring up chaos causes an endorphin rush that diverts us from a state of dead calm. When we bury feelings, they are buried alive and we hear them clawing away at us. Quiet time is get-busy time. Busy is sometimes an excuse: "Sorry I am late, but my house is on fire!" Real life has some stress; that's natural. It pumps adrenaline and helps us focus and function. As addicts, we dramatize our own lives and we often buy into emergencies and tragedies that are figments of our imagination.

It is helpful to look at "Easy Does It" backward. "It" is an acknowledgement that we can do only one thing well at a time—multitasking may be just another misperception. "Does" or "do" is the simple discipline of taking action, instead of dwelling on things. "Easy" is the feeling we get, the sense of mastery, once we are in the routine of dealing with our chores or dilemmas. When we get intoxicated by drama we remind ourselves, "Easy does it." Peace and effectiveness come from steady effort at the chore, staying in the moment and not worrying about results. The hero we are waiting for to save the day is found in flexing our own integrity muscles. Relief comes from doing, incorporating work, rest and play in balance.

Was meditation left until Step Eleven because fidgety addicts in early recovery can't chill out? Maybe if the Steps were derived from Eastern philosophy there would be a meditation for each Step. We have a huge advantage over our Twelve Step ancestors.

Can I learn to slow down and get more done? No matter how much sand is in the top of an hourglass, just one grain at a time passes through the neck of the timepiece. Why do I rush?

# November 2

*"The truth shall set you free,*
*but not until it is finished with you."*

*Heard around the rooms*

---

When many of us came to the rooms, we weren't envious of many in this outfit of losers but we wanted to be liked. Some of us came to be known as nice guys and go-to gals. The attention that we received from others fed an old unmet need. With our low self-esteem, approval was better than integrity—at least we knew how to people-please. We wanted approval and we were willing to do anything to get it. We belonged here, or we were getting what we needed. When we don't know who we are or what we want, approval is intoxicating. Some of us bottom out as a result of people-pleasing. Quiet desperation and passive-aggressiveness will make sober life as unmanageable as ever. Selling out for approval comes with chronic dependency. We despise ourselves and start to resent others.

Alternatively, some of us have a "cut me—I don't bleed" persona that tells people to keep their distance. This gimmick is one of self-sufficiency. No need to smile or play nice for this lone wolf. Belligerence and cynicism are so much easier than being two-faced. These are just a couple of façades that hide the truth—from others and, if we've bought into the role, from ourselves. Our own value systems are sometimes lost in translation. That is, if we ever had the self-image to form boundaries and standards we could call our own.

Addiction and deceit are so interwoven. To whatever extent we journey past our masks, our damage, and make peace with who we are, we will find a new freedom and happiness. Our damage will define us, but it won't be our only defining characteristic. The end game is the strength that comes with fearlessness. When we come to terms with the truth, it isn't so bad and we have nothing to hide.

Do I have the conviction that the truth will set me free? Do I know that every new bottom can be a springboard to better living?

## November 3

*"Whatever course you decide upon, there is always someone to tell you that you are wrong. There are always difficulties arising which tempt you to believe that your critics are right. To map out a course of action and follow it to the end, requires some of the same courage which a soldier needs."*

*Ralph Waldo Emerson (1803–1882)*

---

Emerson may have had Attention Deficit (Hyperactivity) Disorder (ADD, ADHD), a label that is in search of a new name. It isn't a disorder; it's the end of a spectrum.[93] Someone who is over 6' 4" needs certain accommodations but his or her height doesn't have to be corrected. Everyone has some height, but only a small percentage of us are over 6' 3". According to Rick Green, kids with ADHD and ADD are paying attention 50% of the time while average children pay attention 80% of the time.[94] The way doctors and educators were taught to deal with kids with ADHD when the label first hit the street is being called malpractice by some advocates. Kids have been medicated, ridiculed, shamed, and treated as intellectually inferior. Other noteworthy ADD (ADHD) personalities in the company of Emerson may include Agatha Christie, Abraham Lincoln, Prince Charles, Henry Ford, Beethoven, Mozart, Virginia Wolf, Michael Jordan, Babe Ruth, Robin Williams, Christopher Columbus, Ann Bancroft, Salvador Dali, John Lennon, Vincent Van Gogh, Benjamin Franklin, Sir Isaac Newton and Pablo Picasso.[95] These people were likely problem students, hard to be married to, and may also have exhibited concurrent issues such as dyslexia, Obsessive/Compulsive Disorder or addiction. Many addicts have hyperactivity or difficulty with attention or memory. Many of us used addiction or preoccupation (such as gambling or romance) to cope—cope poorly, in most cases.

So when Emerson is saying that others will tell us we're wrong and want us to fit a norm in rigid institutions, we can feel his frustration. Many people with ADD go on to greatness. Many more have their creativity and joy sucked out of them by a system that prefers conformity and obedience.

Do I know that in a program that encourages adaptation for the sake of surviving and thriving, I should never deny my true nature or lean on others to conform? Inner truth trumps social order.

# November 4

*"Every reader finds himself. The writer's work is merely a kind of optical instrument that makes it possible for the reader to discern what, without this book, he would perhaps never have seen in himself."*

*Marcel Proust (1871–1922)*

---

We have not been directly empowered by the fellowship, the program or any counselor. Reading material, the experiences of others and even a favorite song can inspire us and/or provide hope or direction but nothing happens without our willingness and drive. There is no muse without the artist. Nothing is found or discovered without the seeker. We are the creators, as well as the followers.

We hear "It's a selfish program," which might not seem like a good thing for self-centered addicts. Oh, we can be selfish—we can use people, take more than our share, or waste hours thinking that everyone would be happier if they could just save time and see it our way. What is meant by a *selfish* program is that we have to take responsibility for our recovery, not delegate it to someone else. No amount of love or concern from others can do our inventory for us, meditate for us or get us to meetings. We have to do it. No one is going to check our Twelve Step homework; everyone else is working a *selfish* program. If we keep saying "Tomorrow I will get started," no one is going to make us do our work, find us a job, mend our bad relationships or hold us accountable.

The flip side of a selfish program is that nothing and no one can take our recovery from us. Our recovery isn't event or outcome driven. It is ours to keep or to turn away from.

Do I understand that the freedom that comes from recovery demands personal responsibility? Am I waiting for something to happen? Do I feel responsible for myself? Do I feel free?

## November 5

*"We have ceased fighting anything or anyone—even alcohol.*
*For by this time sanity will have returned. We will seldom be*
*interested in liquor. If tempted, we recoil from it as from a hot*
*flame. We react sanely and normally and we will find that this*
*has happened automatically."*

Alcoholics Anonymous 84, 85

---

With few exceptions, during the early months of recovery we boycott people, places and things that tempt or trigger us. No matter what spell addiction or codependence had on us, the day will come when we will be free to go where we want and do what we want. Some members prefer Twelve & Twelve rooms for their social lives while demonizing places, activities and friends they consider bad influences. "Don't fly with the crows if you don't want to be shot at" is a mantra for many. It may be that the lifestyle associated with our old haunts just has no appeal anymore.

But eventually, if our sports team wins big and everyone wants to celebrate, we can go have fun without feeling out of place. Maybe our favorite musical act is performing at a place where we have had bad experiences. Maybe family get-togethers can be triggering. We talk it through with a friend or take a friend along. If we are unsure, we meditate on it or take a rain-check. Some of us get all worked up before an outing into a "slippery" place and we do fine, but then find our guards down a day or two later. Our minds play tricks with us; it is like a delayed reaction.

Freedom means having my choices back, about people, places and behavior. Do I see that my recovery gives me more choices or does it impose more limits?

# November 6

*"We are not in a position in which we have nothing
to work with. We already have capacities,
talents, direction, missions, callings."*

*Abraham Maslow (1908–1970)*

---

As a psychologist, Maslow saw two faces of human nature—the sick and the healthy. He thought that Freud already covered the sick face of the human experience so he paid attention to healthy psychology. The Twelve Steps challenge us to face the destructive facets of our conditions. We don't adopt a morbid preoccupation with our flaws, yet to ignore these facets of addiction could sentence us to repeat history. Today we add context and consider that even at our worst we are never without our marvelous characteristics, too. Maslow understood the vital need for each of us to accentuate the positive.

Each of the shortcomings that we try to shed contains the DNA of our best attributes too. In a way, *character defects* are just the negative manifestations of personality traits. Why not devote soul-searching and fearless inventory to our unique assets? Sobriety can involve living in the solution, not just fending off the problem. Do we feel a higher purpose guiding us as a result of recovery? What good and unique qualities can we bring to a higher purpose? Without being grandiose we can be proud of our uniqueness and apply it to the world we live in to make a positive difference in small ways.

Right here and right now, can I appreciate the qualities, purpose and strength I have? Do I have a clear answer if I am asked, "What's so special about you?"

## November 7

*"A common characteristic of people with compulsive behaviors is our tendency to get ahead of ourselves. We want all things to happen on our timetable and are terribly impatient with ourselves, with little or no regard for our internal rhythms. Our minds seem to refuse to take things one at a time."*

A Skeptic's Guide to the 12 Steps *by Phillip Z.*

---

Phillip Z. looks at the Steps from both an Eastern philosophical and a Western psychological angle. With candor, this author and psychologist shares his battles with preconceptions, life, addiction and recovery.

"First things first" and "Easy does it" are catch-phrases that AA added to its treasure chest of wisdom. The founders understood that meditating or praying were tricky for the short-circuited brain of a newcomer. Slogans are bite-sized meditations. Simple mantras are a good starting point on the lifelong journey of rewiring minds that are predisposed to addictive, escapist and obsessive thinking.

Impatience, like boredom, irritation or fidgetiness, can be gradually reduced, but we have to be realistic and gentle with ourselves. We have been *rebellion-dogging* it for a long time. Peaceful, "sober" living isn't going to be easy while we are still predisposed to only two psychic speeds—full speed ahead and reverse. If there was an option for intense-meditation or extreme-spiritual-living, these options might come more naturally than balance. Our all-or-nothing tendencies have to make nice with some new strategies if we are to avoid stagnation. Employing a beginner's mind opens our eyes to new ways of seeing that give us options beyond our impulsive thoughts, which tend to trigger impulsive actions.

I don't expect to go from squirrel-cage inmate to power-of-example Yogi in one try, do I? Like learning a new language, learning mindfulness will feel awkward and take time. If I can be focused and calm for one or two minutes, maybe one day focus and calm can become my habit.

*"Meditation is the dissolution of thoughts in eternal awareness or pure consciousness without objectification, knowing without thinking, merging finitude in infinity."*

*Swami Sivananda (1887–1963)*

---

As part of the legend of Siddhartha (Prince) Gautama, the Buddha, a story is told of seekers who came to learn from the Buddha. Buddha was asked, "Are you a god?" and he said, "No." He was asked if he was a saint, a prince, a prophet and his answer was, "No," "no" and "no." "Well then, what are you?" the pilgrims cried out. "I am awake," said Buddha.

Some of us incorporate meditation into our lives as a ritual and some of us use it as a pill to cure a headache (take as needed). Twelve & Twelve literature speaks to the importance and value of meditation, but is a wee bit shy on how to do it. The good news is that learning about meditation is easy. Search for it online or in a library, or consider a course at a community center. To get the most out of mindful exercises, guidance helps. That said, you can't really meditate incorrectly. It takes time to be proficient, but some benefits come immediately. A rudimentary technique is to eliminate distractions. We can do this by focusing on one simple thing—our breath, a candle flame or the voice of a meditation guide. Meditation is not deep thinking. According to today's Hindu guru, much of the tension and stress in life comes from our minds. We say, "I have a thinking problem." Heightened awareness (being awake) comes from the dissolution of thoughts and judgment.

Regardless of my knowledge of meditation, I can meditate today and gain benefits from it. If I am a beginner I have to start somewhere and learn as I go. Do I rely on my thinking and wit and know-how to solve problems? Meditation will help me set aside my cerebral skills and expand and exercise my intuition to understand my world beyond thinking and judging.

# November 9

*"[The behavior of] people under the influence of cults is similar to that we observe in addicts. Typical behaviour for both includes draining bank accounts, neglecting children, destroying relations with family and losing interest in anything except the drug or cult."*

Keith Henson (born 1942)

---

How cult-like are Twelve Step meetings or members? A society is a group broadly distinguished from other groups by the structured systems, protection, continuity, security and identity available for its members. In a secure, highly cohesive group, members have the freedom to disagree. "Cult" is a pejorative way to describe an organization of ritualistic practices that is authoritative and exploitive.

The textbook *Social Psychology* defines a cult as a group that isolates its members from the mainstream and is characterized by distinctive rituals and its devotion to a god and/or a charismatic leader.[96] Cults separate newcomers from previous social support systems and isolate them with other cultists, where they lose access to counterarguments. The cult offers a new identity and reality. Cults frown on disagreement and consensus helps eliminate any lingering doubts. Lonely, depressed and susceptible to influence, newcomers have their problems defined by the organization. Members are offered a promise of a new tomorrow. The warmth with which the group accepts rookies is appealing. They are encouraged to trust the "master," join the "family" and learn "the way."

Twice *Harper's* Magazine has used the "cult" word in articles about AA, in 1963 and 2011.[97] Though criticized for transferring dependence from booze to meetings, AA promotes free will in members, autonomy for groups and democracy in the fellowship. The "cult" test doesn't fit AA lore per se, yet legitimate criticism has fallen at the doorstep of certain members and meetings who sacralize a rigid interpretation of a suggested program. The cult label could be attributed to any of us who discourage free will, but hey—we can always go to another meeting where the culture is more to our liking.

Do I feel a freedom to choose, or group pressure from meetings and members? Do I ever lean on others to conform?

## November 10

*"Our public relations policy is based on attraction rather than promotion; we need always maintain personal anonymity at the level of press, radio, films, television and all other public media or communication."*

*Overeater's Anonymous, Tradition Eleven*

---

Who knew about the Internet when the Twelve Traditions were first conceived? The Internet is a great way to get recovery information, find or participate in meetings and connect with members all over the world. Traditions are the result of time-tested experiences—Traditions are not rules. Anonymity is a personal decision that comes into play online or anywhere in public. We have no rules about anonymity. The Internet can be a very permanent place to make a statement. It serves us well to "Think, think, think" before we hit send, send, send.

To say that anonymity indiscretions are new to the social media generation is to ignore our history. All of these Traditions are the result of lessons learned from mistakes made as far back as the 1940s. People born into Generation X (1965–1980) or the Millennials that follow will listen to Boomer "war stories" and say, "Anonymity is mine to do with as I see fit. I protect yours. I have no one but myself to answer to." We don't live with the addiction stigma of years ago. We all live more integrated lives now. This is all defendable. There is a humility found in a faceless fellowship. This not only keeps us in check personally, but brings untold comfort to addicts not yet here. Traditions get broken every day and we survive. Even though addiction doesn't have the stigma it once did, everyone has preconceived ideas about addicts and Twelve & Twelve fellowships. We never know how we'll be judged when we disclose. Associating a face and a name with our fellowship can look more like promotion or endorsement than the egoless "we're here if you need us" anonymous Twelve Step attraction. It is worth learning about the wisdom of the ages but when it comes down to it, we choose for ourselves and we respect each other's right to do the same.

Have I ever made judgments about someone else's choices about anonymity? Is anonymity our spiritual foundation? What do I think makes it so?

## November 11

*"Intimacy means that we can be who we are in a relationship, and allow the other person to do the same."*

Dr. Harriet Lerner (born 1944)

---

Intimacy can be applied to a life partner, a child or parent, a sponsee, a coworker, a teammate or a friend. Being who we are requires authenticity and communication. Helping out or letting someone get close in a healthy way is enriching. Intimacy demands perspective, tolerance and generosity.

*Shared* experience does not mean the *same* experience. For example, if a loved one goes missing or dies, everyone in that circle is grieving the loss of the same person. But a male may express this differently than a female just as a child will be having a completely different reaction than a teen or adult—all based on experience, reference points and perspectives. No two people are having identical feelings in response to the same situation. We are cautious about statements like "I know what you're going through" or "I get where you are coming from." How could we?

This gives perspective to "Live and Let Live." We strive for self-transcendence—a state in which we see ourselves *in* the world, not *at the center of* the world. Controlling or aloof people can't cohere or bond with others. Without coherence we have no community. Without intimacy we will live with others but not as part of a whole.

The walls we built between ourselves and others were originally for our protection from what was, or seemed to be, a hostile environment. This is a coping, not a thriving, technique. Without lowering the walls, being authentic and letting others meet us on their terms we can't thrive, because intimacy is a prerequisite to a full life.

Am I up for just being me, today? Do I let others in?

## November 12

*"I don't know who—or what—put the question, I don't know when it was put. I don't even remember answering. But at some moment I did answer Yes to Someone—or Something—and from that hour I was certain that existence is meaningful and that, therefore, my life, in self-surrender, had a goal."*

Dag Hammarskjöld (1905–1961)

---

Today's quote comes from the former secretary-general of the United Nations. Each of our callings may be modest in comparison but it is just as true for us that feeling useful and having purpose makes life worthwhile. Once we have been around the rooms for a while we may get invited to be involved in service. Alternatively, our purpose may take us away from the rooms. We remember how we arrived at the doorstep of this fellowship—beaten, desperate and almost hopeless. What a transformation we have enjoyed. We pay it forward. In our groups, we do this by becoming public information reps or joining conference committees, or we express our gratitude by taking on civic responsibility. Service enhances our sobriety.

Going to meetings is good, but so is giving back to the larger community. Bill Wilson once said that we don't get sober just so we can go to meetings. In preparing for our newfound calling we remember that ending well is as important as getting starting. In transitioning to a new venture we don't want to burn bridges and we remind ourselves that there is no hurry. Abiding by the motto "steady as she goes" might serve us better than diving blindly into uncharted water. We may feel like we are making up for lost time but we are not; we are making the most out of a second chance.

Am I grateful and open to giving back to life? Do I bring value to the fellowship, my family and community? How does that make me feel? A *higher purpose* is no false idol. Can I find satisfaction from purposeful living?

# November 13

*"The basic thing is that everyone wants happiness,
no one wants suffering. And happiness mainly comes
from our own attitude, rather than from external factors.
If your own mental attitude is correct, even if you remain
in a hostile atmosphere, you feel happy."*

*Tenzin Gyatso, the XIVth Dalai Lama (born 1935)*

---

Many psychologists believe in the ability of Twelve & Twelve fellowships to facilitate attitude and behavior adjustments like the one described above. Recovery isn't exactly what we expected. Why not? Is it our attitude? Here are two examples of altered attitudes in recovery: (1) We thought our "drug of choice" freed us, yet it trapped us; (2) We thought sobriety was restrictive, but it opened us up to many more possibilities than before.

What we call an *attitude adjustment*, the pros have been calling *cognitive restructuring* since 1976, when Dr. Aaron Beck first started incorporating Cognitive Behavioral Therapy (CBT) into depression treatment. Since then, CBT has been a leading non-pharmaceutical approach to both depression and anxiety. CBT is known to help us:

1) recognize that thoughts affect emotional response;
2) identify unrealistic beliefs and offer alternative ways of seeing;
3) gain awareness of how beliefs trigger us; and
4) reevaluate beliefs and provide guidelines to reframe our
thinking.[98]

Attitude adjustments counter the harm from dichotomous thinking (labeling things as "good" or "bad"), over-generalizing (drawing conclusions with few facts), magnifying or minimizing problems and arbitrary interference (good old "contempt prior to investigation"). Step work, getting current in meetings, reading, therapy and/or service to others all help alter our attitude.

My attitude has a bearing on my quality of life. Trauma brings stress and suffering but experience shows that post-traumatic gains are possible too. Am I waiting on external factors to make me happy? Can I welcome and/or face all of my life experiences with courage and openness?

# November 14

*"A hobby a day keeps the doldrums away."*
*Phyllis McGinley (1905–1978)*

---

Most of this book focuses on rigorous work, thoughtful activity and meditation. The work of recovery is seemingly endless as we peel away layer after layer of behavior and awareness. Is our recovery becoming learned dependence or self-empowerment?

The goal of recovery is living, and living isn't all work. Life is too important to be taken seriously all the time. What does healthy escapism look like for those of us who have what some refer to as the "addictive gene"? While we are in the process of healing we need play time and personal, indulgent activities that we can look forward to. Both solitary activities and hanging out with friends are nurturing. Because of our impulsive, addictive nature, we had best differentiate between blowing off steam (healthy behavior) and tempting fate (old, unhealthy behavior). Early in recovery it might be better to find new activities that steer us clear of old environments where we may fall prey to old routines. There will come a time in recovery when the slipperiest of settings will have no power over us and we will feel safe and natural. A nightclub is a fun place to see live music or dance but might not be ideal for an alcoholic in early sobriety. Social networking sites and surfing the internet could be refreshing and stimulating for some but may be triggering for sex and love or online gaming addicts.

Ultimately, the reward for working the Steps is that no person, place or thing has power over us. An alcoholic can dance with friends, surrounded by liquor, or a porn addict can surf the web for work or play without temptation. We will discuss play as part of healthy living over the next few days. Life happens *out there*, not just in the rooms.

Am I as devoted to my personal time as I am to my recovery? Am I good at having fun?

# November 15

*"Today is life—the only life you are sure of. Make the most of today. Get interested in something. Shake yourself awake. Develop a hobby. Let the winds of enthusiasm sweep through you. Live today with gusto."*

Dale Carnegie (1888–1955)

---

What are some of the social activities we can turn to when it's time to take a break from self-analysis and service work? For starters, there are sports, crafts, scheduled outings, concerts or dancing. Going to a country fair or a movie are small things that make our lives more enjoyable. Taking a course can stimulate our brains and help us reach out to new people. Activity—social or solitary—might also feed our need for physical health. We may find ourselves involved in fitness, hiking or team sports. Some of us had healthy activities that we dropped in addiction and we may return to those. For others, a whole new way of life may have to be tried. What can we do to shake ourselves awake?

Taking up new hobbies or returning to old ones may become part of our weekly routine. Activities could include new friends in recovery or we may rekindle old relationships. Sometimes activities can help mend damaged relations as part of a living amends. Showing up for loved ones heals misdeeds of the past. Not everything about balanced living can be learned in a book or at a meeting. We have to get out there and try, try again as we find our natural rhythms.

Am I open to living my life with gusto and getting the most out of life? Would I call myself social or do I have to work to make friends and get along with others?

# November 16

*"Spend the afternoon. You can't take it with you."*

*Annie Dillard (born 1945)*

---

Do we tend to think of personal time as self-indulgent? So what? We have to say, "Hey, we earned it" and be our own best friend, by reading for fun or devoting time to learning a hobby, language or new skill. Yesterday we talked about socializing. Today we look at quality time alone.

Solitary activities are forms of self-care and are an essential part of recovery. Those of us who binged and purged bounced between overextending ourselves and isolating ourselves and we now make a distinction between hiding out and enjoying enriching solitude. For some of us, enjoying our own company is no easy task. The thought of a night or weekend alone might cause anxiety. This is all the more reason to develop some healthy solitary activities, separate from recovery activities of meditation, inventory and introspective reading and writing. Going solo might be uncomfortable for some of us and a little too easy for others. The same is true with group activities. Many of us embrace social butterfly mode with ease while others have to push ourselves out of isolation. Taking ourselves out on dates, going to movies or the museum by ourselves, or dining alone can be healing as we treat ourselves to periodic indulgences. Maybe we can get back to books we started or maybe we have books we want to start. It could be painting or poetry that we devote our alone time to. If there's somewhere we always wanted to go, we do. Travelling solo means never having to ask, "Would you like to eat here or there?"

We have no one to impress or cater to. Self-indulgence reinforces our self-worth and demonstrates that we can meet many of our needs without substances, hostages or crutches.

Am I comfortable in my own company? Today, can I plan some time just for me?

# November 17

*"Hobbies of any kind are boring except to people who
have the same hobby. (This is also true of religion,
although you will not find me saying so in print.)"*

Dave Barry (born 1947)

---

We have been looking at activities/hobbies as either being solitary or as ones that involve other group members. Some solitary activities will spawn from new social activities: If we join a band, we need to practice songs on our own. If we learn a new sport we may set time aside for fitness or drills to help us improve in this. A course at a community college might include some study or research that we will do alone. In the same way that group activity can lead to practice we do on our own, solitary activities like writing could lead to social activities like taking courses, attending poetry readings or performing songs or comedy.

What if we overdo our new hobby and our new activities go from being healthy to being compulsive? The truth is that we will never be perfect all the time. Some things we will be able to naturally do in balance. On the other hand, many of us say, "I never started a hobby that didn't become a second career" or "I can turn any healthy activity into a crippling dependency." Let's not be hard on ourselves. Consider the activities we choose, balance our time the best we can and remember that a little over-indulgence in healthy activity isn't a failure; it is to be expected. Slight adjustments can be made as we go along. We might start an activity that we don't see through to the end. So what? This is recreation, not obligation. If we try something outside our normal comfort zone and it is not for us, there is no shame in quitting. Changing our minds does not mean we lack character.

What can I do for myself to get active, be creative and enjoy my life more?

*"Taking the first step is not a matter of reading the words, '...
admitted we were powerless ...' but of impressing them so deeply
on our consciousness that the admitting will be established as
part of our way of thinking and feeling."*

One Day at a Time in Al-Anon

---

Codependency and/or addiction made us feel whole or helped us cope. There are gaping voids in our lives that all our addiction time took up—doing it, thinking about it, swearing it off. A change in scenery, including new recovery friends and lots of meetings, can fill the time void. Misery loves company but so does recovery. Knowing we are not alone makes this dramatic life change seem plausible. We come to understand that our process or substance was not our friend; all that shines is not gold. This admission is more than an intellectual process. When we make a major purchase we tell our friends our intellectual reasons for buying. We rationalize—"It was on sale" or "It's eco-friendly"—but we likely made the purchase for emotional reasons. A visceral epiphany about being powerless will be far more helpful in recovery than an intellectual rationalization. When we feel in our guts that we have been kidding ourselves and that we can get along better in recovery, then we are better protected when a shit storm hits. Al-Anon reminds us that when we face either our own addictions or someone else's vices we need to always remember that we are powerless.

Some of us come to this new way of seeing so slowly that it's our friends who see the change in us first. Some of us get a giddy feeling, as though we've just won the lottery. Be it a spiritual awakening or a rude awakening that does it for us, it's helpful to recognize that the weakest of convictions may see us through and the most dramatic of realizations may wax and wane at times. That's why we do this one day at a time. In time, we own our recovery and no temptress can lure it away. We are powerless, not helpless.

Am I vigilant about accepting powerlessness over not only my compulsion and obsession, but over others in my life, too?

# November 19

*"Everything that irritates us about others can
lead us to an understanding of ourselves."*

*Carl Jung (1875–1961)*

---

The original *Alcoholics Anonymous* text suggests an inventory of resentments, fears and sexual escapades. Carl Jung, who counseled Bill Wilson, might have been the architect of listing resentments against others first. Hey, play to our strengths—what bugs us about others? In each case we are asked to look at our roles and consider more honest ways of scrutinizing our behavior than blaming others. Using these three simple categories (resentments, fears and sex conduct) we can unravel not just a laundry list but the nature of our wrongs.

Some inventories look at the good and bad. We make lists of shameful acts as well as great accomplishments, healthy expressions of fear and anger vs. unhealthy expressions of fear and anger, our history of deception and avoidance vs. examples of bravery and honesty, our qualities as a lover, partner or parent, as well as our shortcomings. Why settle for a recovery that's just good enough?

When taking inventory of our home group and fellowship, in what way could we better serve both the still suffering who are in the rooms now and those who are still to come?

Christopher Hitchens will always be remembered as an example of someone who was constantly searching. In a eulogy, Lawrence Krauss said that his friend Hitchens lived by the credo, "Skepticism, rather than credulity is the highest principle the human intellect can use to ennoble our existence."[99] We ought to follow Hitchens' lead and try daily to combat atrophy and routine.

If I am awaiting my first or tenth writing of Step Four, do I have the task right-sized and do I have a plan, a timeline and deadline? Should I have a clear goal or just go at it with an open mind? Do I see how my reaction to others may be my own characteristics confronting me? What does what irritates me in others tell me about my own shortcomings?

# November 20

*"It's been said there are two ways of being unhappy:*
*One is not getting what you want,*
*and the other is getting what you want."*

Eckhart Tolle (born 1948)

---

Reality wasn't pleasing to us so we took our chances with whatever was behind Door # 2—the illusion of a better way in addiction. That didn't make us happy either. A maladaptive coping system can't be fixed with another flawed coping technique. Consider putting one foot in a bucket of ice and the other in boiling water. This may seem to be balanced living when you average it out, but these opposite extremes won't make us comfortable or happy in real life.

A life driven by ego and longing will invariably include short-lived pleasures and comforts but no lasting happiness. Longing is a cause of malcontent. The delusion that getting what we want will make us happy is a fallacy, a carrot in front of a donkey. In reality, the pursuit of goals seems to make us happier than achieving them.

"That's my ego talking" gets nods and laughs in the rooms. But as we get past our own blasts of egomania, we realize that getting what we desire and not getting what we desire will both be unsatisfying. What about helping others get what they want? A lot of us believe that the needs of others come before our own and servitude may come naturally for us. But will it make us feel adequate? Humility is a balance of modesty and self-esteem. Negative self-esteem was at the root of much of our Step Four list and in Step Six we unload (or upload if we are theistically inclined) the longing and loathing that comes from feeling either entitled or useless. Maybe with greater spiritual fitness we'll catch ourselves saying, "That's my self-esteem talking."

I don't need strokes or stuff to make me feel good enough. Today, can I remind myself that I have value just the way I am?

*"But later on I realized at depth that the great harms
I had done others were not truly regretted. These
episodes were merely the basis for story-telling and
exhibitionism. With this realization came the
beginning of a certain amount of humility."*

Bill W. A.A. Grapevine, *June 1961*, As Bill Sees It, 311

---

You can dress addicts up, but you have to take them everywhere twice—the second time to apologize. This is a realization made by AA's cofounder after attaining a quarter-century of sobriety—not after the four years he had as he finished the Twelve Steps. To get Step Nine right requires everything learned in the previous Steps. Sometimes we get no second chance to make things right. We take time to assess whether or not we are living in accordance with our values. Ask us, when we're new, about our values. "Values—whose values and what values?" Like chameleons, we were willing to act as if, to gain approval or feel in control. This juncture of recovery isn't about meeting our needs or about being in the spotlight—"Look at me, making amends." Step Eight lists who (and how) we betrayed and manipulated. Can we now be trusted? Have we taken ownership of our misdeeds without making addiction the scapegoat? Can we empathize with those we have harmed? If we try seeing ourselves through another's eyes, can we write the "victim impact statement" that they would write? Do we understand what our actions felt like? Bill, at this stage of his recovery, was pained to see how egotistical behavior may still be rooted in our motivation to do this crucial Step. Coming to terms with our own narcissism ranks up there with hugging a cactus or cleaning latrines—it's not pleasant.

It's true that we arrive at the doors of this fellowship without much credibility to speak of. We don't even trust ourselves. Within months we may win over many who see that we are committed to better living. But when we present ourselves in Step Nine, we need a higher level of spiritual fitness.

Do I know that this is about them and not about my tireless journey in recovery? Do I understand and regret the damage done? How will I make restitution?

# November 22

*"Faith is believing what you know ain't so."*

*Mark Twain (1835–1910)*

---

As much of a party as it is to point out hypocrisies in others, there is something to be gained by challenging our own hard and fast beliefs. Some who subscribe to institutional dogma may do so to relieve anxiety and fit in with the crowd. If push came to shove, these "believers" wouldn't stand by their myths, but so what? The meaning is in the metaphors.

Faith is a curious liberty in Twelve Step groups, considering how much latitude we are given. If you have an outrageous higher power concept you might get some laughs but you won't get picketed by evangelists. For some of us, faith in a higher power is intuitive. It is felt so strongly it doesn't have to be articulated to be believed. Some of us don't need a creator to explain the unknown; the universe is fascinating enough. Just coming to a second meeting was an extreme leap of faith for any of us. The program looked like quackery but we hoped something would rub off and relieve our temptation to relapse. We may have attended the first meeting out of morbid curiosity or as part of a negotiation to get the heat off. But coming back—that takes faith.

Are we better off to be skeptical or to have faith? Comedian Tim Minchin says, "Science adjusts its views based on what's observed. Faith is the denial of observation so that belief can be preserved." If the best rhyme wins, go with skepticism. But if we identify as either skeptical or faithful, we will find what we need in the fellowship and program. But either approach has its limits too. Even an alcoholic cosmologist wrestles with denial. We can't be looking left and right at the same time; we always have a blind spot. Addiction is very democratic—it doesn't care about our IQ, skin color or socioeconomic status. It can kill us all.

Throughout recovery, we periodically take inventory of our beliefs, testing them for authenticity. How are they working for us so far? Few people retain the same belief systems they had when they first got here. A willingness to try new things keeps rigidity from setting in.

When I was new, I had to trade in some beliefs for new ideas and practices. Am I still amenable to challenging my morals, beliefs and tendencies?

## November 23

*"Enjoy your achievements as well as your plans. Keep interested
in your own career, however humble; it is a real possession
in the changing fortunes of time. Exercise caution in your
business affairs, for the world is full of trickery. But let this not
blind you to what virtue there is; many persons strive for high
ideals, and everywhere life is full of heroism."*

Max Ehrmann (1872–1945)

---

This quote from *Desiderata* is a worthy mantra for any addict or codependent. We should not be naïve about a world rife with predators and opportunists. Nor should we grow so tired and discouraged that we think, "What's the use? We are all going to hell in a hand basket." There is goodness in even the darkest of places. Heroism can make tomorrow's history books and it happens anonymously all around us. In doing a daily inventory we see how, where and when we react to our lives with right actions vs. selfish or reactive impulses. Right actions feel good and feeling good gives us such an advantage in bringing balance and optimism to the day before us.

Life is finite. When we look at life two-dimensionally, the starting point and eventual end point are anxiety-provoking. To assuage that anxiety we can invest in the popular hope of an afterlife that our soul transcends into. For some of us, this magical thinking is a departure from reason and to part with reason is to part with sober living. Regardless of what our crystal balls tell us about the hereafter, we can agree that despite the finitude of time on earth, the depth of our experience is potentially infinite. We can live an eternity in each of our moments. How deep is this moment and to what extent can we breathe it in? The more we appreciate that which is in our peripheral vision and the more we feel connected to the people and the planet, the more our capacities for awe expand.

Are there setbacks and disappointments and injustice in my life? Am I better at spotting them than the wonder in each moment, the virtue and heroism that is going on all around me? Am I awake?

# November 24

*"Nothing sways them from their habit—not illness,*
*not the sacrifice of love and relationship, not the*
*loss of all earthly goods, not the crushing of their dignity,*
*not the fear of dying. The drive is that relentless."*

*Dr. Gabor Maté (born 1944)*

---

Maté, author of *In the Realm of Hungry Ghosts*, challenges the perception that addiction is a choice. The collective comfort of the choice model maintains that if addicts are making moral compromises by choice then society is not responsible. Maté's book challenges the popular criminal justice assumption that drug addicts are culpable because they choose to do drugs. Does that make sense? People *choose* addiction, alienation and premature death? Below the mental illness or self-destructive addiction is conflict and anguish that addiction is treating. So the question is not "why the addiction?" but rather, "why the pain?" Opiate addicts self-medicate, which is in keeping with the way our medical community reduces suffering. Soldiers in battle, exposed to potentially traumatic incidents, are given morphine so they are less likely to suffer from a Post-Traumatic Stress Disorder (PTSD). People in hospitals are given opiates by responsible doctors to manage pain. A drunkard is described as someone who feels no pain. Addicts medicate pain, depression, grief and shock. They may not know they have a disorder and they may not be able to articulate or understand their condition but they are taking evasive actions to deal with the symptoms.

"The Doctor's Opinion" in the 1939 printing of *Alcoholics Anonymous* was insightful and still rings true today. Critics inside AA would have preferred that the 1976 and 2004 reprint offered AA members a second opinion. With due respect to Dr. Silkworth, *more has been revealed*. We found something wholesome which was good. Have we stopped seeking with the same zeal? It is not disrespectful to those who have come before us and done so much for us to show that the courage they taught us has enabled us to reach further.

Do I ever judge other addicts as weak? Do I see past my addiction symptoms? Was I medicating pain?

# November 25

*"You can have such an open mind that it is too porous to hold a conviction."*

*George Crane (1901–1995)*

---

Water is a key to life but too much of it will drown us. An open mind is good but an empty mind is not so good. On the one hand, conviction is the cornerstone of a meaningful life, but self-righteousness could see us trading in a life of meaning for anger management classes. However, having no conviction is to be adrift in a sea of indecision.

Any of us who change our approach to recovery every time we read a new book ought to review the story of the Greek nymph, Echo. Helena had been sufficiently distracted by Echo's incessant babbling and Zeus took the opportunity to go bang every other goddess that giggled. The hurt and pissed off Helena blamed Echo for Zeus' indiscretions. Helena cast a spell on Echo so that all she could say was that which was said to her. Poor Echo. Later she would fall in love with Narcissus, which should have been a perfect match—Narcissus hearing every precious word of his echoed back. The novelty wore off and he dumped her. Echo's heart bled and she pined in the meadows until there was nothing left but her echoing voice.

Amiable people have many great qualities but everyone needs their own identity. If core beliefs like "other people's needs are more important than mine" or "if you really knew me you would reject me" trigger us unconsciously, we may mimic others instead of expressing our own unique voices. Many addicts are chameleons who blend in instead of standing out. If fear of rejection is more of a motivator than standing up for our convictions, we will be like Echo—without unique definition.

Standing for something means I don't fall for just anything. Am I self-assured and decisive? Can I make tough decisions without procrastination? When it's time to take a side and stand up for what I believe in, do I look left and right to see how others are leaning before I stick my neck out?

## November 26

*"There is never a sudden revelation, a complete and tidy explanation for why it happened, or why it ends, or why or who you are. You want one and I want one, but there isn't one. It comes in bits and pieces, and you stitch them together wherever they fit, and when you are done you hold yourself up, and still there are holes and you are a rag-doll, invented, imperfect."*

Wasted: A Memoir of Anorexia and Bulimia,
*Marya Hornbacher (born 1974)*

---

Is trauma a misfortune from which there is no healing or is it a springboard to a higher spiritual plane? We often hear that members are glad that they suffered on the mean streets of addiction because this brought them to their knees and they were able to find recovery, which is infinitely meaningful and rewarding. Psychologists measure "Quality of Life" in the recovery community at different stages of sobriety. Clearly we feel better after a few years clean and sober compared to when we lived in addiction, but the notion that we are further ahead than if we had never suffered through addiction and found recovery is purely subjective.[100] We may perceive that we are better off, but our perceived quality of life could easily be attributed to the maturity of aging as opposed to the *gift* of addiction. Most everyone feels more acceptance and peace as they mature. We practice the program but there is no finish line and no one expects us to be perfect. Suggesting that our hardships put us ahead of the rest is a pleasant narrative to give purpose to our suffering. But what's wrong with being equal to all the "rag dolls" of the world?

Post-traumatic life, as described by Hornbacher, is no Shangri-La. It is good to see gains along with the rubs that life will bring. It is good to make the most of the cards we have been dealt. But when we see ourselves on a higher plane than "earth people" we have built a sandcastle in the sky and moved into it. And if we are constantly depressed or delusional, we are not emotionally healthy. We strive for objectivity. Unconditional acceptance brings with it a strength that is sustainable. We don't need to overcompensate anymore.

Do I see the upside to rigorous honesty? Can I be positive or optimistic without deluding myself? Through the balance of November, we will explore perception and truth further.

# November 27

*"At the moment of profound insight, you transcend both appearance and emptiness. Don't keep searching for the truth; just let go of your opinions."*

Seng-Ts'an (Died 606)

---

This patriarch of Zen suffered from leprosy. Seng-ts'an's guru, Hui-k'o, gave him a unique view of suffering and truth which inspired the poem "The Mind of Absolute Trust," which today's quote comes from.[101] To be beyond opinions and expectations is to be peaceful. Without judgment about yesterday, today or tomorrow, what's to worry about? For those of us dominated by our cerebral filter, this ideal is an eye-roller. If we feel our way through life, this statement may sound obvious.

Carl Jung wrote of four ego-functions. Imagine being in the hub of a wheel with four spokes spread out—Feeling, Thinking, Intuition and Sensation. These are the four ways Jung says we interpret reality and respond to it. Most of us rely on one ego-function and back it up with a secondary ego-function.

Thinkers back up their thesis statements with phrases such as "Seeing is believing," relying on their senses for validation. Seeing is a partial truth, and involves jumping to conclusions based on what we see, blind to the expanse of what cannot be seen. Feeling people judge the world on the basis of what is pleasant or what is not. They defend their positions using hunches or intuition. Theists or nonbelievers may *know* that their beliefs are true, not from irrefutable evidence but because of the evidence they perceive from their ego-function of preference. The feelers trust their intuition; the thinkers face the facts. Agnostics don't have inescapable evidence or strong feelings either way. Their search continues. The *apatheist* (who is apathetic) doesn't know and doesn't care. If irrefutable proof for or against god was discovered today, it wouldn't change how they conduct themselves tomorrow. They "transcend both appearance and emptiness" and how they live their lives isn't dependent on the great existential questions.

Do I know that truth isn't out there beyond my reach? Can I see how it is buried under my opinions? Is there a better way to live my recovery program—relying on my thoughts or feelings? Just for today, can I set my biases free for a while and see what I find?

## November 28

*"We are continually faced with great opportunities which are brilliantly disguised as unsolvable problems."*

*Margaret Mead (1901–1978)*

---

Lee Iacocca, the infamous industrialist, is credited with almost the same quote, using "insoluble problems" instead. Insolvable, unsolvable, insoluble—we have a lot of words to choose from when we want to give up. Yet CEOs like Iacocca, anthropologists like Mead and addicts like us can all report that many things that once seemed insurmountable have been tamed and our problems have been converted into assets. Ask a long-time member if they regret being an addict or codependent. Has the admission of powerlessness translated into a handicap or an opportunity? Most members with long-term recovery don't regret being addicts. Addiction led to a program which became a better way of life. The quality of life, now, is a gift in spite of the cost then.

Life doesn't stop sending us brilliantly disguised opportunities in recovery. The quality—not the quantity—of problems improves with time. We may agonize over the frustration of learning how to play the guitar or of choosing one vacation destination over another. Of course there will continue to be troubles, too. We or our loved ones may be unexpectedly diagnosed with an illness. Losing a job or an intimate relationship are events we will likely have to face. These attention-getters leave us at the crossroads of life without clear direction. If we deem hardships to be unsolvable, let's remember that this label is an opinion (perception) and not fact (truth).

Am I quick to haplessly resign myself to considering new challenges unsolvable? The program is full of motivating stories of overcoming insurmountable odds. Biographies and stories of others who have changed the course of history with faith and persistence give me perspective. Would it be worth my time to read one or two biographies each year?

# November 29

*"Emulation is better than envy."*

*Hindu saying*

---

Resenting others for what they have won't help drive us toward what we want for ourselves. Envy, when left unchecked, will lead to self-pity, which isn't one of those forces that brings out the best in us. So, when we feel a twinge of envy, be it for another's smooth demeanor or the cool toys they have, why not do as they do? Emulation may help us get what they have.

A great many things we desire can be ours if we really want them. That said, we can't have everything we fancy, just because we wish for it. Some limits are facts of life. When we truly understand what it would take to emulate those who have what we want, we may conclude it's not worth the sacrifice needed to obtain it. It isn't how she or he whom we envy acts today that matters; what were the steps this person took to arrive at this place?

We sometimes hear "stick with the winners" in the fellowship, which reminds us of two things (i) we are susceptible to picking up on the habits of those around us and (ii) we can choose who will have the greatest influence on us by altering our surroundings. Emulating those in meetings who have what we want has reliable benefits. Acting *as if* employs the adage that we can act our way into right-thinking more easily than we can think our way into right-acting. Ultimately, finding our rightful paths and sticking to them makes more sense when we think about it than investing creative energy in what we don't have. But still, dream away—it can relieve the pain of the moment to imagine a better life. Even while dealing with trauma, we can visualize not regretting this past at some future point. There may be such a thing as post-traumatic gain as well as stress and loss.

What do I want? Who do I have to emulate to get what I want?

*"Sometimes one of the hardest questions to answer in life is 'what do I really want?' We keep ourselves so busy doing what we have to do that we don't get around to asking ourselves what we want to do. And sometimes we don't know how to differentiate between what we really want and what we think we should want."*

*"Visions", Debtors Anonymous*

---

"If I had ten million dollars (pounds, euros) ..." How would we finish that sentence? If we could do whatever we wanted today, what would it be? What does that say about us? More than fear of failure or not being in touch with our values, debt or financial circumstances are often the (perceived) obstacles between us and our bliss. We all think we are going to get out of debt. Here are some interesting quotes about debt from around the world: (i) "Promises make debt; debt makes promises" (Dutch Proverb); (ii) "Before borrowing from a friend, decide which you need most" (Joe Moore); (iii) "Tis against some men's principle to pay interest, and seems against others' interest to pay the principle" (Benjamin Franklin); (iv) "A hundred wagon loads of thoughts will not pay a single ounce of debt" (Italian Proverb). The final quote comes from Adam Smith, author of *Wealth of Nations*, who said, "What can be added to the happiness of a man who is in health, out of debt and has a clear conscience?"

What is there about the Twelve Steps of recovery that isn't covered in Smith's proposition? We regain our health and we take inventory sufficient to clear our debt and our conscience. If our program is intact but we don't feel free, happy and joyous, maybe our relationship with money is out of sorts. The urgency to own stuff and have it now is promulgated by our culture. In the USA, tax incentives for mortgage debt have been around since the 1930s. The idea was that debt enslaved—a man with a mortgage won't go on strike. It was a way to control a worker for his or her working years.

Between money and me, who's the slave and who's the master? What do I really want?

# December 1

*"In the Buddha's life story we see the three stages of practice: Morality comes first, then concentrated meditation, and then wisdom. And we see that the path takes time."*

*Tenzin Gyatso, the XIVth Dalai Lama (born 1935)*

---

Who remembers when clean and sober sounded like a punishment for admitting we were addicts? Long before we can aim for morality we need an adjustment to our attitude about recovery. More reality isn't any prize for an addict. Once we see some hope and value in recovery, then morality, obedience to a plan for living—be it religion or any recovery model—can be a good start. With maturity we will find our own unique values. The first Steps are a coming to terms with the fact that our modus operandi isn't all that manageable. Steps Four to Nine involve moral reconstruction. Meditation isn't formally introduced until Step Eleven, but what are the preceding steps if not soul-searching?

Wisdom or a *spiritual awakening à la* the Steps may be a white light experience, a series of rude awakenings or the "educational variety," as described by William James in Appendix II of *Alcoholics Anonymous*. The process takes time—not time we *find* but time we *make*. Who has extra time? Wellness becomes a priority so we apply ourselves. An attitude adjustment has replaced the self-deceit and street wit that once kept us alive. We don't feel *holier than thou*—in fact, we feel quite humbled. The beginning of finding wisdom includes coming to grips with how much there is still to know.

When overwhelmed by our lives, we are reminded that no matter how much sand sits in the top bulb of the hourglass, only one grain at a time passes through the neck. Our lives have a natural rhythm that we can neither halt nor accelerate. We can rush around in circles, but we don't alter the pace of life.

Have I gone through stages in my recovery? Can I avoid both delaying and rushing my own progress? Recovery is a way of life, not a crash course in feeling better and reaping rewards.

# December 2

*"The most beautiful thing we can experience is the mysterious.*
*It is the source of all true art and science. He to whom this*
*emotion is a stranger, who can no longer pause to wonder and*
*stand rapt in awe, is as good as dead: his eyes are closed. This*
*insight into the mystery of life, coupled though it be with fear,*
*has also given rise to religion. To know what is impenetrable*
*to us really exists, manifesting itself as the highest wisdom*
*and the most radiant beauty which our dull faculties can*
*comprehend only in the most primitive forms—this knowledge,*
*this feeling is at the centre of true religiousness.*
*In this sense, and in this sense only,*
*I belong in the ranks of the devoutly religious men."*

*Albert Einstein (1879–1955)*

---

Humans, unlike other members of the animal kingdom, have the capacity for awe and dread. Edwin Hubble (1889–1953) was the first cosmologist to establish that the universe is expanding. The deeper the Hubble telescope sees into space, the further we see back in time. The light from the stars we see, light years away, is a snapshot from a distant past. That is awesome. We can see into the past. Our minds allow us to imagine a myriad of possible futures, too—the good stuff and the bad. No matter how magical our future may be, we know it ends. That's where dread comes in. Humans can dwell on the past, the future and our inescapable finitude. Imagine a family pet getting excited by the Hubble images or fantasizing about its own death. Sure, every living thing fights to survive and will avoid death. But it's hard to imagine a healthy, well-fed apartment cat worrying about how she or he is going to die.

Einstein is talking about the place where dread and awe meet, where religion is created. What assuages anxiety about uncertainty more than the promise of reincarnation or eternity in heaven? To some, religion offers spiritual procrastination and avoidance of untenable realities. Modern spirituality offers a create-your-own God of our imagination. In the same way religion is an immortality project, nonbelievers also have their own symbols and beliefs that give life purpose. Einstein accepted his place "in the ranks of the devoutly religious," acknowledging his own balancing act between the awe and dread of life's unknown.

Do I feel that all truth will set me free if I am open to it? Do I still wrestle with untenable truths?

# December 3

*"What's really interesting about this 10,000-hour rule is that it applies virtually everywhere. You can't become a chess grand master unless you spend 10,000 hours on practice."*

*Malcolm Gladwell (born 1963)*

---

In the book *Outliers,* Gladwell refers to Anders Ericsson's early-1900s principle which suggests that ten thousand hours, be it three hours a day for ten years, or a five-year full-time job, is what it takes to master anything—from becoming a world-class pianist to becoming a software billionaire. Does this ten thousand hour regimen apply to mastering recovery? We could get *booked* by a Big Book *mucker*, attend a twenty-eight day program and then do a run of ninety meetings in ninety days and still have less than two thousand hours logged. Time and dedication don't guarantee winning an Olympic gold, finding a cure for cancer or staying sober forever. However, this principle is a reminder that mastering life, and mastering it free from addiction or codependency, isn't possible with a half-hearted effort.

The more time we devote to recovery the better we will be. It doesn't mean we won't have setbacks or what some call "emotional slips." At our best, we will still be erring human beings. Is a Twelve Step life a learned dependency or is it self-empowering? In other words, by relying on a program and fellowship, are we replacing our drug of choice with a life-long dependency on a recovery routine? Or does our program and fellowship help us get to the point where we can stand on our own two feet, free from addiction? One thing is for sure—after spending ten thousand hours at something, it will feel very familiar.

Have I put my time into recovery yet? Do I feel anxious about getting results now? As a human I am not an island. How dependent or interdependent am I on people, places and things?

## December 4

*"Normal eaters stop eating when they are full. We do
not. Normal eaters do not hide food and plan how they
will secretly get to it when no one is around. We do.
Normal eaters do not use food to comfort their
insecurities and fears or to prove a fleeting escape
from worries and troubles. We do. Normal eaters do not
feel guilt and shame about their eating. We do."*

*"A Plan of Eating," Overeaters Anonymous*

---

Binging and purging behavior can play out in poker, exercise, saving, spending, drugs, work and sex. All people blow off a little steam or go overboard sometimes. Anyone will have a "hangover" from overdoing it but does that make us addicts? Non-addicts don't feel ashamed after misbehaving. When non-addicts behave outside of their value system, they make adjustments and are likely never to repeat the behavior. The guilt and shame described above about eating can be applied to any Twelve Step discipline. If we do something that makes us feel less worthy and swear we will never do it again, but do, this could be a problem and it could be progressive.

Some members will quip, "If you're not a member of at least four fellowships by ten years of sobriety, you're in denial." For others, spreading time between so many fellowships could be called a compulsion of its own. It's a personal choice and others' opinions matter little. We all take responsibility for when, where and why we are going—or why we are avoiding. What is there to lose in testing the waters of another fellowship if our behavior is suspect?

When I see questionable behaviors in myself to whom do I turn? Who do I know who will be neither neurotic nor enabling?

# December 5

*"Friendship is unnecessary, like philosophy, like art ...
It has no survival value; rather it is one of those
things that give value to survival."*

C. S. Lewis (1898–1963)

---

Fellowship is unnecessary. Steps are unnecessary. People can recover without them—some have to and some prefer to. But for a large number of us, our friends in recovery "give value to survival." We know the Pollyanna platitude, "Recovery is its own reward." When we are in pain this quip has us rolling our eyes but the point is that when life sucks, being whatever we define as *sober* means we have at least broken even on the day. Add to that a friend online, on the phone or at a meeting—then our survival has value. Someone who has been through what we have been through telling us that "this too shall pass" adds value and comfort. Hearing from someone in worse shape than us can help too. Connection adds context in a way that working the program or struggling through the day alone cannot.

Is it happiness or purposefulness that gives life value? Psychologists report that priorities change throughout life. A young adult will report high happiness scores, enjoying freedom from the rules of a parent's home. But their lives don't have much meaning. Then career or family happens. Happiness scores fall prey to stress and routine but a sense of meaning registers higher in this stage of life. Then comes retirement and/or empty-nest-syndrome and meaning diminishes but happiness returns with a more carefree life.[102] Fellowship can give meaning to life—throughout life. We work the Steps and take an interest in the lives of others. So long as we don't retreat into meetings as an escape from the outside world, fellowship can help us establish healthy boundaries and meaningful relationships.

Who are the key people in my recovery network? Do I balance friendships in and out of the fellowship? Am I the type of member who reaches out the hand of friendship as an act of love that asks nothing in return?

# December 6

*"Any time you do something from the heart,*
*people just know it."*

Brad Paisley (born 1972)

---

Step Nine (making amends) is a delicate matter, asking us to be more mindful than gung-ho. Motives have to be considered. What do we have to gain or lose from the outcome? Have we learned humility from Step Seven? Some of us have heard Steps Six and Seven read so many times that when we get to working them we may feel like we've been there—done that. "Yes I am entirely ready to shed my shortcomings and embrace my true nature and oh yeah, humility, I see the benefit of that—I will right-size my self-image and become a fabulous power of example to newcomers. I got it—what's next?" Steps Six and Seven are not intellectual exercises. They are the process of getting in touch with and putting our value systems to work. We identify triggers and interrogate our feelings. With practice we find understanding and compassion. We need to practice these steps. A workbook or a routine of writing and/or meditation might help. Somewhere between ego-deflation and positive self-talk we become something other than victims of addiction. We may be *ready* to make amends.

When we come to do Step Nine we review our Step Eight list and see if we really understand how we victimized others. Well-crafted words are not enough. Communication is said to be 7% words—the rest is tone and body language. Words won't hide insincerity, impurity of intention or a habitual need to control the agenda. Our reaching out has to be pure in intent to be heard and felt by those who don't trust us. We may or may not be forgiven; the goal is to take ownership and express regret for the harm or neglect we have inflicted. Some victims have passed away or moved away and can't be found. An unsent letter may be the best we can do.

Who do I go to for help to test my motives and my readiness? Does "Easy Does It but Do It" have more meaning now? Am I doing Step Nine just from my head or am I acting from my heart?

# December 7

*"We are being destroyed by our knowledge, which
has made us drunk with our power.
And we shall not be saved without wisdom."*

*Will Durant (1885–1981)*

---

In 1929, in *The Mansions of Philosophy: A Survey of Human Life and Destiny*, Durant noted that the culture of the day had grown superficial, and knowledge had become a danger. Back then, we had become enthralled by what we could do mechanically and how our purpose had become lost in the shuffle. OMG, what would he have thought of social media and hundreds of TV channels? Today, an example of superficiality might include capturing moments digitally to share with friends online, while missing the first-hand experience ourselves. The signal-to-noise ratio is so low today that people don't distinguish entertainment from information. "Celebrity news" and "reality TV" are oxymorons that are part of our lexicon. Maintaining a sober head in a world of chaos isn't a new challenge. Dysfunctional group-think is a century-old problem, maybe older. Maybe it is a defining quality of humans.

How does this quote apply inside the fellowship? It warns us about becoming drunk on dogma or confusing knowhow with compassion. When we rattle off cliché after cliché, both masterfully and mindlessly, we may get a buzz from approving nods in a meeting. But can we say it in plain language? The words we quote from the text may have proven themselves to be wise—even universal—truths. Still, every great truth has a convincing rebuttal. It's good for our grey matter to challenge all of our own *noble truths*. Our biases predispose us to seek evidence that supports our opening positions and deny even overwhelming evidence to the contrary. Open minds, skeptical of even our most heartfelt convictions, are our best defense against our own tendency toward confirmation bias.

Do I see that knowledge is stagnant and wisdom is a humble search for more truth? Do I ever power-trip? Do I promptly admit when I am *right* and expect recognition and approval?

## December 8

*"I want you to be concerned about your next door neighbor. Do you know your next door neighbor?"*

*Mother Teresa (1910–1997)*

Sometimes we hear about a natural disaster across the country or the world. We commit to a random act of kindness and we help out with clothes or money. What does that tell us about ourselves? Something good, we hope. It is good to help when duty calls.

Mother Teresa challenges us to ask if our disaster-response-readiness is in tune to the less dramatic events, and for those closer to home. When we witness quiet desperation in our regular travels, why not ponder small but meaningful ways to help? It may be our next-door neighbor whom we take for granted and never get to know. Taking this message to heart, we don't suddenly and rudely violate people's boundaries, but maybe we can start to break the ice with a smile, by saying "Hello, how are you? I live next-door and I have never introduced myself."

Let's consider the newer member at our meeting whom we never took the time to get to know because we figured someone else had taken them under their wing. Longtime members still have problems, too. We put them on pedestals and maybe they don't do too much to deter this, but crisis, dread, doubt and despair come at any time in life and any time in recovery.

Am I my sister's or brother's keeper? What can I do or say to demonstrate my concern for others? Do I ever try to do a good deed anonymously? Can I do something for someone today without getting caught?

## December 9

*"We don't see things as they are; we see things as we are."*

*Anaïs Nin (1903–1977)*

---

It's been said that the best situation a lawyer can ask for in a trial is a witness. The worst thing the lawyer can have is two witnesses. Any two people are going to see, remember or experience the same situation differently. Two witnesses are bound to contradict one another. Observations and recollections will be based on what each person saw unfold and will be colored by assumptions, reference points and life experience—in other words, how each of them are.

Today's quote sheds a light on how we relate to emotionally-charged events from our past, be it early childhood or a day and a half ago. Let's try to view the events from different vantage points rather than just as *we* are. New ways of seeing will make problematic mysteries look like obvious truths with obvious solutions. We may uncover old automatic patterns that are interfering with enjoying our lives to the fullest. Or we could gain perspective on an old sorrow that shines a light on today's anxieties.

Today's quote also talks to us about empathy. It's easy to identify with someone else's experience and jump to conclusions about what an experience means for them—it must mean for them what it means for us. No matter how similar our encounters—they may seem to be identical experiences—with quizzical minds, we see how our experiences are similarly caused, but have different effects. Everyone at a funeral is missing the same person but the spouse, sibling, grandchild and all the rest are having unique experiences. The advice we offer to others tends to be based on what works for us.

Today, do I see things the way they are? Am I sure about that? How about the people in my life—do I see them as unique?

## December 10

*"Anonymity is the spiritual foundation of all our traditions,*
*ever reminding us to place principles before personalities."*

Tradition Twelve [103]

---

What is more spiritual than humility and what sustains humility more than anonymity? A wholesome exercise is to do good deeds anonymously, once a week or so. We could clean the car headlights of a member we resent or we can anonymously donate to a cause in place of an amends we can't otherwise make. Anonymity and humility can ease tension and flex our character muscles. In public we guard the names of others. Our own anonymity is ours to do with as we see fit. We do our homework before side-stepping any Tradition to avoid the same regrets others have suffered. Also, if we serve on committees or have some years of recovery we don't have to fit our title or qualifications into conversation at every meeting. Our name is out there, within the fellowship, should people need us. Our deeds—our service accomplishments, if you will—can be kept anonymous. We don't do it for recognition.

"Principles before personalities" is one of the concepts that we aim to incorporate into meetings all the time. It's said that "If you haven't met anyone you don't like in the fellowship, you need to go to more meetings." Members will rub us the wrong way, but would that stop us from helping them? This is one way we practice this Tradition. Another is by choosing the right members for service tasks—not the most popular. When we bring these principles into the rest of our lives, outside the rooms, others may think we are sages—imagine that!

Are the principles behind the Traditions something that I incorporate in all areas of my life today? Who annoys me and what does that tell me about me? What good can I do anonymously today?

# December 11

*"People spend a lifetime searching for happiness;
looking for peace. They chase idle dreams, addictions,
religions, even other people, hoping to fill the
emptiness that plagues them. The irony is the only
place they ever needed to search was within."*

Ramona L. Anderson (1887–1949)

---

Life is full of irony: tripping over the crutches and spraining our ankles; crashing a car into a tow-truck; drinking to forget only to be haunted; saying we would rather be dead than sober only to find that, in recovery, we felt alive for the first time. The commercial world of self-help plays into our quest to find happiness. One more book, and a weekend seminar, and wealth and love will fill our lives. Some of us hope that magical qualities in other members will rub off on us.

Happiness is a feeling—a legitimate and sincere state that comes and goes. It is not a reward for eating our vegetables or a measure of our successes. We do not command our feelings any more than our thoughts and sensations. They rush in like a wave and then recede. Some feelings lap up along the shore, barely tickling us, and others have tidal wave-like consequences. Either way, tomorrow will be different. Happiness, sadness, anger and fear wash over us and recede throughout our lives.

Drugs, infatuation, religious fanaticism and day-dreaming are all fool's gold forms of happy-making. As a drink is to a social drinker, periodically indulging in wishful thinking breaks monotony and relieves stress. Addicts may expect too much from escape, losing touch with reality. Some things we subjectively judge as positive and some as tragic. Getting rejected at a job interview might be a net gain or net loss, depending on what happens tomorrow. But we tend to treat the event as personal rejection or good fortune. Because of expectations and/or judgments a circumstance becomes an emotionally-charged issue.

There is no get-happy Step. There isn't even a get-un-sad Step. Can I see that sadness isn't failure any more than happiness is proof that I have recovered? When happiness hits me, chances are I will be busy doing something other than searching for *the secret road to happiness*. Isn't that ironic?

# December 12

*"Speak when you are angry—and you'll make the best speech you'll ever regret."*

*Laurence L. Peters (1919–1988)*

---

The *rageaholic* raises the stakes by raising the volume. We can be cruel and manipulative, dressing up our demands as "seeking justice." Everyone wants control and resists being controlled. As humans, we resort to verbal violence to get our way. Even if we don't use threatening gestures or suggestions, just the increased volume is a primitive way of expressing our issues around control. Do our outbursts express ourselves authentically or are we fighting dirty? How we feel after *laying it on the line* will tell us if we acted rightly. Did we feel good about ourselves or regretful?

Anger is the most misunderstood of feelings. If we internalize anger, it seeps out as passive-aggressive, sarcastic or judgmental barbs. We may find ourselves saying, "I'm not angry—really." We feel smug because we don't start screaming like "so and so" does. Anger is not a wrong feeling. Experiencing and expressing emotion is healthy and human. Regret comes from *acting on*—not from *feeling*—anger. Anger gives us clarity and strength. It is a survival instinct dating back to our primitive roots when quick decisions had to be made: fight, flight or freeze. The feeling of anger takes only a few minutes to wax and wane. People who say they have been angry for weeks have really been ruminating, not angry—we call this "holding resentments." Like laughter or orgasm, anger gets intense, then passes. Dramatic emotional sensations do not automatically require impulsive, dramatic reactions. Feelings and sensations pass through us like ideas and options swirl through our brain. Brains work overtime when we are emotional, so let's take advantage of our heightened awareness. But feelings are visceral; they are to be experienced, not intellectualized.

How do I get angry? What and who trigger me? Do I dump my feelings with impunity or do I repress them? What are the consequences of acting out? What are the consequences of holding back?

# December 13

*"One of the ways of surrendering freedom is to actually have convictions. And a way of further surrendering freedom is to spend quite a bit of time acting on those convictions."*

Jonathan Franzen (born 1959)

---

Anyone who knows this author's devotion to art would question his commitment to balanced living. He spent nine years writing the book *Freedom*, without holidays or much recreation. Franzen's dedication to art is an enslavement he would prefer to freedom. We often look at recovery and addiction in opposite lights—addiction was manic (or depressive) and compulsive, so recovery should be long walks on the beach or curled up with a book. Recovery releases us from enslavement. Our new freedom is ours to do with as we see fit. If we want to trade in our freedom for a calamitous cause, we go for it. We need not be afraid of extreme behavior, so long as we maintain our sanity and our power of choice. Music, painting, travel and many other ways we spend our time don't come with early to bed, early to rise, three square meals per day and a white picket fence.

How do we differentiate obsessive-compulsive behavior (unhealthy living) from getting lost in a noble calling? Our inner voices guide us. Checking with a sponsor or a confidant might not hurt either. Do we start slow and see how it goes or do we jump right in? The all-or-nothing drama from our past doesn't have to dictate how we follow our bliss. How calm or dramatic our lives are will not determine whether they are good or bad. Good living is meaningful living. Pleasure and accolades aren't something we desperately seek for reassurance when our lives our chock-full of meaning. Are we living in accordance with our true values?

What limits do I impose on my life because I am an addict? Are these healthy limits? Are they necessary? Put another way, what are the limits and freedoms of my recovery?

# December 14

*"Tibetan lamas warn of winding up in the god realm—blissed out for incalculable aeons—until good karma becomes exhausted and we wind up back at square one.*
*Square one sucks. I was addicted to silence for a long time in Zen, and it was one of the factors that led to my eventual relapse. As an addict, I need to be free of attachments— especially attachments to states of mind."*

The 12-Step Buddhist *by Darren Littlejohn*

---

Is too much of a good thing a bad thing? *Extreme sobriety* and intense peacefulness might be something we call a Century Twenty-One hybrid awakening. The acid test is: "So how is that working for you so far?" In *The 12-Step Buddhist*, Littlejohn gives a candid account of his experience seeking balance while pushing himself throughout decades of recovery, therapy and Buddhism. As we see from the excerpt above, more isn't always better.

Every misadventure in our journey is another *no matter how far down the road we go, we will see how our experience can benefit others* arrow in our quiver. Addiction was an innocent wrong turn in our lives of seeking. We truly thought we found the answer to everything in our drug of choice. In sobriety we replace the void with meetings, people, gadgets, exercise, books, conferences, brownies, frappuccinos and romantic intrigue—new post-addiction stuff to fill our spiritual voids. Longing and loathing, control and approval—these are the lifelong barometers of our spiritual health. We want to be cured. We want to be better, so we think that a new state of mind will free us forever. In truth, it is still a one-day-at-a-time journey that involves making slight adjustments and doing our best.

When I am rigid and demanding with myself, am I not judgmental or hard on others? Can I remember that wearing life like a loose garment is better for me than thinking in absolutes? Do I value balance or do I always want more of the good stuff?

# December 15

*"Regarding having a relationship with someone in the fellowship, the odds are good, but the goods are odd."*

*Heard around the rooms*

---

Here's an acronym from the *Heard Around the Rooms* handbook: RELATIONSHIP means Really Exciting Love Affair Turns Into Outrageous Nightmare; Sobriety Hangs In Peril (or Seek Help In Program, depending on the region of the world where we attend meetings). Dating when we are new isn't a moral issue. You would never hear a chemotherapy patient being told, "Don't talk to boys until your cancer is gone." Addiction has triggers that other illnesses don't have, so recovery is fraught with well-intentioned advice. Life isn't to be put on hold to get clean and sober. Life and recovery happen in concert with each other. More caution, less compulsion is the general idea. Do boundaries punish or purify us? Temporary fasts, celibacy and any other form of spiritual cleansing don't ensure sobriety nor do they trigger relapse. Some Sex and Love Addicts Anonymous meetings end with this sobering shot: "Dating between members is not recommended. Dating between members and newcomers is discouraged. Talk among yourselves. Reason it out. Let there be no gossip or criticism, just love and understanding."

It is not solely for the naïve newbie that we suggest sober second thought before jumping in the sack. It's the long-term member whose sobriety faces new risks. Drama and chaos is just another day at the office for the newcomer. The established member may be more out of her or his element in a whirlwind affair. Over time we see that for every unwritten rule in the rooms there are undeniable exceptions. We all have our own experiences. Let's share them and keep our opinions, advice and moralizing to ourselves. Helping other members find what is true for themselves is so much more helpful than imposing our boundaries or values on them.

Do I have clear sex conduct rules for myself? If so, do I think everyone should live by them? Do I ever hear myself saying "Now listen to me if you want to stay sober..."?

# December 16

*"It is not the end of the physical body that should worry us. Rather, our concern must be to live while we're alive—to release our inner selves from the spiritual death that comes with living behind a façade designed to conform to external definitions of who and what we are."*

*Elisabeth Kubler-Ross (1926–2004)*

---

Chronic Shock Syndrome happens when traumatic experiences occur without the support needed to make sense of them. Symptoms include memory dead-zones, anxiety, depression and emotional numbness. The cause is either abuse or deprivation. In rigid or chaotic environments, children are over-stimulated or under-stimulated; either way, healthy emotional development is derailed. Looking back at our childhood, what were the reward and punishment criteria? What was demanded and what was forbidden? These lists, written and reviewed, reveal valuable clues. What happened when we expressed ourselves? What secrets were we told to keep? None of us get or give perfect parenting. Assessing blame is for another day; today we merely wish to identify dysfunctions that might have led us to seek shelter behind our "external definitions." Professional feedback in reviewing the severity and frequency of abuses and deprivation in a dysfunctional life may be needed to break down the barriers to finding our spiritually alive selves.

We all have some unmet needs and we have emotional defenses to play hide-and-seek behind. It's a matter of degrees—how often did we suffer and how severe were the occurrences? Fear, shame, anger—what will we find? Shame is so integral to addiction. Shame begets addiction; addiction begets shame. The thickest wall of defense is narcissism. Narcissists have been cut off from being hurt by either how we feel or by how they feel. Any empathy they show is an act. We all have selfishness; how much is the question. It can be a bad habit or it can be a psychotic symptom.

Am I spiritually alive now? What is *expected* and *forbidden* about my behavior, today?

## December 17

*"All truth passes through three stages. First, it is ridiculed.*
*Second, it is violently opposed.*
*Third, it is accepted as being self-evident."*

Arthur Schopenhauer (1788–1860)

---

How did those of us who were confronted about our addictions respond to the suggestion that we were powerless and our lives were unmanageable? "What a joke," might have been a knee-jerk reaction. The best defense was a good offense. A dismissive or hostile reaction to an inconvenient truth is something we call denial—a cliché of our addictive past. And now? We identify as addicts as if it was obvious. The truth of addiction passes through these three stages.

Even in recovery, coming to terms with a new truth is a great challenge. Our innate confirmation biases render us way more likely to argue that we are right than to welcome a new way of looking at things. Hugo Mercier and Dan Sperber, who look at the evolution of human reasoning, illustrate for us how the open mind we associate with the spiritual life has some social and psychological booby-traps.[104] We tend to pick and choose from a wealth of evidence that defends our current prejudices and we easily dismiss convincing evidence that contradicts our point of view.

Political and religious agendas can withstand damning contradictory evidence. A fellowship can wallow in reification when needed change looms. Consumers can minimize their impact on a global crisis. If a breakthrough can be made, the truth feels obvious. Maybe we find the routine and rituals of a meeting comforting now. What was our first impression of meetings? Did we see them as infantile or cult-like? Did we say to ourselves, "No way in hell am I joining this whack-job outfit!"

What are the things I scoff or balk at? What are the things I feel hostile toward? Maybe I am 2/3 of the way to a breakthrough.

# December 18

*"Human beings, who are almost unique in having the ability to learn from the experience of others, are also remarkable for their apparent disinclination to do so."*

*Douglas Adams (1952–2001)*

Smart people learn from their own mistakes; the wise also learn from the mistakes of others. There is a wealth of experience/wisdom in our meetings and literature. Modern psychology, spiritual teachings and the wisdom of the ages are key strokes away or, at most, involve an excursion to a library. Ego persuades us that these other blowhards aren't worth their salt; we are self-sufficient. We think we're on a mission from God but it's really an ego trip. A member of a 100% abstinence program may have a strong opinion about harm reduction or moderation management programs without doing any research or having any firsthand experience. This closed-mindedness is only a problem if it leads to preaching that these alternatives are good for nothing.

Maybe there are other Twelve & Twelve fellowships that we were meaning to get to one day. When considering attending another fellowship, a member may say, "Yeah, I asked my sponsor about that and she/he said, 'Eleven of the Steps are exactly the same; we have everything we need here.'" Imagine that—we use someone else's disinclination as a higher authority, convincing ourselves we did all the research needed. Really, no one else can tell us if we should try another program. If we aren't sure, attending six or seven meetings with an open mind should set us straight. Learning opportunities aren't available solely from those whom we deem to be qualified teachers. How many members do we disqualify, saying, "Yes, I am restless and seeking but you have nothing to offer me"?

Do I have the humility to know that answers can come from the most unexpected places? Not knowing doesn't make me inadequate; I am always learning. Can I learn from the experiences of others?

## December 19

*"All of us have been affected by our past, but none of us have to be VICTIMS of the past. In order to recover or change things for the better, the more clearly and more accurately we can diagnose what is wrong, the better chance we have of remedying the situation."*

Earnie Larsen (1939–2011)

---

Adult Child Syndrome (ACS) is found to be at the root of many coping problems. Here are seven common characteristics of ACS: (1) repeatedly becoming involved in failed relationships, (2) being violent or staying in violent relationships, (3) developing an eating disorder, (4) being excessively apologetic, (5) having difficulty making commitments, (6) developing an intimacy disorder and (7) having difficulty relaxing and having fun.[105] No parent or community is perfect. We can't avoid a few emotional scrapes and bruises along the way.

If we don't understand our histories we are destined to repeat them. If life is good and we play nice with others, no problem. If a glass wall seems to stand between us and our dreams, we look for causes and effects that may be in play. Alcoholic homes don't have a monopoly on dysfunction. Anywhere that excess or rigidity flourishes, disturbing and conflicting messages can be found: "Don't trust" and "Stay quiet" are a couple of examples. Neurotic family life may be what we have boxed up, taped up and classified as our ancient history. But if any of the seven symptoms ring a bell, out of sight might not assure us that these problems are out of mind. ACS is a syndrome that tells us we don't have a syndrome. When it's our fault, we blame; when it's not our fault, we feel responsible. We refuse to deal with our past, dismissively saying, "Oh, that's so self-indulgent. I am done with navel-gazing." We may be afraid of what we uncover if we take a good look.

Earnie Larson was well known for his work in the ACS field. Hurt people hurt people. If we have family histories of inadequate parenting we risk repeating these patterns. It isn't about assessing blame; we want to understand, be aware, heal what we can and better manage the remaining damage.

Do I relate to any of the seven symptoms? It's never too late to have a happy childhood.

# December 20

*"Clarity of mind means clarity of passion, too;*
*this is why a great and clear mind loves ardently*
*and sees distinctly what it loves."*

*Blaise Pascal (1623–1662)*

---

Today's author, a mathematician, physicist, inventor, writer and Catholic philosopher, describes the clear and loving mind from many perspectives and disciplines. Language has certain shortcomings as a means of communication. Two people can't conclude that the color yellow looks exactly the same to both of them. When physicists want to speak the truth, a mathematical formula, not language, is their preferred means of communication. A musician may prefer the chords on a piano to tell us how they feel. A social worker tells two lovers, "You can't love anyone else unless you love yourself." Pascal says we can't love ardently until we clear our minds. Clarity offers resolution. Clarity doesn't come on our own terms and sometimes we have to live with or work around havoc or uncertainty.

The Twelve Steps are one way to clear our minds of old clutter and manage current events better. With clarity, what was once *the bondage of self* loosens up to be more like enlightened self-interest. We aren't entirely selfless, but clarity empowers our gut instincts to let us know when to look inward more, and when to move on. We learn that love is as much an action as a feeling, freely given with no conditions. Steps Ten through Twelve involve both the constant practice of self-care (loving ourselves) and practicing to be a better human being for all concerned.

"We will intuitively know how to handle situations which used to baffle us."[106] Does love still baffle me? Have my heart and head cleared somewhat? Is my head like a school bus filled with emotionally disturbed children, speaking several foreign languages? Or do I feel peace?

# December 21

*"Applauding me for quitting [drinking] is sort of like giving a trophy to a cowboy with hemorrhoids for not riding his horse."*

*John Larroquette (born 1947)*

---

Do we ever think we should get special treatment because we are in recovery? When asked about our lead feet on the highway, our unpaid parking tickets, our backlog of taxes or our tardiness at work, do we say, "The rules don't apply to me—I have a handicap"? Some of us will be tempted to point the finger at others as we review this list of rationalizations. Some will feel irritated just reading this, wondering why a book of helpful ideas suddenly started nagging. Around AA coffee pots there has long been a distinction between dry and sober alkies. Quitting mitigates the damage. Let's not forget that any sobriety is good sobriety. Contented sobriety is optional. The "dry" state involves white-knuckling, restlessness, discontentedness, and is excruciating. It's not deadly, but it can get old after a while.

Sobriety is not a punishment for admitting our addictions! There is a pay-off or an emotional lift that comes from right living. Going to meetings can keep us on the wagon. To change from dry to sober we have to confront our crazy-making thoughts and impulsive and/or ingrained behaviors. We try therapies, the Steps, new skills or anything else that takes us out of our comfort zones. For some of us, that means becoming less self-reliant. We use the telephone. If we are averse to calling virtual strangers to talk about our problems, we practice with quick calls just to say "Hi." If we just can't stand the alone-time needed to make lists like in Step Four, we suck it up and do it anyway. If we are uncomfortable going to new meetings, we find running mates to travel with. We can mix it up with a weekend conference or a road trip.

Sobriety doesn't earn me a gold star for completing anything. But hasn't it been rewarding, so far? Am I getting *too* comfortable? Do I keep encouraging myself?

## December 22

*"Question with boldness even the existence of a God;
because if there be one, he must more approve of the
homage of reason than that of blindfolded fear."*

Thomas Jefferson (1743–1826)

---

Question with boldness this book, the Big Book and everything. Ironically, the quote considering contempt prior to investigation, found in "The Spiritual Experience" appendix in *Alcoholics Anonymous,* and which is all about coming to erroneous conclusions, was erroneously attributed to Herbert Spencer.

Spencer's contemporary, Erving Goffman (1922–1982), was a proponent of *symbolic interactionism.* This refers to the assignment of meanings to things, people and ideas as well as to how we relate to them. Faith and skepticism are emotionally-charged words to many. It isn't so much how these words are defined in the dictionary as it is what they symbolize to each of us. Yin and yang are interdependent, opposite forces that work in reciprocal dependency as part of a whole, like the conscious and subconscious or the material and spiritual world.

Skepticism is the opposite of dogmatism, not the opposite of faith. Skepticism is neither cynical nor dismissive. Like a curious child, the skeptic is searching and asking why. The dogmatic is closed to inquiry. The faithful have nothing to fear from doubt. New information is likely to alter their worldview slightly, not change it. When we discovered the world was not a perfect sphere, we didn't go back to seeing it as flat; we made a slight adjustment. It may be hard for doubters to define their own beliefs without referencing a deity—identifying with what they don't believe. Conversely, religion could not have grown quickly without the constant outside pressure of atheism. In recovery circles, we are a community of equals, different from and dependent upon each other. The theist and atheist both use the Twelve Steps as symbols of recovery but because of divergent worldviews, each will interact with the program differently. In our meetings, our differences don't put our aims at odds. On the contrary, our differences make us whole and keep us all "question[ing] with boldness."

Don't my beliefs today differ from the beliefs I held when I got here? They may change again. Do I rate people in a hierarchy of beliefs? Am I boldly skeptical or instantly dogmatic?

## December 23

*"We are not here to see through each other,*
*we are here to see each other through."*

*Heard around the rooms*

---

No one in the program is going to fix us, run our rat race, or work our Steps for us. On the other hand, recovery is not a solitary experience. At meetings, we are likely going to form some of the most significant relationships of our lives. As we feel safer in meetings and become more candid, we will be hard pressed to find a problem that someone else doesn't have experience with. Each of us does our own work and faces our own demons. No one checks our homework and we don't crowd-surf through life, supported by the program. It takes all kinds of people to make a fellowship and we work all kinds of programs. Not everyone is there just for us, placed there by God for the express purpose of making us happy. But somehow, we find who and what we need. Even those we deem useless today may have a few things to teach us when we are ready. We play nice when we can and when we disagree we work it out; we see each other through. If we don't let people in, if we don't form an inner circle in the program, we are missing out on one of the greatest benefits of recovery—fellowship. If we travel, there are no strangers in Twelve Step rooms, only friends we haven't met yet.

Can we go to too many meetings? Absolutely—moderation rules! Early recovery may require an intense regimen of attending meetings and socializing with program people, but meetings can become a new crutch. We may feel a sense of mastery from the ease with which we "talk shop" and it is a warning sign if we don't easily establish friendships outside of meetings. Familiarity breeds contempt so if we're always at meetings, always seeing the same people, these meetings will soon become the problem. One member says, "I owe my life to the program and my closest friends are found here, but I don't live here. I come here to get better and then get back to my life, which is out in the world."

Do I think I am expected to see through others? Do I ever wish they could see through me?

# December 24

*"Let's not forget that the little emotions are the great captains of our lives and we obey them without realizing it."*

*Vincent Van Gogh (1853–1890)*

---

Anyone who says that they choose their thoughts, feelings and/or sensations will lie to us about other things too. Let's stop thinking for one minute. Sixty seconds of no more thoughts—go ahead; take control in three, two, one, zero _____!

So, how did we all make out? Ten seconds in, how many of us wondered (thought), "How much longer?" As Vinnie says, we are directed by feelings, thoughts and sensations—not the other way around. Feeling doubt doesn't mean that something is wrong. Our world doesn't evaporate because we feel impending doom. Feeling like masters of the universe may not last the whole day either. Feelings are not facts, but what would life be without them? Recovery is about being authentic— flawed but striving. Recovery never demands perfection. We don't break the tape at life's finish line to an outbreak of applause, nor will we often spend all day cross-legged, mindfully exploring our thoughts and feelings with unwavering minds. We have things to do—ready or not, here they come. We work at living in the moment, slipping in and out, experiencing, resisting, feeling and breathing.

Some say that feelings and sensations are psychic postcards from our subconscious. Others speculate that we're part of a larger collective consciousness (which might explain all those voices in our heads). Belief and infinite possibilities aside, we aren't likely to have it all figured out today or in our lifetime. We live our lives with ever-improving imperfection. Domination of emotion is a pleasant but delusional idea. It's enough to have awareness when we are being triggered or taken for a ride by them.

Welcome: thoughts, feelings and sensations—where are you taking me today?

# December 25

*"Chaos and Order are not enemies, only opposites."*
*Richard Garriott (born 1961)*

Many of us resist the word "insanity" in Step Two. Teen Addiction Anonymous drops the word: "I have found a power that is greater than I am which can restore my sense of peace." Denial and delusion come from addictive and co-addictive impaired thinking. We think we can control that which we cannot. We feel helpless or overwhelmed by problems that are easily solved a little at a time. Peace will continue to elude us if we accept that we are powerless regarding addiction yet persist in delusion in other areas. Awakening can be called *spiritual* or simply *natural,* it can be mystical or educational, but cognitive dissonance must give way to reality and reason at every stage of recovery.

Reality distortions are coping techniques for a hostile, untenable world. The same creative skills we utilized in the chaos of addiction may serve us well once again in recovery. We have to understand our coping mechanisms so they don't enslave us. Patrick Carnes points out three blocks—ignoring, distorting and lacking reality.[107] Denying warning signs is an example of ignoring reality. Selective memory is sometimes a manipulation or a smokescreen. Other times things aren't remembered the way they happened. Old timers will say "Half of what I remember never happened." In some areas of our lives we have total memory loss, due to trauma, black-outs or psychic distortions. Some of these memories may take years to come back—if they ever do. We are all here because we are not *all there.* We must find balance between chaotic extremes and getting all anal-retentive about order.

Do I take issue with the word "insane" in Step Two, or with any of the other references to my behavior? How do I describe my addictive thinking and behavior? I can pick a different word if I don't like the way a Step is written. What does sane and peaceful living look like today? Chaos will return in recovery. It is not a punishment or a sign of inadequacy. Shit happens, right?

# December 26

*"He that is possessed with a prejudice is possessed with a devil, and one of the worst kinds of devils, for it shuts out the truth and often leads to grievous error."*

*Tryon Edwards (1809–1894)*

---

This American theologian is talking about chronic prejudice. Simple prejudice is caused by ignorance; information cures ignorance. When assumptions or preconceived ideas about someone or something are confronted by the truth, our prejudices are removed. Imagine if addiction could be cured with information. What stops us from seeking help when presented with the facts? Is it ... Satan? "The devil made me do it!" We often personify *the addict* in us as someone or something else with evil intent: "While I am at a meeting, my disease is doing push-ups, just waiting for a moment of weakness." We have a devilish time facing the truth about addiction. As long as recovery sounds like a punishment for admitting we are addicts or alcoholics we tend to proclaim that things aren't that bad. We call this denial.

After tackling denial in Step One, we stay vigilant about the constant risk of new prejudices that lead "to grievous error." We can find ourselves emotionally involved and blindsided by an argument or cause we feel invested in. Our "mission from God" might be self-will run riot, even if people agree with us. We speak of truth and integrity while intolerance and self-justification are brewing inside us.

Flawed logic has been around for as long as humans have been arguing. Innuendo invites the listener to draw conclusions they will never state explicitly. Founders warned that if our fellowship is destroyed, it will be from within. This warning may be quoted to manipulate others to draw conclusions about a proposed course of action that can't be substantiated as being harmful or threatening. Omission, exaggeration and appealing to false authority all come into play when any of us are hiding an agenda beneath our *loving appraisal.*

Am I being blinded by stubborn denial or pride today? Am I overconfident about my brand of truth?

## December 27

*"Integrate what you believe in every single area of your life. Take your heart to work and ask the most and best of everybody else, too."*

*Meryl Streep (born 1949)*

---

When we "integrate what [we] believe" in Steps Ten through Twelve, taking stock of each day, meditating about greater consciousness, and practicing these principles in our lives, we are living the program. On some days, shame, self-doubt and incessant self-seeking are kept at bay and instead we know how to handle situations as promised in *Alcoholics Anonymous*. This sense of freedom may not last an entire day, but still, we can enjoy feeling in the flow; we are challenged and we feel capable. We can expect the best and whatever that best turns out to be is fine with us. We are in the moment. Humility, honesty and taking inventory are more than bandages on days like this; we have integrated these principles and they are our habits. We exude trustworthiness and calmness. We feel like we can lead if called upon but we don't feel power-lust.

We can "ask the most and best of everybody else." We live and let live by example. As the Buddhists teach us, we wish others well; we want the best for friends and foes. We aren't demanding but we expect the best for everyone. We all do our best when we feel our best. So we treat people well—we show our gratitude and we are quick to recognize other people's abilities and contributions. Rebellious children will stand their ground against a bossy-cow of a parent or teacher. But enthusiasm and well-wishing is contagious. If we put our hearts into what we do, it might feel phony for the first few minutes, but just as it is hard to feel sad when we force a smile upon our faces, acting with love leads to feeling the love.

I have probably said, "reality—what a concept!" But do I know that reality is what I make it? A concept never becomes a reality unless it is lived and practiced. Do I "ask the most and best" of myself and others?

*"The Eighth Step is the beginning of a process that lets us feel equal to others. Instead of feeling shame and guilt, instead of feeling forever 'less than,' we become able to look people in the eye. We won't have to avoid anyone. We won't have to be afraid we'll be caught and punished for some neglected responsibility. We'll be free."*

The Narcotics Anonymous Step Working Guide, 55

---

We have been the center of attention in the first seven Steps. In Step Eight, we look at our roles as secondary characters in the lives of others. We look at how our misdeeds and manipulations, passive or overt, impact people. We put ourselves in their shoes and imagine the pain caused by our misdeeds. We meditate about it or write about it. We are the antagonists in this version of our narratives. They are the protagonists as we walk a mile in their shoes, seeing ourselves through their eyes.

By becoming better people, some of this work has already, inadvertently, been done. Being further along in our recovery than we were at Steps Four and Five, we may not have the same urgency to get this burden off our back. Complacency can set in. We have already benefited enormously from the first half of the Steps. It's easy to feel tired of all this list-making and thoroughness. We see the obvious benefit from making things right—our values are clearer than ever now. Most of the resistance about making a list of people we had harmed comes from looking ahead to Step Nine. We are not stupid; we have already imagined ourselves, the perpetrators, at the mercy of our victims. Yes, some of these people victimized us, too. We are getting ahead of ourselves if we think about making amends right now. No one is saying we have to make amends to everyone we write about in Step Eight. This Step is about our understanding and willingness. We spend some time with the list of people we have harmed to really understand what our roles in their lives have meant to them.

Do I have preconceived ideas of how this amends-making will go? Do I feel resistant to taking this Step? Will I persevere through my reluctance all the way to the end?

# December 29

*"I put a dollar in a change machine. Nothing changed."*

George Carlin (1937–2008)

---

Comedians offer a look at life from a different angle. Assumptions need to be disturbed. The idea we have about a change machine sets us up for a laugh because George Carlin innocently assumes something very different. We have biases that save us time with many of life's seemingly small decisions, but these time-savers can be perspective-stealers. Assumptions limit our peripheral vision. We assume so-and-so should solve a problem our way because we don't see that her or his personality or circumstances are considerably different. Binary thinking paints a picture of people who agree with our perspectives as being wise and open-minded and those who oppose us as deluded or sinister.

If we struggle with Step Four, a member might say, "Go back to Step Three; unfinished business awaits you there." That may be true, but it might be that a lack of initiative in Step Four is the result of having glossed over Step Two or even Step One. If we haven't had a visceral experience surrounding our powerlessness and insanity, why would we feel an urgent need to clean house? What's the hurry if addiction is just a bad habit, as opposed to a symptom of underlying psychic trouble that is still lurking? If Step Nine isn't going as expected, it might not have everything to do with the thoroughness of the Step Eight list. We might not have the visceral ego-deflating humility that focus on Step Seven offers. Nor could we do a proper amends list if our personal inventory was skimped on.

The Steps are not an intellectual process. They are implemented and then understood later. Just like we can't learn swimming from a book alone, we learn the Steps by jumping in, getting wet and splashing around.

I put my money in the Seventh Tradition basket—did I change? May I never take myself too seriously.

# December 30

*"Goals too clearly defined can become blinders."*
Mary Catherine Bateson (born 1939)

It is said that no one is too stupid to get our program. But some of us act like we're too smart to get the program. We like to save time and skip to the last chapter. We set goals with clearly defined outcomes. Maybe it's better for us to focus on the effort and not the result. Is it not good enough for us to seek? Why define what we expect to find?

The *beginner's mind* is a mindfulness practice employed to observe our unfolding lives. We can apply this mindset at any age and at any time. Newcomers to our programs don't talk in our clichés. They have to listen attentively to everything. They might not agree with what they hear but they are listening more intently than some old farts. In so doing, they are more present to what is being said or read. Beginners won't hear the same thing and draw the same conclusion as the rest of the room. Auto-pilot thinking is not an option when you are hearing or experiencing new stimuli. A newcomer has a beginner's mind.

Anthropologist Mary Catherine Bateson is a fellow of a think-tank called the International Leadership Forum, which tackles major issues facing society. After we heal catastrophes such as addiction, we may start directing these practices at more global affairs. We may apply these principles to a community revitalization project or to global literacy. Our objectives are important but so are our attitudes—we need not be too hung up on clearly defined goals.

Can I "think, think, think" my way slowly and reevaluate as I go, instead of limiting myself with rigid goals?

# December 31

*"Let us never fear needed change. Certainly we*
*have to discriminate between changes for the worse*
*and changes for the better. But once a need becomes*
*clearly apparent in an individual, in a group, or in A.A.*
*as a whole, it has long since been found out that we*
*cannot stand still and look the other way.*
*The essence of all growth is a willingness to change for*
*the better and then an unremitting willingness to*
*shoulder whatever responsibility this entails."*

Bill W. A.A. Grapevine July 1965, As Bill Sees It 115

---

The tragic flaw of the Titanic may have been, in part, the over-confidence of her stewards. The captain and crew felt invincible. A little humility could have changed history. AA's cofounder warns us about this type of complacency. Do we tend to get defensive about our fellowship—"If it ain't broke, don't fix it"? If extraordinary changes in our fellowship will make us more attractive and more effective, let's not be afraid or prideful. Wanting things to stay the same is egotistical. We are comfortable with the familiar; it suits us. Courage to change is a form of maturity. If the change we try isn't working out, there's no shame in trying again. We do not need to be perfect. We need to be willing to try and ready to bend.

Fear and desire are the most basic of all human motivators. Of these, fear of loss is more of a deterrent than desire for gain is a motivator. This is why an *informed* group conscience will more often vote to keep things the same over adopting proposed changes. Fear is no less fateful than over-confidence.

At the end of the calendar year it is customary to take both a personal and collective inventory, to see how we could have done better and how we can best prepare ourselves to meet the challenges yet to come. It doesn't hurt to take stock of what we have done right this year, too. Celebrating growth is fitting for this time of year.

This year, did I face the challenge of change with courage? Will I continue to try, try again?

# NOTES

[1] According to Alcoholics Anonymous Public Information at the General Service Office in 2012, AA has authorized five hundred fellowships/organizations to use the Twelve Steps for their own purposes.

[2] *Alcoholics Anonymous Comes of Age*, 81.

[3] *Twelve Steps and Twelve Traditions*, 63.

[4] Arthur S. et al, "Alcoholics Anonymous (AA) Recovery Outcome Rates": AA's worldwide population in 1991 was 2,047,250. The low point over 20 years was 1,790,169 in 1995 and the high point, 2,215,239 in 2002; *Box 4-5-9*: The population is 2,133,842 as of the January 2012 survey, accessed November 26, 2013, http://www.aa.org/en_pdfs/en_box459_summer12.pdf.

[5] Kurtz, *Not God: A History of Alcoholics Anonymous*, Note 67: February 6, 1961 letter from Bill W. to Howard E., "As time passes our book literature has a tendency to get more and more frozen, a tendency for conversion into something like dogma, a human trait I am afraid we can do little about. We may as well face the fact that A.A. will always have its fundamentalists, its absolutists, and its relativists."

[6] *The Pew Forum on Religion and Public Life 2012 survey: accessed November 26, 2013,* http://www.pewforum.org/Unaffiliated/nones-on-the-rise.aspx

[7] In 2011 The British Humanist Organization and YouGov Plc in Scotland both reported on survey results showing a decrease in the number of religious adherents compared to the previous survey period. http://humanism.org.uk/2011/03/20/news-771/ (accessed December 20, 2012) and CBC (June 3, 2008) reported on Harris-Decima's findings that 25% of Canadians say they do not believe in god. http://www.cbc.ca/news/canada/story/2008/06/03/f-religion-poll.html (accessed November 26, 2013).

[8] Kunstler, *Too Much Magic*, chap. 1.

[9] For further information about Alice Miller's books (accessed November 26, 2013): http://www.alice-miller.com/index_en.php.

[10] Bill W., "Concept V," *The A.A. Service Manual Combined With Twelve Concepts of World Service*, 22 -24.

[11] Transactional Analysis started with a Canadian-born American psychiatrist, Eric Berne, who wrote the book, *Games People Play.* The

Drama Triangle is a Transactional Analysis (TA) model introduced by Stephen Karpman. In this model, three primary roles are explored: Persecutor, Victim and Rescuer. Each role has specific rituals, behaviours and characteristics. Most addicts and codependents have one role they identify most strongly with but these roles can change, sometimes in different relationships and sometimes over the course of one conversation. The rationalizations that hold these constructs together are subjective and affected by who we think we are, what our roles in life are and by the roles of others in our lives. Persecutors blame, find fault, impose limits and expectations, threaten and take advantage of others, sometimes sadistically or with a self-justified sense of entitlement. Chronic persecutors may have a narcissistic personality disorder. Victims feel sorry for themselves, define themselves by the abuse they take, and blame the Persecutor for failures or shortcomings in their own lives. Victims may have a persecution complex, believing the whole world is out to get them. A Victim is very attached to their role as an excuse for underachievement. This person may feel guilty and take comfort in being victimized as a form of penance. Victims don't take responsibility for their happiness or choices in life. Rescuers drop everything to help others. Rescuers resent the burden of others but keep Victims dependent on them to satisfy their own roles or scripts. Rescuers feel guilty if they don't step in, often believing they are carrying the weight of the world on their shoulders. Rescuers are defined by little else and welcome the role as an excuse to underachieve in their own lives. People in the Rescuer role may be passive-aggressive; they may fantasize about being recognized for heroism without owning up to it. For further information about the Drama Triangle, accessed November 26, 2013: http://www.karpmandramatriangle.com/.

[12] *Twelve Steps and Twelve Traditions*, 129.

[13] Rifkin's *The Empathic Civilization* challenges the notion that humans are self-serving, with winner-take-all attitudes. He argues that people are communal and cooperative, and the ideas he puts forth are not unlike the Twelve & Twelve tenet that we, as members of a fellowship, are interdependent. For further information about Rifkin's *The Empathic Civilization*, accessed November 26, 2013: http://empathiccivilization. com/.

[14] Carnes, *A Gentle Path Through the Twelve Steps*, 127–130.

[15] The Hierarchy of Needs, first proposed in Maslow's 1943 paper, "A Theory of Human Motivation," contends that after humans meet basic needs, they seek to satisfy successively higher needs. Maslow's Hierarchy of Needs is often depicted as a pyramid with "deficiency

needs" (physiological and security needs) at the bottom and "growth needs" (social, esteem and self-actualization needs) at the top. While deficiency needs must be met, growth needs continually shape behavior once all the needs that are lower down in the pyramid are satisfied. Community, belonging, acceptance and self-respect are all needs that, if not met, cause psychological problems. Maslow, *Motivation and Personality*.

[16] Rule 62 is that we not take ourselves too damn seriously. In *Twelve Steps and Twelve Traditions,* we learn the origins of Tradition Four: "Each group should be autonomous except in matters affecting other groups or A.A. as a whole." A story is told of an AA member with stars in his eyes who conceived of a great club house that would offer fellowship, treatment, meetings and financial help to alcoholics. Promoters sought the blessing of General Service Office, who recommended against the idea while insisting they had no rule against it. The club house was an elaborate scheme and there were 61 rules. The plan flopped. The promoter sent a letter to New York admitting that he wished that he had listened to the suggestions and voices of experience. In that letter, he included what he had learned, Rule 62. *Twelve Steps and Twelve Traditions*, 149.

[17] Maté, *When The Body Says No,* 195 -196.

[18] White and Dolan, "Accounting for the Richness of Daily Activities." Accessed November 26, 2013, http://pauldolan.co.uk/wp-content/uploads/2011/07/Accounting-for-the-rishness-of-daily-activities.pdf.

[19] Wilson, Bill. *As Bill Sees It,* 67.

[20] Pew Research Centre, "Concern About Extremist Threat Slips in Pakistan," accessed November 14, 2013, http://www.pewglobal.org/files/pdf/Pew-Global-Attitudes-2010-Pakistan-Report.pdf.

[21] *Alcoholics Anonymous,* 58-59.

[22] Dopamine is a neurotransmitter that defines the pleasure pathways in the brain. All drugs/processes release dopamine at higher levels than regular life pleasures, making them seem more rewarding.

[23] For further information about Stockholm Syndrome: "The Free Dictionary," accessed November 26, 2013. http://medical-dictionary.thefreedictionary.com/Stockholm+Syndrome

[24] *Twelve Steps and Twelve Traditions,* 132, Tradition Two: "For our group purpose there is but one ultimate authority—a loving God as He may expresses Himself in our group conscience. Our leaders are but trusted servants; they do not govern."

[25] National Institute on Alcohol Abuse and Alcoholism, "Interventions for Alcohol Use and Alcohol Use Disorders in Youth," accessed November 26, 2013, (http://pubs.niaaa.nih.gov/publications/arh283/163-174.htm) "In 2002, only 16% of the 1.4 million youth ages 12 to 17 estimated to have alcohol use disorders reported receiving any type of service for these problems."

[26] Ibid.

[27] Peck, *The Road Less Travelled*, 67.

[28] Tradition Eleven (long form), states, "Our relations with the general public should be characterized by personal anonymity. We think A.A. ought to avoid sensational advertising. Our names and pictures as A.A. members ought not be broadcast, filmed, or publicly printed. Our public relations should be guided by the principle of attraction rather than promotion. There is never need to praise ourselves. We feel it better to let our friends recommend us." *Twelve Steps and Twelve Traditions*, 192.

[29] Keen, "Constructing a Spiritual Bullshit Detector," *Hymns To An Unknown God*, 110–115: In the chapter, Keen encourages seekers to listen to the wise, but not to quote them verbatim. All that shines blinds, so Keen also suggests watching out for the overwhelming or captivating. We should avoid spiritual teachers who demand obedience, denounce skepticism, don't live by the same standards they expound and who expect us to put the program ahead of family, career or other priorities. If our would-be guru is a zealous cheerleader, that's another warning. Inasmuch as being self-absorbed is micro-idolatry, talking about one's [Twelve Step] program as being superior or a divinely inspired treatment is a form of macro-idolatry. We should do a reality check any time we hear ourselves making sweeping claims that are not substantiated. That would be an early sign of *bleeding-deconism*.

[30] The Story of Stuff is the material economy explained in a kind of Fourth Step inventory of our stewardship of planet Earth and/or our own home and family by Tides Foundation, Funders Workgroup for Sustainable Production and Consumption and Free Range Studios. The narrator is Annie Leonard. For more information go to http://www.storyofstuff.org/ (accessed November 26, 2013).

[31] The brain's reward system, or "Go!" system as named in the HBO documentary Addiction, is a part of our natural instinct to seek out what we need for survival, be it food, shelter or reproduction. The risk system in the frontal lobe of the brain, the "Stop!" system, evaluates risks and warns us about leaping before we look or entering a dark cave where we

hear growling and snarling. These systems work together. "That looks good. Is it worth the risk?" We weigh consequences and decide if and when to go for something that is both rewarding and potentially risky. "With addicts, however, it is as though [the risk/reward systems] have become functionally disconnected. It is as though the 'Go! system' is sort of running off on its own, is a rogue system now and is not interacting in a regular, seamless integrated way with the 'Stop!' system," says Anna Rose Childress, PhD, of the University of Pennsylvania School of Medicine. The "Go! system" can be triggered so quickly that we're unaware of it, and can and will move us to take action before the risk ("Stop!") system can mount a defense or even become engaged.

[32] Csikszentmihalyi, *Finding Flow*. Permission to use chart granted by Copyright Clearance Center on behalf of Perseus Books Group License Number: 2984231236182 granted September 8, 2012.

[33] Bretherton, "The Origins of Attachment Theory," *Developmental Psychology* 1992, 759–775: John Bowlby coined the term "attachment theory" after studying delinquents and homeless children. He discovered that the foundation of successful social, emotional and cognitive development depended on a continuous, caring and secure attachment relationship between the child and caregiver. "Mary Ainsworth's innovative methodology not only made it possible to test some of Bowlby's ideas empirically but also helped expand the theory itself and is responsible for some of the new directions it is now taking." People who suffer from oppositional defiant disorder and post-traumatic stress disorder commonly show an absence of secure and healthy attachment. Criminalized violent offenders have a shockingly high rate of attachment disorder.

[34] *Twelve Steps and Twelve Traditions*, 189.

[35] TheWeek.com, Editorial Staff, April 13, 2012, "The rise of atheism in America," accessed November 26, 2013, http://theweek.com/article/index/226625/the-rise-of-atheism-in-america: "Between 1.5 and 4 percent of Americans admit to so-called 'hard atheism,' the conviction that no higher power exists. But a much larger share of the American public (19 percent) spurns organized religion in favor of a non-defined skepticism about faith. This group, sometimes collectively labeled the 'Nones,' is growing faster than any religious faith in the U.S. About two thirds of Nones say they are former believers." The data came from Win-Gallup International Global Index of Religiosity and Atheism – 2012 (http://redcresearch.ie/wp-content/uploads/2012/08/RED-C-press-release-Religion-and-Atheism-25-7-12.pdf, accessed November 26, 2013), which reports that 59% of people consider themselves

religious, 23% not religious and 13% are atheists worldwide. The religious population in the USA dropped from 73% to 60% between 2005 and 2012. Countries included with the lowest number of believers in a God or higher power include Australia, Austria, Czech Republic, Canada, China, France, Ireland, Japan and Scandinavian countries.

[36] "Adult Children of Alcoholics," accessed November 26, 2013. http://www.renascent.ca/2012/04/adult-children-of-alcoholics/.

[37] Adult Children of Alcoholics literature and website provide a self-diagnostic lists of symptoms called "The Laundry List," accessed November 28, 2012. http://www.adultchildren.org/lit/Laundry_List. php. Claudia Black, Earnie Larsen and John Bradshaw are some of the specialists in Adult Children (of Alcoholics) issues.

[38] *A Skeptic's Guide to the 12 Steps* is Philip Z.'s first person recovery journey as well as a clinical explanation of the Twelve Step process from Jungian and transpersonal psychology, Buddhism, Eastern philosophy and his faith of birth, Judaism. Phil Z. is an Overeaters Anonymous member, atheist and psychotherapist. For further information: http://www.hazelden.org/OA_HTML/ibeCCtpItmDspRte. jsp?a=b&item=4009.

[39] Wilson, *As Bill Sees It*, 86.

[40] "Special Populations and Co-occurring Disorders," accessed November 26, 2013, http://www.niaaa.nih.gov/alcohol-health/special-populations-co-occurring-disorders.

[41] *Twelve Steps and Twelve Traditions*, 146.

[42] Olson, "FACES IV & the Circumplex Model: Validation Study" *In Press, Journal of Marital and Family Therapy*, accessed November 29, 2012. http://facesiv.com/pdf/facesiv_validation_2010.pdf.

[43] AA pamphlet P-17, "A.A. Tradition—How It Developed" summarizes Bill W.'s Grapevine articles from 1946 to 1947. Bill writes, "The number of membership rules which have been made (and mostly broken!) are legion" and goes on to say, "The way our 'worthy' alcoholics have sometimes tried to judge the 'less worthy' is, as we look back on it, rather comical."

[44] Connock et al, "Methadone and buprenorphine for the management of opioid dependence: a systematic review and economic evaluation," accessed November 26, 2013, http://www.ncbi.nlm.nih.gov/pubmedhealth/ PMH0015139/: This is the summary of a ten year study in the UK, from 1996 to 2005, looking at the effectiveness of different treatment regimens for opioid addicts.

[45] "Books That Shaped America' Exhibition to Open June 25," last modified July 2, 2012, accessed November 26, 2013, http://www.loc.gov/today/pr/2012/12-123.html.

[46] Buddhists announce to AA that they would love to be part of AA, yet they would be replacing the word "god" with "good" so that the practice of the Steps could be compatible with their non-theistic belief. In 1957, Bill writes: "To some of us, the idea of substituting 'good' for 'God' in the Twelve Steps will seem like a watering down of A.A.'s message. But here we must remember that A.A.'s Steps are suggestions only. A belief in them, as they stand, is not at all a requirement for membership among us. This liberty has made A.A. available to thousands who never would have tried at all had we insisted on the Twelve Steps just as written." *Alcoholics Anonymous Comes of Age*, 81.

[47] "Interview: A Doctor Speaks," *AA Grapevine, Vol. 57, No. 12 (May 2001)*.

[48] Thailo, "An Atheist's Guide to Twelve-Step Recovery from Substance Addiction," accessed November 26, 2013, http://everything2.com/title/12-step+program?author_id=2018863#thalio.

[49] Peabody's *The Common Sense of Drinking* was a primary text for AA members and their families prior to the completion of Alcoholics Anonymous. Peabody was a recovered/recovering alcoholic himself who treated alcoholism in Boston and New York City. Many of the ideas and attitudes about addiction and recovery that were made famous in the Big Book were borrowed from Peabody's secular approach. This 190 page book is available online, accessed November 26, 2013: http://www.aabibliography.com/pdffiles/CommonSenseDrinkPeabody.pdf.

[50] From Yasmin Anwar, "Findings offer new clues into the addictive brain," accessed November 26, 2013, http://newscenter.berkeley.edu/2011/10/30/addicted-brain/: "Researchers targeted the orbitofrontal cortex and anterior cingulate cortex--two areas in the frontal brain--because previous research has shown that patients with damage to these areas of the brain are impaired in the choices they make. While these individuals may appear perfectly normal on the surface, they routinely make decisions that create chaos in their lives. A similar dynamic has been observed in chronic drug addicts, alcoholics and people with obsessive-compulsive tendencies."

[51] Hain, *Next Generation of Modern Orthodoxy*, 321.

[52] From the documentary *Blind spot: Peak Oil and the Coming Global Crisis* http://www.mediaed.org/assets/products/147/transcript_147.pdf.

[53] Wilson, *As Bill Sees It*, 146.

[54] From Herb Silverman, "Why do Americans still hate atheists?" The Washington Post, May 4, 2011, http://live.washingtonpost.com/why-do-americans-hate-atheists-herb-silverman.html: "Rarely denounced by the mainstream, this stunning anti-atheism discrimination is egged on by Christian conservatives who stridently—and uncivilly—declare that the lack of godly faith is a detriment to society, rendering nonbelievers intrinsically suspect and second class citizens."

[55] This is also referred to as "the narcissism of *minor* differences," referenced and popularized by Freud in his *Civilization and Its Discontents* (1930). Ethnic, cultural or theistic differences can offend or threaten us, undermining our confidence in our own worldviews. This self-doubt compromises our self-worth and perpetuates anxiety. We subconsciously project our anxiety onto others, perceiving their slight differences as aggressive, inferior or evil. To the impartial observers the differences may be unidentifiable but to the individual who is preoccupied with them, perceived differences may dehumanize the other.

[56] Thomsen, *Bill W: The absorbing and deeply moving life story of Bill Wilson, co-founder of Alcoholics Anonymous*, 340.

[57] Rank, *Art and Artist*, 133. Before new-age, before beatnik culture, Rank was tripping out on Art and its capacity to lend insight into the human condition.

[58] Causa sui, a Latin word meaning caused from/by the self, is a contentious theory used to explain the cause of who we are and what we do. Spinoza applied this idea to philosophy, using it to explain Pantheism: God is not up there but rather God is everywhere, omnipresent as well as omnipotent. Psychoanalysts theorize that many of our surface coping mechanisms are caused by subconscious fears such as the fear of death. Much of our human activity and social interaction is motivated by a subconscious need to assuage anxiety. Religious convictions that include belief in an afterlife or reincarnation are examples of social constructs that combat fear of death with symbols of immortality. Not everyone is or has been aboard the causa sui band-wagon. Nevertheless, causa sui is still alive and well in academic debate, considered by many a means to understanding subconscious motivations. Causa sui definition from Philosophy Dictionary, accessed November 26, 2013: http://www.ditext.com/runes/c.html.

[59] The theory of cognitive dissonance was introduced in 1957 by Leon Festinger. When we hold two ideas that conflict with one another

this causes tension; something has to give. When we are addicted to something that is killing us and we know in our hearts that we have to stop, tension is created when the craving starts. We want to get high or numbed out. We also know we will regret it in the morning. Either we have to curb our behavior or alter our values so that actions and cognition are in agreement (cognitive consonance). We try to relieve the tension by kidding ourselves. Failing to confront and resolve the conflict often leads to denial as we futilely attempt to get what we want without feeling the pang of the consequences. Buyer's remorse is an example of cognitive dissonance. We spend more than we can afford in order to get what we really want and then we feel the burden of debt. We really, really want something—that's true. We really, really can't afford it—that's also true. Something has to give to come into accordance with reality or we have to craft a distorted reality and deny the facts. More information at http://www.simplypsychology.org/cognitive-dissonance. html (accessed November 26, 2013).

[60] Ernest Becker's (1924 – 1974) *Denial of Death and Escape from Evil* examine how fear of death is always freaking out in the subconscious, regardless of how calm we are at the conscious level. Becker's body of work expands on ideas put forth by predecessors Rank, Kierkegaard, Freud, Hegel, Wilhelm Reich, Norman O. Brown and Erich Fromm. The importance we place on society and the contributions we make to it, by way of procreation, athletic, academic, professional or social achievements are, in part, symbolic. What these activities and constructs symbolize for us is immortality. The motivation for such symbols is dread, whether conscious or subconscious (ego). We know that we are finite and that death is inevitable. Ego's micro-idolatry finds our mortality untenable and to deny or assuage this inconvenient truth, immortality symbols such as a family lineage, a legacy or noble society are gimmicks that help us avoid facing death. Religion is pervasive in culture because it offers the promise of literal immortality in the form of reincarnation or afterlife. Ernest Becker argued that no matter how effective these symbols are at comforting us, alternative worldviews will shake us out of our daydreams and threaten the macro-idolatry of our symbols, and this triggers our death-anxiety. We tend to project our anxiety upon those who hold alternative worldviews and we act out in ways ranging from ridicule to persecution to genocide. Today much of human conflict—political and religious—is triggered, according to Becker, by the subconscious threat that one opposing worldview poses upon those who hold another. For further information, see Patick Shen and Greg Bennick's documentary *Flight From Death: The Quest for Immortality* (2003).

[61] Terror Management Theory (TMT) is inspired by the writings of Ernest Becker and undertakes to corroborate theories presented in Becker's work, including *Denial of Death*. Psychologists Jeff Greenberg, Tom Pyszczynski, and Sheldon Solomon conduct experiments to test people's prejudices and other social tendencies. Based on the premise that at our core we fear our death and that much of our social activity is designed to ignore or deny our finitude, these experimenters see what happens when people are reminded of their own mortality. The findings are that people tend to react aggressively when death anxiety is promoted. For more on TMT visit www.tmt.missouri.edu (accessed November 26, 2013) or www.ernestbecker.org (accessed November 26, 2013). Sources: July 2011 interview with Sheldon Solomon, Professor of Psychologist, Skidmore College; Becker, *Denial of Death, Escape from Evil; Flight From Death: The Quest for Immortality* (2003) documentary.

[62] *Twelve Steps and Twelve Traditions*, 149.

[63] *Twelve Steps and Twelve Traditions*, 155.

[64] *Alcoholics Anonymous* 59: "Admitted to God, to ourselves, and to another human being the exact nature of our wrongs."

[65] "Top Gun," CBC, *The Fifth Estate,* broadcast March 6, 2009, accessed November 26, 2013, http://www.cbc.ca/fifth/2008-2009/top_gun/: This episode features a family devastated by the loss of their son, who ran away from home after his parents confiscated his Xbox. Gaming is considered by some scholars and clinicians to be an impulse control disorder like compulsive gambling or internet addiction. The Council On Science and Public Health reported to the American Medical Association in 2005 in the Entertainment Software Association Survey playing for more than two hours per day is considered gaming overuse.

Kravets, David. "Addicted Gamer Sues Game-Makers, Says He is 'Unable to Function,'" *Wired Magazine* (August 2010), accessed November 26, 2013, http://www.wired.com/threatlevel/2010/08/ lineage11-addiction/: A gamer who reportedly played 20,000 hours over five years believes he should have been warned by the video game maker.

Tran, Mark, "Girl starved to death while parents raised virtual child in online game," *The Guardian* (March 5, 2010), accessed November 26, 2013, http://www.guardian.co.uk/world/2010/mar/05/korean-girl-starved-online-game: A Korean couple became obsessed with raising a virtual baby while their daughter was abandoned and unfed.

Young, "Understanding Online Gaming Addiction and Treatment Issues for Adolescents," 355-372: Young reports that symptoms of gaming/video game addiction include lying about how much time one is gaming and thinking about the game during social, work, family and school time. The gamer loses interest in other hobbies and activities. The first detox for gaming opened in the Netherlands in 2006. The American Medical Association finds that 90% of American youth play games and 15% (five million) of them could be addicted. Young advocates restrictions in homes of problem users and family therapy instead of just blaming the addict. The cause of the addiction may have been tensions, patterns and interactions at home. Accessed November 14, 2013: http://www.cbc.ca/player/Shows/Shows/the+fifth+estate/ID/1368429043/?page=12.

[66] See endnotes 60 and 61.

[67] Thomas, "How to beat denial—a 12-step plan." *The Ecologist*, accessed November 26, 2013, http://www.theecologist.org/investigations/climate_change/268964/how_to_beat_denial_a_12step_plan.html.

[68] 2012 findings indicate 23.5 million American adults are overcoming an involvement with drugs or alcohol that they once considered to be problematic. According to the new survey funded by the New York State Office of Alcoholism and Substance abuse (OASAS), 10% of adults surveyed said yes to the question, "Did you once have a problem with drugs or alcohol, but no longer do? "Ten Percent of American Adults Report Being in Recovery from Substance Abuse or Addiction," accessed November 26, 2013, http://www.oasas.ny.gov/pio/press/20120306Recovery.cfm.

[69] Ahuvia, "Individualism/Collectivism and Cultures of Happiness": For many people, Subjective Well-Being (SWB) is not the attainment of happiness or success. In the West, we tend to see individual happiness as the be-all and end-all. Americans consider 'the pursuit of happiness' a fundamental right. This isn't so important in every culture. Cross-cultural research shows that values like 'enjoying life' and leading 'an exciting life' are stronger in individualistic societies, whereas 'social recognition,' 'preserving my public image,' being 'humble,' and 'honoring parents and elders' are particularly strong in collectivist societies.

[70] *Twelve Steps and Twelve Traditions*, 160: Tradition Seven states, "Every A.A. group ought to be fully self-supporting, declining outside contributions."

[71] Logo (Greek for "meaning") therapy and Existential Analysis are the basis of Viktor Frankl's (*Man's Search for Meaning*) work. Logotherapy focuses on meaning in life. In the grand scheme of things, happiness is less about pleasant thoughts and experiences, and more about feeling that our lives and contributions are meaningful. For further information:

Viktor Frankl Institute, accessed November 26, 2013, http://logotherapy. univie.ac.at/e/index.html.

[72] From 40 members in 1938, AA grew to 10,000 members in 325 groups by 1944. Between 1981 and 1982 AA reached one million members. By 1991, AA membership reached 2.1 million members and remained at about the same level for twenty years leading up to January 1, 2012. Over half the groups and members are in the USA. By contrast, the general population of the United States reached 312 million in 2012, up 25% from 250 million in 1991. So as a percentage of the population, AA members are on the decline. A.A.'s population estimate from Box 4-5-9, Summer of 2013 Vol. 57, No. 2 is 2,131,459 members.

| Year | Members | Groups |
|------|---------|--------|
| 1941 | 2,000 | 200 |
| 1951 | 120,000 | 4,436 |
| 1961 | 176,474 | 9,305 |
| 1971 | 329,429 | 17,776 |
| 1981 | 937,212 | 47,797 |
| 1991 | 2,119,744 | 96,458 |
| 2001 | 2,214,978 | 100,131 |
| 2011 | 2,133,842 | 114,070 |

If the world convention is a show of membership momentum, attendance doubled from New Orleans (1980) to Montreal (1985), which saw 45,000 people in attendance. The AA World Conference grew again in Seattle and peaked five years later with 56,000 attending San Diego (1995). Numbers dropped in Minneapolis (2000) and Toronto (2005) didn't match Montreal's numbers, with 44,000 in attendance. San Antonio numbers in 2010 were 53,000, up from two sagging back-to-back quinquennium celebrations but not matching the peak attendance of the 1995 world conference.

Conference attendees data taken from the AA Timeline, accessed November 26, 2013, http://www.aa.org/aatimeline/. 2011 statistics from From *Box 459* 58, (Summer 2012): 2. All other statistics from Arthur S. et al, "Alcoholics Anonymous (AA) Recovery Outcome Rates."

[73] Kurtz, *The Collected Ernie Kurtz*, 20: In response to an AA member who wrote GSO about the Cain letter, Bill W. wrote to Betty R. in 1963, "Despite its petulant and biased nature, the piece did contain some half-truths. It certainly applied to some A.A.'s at some place at some times! Therefore it should help us take heed of these natural tendencies."

[74] Accessed November 26, 2013, http://www.hindsfoot.org/steps6.html. This version of the six steps comes from a note from Bill Wilson to Ed (presumably Ed Dowling). He scribbled down what he once did for other drunks as there was not yet a book to give them. There are other versions of the six step program and that's just the point—they are ideas that if followed were effective for many. They were not cast in stone. A longer version of the six step program can be found in *Pass it On*, 197.

[75] *Box 4-5-9's 2005 Holiday issue (Vol. 51, No.6, 7–8)* includes an article, "Big Book Study Guides: Reviewing a Position Paper" wherein they make note of the 1977 Study Guide Position Paper. The article starts by saying, "Sober alcoholics are notorious for refusing to be told what to do, say or think. The Steps are 'suggested' and experienced sponsors are wise enough not to give newcomers hard and fast directives. Yet paradoxically, a surprising number of members seek out and rely on study guides when they begin delving into A.A. literature." AA has never produced such a guide; many outside entities have done just that and weekend retreats with self-appointed bishops and cardinals teaching and interpreting are not uncommon. A former member of AA's Board of Directors is quoted as saying, "Placing guidelines on paper seems to say, 'This is the way—the only way.'" For that reason, AA has never created such a guide.

[76] W., Bill, "The Individual In Relation to A.A. as a Group," *AA Grapvine*, 2. July 1946.

[77] Swegan and Chestnut, *The Psychology of Alcoholism.*

[78] Kurtz, *Not God: A History of Alcoholics Anonymous*, 300, note 67.

[79] *Alcoholics Anonymous*, 58.

[80] For further information on subjective well-being (SWB), see endnote 69.

[81] Jack Alexander was a writer for *The Saturday Evening Post*. Jim first broached the subject of an article about AA to Alexander. Jack Alexander was a notorious racket-buster as a journalist and the Post thought that AA might be a racket deserving of exposure. The outcome was quite the contrary. Jack was impressed with AA and his article in 1941 gave Alcoholics Anonymous its first national media attention, spring-boarding membership from 2,000 in 1941 to 6,000 in 1942 and 10,000 by the end of 1944. (See Arthur S. et al, "Alcoholics Anonymous (AA) Recovery Outcome Rates.") There is a Jim B. talk from 1957 in San Diego where he tells the story himself: http://rebelliondogspublishing. com/rebellinks.cfm, accessed November 26, 2013. A.A. offers pamphlet P-12, "The Jack Alexander Story" which is a reprint of the story in

*The Saturday Evening Post* and can be viewed here: http://aa.org/pdf/products/p-12_theJackAlexArticle.pdf (accessed November 26, 2013).

[82] Steve W. Rawlings of the United States Census Bureau posted a report measuring household trends from 1970 to 1994 which revealed that in 1970 married couples with children accounted for 40.3% of households. By 1994 that percentage had dropped to 25.9%: http://www.census.gov/prod/1/pop/profile/95/p23-189.pdf, accessed November 14, 2013.

D'Vera Cohn, "Census 2010 News Stories: The Changing Family," Pew Research Center, http://www.pewsocialtrends.org/2011/06/23/census-2010-news-stories-the-changing-family/, accessed November 26, 2013: The Census Bureau shows that in California in 2010 married men and women living with their children declined to 23.4%. For further information: http://nces.ed.gov/programs/digest/d07/tables/dt07_018.asp (accessed November 26, 2013).

[83] *Twelve Steps and Twelve Traditions*, 172.

[84] Harvey, *Grieving For Dummies*, 311–316.

[85] Richard Ridderinkhof, professor of neurocognitive development and aging at the University of Amsterdam, reports that heavy drinking alters our brains. This has an immediate and maybe lasting impact on decision making, problem solving and social behavior. The affected portions of the brain are the frontocerebellar circuitry and the hippocampus. "How much can the brain recover from years of excessive alcohol consumption?" *Scientific American,* September 2011, accessed November 26, 2013. http://www.scientificamerican.com/article.cfm?id=how-much-can-the-brain-recover.

[86] 53% of drug users have concurrent mental disorders; 30% of mental health patients have substance abuse problems, from *Quick Facts: Mental Health and Addiction in Canada, Third Edition*, accessed November 26, 2013: http://www.mooddisorderscanada.ca/documents/Media%20Room/Quick%20Facts%203rd%20Edition%20Eng%20Nov%2012%2009.pdf.

[87] Kabat-Zinn, *Full Catastrophe Living*, 31–46: The Chapter "The Attitudinal Foundations of Mindfulness Practice" includes Non-judging, Patience, Beginner's Mind, Trust, Non-striving, Acceptance and Letting Go, as well as the monkey story.

[88] Germer, Christopher. "You Gotta Have Heart," *Psychotherapy Networker* 30, Issue 1,(January/February 2006):DocumentPSYNET0020060502e2110000o.

[89] *Pass It On, 165–166.*

[90] *Twelve Steps and Twelve Traditions*, 176: "Tradition Ten: Alcoholics Anonymous has no opinion on outside issues; hence the A.A. name ought never be drawn into public controversy."

[91] See endnote 11 for further information about Transactional Analysis (TA).

[92] *Alcoholics Anonymous*, 63.

[93] For further information about AD/HD (accessed November 26, 2013): http://www.ncbi.nlm.nih.gov/pubmedhealth/PMH0002518/.

[94] From CBC radio program "Fresh Air," September 8, 2012, accessed November 26, 2013., http://www.cbc.ca/video/news/audioplayer. html?clipid=2277481493.

[95] Attention Deficit Disorder (ADD) or Attention Deficit Hyperactivity Disorder (AD/HD) comes with a variety of symptoms and severity. The list of *diagnosed* people should be taken lightly; many have been diagnosed posthumously. Disagreement rages on about these displayed characteristics being a disorder. List of AD/HD famous people came from http://add.about.com/od/famouspeoplewithadhd/a/famouspeople. htm (accessed November 26, 2013).

[96] Myers and Spencer, *Social Psychology*, 140.

[97] Psychologist Dr. Arthur Cain wrote "Alcoholics Anonymous: Cult or Cure?" for *Harper's Magazine* in February 1963 (and later in the *Saturday Evening Post*, September 19, 1964, wrote "Alcoholics Can be Cured—despite AA"). Dr. Cain blamed AA and AA mentality for holding science and research back. He considered the dependence on meetings cult-like. January 2011, relative newcomer and writer Clancy Martin wrote "The Drunk's Club: The Cult that Cures." This second generation AA tells of how he was told by his father that "the problem with AA is it's become a religion," and he goes on to state that "AA is deeply, perhaps irredeemably infused with a moral view of alcoholism." He outs AA for closed-mindedness to pharmaceuticals and psychiatry as part of recovery, while he notes that many members had said outside of a meeting that they were being treated for concurrent disorders or taking medication to help fend off withdrawal or craving.

[98] The following article "examines alcoholism as a thought disorder and cognitive restructuring as an effective model of treatment" (Steigerwald and Stone, "Cognitive Restructuring and the 12-Step Program of Alcoholics Anonymous," accessed November 26, 2013): http://www. ncbi.nlm.nih.gov/pubmed/10349605.

[99] Lawrence Krauss, author of *The Physics of Star Trek*, *Fear of Physics*

and *A Universe from Nothing: Why There is Something Rather than Nothing*, remembers Christopher Hitchens (1949 – 2011). Krauss jokingly says he was proud to be called "Hitch's" personal physicist. In a eulogy to Christopher Hitchens, Krauss writes, "Christopher was a beacon of knowledge and light in a world that constantly threatens to extinguish both. He had the courage to accept the world for just what it is, and not what we would like it to be. That is the highest praise I believe one can give to any intellect. He understood that the universe doesn't care about our existence, or our welfare, and epitomized the realization that our lives have meaning only to the extent we give them meaning." To read the rest of the eulogy, visit http://old.richarddawkins.net/articles/644326-remembering-christopher-hitchens (accessed November 26, 2013).

[100] In Laudet's study "The Case for Considering Quality of Life in Addiction Research and Clinical Practice" (44–55) over 300 addicts in recovery answered questionnaires to establish their Quality of Life (QoL). They were asked questions about satisfaction with work, relationships, financial comfort, mobility and concentration. Participants' answers were given on a scale from one to ten. Self-reporting recovering addicts/alcoholics had scores that gradually rose higher from six months to three years of sobriety, after which time they petered off slightly. (<6mo: 6.75, 6 mo to 18 mo: 7.51, 18 mo to 36 mo: 8.13, >36 mo: 8.05). Results show that people in recovery have higher subjective well-being (self reported quality of life) compared to their time in substance abuse/relapse. Recovering addicts were compared to a control group. In the World Health Organization 2006 QoL survey, (normal) respondents scored higher than early sobriety participants and lower than stable recovery respondents. In their conclusion they note, "we did not have a control group of active drinkers to compare against, and so we cannot assume that QoL is higher in abstinent than in continuing drinkers from the current study. There is also a relationship with age—both in terms of older participants reporting higher QoL and that they are more likely to be in the 'stable recovery' group, and we would suggest that future prospective research may need to investigate the age effects in maturing out of alcohol problems." For further information on this subject: Hibbert and Best, "The Case for Considering Quality of Life in Addiction Research and Clinical Practice." *Drug and Alcohol Review* 30 (1) (January 2011): 12-20.

[101] *The Mind of Absolute Trust* (Early Zen Poetry of Seng-ts'an), accessed November 26, 2013. http://www.selfdiscoveryportal.com/cmSengTsan.htm.

## End Notes

[102] Diener et al, "Looking Up and Looking Down," *Personality and Social Psychology Bulletin,* 437–445.

[103] *Twelve Steps and Twelve Traditions*, 184.

[104] Mercier and Sperber, "Why do humans reason? Arguments for an argumentative theory," accessed November 26, 2013, http://ram.mrtc. ri.cmu.edu/_media/papers/arguments_for_an_argumentative_theory. pdf.

[105] Larsen, *Why Do I Feel This Way?*

[106] *Alcoholics Anonymous*, 83-84.

[107] Carnes, *A Gentle Path Through the Twelve Steps*, 127-130.

# BIBLIOGRAPHY

*Addiction*, documentary film (2007), HBO Documentary Films in association with the Robert Wood Johnson Foundation, The National Institute on Drug Abuse, The National Institute on Alcohol Abuse and Alcoholism, produced by John Hoffman, Susan Froemke, directed by Jon Alpert et al.

Ahuvia, Aaron C. "Individualism/Collectivism and Cultures of Happiness: A Theoretical Conjecture of The Relationship between Consumption, Culture and Subjective Well-Being At the National Level," Journal of Happiness Studies (January 2002), 3 (1), 23-36.

Alcoholics Anonymous. "A.A. Tradition: How it Developed by Bill W.", New York: Alcoholics Anonymous World Services, Inc., 1983.

Alcoholics Anonymous. *Alcoholics Anonymous 3rd Edition*. New York: Alcoholics Anonymous World Services, Inc., 1991.

Alcoholics Anonymous. "Alcoholics Anonymous 2007 Membership Survey." New York: Alcoholics Anonymous World Services, Inc., 2008.

Alcoholics Anonymous. "Alcoholics Anonymous 2011 Membership Survey." New York: Alcoholics Anonymous World Services, Inc., 2012.

Alcoholics Anonymous. *Alcoholics Anonymous Comes of Age*. New York: Alcoholics Anonymous World Services, Inc., 1985.

Alcoholics Anonymous. Box 459: News and Notes from the General Service Office of A.A., Vol. 50, No.2 April-May 2004. New York: Alcoholics Anonymous World Services, Inc.

Alcoholics Anonymous. Box 459: News and Notes from the General Service Office of A.A.58, No.2 (Summer 2012), New York: Alcoholics Anonymous World Services.

Alcoholics Anonymous. *Living Sober*. New York: Alcoholics Anonymous World Services, Inc., 2004.

Alcoholics Anonymous. *Pass it On: The story of Bill Wilson and how the A.A. message reached the world*. New York: Alcoholics Anonymous World Services, 1984

Alcoholics Anonymous. The A.A. Service Manual combined with Twelve Concepts for World Service by Bill W. 2010-2011 Edition. New York: Alcoholics Anonymous World Services, 2010.

Alcoholics Anonymous. *Twelve Steps and Twelve Traditions*, New York: Alcoholics Anonymous World Services, 1990.

Alexander, Jack. "Alcoholics Anonymous." Accessed December 4, 2012, http://aa.org/pdf/products/p-12_theJackAlexArticle.pdf.

Anderson, Stephen A. and Ronald M. Sabatelli. *Family Interaction: A Multigenerational Developmental Perspective, 3rd Edition*. Boston: Pearson, 2003.

Anuff, Joey and Gary Wolf. *Dumb Money: Adventures of a Day Trader*. New York: Random House, 2000.

# Bibliography

Anwar, Yasmin. "Findings offer new clues into the addicted brain."UC Berkeley New Center, October 30, 2011, checked November 28, 2012, http://newscenter.berkeley.edu/2011/10/30/addicted-brain/.

Augustine Fellowship, The. "For the Professional: Information about S.L.A.A." Boston: The Augustine Fellowship, Sex and Love Addicts Anonymous, Fellowship-Wide Services, 2004.

Augustine Fellowship, The. *Sex and Love Addicts Anonymous*. Norwood: Sex and Love Addicts Anonymous, Fellowship-Wide Services Inc., 2004

B., Mel and Michael Fitzpatrick. *Living the Twelve Traditions in Today's World*. Center City: Hazelden, 2012.

Becker, Earnest. *Denial of Death*. New York: Free Press Paperbacks, 1997.

Becker, Earnest. *Escape from Evil*. New York: The Free Press, 1975.

Benyo, Richard. *The Masters of the Marathon*. New York: Atheneum, 1983.

Berger, Janice. *Emotional Fitness: Discover our natural healing power*. Toronto: Prentice Hall Canada, 2000.

Berger, Peter L., Luckman, Thomas. *The Social Construction of Reality: A Treatise in the Sociology of Knowledge*. Garden City: Random House, 1966.

Berne, Eric. *Games People Play: the Psychology of Human Relations*. New York: Ballantine Books, 1973.

Berne, Eric *Transactional Analysis in Psychotherapy*. New York: Souvenir Press, 1996.

Bretherton, Inge. "The Origins of Attachment Theory: John Bowlby and Mary Ainsworth" Developmental Psychology 28, No. 5, (1992): 759–775.

Brooks, David. The Social Animal. New York: Random House, 2011.

Cain, Arthur H. "Alcoholics Anonymous: Cult or Cure?" Harper's (February 1963): 48–52.

Cain, Arthur H. "Alcoholics Can Be Cured--Despite A.A." Saturday Evening Post 237, #32 (September 19, 1964): 6–11.

Cameron, Julia. *The Artist's Way*. New York: Penguin Group, 2007.

Carver, Charles and Michael F. Scheier. *Perspectives on Personality, 5th Edition*. Boston: Pearson Education, 2004.

Carnes, Patrick. *A Gentle Path Through the Twelve Steps*. City Center: Hazelden, 2005.

Connock, M. et al. "Methadone and buprenorphine for the management of opioid dependence: a systematic review and economic evaluation." (2007), accessed December 19, 2013, http://www.ncbi.nlm.nih.gov/pubmedhealth/PMH0015139/.

Csikszentmihalyi, Mihaly. Flow: *The Psychology of Optimal Experience*. New York: Harper and Row, 1990.

Davis, Kenneth C. *Don't Know Much About Mythology*. New York: Harper Collins, 2005.

DeNeve, Kristina M. and Harris Cooper. "The Happy Personality: A Meta-Analysis of 137 Personality Traits and Subjective Well-Being" Psychological Bulletin 124, No. 2 (1998): 197-229.

Diener, Ed et al. "Looking Up and Looking Down: Weighting Good and Bad Information in Life Satisfaction Judgments." PSPB 28, No. 4 (April 2002): 437–445.

Durant, Will. *The Mansion of Philosophy: A Survey of Human Life and Destiny*. New York: Simon & Schuster, 1941.

Flight From Death: *The Quest for Immortality*, documentary film (2003), directed by Patrick Shen, written by Patrick Shen and Greg Bennick, produced by Transcendental Media.

Follette, Victoria M. and Jacqueline Pistorello. *Finding Life Beyond Trauma*. Oakland: New Harbinger, 2007.

Frankl, Viktor. *Man's Search for Meaning*, Simon & Schuster, 2006.

Freud, Sigmund. Civilization and Its Discontents. New York: W.W. Norton, 2005.

Gamblers Anonymous. *Sharing Recovery Through Gamblers Anonymous*. Los Angeles: Gamblers Anonymous, 1984.

Gerber, Alex Jr., *Wholeness On Education*, Buckminster Fuller, and Tao. Kirkland: Gerber Educational Resources, 2001.

Germer, Christopher. "You Gotta Have Heart," Psychotherapy Networker 30, Issue 1, (January/February 2006): Document PSYNET0020060502e2110000o.

Greenberger, Dennis and Christine Padesky. *Mind Over Mood: Change How You Feel by Changing the Way You Think.* New York: The Guilford Press, 1995.

Haberman, Arthur. *The Making of the Modern Age, 2nd Edition*. Toronto: Gage Educational Publishing, 1987.

Haidt, Jonathan *The Righteous Mind: Why Good People are Divided by Politics and Religion*. New York: Pantheon Books, 2012.

Hain, Schmel. *The Next Generation of Modern Orthodoxy*. San Francisco: Michael Scharf Publication Trust of the Yeshiva Univ. Press, 2012.

Hartigan, Francis. *Bill W.: A Biography of Alcoholics Anonymous Cofounder Bill Wilson*. New York: Thomas Dunne Books, 2000.

Harris, Thomas A. MD. *I'm OK, You're OK*. New York: Galahad Books, 1967.

Harvey, Greg. *Grieving For Dummies*. Indianapolis: Wiley Publishing Inc., 2007.

Havamal: *The Sayings of the Vikings*. Reykjavik: Gudrun Publishing, 2006.

Hedges, Chris. *Empire of Illusion: The End of Literacy and the Triumph of Spectacle*. New York: Nation Books, 2009.

Hendricks, Gay, PhD and Kathlyn Hendricks, PhD *Conscious Loving*. New York: Bantam Books, 1992.

Hibbert, Louise J. and David W.Best. "The Case for Considering Quality of Life in Addiction Research and Clinical Practice." Drug and Alcohol Review 30 (1) (January 2011): 12-20.

Hitchens, Christopher. *God is Not Great: How Religion Poisons Everything*. Toronto: McClellend Steward Ltd., 2007.

# Bibliography

Hornbacher, Marya. *Waiting: A Nonbeliever's Higher Power*. City Center: Hazelden, 2011.

Ignatieff, Michael. *The Warrior's Honor: Ethnic War and the Modern Conscience*. Toronto: Viking Penguin, 1998.

"Interventions for Alcohol Use and Alcohol Use Disorders in Youth." National Institute on Alcohol Abuse and Alcoholism, accessed December 4, 2012, http://pubs.niaaa.nih.gov/publications/arh283/163-174.htm.

James, Muriel and Dorothy Jongeward. *Born to Win: Transactional Analysis With Gestalt Experiments*. Cambridge: Perseus Books, 1996.

Jampolsky, Lee. *Healing the Addictive Mind*. Berkeley: Celestial Arts, 1995.

Jung, Carl. *Man and His Symbols*. New York: Dell, 1968.

Kabat-Zinn, Jon. *Full Catastrophe Living: Using the Wisdom of Your Body and Mind to Face Stress, Pain, and Illness*. New York: Bantam Dell, 2005.

Karpman, Stephen. "Fairy Tales and Script Drama Analysis," *Transactional Analysis Bulletin* 7, No. 26, April 1968, 39 - 43.

Keen, Sam. *Hymns To An Unknown God: Awakening the Spirit in Everyday Life*. New York: Bantam Books, 1995.

Kunstler, James Howard. *Too Much Magic: Wishful Thinking, Technology and the Fate of the Nation*. New York: Atlantic Monthly Press, 2012.

Kurtz, Ernest. *The Collected Ernie Kurtz*. Bloomington: iUniverse, 2008.

Kurtz, Ernest. *Not God: A History of Alcoholics Anonymous*. Center City: Hazelden Educational Material, 1979.

Kurtz, Ernest, PhD, and Katherine Ketcham. *The Spirituality of Imperfection: Storytelling and the Search for Meaning*. New York: Bantam Books, 2002

Laudet, Alexandre B. "The Case for Considering Quality of Life in Addiction Research and Clinical Practice." *Addiction Science & Clinical Practice* 6, Vol. 1(July 2011): 44–55.

Larsen, Earnie. *Why Do I Feel This Way?* St. Paul: International Marriage Encounters, 1986.

Levitt, Steven B. and Stephen J. Duner. *Freakonomics: A Rogue Economist Explores the Hidden Side of Everything*. New York: Harper Collins, 2005.

Levitt, Steven B. and Stephen J. Duner. *Super Freakonomics: Global Cooling, Patiotic Prostitues and and Why Suicide Bombers Should Buy Life Insurance*. New York: Harper Collins, 2009.

Martin, Clancy. "The Drunk's Club: The Cult That Cures," *Harper's* (January 2011): 27–38.

Maslow, Abraham. *Motivation and Personality*. New York: Harper & Row, 1970.

Maslow, A. H. "A Theory of Human Motivation." *Psychological Review* 50 (1943): 370–396.

Maté, Gabor. *In the Realm of Hungry Ghosts: Close Encounters with Addiction*. New York: Alfred A. Knopf, 2008.

Maté, Gabor. *When The Body Says No: The Cost of Hidden Stress.* Toronto: Random House, 2003.

Mercier, Hugo and Dan Sperber. "Why do humans reason? Arguments for an argumentative theory." Behavioral and Brain Sciences 34 (2011): 57-111. doi:10.1017/S0140525X10000968.

Milam, James R, and Katherine Ketcham. U*nder the Influence: A Guide to the Myths and Realities of Alcoholism.* Seattle: Madrona, 1981.

Miller, Alice. *The Drama of the Gifted Child: The Search for True Self.* New York: Farrar, Straus and Giroux, 1970.

Miller, Alice. *Thou Shalt Not Be Aware: Society's Betrayal of the Child.* New York: Farrar, Straus and Giroux, 1984.

Myers, David G. and Steve J. Spencer. *Social Psychology, 2nd Canadian Edition.* Toronto: McGraw Hill Ryerson, 2004.

Narcotics Anonymous. *Narcotics Anonymous, 5th Edition.* Chatsworth: Narcotics Anonymous World Services Inc., 1987.

*Narcotics Anonymous. It Works: How and Why,* Van Nuys: Narcotics Anonymous World Services Inc., 1993.

Nietzche, Friedrich. *Beyond Good and Evil.* New York: Random House, 1989

Olson, David H. "FACES IV & the Circumplex Model: Validation Study." In Press, Journal of Marital & Family Therapy (2010), accessed November 28, 2012, http://facesiv.com/pdf/facesiv_validation_2010.pdf.

*One Day at a Time in Al-Anon.* New York: Al-Anon Family Group, 1979.

Peabody, Richard R. T*he Common Sense of Drinking.* Boston: Little Brown, 1930.

Peck, M. Scott. *The Road Less Travelled.* New York: Simon & Schuster, 1978.

Pew Reseach Center. " 'Nones' on the Rise: One-in-Five Adults Have No Religious Affiliation." Washington: The Pew Forum on Religion and Public Life, October 9, 2012, accessed November 26, 2013, http://www.pewforum.org/Unaffiliated/nones-on-the-rise.aspx.

Piirto, Jane PhD *Understanding Creativity.* Scotsdale: Great Potential Press, 2004.

Powell, John. *Why Am I Afraid to Tell You Who I Am?* Grand Rapids: Zondervan, 1999.

Rank, Otto. *Art and Artist: Creative Urges and Personality Development.* New York: W. W. Norton Company, 1989.

Ridderinkhof, Richard. "How much can the brain recover from years of excessive alcohol consumption?" Scientific American (September 2011), accessed December 3, 2012, http://www.scientificamerican.com/article.cfm?id=how-much-can-the-brain-recover.

Rifkin, Jeremy. *The Empathic Civilization: The Race to Global Consciousness in a World in Crisis.* New York City: Penguin Group, 2009.

S., Arthur et al. "Alcoholics Anonymous (AA) Recovery Outcome Rates." January 1, 2008.

# Bibliography

Schmuck, Peter, Kasser, Tim Ryan, Richard M. "Intrisic and Extrinsic Goals: Their Structure and Relationship to Well-Being in German and U.S. College Students," Social Indicators Research 50: 225 - 241 (2000)

Silverman, Herb. "Why do Americans still hate atheists?" Live Q & A Washington Post (May 4, 2011), accessed December 19, 2013, http://live.washingtonpost.com/why-do-americans-hate-atheists-herb-silverman.html.

Soccio, Douglas J. *Archetypes of Wisdom, 5th Edition*. Belmont: Wadsworth/Thomson Learning, 2004.

Solomon, Sheldon (Professor of Psychology Skidmore College, Terror Management Theory researcher, author *In the Wake of 9/11: the Psychology of Terror)*, in discussion with author July 2011.

Sowell Thomas. *A Conflict of Vision: Ideological Origins of Political Struggles*. New York: Basic Books, 2002.

Strathern, Paul. *Dr. Strangelove Game: A Brief History of Economic Genius*. Toronto: Knopf, 2001.

Steigerwald, F. and D. Stone. "Cognitive restructuring and the 12-step program of Alcoholics Anonymous," The Journal of Substance Abuse Treatment 4, (June 16 1999): 321-327.

Stein, Murray. "Individuation: Inner Work." Journal of Jungian Theory and Practice 7, No. 2 (2005): http://www.junginstitute.org/pdf_files/JungV7N2p1-14.pdf, accessed November 26, 2013.

Swegan, William E. and Glenn F. Chestnut, PhD *The Psychology of Alcoholism*. Bloomington: iUniverse, 2003.

Thomas, Pat. "How to beat denial—a 12-step plan." The Ecologist. (December 1, 2006), accessed November 26, 2013, http://www.theecologist.org/investigations/climate_change/268964/how_to_beat_denial_a_12step_plan.html.

Thomsen, Robert. *Bill W.: The absorbing and deeply moving story of Bill Wilson, co-founder of Alcoholics Anonymous*. New York City: Harper & Row, 1975

Vaillant, George. "A Doctor Speaks: An interview with George E. Vaillant, MD" AA Grapevine 57, No. 2 May 2001, Vol. 57, No. 12.

W., Bill. "The Individual in Relation to A.A. as a Group," AA Grapevine III, No. 2 (July 1946): 2, 6.

Weiten, Wayne. *Psychology Themes and Variations 6th Edition*. Belmont: Wadsworth/Thomson Learning, 2004.

White, Matthew P. and Paul Dolan. "Accounting for the Richness of Daily Activities." Psychological Science 20, No. 8 (August 2009): 1000–1008, accessed November 28, 2012, http://pauldolan.co.uk/wp-content/uploads/2011/07/Accounting-for-the-rishness-of-daily-activities.pdf.

Wilber, Ken. *No Boundaries: Eastern and Western approaches to personal growth*. Boulder: Shambhala Publications, 1981.

Williams, Mark et al. *The Mindful Way through Depression: Freeing Yourself from Chronic Unhappiness*. New York: Guilford Press, 2007.

WIN-Gallup International. "Global Index of Religiosity and Atheism—2012," accessed December 4, 2012, http://www.wingia.com/web/files/richeditor/filemanager/Global_INDEX_of_Religiosity_and_Atheism_PR__6.pdf.

Young, Kimberly. "Understanding Online Gaming Addiction and Treatment Issues for Adolescents." The American Journal of Family Therapy 37 (2009): 355-372.

Z., Philip. *A Skeptic's Guide to the 12 Steps*. Indianapolis: Hazelden, 1990.

# INDEX

# Index

# Index

# Index

58825258R00226

Made in the USA
Charleston, SC
19 July 2016